FORMULATION AND IMPLEMENTATION OF COMPETITIVE STRATEGY

The Irwin Series in Management and The Behavioral Sciences
L. L. Cummings and E. Kirby Warren   Consulting Editors

Consider — value of
   Firm falling short of goals
   going in too many directions
   experienced mgt. as future network
   bonding of those who had worked together.

Airline — food transport

FORMULATION AND IMPLEMENTATION OF COMPETITIVE STRATEGY

John A. Pearce II
School of Business Administration
George Mason University

Richard B. Robinson, Jr.
College of Business Administration
University of South Carolina

1988   Third Edition

IRWIN
Homewood, Illinois 60430

© RICHARD D. IRWIN, INC., 1982, 1985, and 1988

All rights reserved. No part of this publication may be
reproduced, stored in a retrieval system, or transmitted,
in any form or by any means, electronic, mechanical,
photocopying, recording, or otherwise, without the prior
written permission of the publisher.

Acquisitions editor: William R. Bayer
Project editors: Jean Roberts and Karen Smith
Production manager: Bette Ittersagen
Compositor: Arcata Graphics/Kingsport
Typeface: 10/12 Century Schoolbook
Printer: R. R. Donnelley & Sons Company

ISBN 0–256–06251–X

Library of Congress Catalog Card No. 87–82170

Printed in the United States of America
    4 5 6 7 8 9 0 DO 5 4 3 2 1 0 9

To Mary Frances and Jack Pearce
Mattie Robinson and Frank Fletcher

PREFACE

The third edition of this book is the culmination of 10 years of diligent work on the part of many people. This preface is designed to provide you with an overview of the content of the third edition and to recognize the many contributors to it. To do this we have divided the preface into three sections. The first section is addressed to the student and is designed to give this first-time user a concise overview of the structure and content of the book. The second section is addressed to the instructor and is designed to give the person familiar with our previous editions a sense of what is new. The third section acknowledges the many contributors to this ongoing project.

To the Student

Formulation and Implementation of Competitive Strategy, third edition, is a book designed to introduce you to the critical business skills of planning and managing strategic activities. It incorporates two teaching approaches: text and a cohesion case.

The text portion of this book provides you with a readable, up-to-date introduction to the management of strategy in the business enterprise. We have tried to integrate the work of strategic management theorists, practitioners, and researchers with a strong emphasis on real-world applications of strategic management concepts. To further this aim, we have included Strategy in Action reports across 13 chapters which give current examples of the application of key concepts by well-known business firms.

The structure of the text material is guided by a comprehensive model of the strategic management process. The model will help you acquire an executive-level perspective on strategy formulation and implementation. It provides a visual display of the major components of the entire process and shows both how they are conceptually related and how they are sequenced through the process.

The major components of the model are each discussed in depth in separate chapters, thereby enabling you to acquire detailed knowledge and specific skills within a broad framework of strategic management. The use of the model is also extended to the Cohesion Case, where you will be guided in disciplined, systematic, and comprehensive study of an actual strategic dilemma.

The Cohesion Case offers a particularly unique feature designed to aid both the student and the teacher of strategic management and business policy. We have taken a well-known, multi-industry firm—Holiday Inns, Inc.—and used it as the basis of an in-depth case study to illustrate in detail the application of the text material. To do this, we provide a cohesion case section at the end of each chapter which applies the chapter material to the company. The Holiday Inns, Inc., case offers a clear illustration of the corporate, business, and functional levels of strategy—so important to the understanding of strategic management in today's corporate environment.

The Cohesion Case offers several benefits to the reader:

It provides a continuous illustration of the interdependence of the various parts of the strategic management process by using the same enterprise throughout the chapters.

It provides a useful aid in understanding the text material when the primary emphasis in the course is to be on case studies or other nontext analysis.

It provides a useful aid in preparing for the case analysis component of the course, in the event that the instructor prefers to emphasize the conceptual material.

It offers an in-depth basis for class discussion of strategic management concepts, application, and ideas for any classroom pedagogy.

To the Instructor

This third edition of *Formulation and Implementation of Competitive Strategy* provides a thoroughly revised, state-of-the-art treatment of the critical business skills of planning and managing strategic activities. We have reorganized our treatment of strategic management into 13 chapters; added critical pedagogical features; condensed the material into fewer pages; expanded the number of "real-world" examples; condensed and updated the Cohesion Case; and further incorporated the work of contemporary scholars into our coverage of strategic management. We feel confident you will find the material well organized, laden with current examples, and reflective of new contributions in the strategic management literature while retaining a structure guided by our time-tested model of the strategic management process.

We have revised and condensed the Cohesion Case while retaining Holiday Inns, Inc., as the company that we examine. We have been pleased with the response of both students and instructors to this innovative, pedagogical feature we pioneered in this book. While the Cohesion Case has been recognized by many as one of the unique pedagogical advances in business policy this decade, we have endeavored to add still more self-teaching aids to this edition.

We have expanded our strategic management teaching package for this edition. In our second edition, we pioneered the use of computer-assisted strategic analysis with the introduction of *Strategic Analyst* to accompany our textbook. *Strategic Analyst* allowed the student to conduct a computer-based, systematic analysis of the strategic options available to a business and do so with built-in linkages to our text. *Strategic Analyst* is still available with this third edition.

Other components of our teaching package include a totally revised and enhanced *Instructor's Manual;* a set of four-color teaching transparencies; a computerized version of our test bank; *Strategic Management: Strategy Formulation and Implementation,* a hardback offering text and case coverage of strategic management identical to that in this book; *Company and Industry Cases in Strategy and Policy;* and a paperback offering 28 cases and industry notes. Each of these components of our teaching package offers the instructor optimal, integrated flexibility in designing and conducting the strategic management course.

Changes to Our Text Material

The literature and research comprising the strategic management field have been developing at a rapid pace in recent years. We have endeavored to create a third edition that incorporates major developments in this literature while keeping our focus centered on a simple, understandable framework through which students can begin to grasp the complexity of strategic management. Several text revisions or additions you should be aware of are described below:

- A new chapter has been added covering international issues and strategic management in an international setting.
- The three-chapter set on external analysis has become four chapters plus a supplement on sources of industry data. Separate chapters now cover the nature of external environments, environmental forecasting, industry analysis, and the international business setting. While the number of chapters is expanded, the material has been condensed and streamlined, affording a concise, practical treatment.

- A major new section has been added on the topic of "strategic control." Three basic types of strategic control and ways to use them are highlighted in this material.
- Organizational culture as a central dimension of strategy implementation has received significantly greater attention in Chapter 12 of this edition. Several useful analytical concepts and techniques that aid identification and management of the strategy–culture interface are incorporated to aid the student in understanding the culture concept.
- Two useful supplements now accompany our text material. A revised guide to financial analysis is provided following Chapter 8—Internal Analysis. It provides perhaps the most thorough and easy-to-use guide to quantitative analysis of financial and operating information available in any strategic management text. A guide to industry information sources follows Chapter 5—Environmental Forecasting. It has been revised and updated for this edition. Students will find it most helpful in rapidly orienting them to where and how to get company and industry data.
- We have increased the number of Strategy in Action Illustration Capsules by 30 percent. The text material now contains 43 of these illustration vignettes, 35 of which are new to this edition. Each Strategy in Action provides a contemporary business example of a key chapter topic to interest the student and aid learning.
- Our popular Cohesion Case feature has received considerable attention this edition. We have continued the use of a well-known, multi-industry firm—Holiday Corporation (Holiday Inns, Inc.)—as an in-depth case study to illustrate in detail the application of the text material. We also continue to provide cohesion case sections at the end of each chapter, which apply chapter material to the Holiday situation. We have updated the material about Holiday Corporation, and we have streamlined and shortened its presentation, making this feature even more appealing and useful.

In conclusion, we are confident you will find the text material in this third edition well organized, concise, filled with current examples, and consistent with the current theory and practice of strategic management.

Acknowledgments

The development of this book through three editions has been greatly enhanced by the generous commitment of time, energy, and ideas from the following people:

Sonny S. Ariss, University of Toledo
Robert Earl Bolick, Metropolitan State University

William E. Burr II, University of Oregon
E. T. Busch, Western Kentucky University
Richard Castaldi, San Diego State University
Larry Cummings, Northwestern University
William Davig, Auburn University
Peter Davis, University of Oregon
Greg Dess, University of Texas at Arlington
Marc J. Dollinger, University of Kentucky
Liam Fahey, Northwestern University
Elizabeth Freeman, Portland State University
Diane J. Garsombke, University of Maine
J. Michael Geringer, Southern Methodist University
Peter G. Goulet, Hawkeye Consultations and University of Northern
    Iowa
Don Hambrick, Pennsylvania State University
Richard C. Hoffman, College of William and Mary
Troy Jones, University of Central Florida
Jon G. Kalinowski, Mankato State University
Kay Keels, University of South Carolina
Michael Koshuta, Valparaiso University
Myroslaw J. Kyj, Widener University of Pennsylvania
Joseph W. Leonard, Miami University, Ohio
Edward L. McClelland, Roanoke College
Patricia McDougall, Georgia State University
John G. Maurer, Wayne State University
S. Mehta, San Jose State University
Richard R. Merner, University of Delaware
Cynthia Montgomery, University of Michigan
Stephanie Newell, Bowling Green State University
Kenneth Olm, University of Texas at Austin
Benjamin Oviatt, Clemson University
Joseph Paolillo, University of Mississippi
G. Norris Rath, Shepherd College
Paula Rechner, University of Illinois
Les Rue, Georgia State University
J. A. Ruslyk, Memphis State University
Scott Snell, Michigan State University
James S. Snyder, North Adams State College
Arien A. Ullmann, SUNY at Binghamton
William C. Waddell, California State University, Los Angeles
Bill Warren, College of William and Mary
Kirby Warren, Columbia University
Michael White, University of Tulsa
Frank Winfrey, University of Wisconsin
Robley Wood, Virginia Commonwealth University

The valuable ideas, recommendations, and support of these outstanding scholars and teachers have added quality to this book.

Because we are affiliated with two separate universities, we have two sets of co-workers to thank.

The growth and dynamic environment at George Mason University have contributed directly to the development of this edition. Valuable critiques and helpful recommendations have been made by strategic management faculty Carolyn Erdener, Keith Robbins, and Shaker Zahra, and by colleagues Bill Bolce, Debra Cohen, Joe English, Ellen Fagensen, Freda Hartman, Eileen Hogan, Ken Kovach, Steve Patrick, and Hank Sims. For his gracious support and personal encouragement, we also wish to thank Coleman Raphael, Dean of George Mason University's School of Business Administration and Chairman of the Board of Atlantic Research, Inc. For their excellent secretarial assistance, we most sincerely appreciate the work of Debbie McDanial, Sondra Patrick, and Luci Rosinski.

We are especially grateful to LeRoy Eakin, Jr., and his family for their generous endowment of the Eakin Endowed Chair in Strategic Management at George Mason University that Jack holds. The provisions of the Chair have enabled Jack to continue his dual involvements with this book and strategic management research.

The stimulating environment at the University of South Carolina has contributed to the development of this book. Thought-provoking discussions with strategy colleagues Alan Bauerschmidt, Carl Clamp, Jim Chrisman, Herb Hand, John Logan, Bob Rosen, Bill Sandberg, and David Schweiger gave us many useful ideas. We also want to recognize the important input of doctoral candidates Kay Keels, Frank Winfrey, Jacob Weber, Lanny Herron, and Julio DeCastro in the development, class testing, and refinement of selected business case studies. Likewise, we want to thank James F. Kane, Dean of the College of Business Administration; James G. Hilton, our Associate Dean; and Joe Ullman, Program Director in Management, for their interest and support. Our sincere appreciation also goes to Sandra Murrah for her help in preparing this manuscript and in solving endless logistical problems.

In using this text, we hope that you will share our enthusiasm both for the rich subject of strategic management and for the learning approach that we have taken. We value your recommendations and thoughts about our materials. Please write Jack at the School of Business Administration, George Mason University, Fairfax, Virginia 22030, or Richard at the College of Business Administration, University of South Carolina, Columbia, South Carolina 29208.

Jack Pearce
Richard Robinson

ABOUT THE AUTHORS

John A. Pearce II, Ph.D., is the holder of the Eakin Endowed Chair in Strategic Management in the School of Business Administration at George Mason University (Fairfax, VA 22030, 703-323-4361) and Chairman of the school's Management Department.

Professor Pearce has published more than 100 journal articles, invited book chapters, and professional papers in outlets that include *Academy of Management Executive, Academy of Management Journal, Academy of Management Review, California Management Review, Journal of Business Venturing, Sloan Management Review,* and the *Strategic Management Journal.* He has served on the editorial boards of four journals, and he is currently the Consulting Editor in Strategic Management for the *Journal of Management.* Professor Pearce is also the coauthor or coeditor of 17 texts, proceedings, and supplements for publishers that include Richard D. Irwin, Inc., McGraw-Hill, Random House, and the Academy of Management.

Elected to more than a dozen offices in national and regional professional associations, Professor Pearce has served as Chairman of the Academy of Management's Entrepreneurship Division, Strategic Management and Entrepreneurship Track Chairman for the Southern Management Association, and Strategy Formulation and Implementation Track Chairman for the Decision Sciences Institute. He is also the 1989 President-elect of the Southern Management Association.

An active consultant and management trainer, Professor Pearce specializes in helping executive teams to develop and activate their firms' strategic plans.

Richard B. Robinson, Jr., Ph.D., is currently Professor of Strategy and Enterpreneurship in the College of Business Administration at the University of South Carolina (Columbia, SC 29208, 803-777-5961).

Professor Robinson has published more than 100 journal articles, invited chapters, and professional papers in outlets that include the *Academy of Management Journal, Strategic Management Journal, Academy of Management Review, Journal of Business Venturing, Journal of Small Business Management,* and the *Personnel Administrator.* He is also coauthor or coeditor of 16 texts, proceedings, and supplements for publishers that include Richard D. Irwin, Inc., McGraw-Hill, Random House, and the Academy of Management.

Professor Robinson is the recipient of several awards in recognition of his work in strategic management and entrepreneurship. Sponsors of these awards include the Heizer Capital Corporation, the Academy of Management, the Center for Family Business, the National Association of Small Business Investment Companies, the Southern Business Administration Association, the Small Business Administration, the National Venture Capital Association, and Beta Gamma Sigma. He has also held offices in the Academy of Management, the Southern Management Association, and the International Council of Small Business. Professor Robinson is an active consultant in the strategic management of growth-oriented ventures.

CONTENTS

FORMULATION AND IMPLEMENTATION OF COMPETITIVE STRATEGY

STRATEGIC MANAGEMENT MODEL

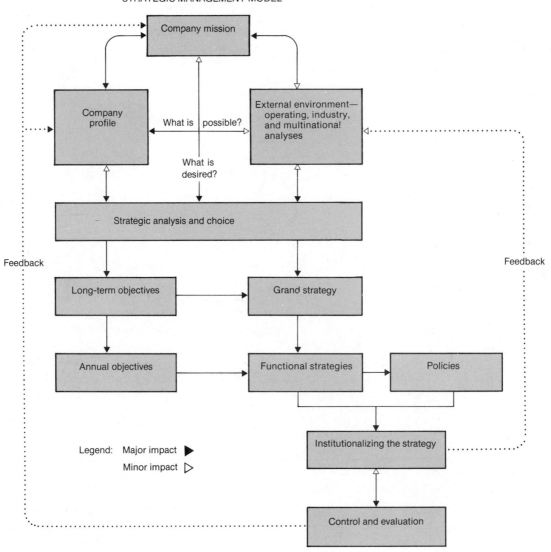

PART ONE

Overview of Strategic Management

The first two chapters of this text provide a broad introduction to strategic management. They describe the nature, need, benefits, and terminology of the processes for producing and implementing major plans directing business activities. Subsequent chapters then provide greater detail.

Chapter 1, The Nature and Value of Strategic Management, emphasizes the practical value of a strategic management approach for a business organization and reviews the actual benefits for companies that have instituted strategic management. The critical activities of strategic management are then presented as a set of dimensions that can be used to distinguish strategic decisions from other planning tasks of the firm.

Chapter 1 stresses the key point that, in many companies, strategic management activities are undertaken at three levels: corporate, business, and functional. The distinctive characteristics of strategic decision making at each of these levels are discussed; these characteristics will serve as the basis for later observations concerning the impact of activities at different levels on company operations.

The extent to which formality is desirable in strategic management is another key point in Chapter 1, as is the alignment of strategy makers with particular activities in the overall process of strategy formulation and implementation. It is shown that it is possible to assign areas of decision-maker responsibility, and an appropriate degree of formality in strategic activities is suggested. The factors determining these conclusions are discussed in detail.

A final section in Chapter 1 reviews the results of research in business organizations. The studies convincingly demonstrate that companies utilizing strategic management processes often enjoy financial and behavioral benefits that justify the additional costs involved.

Chapter 2 presents a model of the strategic management process. The model is representative of approaches currently used by strategic planners and will serve as an outline for the remainder of the book in that each subsequent chapter is devoted to an in-depth discussion of one of the major components of the model. Each of the individual components is carefully defined and explained in Chapter 2, as is the process by which the components are integrated to produce cohesive and balanced results. The chapter ends with a discussion of the practical limitations of the model and the advisability of tailoring the general recommendations suggested to the unique situations confronted in actual business practice.

1

The Nature and Value of Strategic Management

The complexity and sophistication of business decision making requires strategic management. Managing various and multifaceted internal activities is only part of the modern executive's responsibilities. The firm's immediate external environment poses a second set of challenging factors. This environment includes competitors whenever profits seem possible, suppliers of increasingly scarce resources, government agencies monitoring adherence to an ever-growing number of regulations, and customers whose often inexplicable preferences must be anticipated. A remote external environment also contributes to the general yet pervasive climate in which a business exists. This environment consists of economic conditions, social change, political priorities, and technological developments, each of which must be anticipated, monitored, assessed, and incorporated in top-level decision making. However, these influences are often subordinated to the fourth major consideration in executive decision making—the multiple and often mutually inconsistent objectives of the stakeholders of the business: owners, top managers, employees, communities, customers, and country.

To deal effectively with all that affects the ability of a company to grow profitably, executives design strategic management processes they feel will facilitate the optimal positioning of the firm in its competitive environment. Such positioning is possible because these strategic processes allow more accurate anticipation of environmental changes and improved preparedness for reacting to unexpected internal or competitive demands.

when concept impt? late 1970s?

5

Broad-scope, large-scale management processes have become dramatically more sophisticated since the end of World War II, principally as a reflection of increases in the size and number of competing firms; of the expanded intervention of government as a buyer, seller, regulator, and competitor in the free enterprise system; and of greater business involvement in international trade. Perhaps the most significant improvement in management processes came in the 1970s as "long-range planning," "new venture management," "planning, programming, budgeting," and "business policy" were blended with increased emphasis on environmental forecasting and external as well as internal considerations in formulating and implementing plans. This all-encompassing approach is known as *strategic management* or *strategic planning*.[1]

Strategic management is defined as *the set of decisions and actions resulting in formulation and implementation of strategies designed to achieve the objectives of an organization*. It involves attention to no less than nine critical areas:

1. Determining the mission of the company, including broad statements about its purpose, philosophy, and goals.
2. Developing a company profile that reflects internal conditions and capabilities.
3. Assessment of the company's external environment, in terms of both competitive and general contextual factors.
4. Analysis of possible options uncovered in the matching of the company profile with the external environment.
5. Identifying the desired options uncovered when possibilities are considered in light of the company mission.
6. Strategic choice of a particular set of long-term objectives and grand strategies needed to achieve the desired options.
7. Development of annual objectives and short-term strategies compatible with long-term objectives and grand strategies.
8. Implementing strategic choice decisions based on budgeted resource allocations and emphasizing the matching of tasks, people, structures, technologies, and reward systems.
9. Review and evaluation of the success of the strategic process to serve as a basis for control and as an input for future decision making.

As these nine areas indicate, strategic management involves the planning, directing, organizing, and controlling of the strategy-related decisions and actions of the business. By strategy, managers mean their *large-scale, future-oriented plans for interacting with the competitive environment to optimize*

---

[1] In this text the term *strategic management* refers to the broad overall process because to some scholars and practitioners the term *strategic planning* connotes only the formulation phase of total management activities.

achievement of organization objectives. Thus, a strategy represents a firm's "game plan." Although it does not precisely detail all future deployments (people, financial, and material), it does provide a framework for managerial decisions. A strategy reflects a company's awareness of how to compete, against whom, when, where, and for what.

Dimensions of Strategic Decisions

What decisions facing a business are strategic and therefore deserve strategic management attention? Typically, strategic issues have six identifiable dimensions:

Strategic Issues Require Top-Management Decisions.   Strategic decisions overarch several areas of a firm's operations. Therefore, top-management involvement in decision making is imperative. Only at this level is there the perspective for understanding and anticipating broad implications and ramifications, and the power to authorize the resource allocations necessary for implementation.

Strategic Issues Involve the Allocation of Large Amounts of Company Resources.   Strategic decisions characteristically involve substantial resource deployment. The people, physical assets, or moneys needed must be either redirected from internal sources or secured from outside the firm. In either case, strategic decisions commit a firm to a stream of actions over an extended period of time, thus involving substantial resources.

Strategic Issues Are Likely to Have a Significant Impact on the Long-Term Prosperity of the Firm.   Strategic decisions ostensibly commit the firm for a long period of time, typically for five years; however, the time frame of impact is often much longer. Once a firm has committed itself to a particular strategic option in a major way, its competitive image and advantages are usually tied to that strategy. Firms become known in certain markets, for certain products, with certain characteristics. To shift from these markets, products, or technologies by adopting a radically different strategy would jeopardize previous progress. Thus, strategic decisions have enduring effects on the firm—for better or worse.

Strategic Issues Are Future Oriented.   Strategic decisions are based on what managers anticipate or forecast rather than on what they know. Emphasis is on developing projections that will enable the firm to select the most promising strategic options. In the turbulent and competitive free enterprise environment, a successful firm must take a proactive (anticipatory) stance toward change.

too often reactive

Strategic Issues Usually Have Major Multifunctional or Multibusiness Consequences.   A strategic decision is coordinative. Decisions about such factors as customer mix, competitive emphasis, or organizational structure necessarily involve a number of a firm's strategic business units (SBUs), functions, divisions, or program units. Each of these areas will be affected by the allocation or reallocation of responsibilities and resources related to the decision.

Strategic Issues Necessitate Considering Factors in the Firm's External Environment.   All business firms exist in an open system. They impact and are impacted by external conditions largely beyond their control. Therefore, if a firm is to succeed in positioning itself in future competitive situations, its strategic managers must look beyond the limits of the firm's own operations. They must consider what relevant others (e.g., competitors, customers, suppliers, creditors, government, and labor) are likely to do.

Three Levels of Strategy

The decision-making hierarchy of business firms typically contains three levels. At the top is the corporate level, composed principally of members of the board of directors and the chief executive and administrative officers. They are responsible for the financial performance of the corporation as a whole and for achieving the nonfinancial goals of the firm, for example, corporate image and social responsibility. To a large extent, orientations at the corporate level reflect the concern of stockholders and society at large. Particularly in multibusiness firms, one duty of those at the corporate level is to determine the businesses in which the company should be involved. Further, corporate officers set objectives and formulate strategies that span the activities of individual businesses in the corporation and the functional area of these businesses. By adopting a portfolio approach to strategic management, corporate-level strategic managers attempt to exploit their distinctive competencies within their industries while typically planning over a five-year time horizon.

The second rung of the decision-making hierarchy is the business level, composed principally of business and corporate managers. These managers must translate the general statements of direction and intent generated at the corporate level into concrete, functional objectives and strategies for individual business divisions or SBUs. In essence, business-level strategic managers must determine the basis on which a company can compete in the selected product–market arena. While so doing, they strive to identify and secure the most profitable and promising market segment. This market segment is the fairly unique piece of the total market that the business can claim and defend because of competitive advantages. Every corporation, even the largest multinational, depends on the strength of market segments for continuing viability.

The third rung is the functional level, composed principally of managers

Figure 1–1
Alternative strategic management structures

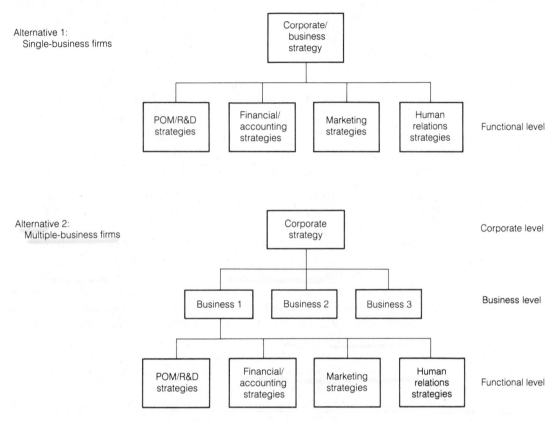

of product, geographic, and functional areas. It is their responsibility to develop annual objectives and short-term strategies in such areas as production, operations, and research and development; finance and accounting; marketing; and human relations. However, their greatest responsibilities are in the implementation or execution of a company's strategic plans. While corporate and business-level managers center their planning concerns on "doing the right things," managers at the functional level must stress "doing things right." Thus, they directly address such issues as the efficiency and effectiveness of production and marketing systems, the quality and extent of customer service, and the success of particular products and services in increasing their market shares.

Figure 1–1 depicts the three levels of strategic management as they are actually structured in practice. In alternative 1 the company is engaged in only one business and the corporate and business-level responsibilities are concentrated in a single group of directors, officers, and managers. This particular structure is nearly synonymous with the organizational formats of the small businesses that constitute approximately 95 percent of all business organizations in the United States.

Alternative 2 is a classical corporate structure comprised of three fully operative levels. The suprastructure is provided at the corporate level, with the superstructure at the business level giving direction and support for functional-level activities.

The approach taken throughout this text is best depicted by alternative 2. Thus, whenever appropriate, topics will be covered from the perspective of each level of strategic management. In this way the text presents one of the most comprehensive and up-to-date discussions of the strategic management process.

Characteristics of Strategic Management Decisions

The characteristics of strategic management decisions vary with the level of strategic activity considered. As shown in Figure 1–2, corporate-level decisions tend to be value oriented, conceptual, and less concrete than those at the business or functional level of strategy formulation and implementation. Corporate-level decisions are also characterized by greater risk, cost, and profit potential, as well as by longer time horizons and greater needs for flexibility. These characteristics are logical consequences of the more far-reaching futuristic, innovative, and pervasive nature of corporate-level strategic activity. Examples of corporate-level decisions include the choice of business, dividend policies, sources of long-term financing, and priorities for growth.

At the other end of the continuum, functional-level decisions principally involve action-oriented operational issues. These decisions are made periodically and lead directly to implementation of some part of the overall strategy formulated at the corporate and business levels. Therefore, functional-level decisions are relatively short range and involve low risk and modest costs because they are dependent on available resources. Functional-level decisions usually determine actions requiring minimal companywide cooperation. These activities supplement the functional area's present activities and are adaptable to ongoing activities so that minimal cooperation is needed for successful implementation. Because functional-level decisions are relatively concrete and quantifiable, they receive critical attention and analysis even though their comparative profit potential is low.

Some common functional-level decisions include generic versus brand-name labeling, basic versus applied R&D, high versus low inventory levels, general-versus specific-purpose production equipment, and close versus loose supervision.

Bridging corporate- and functional-level decisions are those made at the business level. As Figure 1–2 indicates, business-level descriptions of strategic decisions fall between those for the other two levels. For example, business-level decisions are less costly, risky, and potentially profitable than corporate-

Figure 1–2
Characteristics of strategic management decisions at different levels

	Level of strategy		
Characteristic	Corporate	Business	Functional
Type	Conceptual	Mixed	Operational
Measurability	Value judgments dominant	Semiquantifiable	Usually quantifiable
Frequency	Periodic or sporadic	Periodic or sporadic	Periodic
Adaptability	Low	Medium	High
Relation to present activities	Innovative	Mixed	Supplementary
Risk	Wide range	Moderate	Low
Profit potential	Large	Medium	Small
Cost	Major	Medium	Modest
Time horizon	Long range	Medium range	Short range
Flexibility	High	Medium	Low
Cooperation required	Considerable	Moderate	Little

level decisions, but they are more costly, risky, and potentially profitable than functional-level decisions. Some common business-level decisions involve plant location, marketing segmentation and geographic coverage, and distribution channels.

Formality in Strategic Management

The formality of strategic management systems varies widely among companies. *Formality* refers to the degree to which membership, responsibilities, authority, and discretion in decision making are specified. It is an important consideration in the study of strategic management because degree of formality is usually positively correlated with the cost, comprehensiveness, accuracy, and success of planning.

A number of forces determine the need for formality in strategic management. As shown in Figure 1–3, the size of the organization, its predominant management styles, the complexity of its environment, its production processes, the nature of its problems, and the purpose of its planning system all combine in determining an appropriate degree of formality.

In particular, formality is often associated with two factors: size and stage of development of the company. Methods of evaluating strategic success are also linked to degree of formality. Some firms, especially smaller ones, are *entrepreneurial*. They are basically under the control of a single individual and produce a limited number of products or services. With this mode, performance evaluation is very informal, intuitive, and limited in scope. At the other end of the spectrum, evaluation is part of a comprehensive, formalized,

Figure 1–3
Forces influencing design of strategic management systems

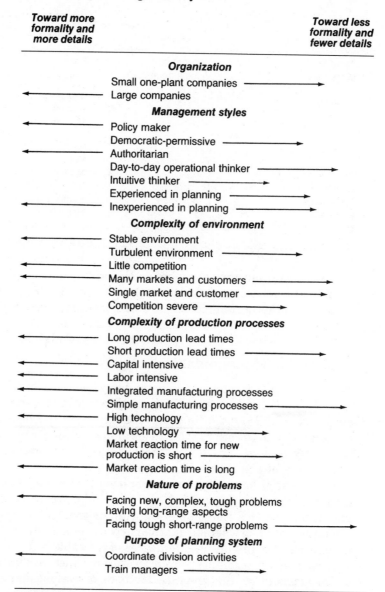

Source: George A. Steiner, *Strategic Planning* (New York: Free Press, 1979), p. 54. Copyright © 1979 by the Free Press, a division of Macmillan Publishing Co., Inc. Reprinted with permission of Macmillan.

Figure 1–4
Hierarchy of objectives and strategies

Ends (What is to be achieved?)	Means (How it is to be achieved?)	Strategic decision makers			
		Board of directors	Corporate managers	Business managers	Functional managers
Mission, including goals and philosophy		√√	√√	√	
Long-term objectives	Grand strategy	√	√√	√√	
Annual objectives	Short-term strategy policies		√	√√	√√
Functional objectives	Tactics			√	√√

Note: √√ indicates a principal responsibility; √ indicates a secondary responsibility.

multilevel strategic planning system. This approach, which Henry Mintzberg called the *planning mode,* is used by large firms, such as Texas Instruments and General Electric. Mintzberg also identified a third mode (the *adaptive mode*) in the middle of this spectrum, which he associated with medium-sized firms in relatively stable environments.[2] For firms in the adaptive mode, identification and evaluation of alternative strategies are closely related to existing strategy. Despite these generalities, it is not unusual to find different modes within the same organization. For example, Exxon might adopt an entrepreneurial mode in the development and evaluation of its solar subsidiary's strategy, while the rest of the company follows a planning mode.

Exxon solar project.

The Strategy Makers

The ideal strategic management process is developed and governed by a strategic management team. The team consists principally of decision makers at all three levels (corporate, business, and functional) in the corporation, for example, the chief executive officer (CEO), the product managers, and the heads of functional areas. The team also relies on input from two types of support personnel: company planning staffs, when they exist, and lower-level managers and supervisors. The latter provide data for strategic decision making and are responsible for implementing strategies.

Because strategic decisions have such a tremendous impact on a firm and because they require large commitments of company resources, they can only be made by top managers in the organizational hierarchy. Figure 1–4 indicates the alignment between levels of strategic decision makers and the kinds of objectives and strategies for which they are typically responsible.

[2] Henry Mintzberg, "Strategy Making in Three Modes," *California Management Review* 16, no. 2 (1973), pp. 44–53.

Figure 1–5
Responsibility relationships in strategic planning

Planning activities	Corporate responsibility		Business responsibility		Functional responsibility
	Top management	Corporate planning department	General management	Staff groups	Departmental planning groups
Establish corporate objectives	△				
Identify performance targets	●	●			
Setting planning horizon	●		●		
Organize and coordinate planning effort		●			●
Make environmental assumptions	△	●	△	●	
Collection information and forecast					
Forecast sales	△		△	●	
Assess firm's strength and weaknesses			△	●	
Evaluate competitive environment			△	●	
Establish business objectives	△		△	●	△
Develop business plans	△	○	△		△
Formulate alternative strategies		○		●	
Select alternative strategies		○	●		
Evaluate and select projects			△	●	
Develop tactics			△	●	
Revise objectives and plans if objectives are not met	△				
Integrate plans		●			
Allocate resources	△				
Review progress against the plan	●		●		
Evaluate plan's effectiveness		●			

Key: △ Approves.
  ○ Reviews, evaluates, and counsels.
  ● Does the work.

Source: Adapted from Ronald J. Kudla, "Elements of Effective Corporate Planning," *Long-Range Planning,* August 1976, p. 89.

The use of company planning staffs has increased considerably since the 1960s. In large corporations, the existence of planning departments, often headed by a corporate vice president for planning, is common. Medium-sized firms frequently employ at least one full-time staff member to spearhead strategic data-collection efforts. Even in smaller or less progressive firms, an officer or group of officers designated as a planning committee is often assigned to spearhead the company's strategic planning efforts.

Precisely what are managers' responsibilities in the strategic planning process at the corporate and business levels? Figure 1–5 provides some answers.

It shows that top management shoulders responsibility for broadly approving each of the six major phases of planning listed. They are assisted in the execution of these responsibilities by the corporate planning department, staff, or personnel, who actually prepare major components of the corporate plan. Top management also reviews, evaluates, and counsels on most major phases of the plan's preparation.

Figure 1–5 further shows that general managers at the business level have principal responsibilities for approving environmental analysis and forecasting, establishing business objectives, and developing business plans prepared by staff groups. The figure clearly indicates the pervasive and potentially powerful influence of corporate planners in the overall strategic management process.

One final, but perhaps overriding, point must be made about strategic decision makers: a company's president or CEO characteristically plays a dominant role in the process. In many ways this situation is desirable and reasonable. The principal duty of a CEO is often defined as giving long-term direction to the firm. The CEO is ultimately responsible for the success of the business and therefore of its strategy. Additionally, CEOs are typically strong-willed, company-oriented individuals with a high sense of self-esteem. Their personalities often prevent them from delegating substantive authority to others in formulation or approval of strategic decisions.

However, when the dominance of the CEO approaches autocracy, the effectiveness of the firm's strategic planning and management processes are likely to be greatly diminished. The advantages of a team-oriented, participative strategic system are obviously related inversely to the CEO's propensity to make major strategic decisions single-handedly. For these reasons, establishment of a strategic management system carries with it an implicit promise by the CEO to provide managers at all levels with the opportunity to play a role in determining the strategic posture of the firm. The degree to which the CEO fulfills this promise is often parallel to the degree of success enjoyed through the use of the strategic management process.

The Interactive and Iterative Flow of the Strategic Process

The strategic management process is sometimes misperceived as involving a unidirectional flow of objectives, strategies, and decision parameters from corporate- to business- to functional-level managers. In fact, the process is highly interactive, that is, designed to stimulate input from creative, skilled, and knowledgeable people throughout the firm. While the strategic process is certainly overseen by top managers—because they have a broad perspective on the company and its environment—managers at all levels have multiple opportunities to participate in various phases of the total process.

Figure 1–6 provides an example of the basic, typical, interactive flow. As indicated by the solid line, strategic management activities tend to follow a formalized pattern of top-down/bottom-up interactions involving planners at all three levels.

Figure 1–6
Strategic planning process cycle

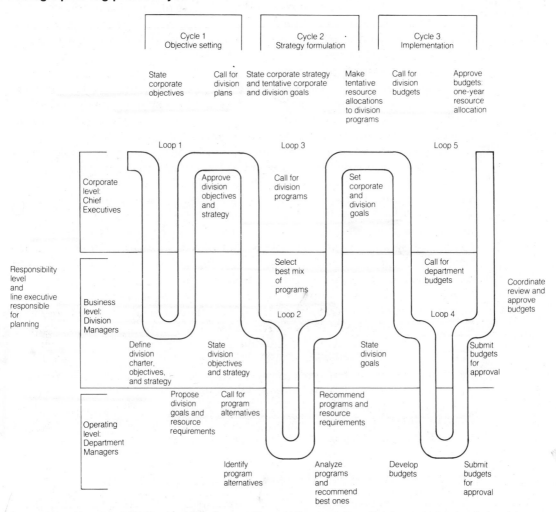

Source: Adapted from Richard F. Vancil and Peter Lorange, "Strategic Planning in Diversified Companies," by permission of the *Harvard Business Review*, January–February 1975.

As indicated by the five loops in Figure 1–6, the strategic management process is also iterative. This means strategic decisions are usually reached only after trial and error. Management expert Peter Lorange illustrates the five iterative loops as follows:

> Loop 1: When the CEO receives inputs indicating where the businesses may be going, he or she may have to reconcile the emerging portfolio pictures with initial tentative objectives. As a result, the CEO may ask

one or more of the businesses to revise their inputs, and may change the original tentative objectives as well. One or more iterations may be necessary before the loop is closed.

Loop 2: In formulating strategy, the business manager may frequently go back to the functional departments and request revisions so that individual programs fit into a more coherent package from the business strategy viewpoint.

Loop 3: When the CEO receives the portfolio of business strategies, he or she may have to recycle one or more of these for revisions to achieve the desired portfolio strategy.

Loop 4: During implementation, a business manager may have to recycle functional proposals so that the overall implementation plan has the desired strategic properties (i.e., becomes a near-term reflection of the longer-term strategy).

Loop 5: Similarly, the CEO might want revisions in one or more of the business implementation plans so that a final overall fit is achieved.[3]

The central point of this discussion is that the team concept is a critical and practiced feature in strategic processes. Managers at various levels have different responsibilities for various parts of the process, but they interact and are interdependent in achieving the final outcome.

Value of Strategic Management

Financial Benefits

The principal appeal of any managerial approach is the expectation that it will lead to increased profit for the firm. This is especially true of a strategic management system with a major impact on both the formulation and implementation of plans.

A series of studies of various business organizations actually measured the impact of strategic management processes on the bottom line. One of the first major studies was conducted by Ansoff, Avner, Brandenburg, Portner, and Radosevich in 1970.[4] In a study of 93 U.S. manufacturing firms, the authors found that formal planners who took a strategic management approach outperformed nonplanners in terms of financial criteria that measured sales, assets, sales price, earnings per share, and earnings growth. The planners were also more accurate in predicting the outcome of major strategic actions.

---

[3] P. Lorange, *Corporate Planning: An Executive Viewpoint* (Englewood Cliffs, N.J.: Prentice-Hall, 1980), p. 62.

[4] H. I. Ansoff, J. Avner, R. Brandenburg, F. E. Portner, and R. Radosevich, "Does Planning Pay? The Effect of Planning on Success of Acquisitions in American Firms," *Long-Range Planning* 3 (1970), pp. 2–7.

A second pioneering research effort was published in 1970 by Thune and House, who studied 36 firms in six different industries.[5] They found that formal planners in the petroleum, food, drug, steel, chemical, and machinery industries significantly outperformed nonplanners in the same fields. Additionally, planners improved their own performance significantly after the formal process had been adopted as compared to their financial performance during the nonplanning years.

Herold later (1972) reported a replication of part of the Thune and House research dealing with drug and chemical companies.[6] His findings supported the earlier study and, in fact, suggested that the disparity between the financial performance of planning and nonplanning firms was increasing over time.

In 1974 Fulmer and Rue published a study of the strategic management practices of 386 companies over a three-year period. The authors found that durable goods manufacturing firms with strategic management were more successful than those without.[7] Their findings did not hold for nondurable and service companies—probably, the authors suspected, because strategic planning among these firms was a recent phenomenon and its effects were not fully realized.

In 1974, Schoeffler, Buzzell, and Heany reported a study designed to measure the profit impact of market studies (PIMS).[8] This PIMS project involved the effects of strategic planning on a firm's return on investment (ROI). The researchers concluded that ROI was most significantly affected by market share, investment intensity, and corporate diversity. The overall PIMS model, which incorporated 37 performance variables, disclosed that up to 80 percent of the improvement possible in a firm's profitability is achieved through changes in the company's strategic direction.

An additional study of widespread impact was reported by Karger and Malik in 1975.[9] Their research—involving 90 U.S. companies in five industries—found that strategic long-range planners significantly outperformed nonformal planners in terms of generally accepted financial measures.

Finally, while most studies have examined strategic management in large firms, a 1982 report found that strategic planning had a favorable impact on performance in small businesses. After studying 101 small retail, service, and manufacturing firms over a three-year period, Robinson found a significant

---

[5] S. S. Thune and R. J. House, "Where Long-Range Planning Pays Off," *Business Horizons,* August 1970, pp. 81–87.

[6] D. M. Herold, "Long-Range Planning and Organizational Performance: A Cross-Validation Study," *Academy of Management Journal,* March 1972, pp. 91–102.

[7] R. M. Fulmer and L. W. Rue, "The Practice and Profitability of Long-Range Planning," *Managerial Planning* 22 (1974), pp. 1–7.

[8] S. Schoeffler, R. D. Buzzell, and D. F. Heany, "Impact of Strategic Planning on Profit Performance," *Harvard Business Review,* March–April 1974, pp. 137–45.

[9] D. W. Karger and Z. A. Malik, "Long-Range Planning and Organizational Performance," *Long-Range Planning,* December 1975, pp. 60–64.

improvement in sales, profitability, and productivity among those businesses engaging in strategic planning when compared to firms without systematic planning activities.[10]

The overall pattern of results reported in these seven studies clearly indicates the value of strategic management as gauged by a variety of financial measures.[11] Based on the evidence now available, organizations that adopt a strategic management approach do so with the strong and reasonable expectation that the new system will lead to improved financial performance.

Benefits of Strategic Management[12]

The strategic management approach emphasizes interaction by managers at all levels of the organizational hierarchy in planning and implementation. As a result, strategic management has certain behavioral consequences that are also characteristic of participative decision making. Therefore, an accurate assessment of the impact of strategy formulation on organizational performance also requires a set of nonfinancial evaluation criteria—measures of behavioral-based effects. In fact, it can be argued that the manager trained to promote the positive aspects of these behavioral consequences is also well positioned to meet the financial expectations of the firm. However, regardless of the eventual profitability of particular strategic plans, several behavioral effects can be expected to improve the welfare of the firm:

1. Strategy formulation activities should enhance the problem prevention capabilities of the firm. As a consequence of encouraging and rewarding subordinate attention to planning considerations, managers are aided in their monitoring and forecasting responsibilities by workers who are alerted to needs of strategic planning.

2. Group-based strategic decisions are most likely to reflect the best available alternatives. Better decisions are probable outcomes of the process for two reasons: first, generating alternative strategies is facilitated by group interaction; second, screening of options is improved because group members offer forecasts based on their specialized perspectives.

3. Employee motivation should improve as employees better appreciate the productivity–reward relationships inherent in every strategic plan. When employees or their representatives participate in the strategy formulation process,

---

[10] R. B. Robinson, Jr., "The Importance of 'Outsiders' in Small Firm Strategic Planning," *Academy of Management Journal*, March 1982, pp. 80–93.

[11] A few additional studies not discussed in the chapter reported mixed results. For a review of both sides of the issue, refer to J. A. Pearce II, E. B. Freeman, and R. B. Robinson, Jr., "The Tenuous Link between Formal Strategic Planning and Financial Performance," *Academy of Management Review*, in press.

[12] This section was adapted in part from J. A. Pearce II and W. A. Randolph, "Improving Strategy Formulation Pedagogies by Recognizing Behavioral Aspects," *Exchange*, December 1980, pp. 7–10, with permission of the authors.

a better understanding of the priorities and operations of the organization's reward system is achieved, thus adding incentives for goal-directed behavior.

4. Gaps and overlaps in activities among diverse individuals and groups should be reduced as participation in strategy formulation leads to a clarification of role differentiations. The group meeting format, which is characteristic of several stages of a strategy formulation process, promotes an understanding of the delineations of individual and subgroup responsibilities.

5. Resistance to change should be reduced. The required participation helps eliminate the uncertainty associated with change, which is at the root of most resistance. While participants may be no more pleased with their own choices then they would be with authoritarian decisions, their acceptance of new plans is more likely if employees are aware of the parameters that limit the available options.

Risks of Strategic Management

While involvement in strategy formulation generates behavior-based benefits for participants and for the firm, managers must be trained to guard against three types of unintended negative consequences. First, while it is readily recognized that the strategic management process is costly in terms of hours invested by participants, the negative effects of managers spending time away from work is considered less often. Managers must be trained to schedule their duties to provide the necessary time for strategic activities while minimizing any negative impact on operational responsibilities.

Second, if the formulators of strategy are not intimately involved in implementation, individual responsibility for input to the decision process and subsequent conclusions can be shirked. Thus, strategic managers must be trained to limit their promises to performance that can be delivered by the decision makers and their subordinates.

Third, strategic managers must be trained to anticipate, minimize, or constructively respond when participating subordinates become disappointed or frustrated over unattained expectations. Frequently, subordinates perceive an implicit guarantee that their involvement in even minor phases of total strategy formulation will result in both acceptance of their preferred plan and an increase in clearly associated rewards. Alternatively, they may erroneously conclude that a strategic manager's solicitation of their input on selected issues will extend to other areas of decision making. Sensitizing managers to these issues and preparing them with effective means of negating or minimizing such negative consequences will greatly enhance the overall potential of any strategic plan.

Executives' Views of Strategic Management

How do managers and corporate executives view the contribution of strategic management to the success of their firms? To answer this question a survey was conducted that included over 200 executives from the Fortune 500, Fortune

Strategy in Action 1–1
Executives' General Opinions and Attitudes

Item	Percent of respondents indicating		
	Agreement	Neutral	Disagreement
1. Reducing emphasis on strategic planning will be detrimental to our long-term performance.	88.7	4.9	6.4
2. Our plans today reflect implementation concerns.	73.6	16.9	9.5
3. We have improved the sophistication of our strategic planning systems.	70.6	18.6	10.8
4. Our previous approaches to strategic planning are not appropriate today.	64.2	16.2	19.6
5. Today's systems emphasize creativity among managers more than our previous systems do.	62.6	20.2	17.2
6. Our strategic planning systems today are more consistent with our organization's culture.	55.6	30.7	13.7
7. We are more concerned about the evaluation of our strategic planning systems today.	54.0	29.7	16.3
8. There is more participation from lower-level managers in our strategic planning.	56.6	18.0	25.4
9. Our tendency to rely on outside consultants for strategic planning has been on the decrease.	50.8	23.0	26.2
10. Our systems emphasize control more than before.	41.3	33.0	25.7
11. Planning in our company or unit is generally viewed as a luxury today.	15.0	13.0	72.0

Source: Adapted from V. Ramanujam, J. C. Camillus, and N. Venkatraman, "Trends in Strategic Planning," in *Strategic Planning and Management Handbook,* ed. W. R. King and D. I. Cleland (New York: Van Nostrand Reinhold, 1987), p. 619.

500 Service, and INC 500 companies.[13] Their responses are summarized in Strategy in Action 1–1.

Overall, the responses paint a very supportive picture of corporate America's view of strategic management. The process is generally seen as instrumental

---

[13] V. Ramanujam, J. C. Camillus, and N. Venkatraman, "Trends in Strategic Planning," in *Strategic Planning and Management Handbook,* ed. W. R. King and D. I. Cleland (New York: Van Nostrand Reinhold, 1987).

to high performance, evolutionary and perhaps revolutionary in its ever-increasing sophistication, increasingly pervasive throughout the firm, action oriented, and cost effective.

In the collective view of the responding executives, strategic management clearly is critical to their individual and organizational success.

Summary

Strategic management was defined as the set of decisions and actions resulting in the formulation and implementation of strategies designed to achieve the objectives of an organization. It was shown to involve long-term, future-oriented, complex decision making necessitating top-management action because of the resources required to formulate an environmentally opportunistic plan.

Strategic management was presented as a three-tiered process involving corporate-, business-, and functional-level planners, and support personnel. At each progressively lower level, strategic activities were shown to be more specific, narrow, short term, and action oriented with lower risks but fewer opportunities for dramatic impact.

The value of strategic management was demonstrated in a review of seven large-scale business studies. Using a variety of financial performance measures, each of these studies was able to provide convincing evidence of the profitability of strategy formulation and implementation. In addition, the chapter identified five major behavioral benefits for the team-oriented, strategic-management-directed firm. Despite some noteworthy behavioral costs, the net behavioral gains justify the approach, almost irrespective of the hope of improved financial performance.

Questions for Discussion

1. Find a recent copy of *Business Week* and read the "Corporate Strategies" section. Was the main decision discussed strategic? At what level in the organization was the key decision made?

2. In what ways do you think the subject matter in this strategic management/business policy course will differ from previous courses you have had?

3. Why do you believe the case method is selected as the best approach for learning the skills needed in strategy formulation and implementation?

4. After graduation you are not likely to move directly into a top-level management position. In fact, most members of your class may never reach that level. Why then is it important for all business majors to study the field of strategic management?

5. Do you expect that outstanding performance in this course will require a great deal of memorization? Why or why not?

6. You have undoubtedly read about individuals who seemingly single-handedly have given direction to their corporations. Is it likely that a participative strategic management approach might stifle or suppress the contributions of such individuals?

Bibliography

Fulmer, R. M., and L. W. Rue. "The Practice and Profitability of Long-Range Planning." *Managerial Planning* 22 (1974), pp. 1–7.

Herold, D. M. "Long-Range Planning and Organizational Performance: A Cross-Validation Study." *Academy of Management Journal,* March 1972, pp. 91–102.

Hofer, C. W., and D. Schendel. *Strategy Formulation: Analytical Concepts.* St. Paul, Minn.: West Publishing, 1978.

Karger, D. W., and Z. A. Malik. "Long-Range Planning and Organizational Performance." *Long-Range Planning,* December 1975, pp. 60–64.

Kudla, R. J. "Elements of Effective Corporate Planning." *Long-Range Planning,* August 1976, pp. 82–93.

Lorange, P. *Corporate Planning: An Executive Viewpoint.* Englewood Cliffs, N.J.: Prentice-Hall, 1980.

Mintzberg, H. "Strategy Making in Three Modes." *California Management Review* 16, no. 2 (1973), pp. 44–53.

Pearce, J. A., II; E. B. Freeman; and R. B. Robinson, Jr. "The Tenuous Link between Formal Strategic Planning and Financial Performance." *Academy of Management Review,* October 1987, pp. 658–75.

Pearce, J. A., II, and W. A. Randolph. "Improving Strategy Formulation Pedagogies by Recognizing Behavioral Aspects." *Exchange,* December 1980, pp. 7–10.

Robinson, R. B., Jr. "The Importance of 'Outsiders' in Small Firm Strategic Planning." *Academy of Management Journal,* March 1982, pp. 80–93.

Schoeffler, S.; R. D. Buzzell; and D. F. Heany. "Impact of Strategic Planning on Profit Performance." *Harvard Business Review,* March–April 1974, pp. 137–45.

Steiner, G. A. "The Rise of the Corporate Planner." *Harvard Business Review,* September–October 1970, pp. 133–39.

————. *Strategic Planning.* New York: Free Press, 1979.

Thune, S. S., and R. J. House. "Where Long-Range Planning Pays Off." *Business Horizons,* August 1970, pp. 81–87.

Vancil, R. F. ". . . So You're Going to Have a Planning Department!" *Harvard Business Review,* May–June 1967, pp. 88–96.

The Cohesion Case

A Unique Learning Aid to Understanding the Strategic Management Process

This section inaugurates a unique feature of this book, the *Cohesion Case* and 13 *Cohesion Case Illustrations*. The purpose of this unique feature is to help you understand the process and the concepts associated with strategic management, which are discussed throughout the 13 chapters in this book. As the word *cohesion* suggests, the objective of this learning aid is to "tie related parts together." Specifically, the objective is to tie together the strategic management concepts discussed in each chapter with an illustration of their practical application in an actual business firm.

To ensure continuity across the 13 chapters, each of the 13 Cohesion Case Illustrations will focus on the same company—Holiday Inns, Inc. This provides you with the added advantage of illustrating each part of the strategic management process within the same firm, thus offering an integrated, consistent picture of the formulation and implementation of a company's strategy. Over 200,000 people have used this Cohesion Case in the last six years as a learning aid in their study of strategic management. The overwhelming sentiment is that it provides a useful, easy-to-understand way of becoming familiar with strategic management.

Holiday Inns, Inc., is the world's leading hospitality company, with interests in hotels/motels, casino gaming, restaurants, and transportation. It was selected as the Cohesion Case for several reasons:

1. Holiday Inns, Inc., is a highly visible, well-known company.
2. Holiday Inns, Inc., is a multibusiness company. Only 54 percent of its revenues come from its lodging chain, with the remainder coming from gaming, restaurants, and transportation. The fact that Holiday Inns, Inc., is a multibusiness company provides the opportunity to apply strategic management concepts at three key levels—corporate strategy, business strategy, and operations strategy.
3. While Holiday Inns, Inc., is a multibusiness company, it is still a relatively simple, comprehendable enterprise. As a result, using this firm facilitates maximum focus on the application of text material and avoids wasting energy on simply trying to understand what the business is about.

The remainder of this section provides the Cohesion Case describing Holiday Inns, Inc. This case is the basis for understanding the Cohesion Case Illustrations. This material should be read thoroughly to gain a familiarity with Holiday Inns. As the remaining chapters (and accompanying Cohesion Case Illustrations) are covered, refer to this case material, occasionally rereading it. Doing this will ensure an adequate foundation for understanding how the components of strategic management, discussed in each chapter, are being applied to Holiday Inns in the respective illustrations.

The first objective in dealing with this Cohesion Case is to become more familiar with the total operation of Holiday Inns, Inc., and to think about the relevance of strategic management to this firm. An illustration is provided at the conclusion of the case to aid in applying the Chapter 1 material to Holiday Inns.

Your instructor may choose to use this Cohesion Case feature as a regular part of your class discussion related to coverage of the chapter materials. An equally viable option used by many instructors is to leave coverage of the Cohesion Case and the 13 Cohesion Case Illustration sections up to you as an optional aid in understanding strategic management. Both approaches work well, and the material is written to accommodate either one.

One final point: The case covers Holiday Inns, Inc., through early 1982. This date was chosen because the early 1980s represented a key decision point in the strategic posture of the firm. Thus, the Cohesion Case Illustrations allow the reader to assume the role of assistant to the president and executive committee at Holiday Inns with the assignment of formulating and implementing a strategy for the 1980s. An update of key actions at Holiday Inns, Inc., is provided at a later point in this book.

Hospitality Co.

The Cohesion Case: Holiday Inns, Inc.

The Businesses of Holiday Inns, Inc.

1   When we think about Holiday Inns, we generally are only considering hotels and motels. However, Holiday Inns, Inc., is a $1.2 billion-per-year diversified multinational corporation. In fact, only 54 percent of total corporate revenues results from hotel operations. The company was structured into four divisions:

1. Hotel group.
   a. Parent company.
   b. Licensees.
   c. International.
2. Transportation group.
   a. Trailways, Inc.
   b. Delta Steamship Lines, Inc.
3. Restaurant group.
   a. Perkins Cake and Steak.
4. Casino gaming.
   a. Atlantic City.
   b. Las Vegas.

2   As Holiday Inns moved into the decade of the 1970s, top management sought to broaden its hotel-intensive earnings base. Under the leadership of Kemmons Wilson, Holiday Inns' founder, the mission was redefined from being a food-and-lodging company to a travel and transportation-related company. This definition led to the four business groups.

3   A reexamination and possible restructuring of the company's operations was being considered as the company's executives devised a strategy for the 1990s. The thrust of the reexamination involved both the basic mission of the company and the missions and appropriateness of its business groups. Exhibit 1 provides some insight into operations at Holiday Inns, Inc., from a financial perspective through 1981. The next several sections briefly describe the operations of the four business groups that make up Holiday Inns, Inc.

Hotel Group

4   Hotels that are part of Holiday Inns, Inc., are segregated into two groups. The hotels in the first group are company owned, and those in the second group are franchisee owned and operated. The Holiday Inns system continued to reflect the company's

This 1988 revised edition of the Holiday Inns, Inc., case was prepared by Richard Robinson, University of South Carolina. © Richard Robinson, 1988.

Exhibit 1
Financial information on each business group ($ millions)

	1979	1980	1981
Revenues			
Hotel	$ 784	$ 849	$ 853
Gaming	1	201	388
Restaurant	30	93	96
Transportation	278	377	413
Products and other	19	13	13
	$1,112	$1,533	$1,765
Operating income			
Hotel	$ 137	$ 155	$ 171
Gaming	1	24	56
Restaurant	3	4	6
Transportation	17	48	46
Products and other	11	7	11
	$ 169	$ 238	$ 290
Identifiable assets			
Hotel	$ 651	$ 712	$ 749
Gaming	30	451	573
Restaurant	98	97	92
Transportation	234	268	254
Products and other	226	152	147
	$1,239	$1,680	$1,815
Capital expenditures			
Hotel	$ 111	$ 122	$ 127
Gaming	—	61	29
Restaurant	12	11	2
Transportation	2	6	6
Products and other	8	7	6
	$ 133	$ 207	$ 170
Depreciation and amortization			
Hotel	$ 45	$ 49	$ 53
Gaming	—	10	18
Restaurant	1	5	4
Transportation	8	8	9
Products and other	2	2	3
	$ 56	$ 74	$ 87

original emphasis on franchising. In 1981, 82 percent of the system was operated by franchisees—independent businesspeople or companies—while Holiday Inns, Inc., operated the remaining 18 percent. The Holiday Inns system has maintained an approximately 80/20 franchised-to-company-owned ratio since the chain was started. Exhibit 2 shows a breakdown of the Holiday Inns system by these two groups.

Exhibit 2
Hotel group

	1979	1980	1981	5-year compound growth rate[†] (percent)	10-year compound growth rate[‡] (percent)
Hotels at year-end					
Company owned or managed	246	240	229	(4.5)%	(2.3)%
Licensed*	1,495	1,515	1,522	1.3	3.5
Total system	1,741	1,755	1,751	0.4	2.5
Rooms at year-end					
Company owned or managed	55,821	56,141	55,285	(1.1)	.7
Licensed	240,430	247,437	252,828	2.8	5.4
Total system	296,251	303,578	308,113	2.1	4.4
Occupancy (company owned)	73.8%	71.5%	69.2%	—	—
Average rate per occupied room (company owned)	$32.65	$36.80	$40.79	13.0	9.5

* Licensed means franchised.
[†] Since 1976.
[‡] Since 1971.

5   Holiday Inns' commitment to the ownership and operation of properties provided a basis for innovation and leadership in the marketplace; for example, company-operated hotels provided an extensive research base for the development of marketing information, operating procedures, and marketing techniques. The company claimed that its 200-plus properties provide a solid, diverse base from which to build and improve operating expertise.

6   As shown in Exhibit 2, the number of company-owned hotels has steadily decreased. This reflects Holiday Inns' emphasis on removing older properties from its system. Commenting on this trend, Roy Winegardner, chairman of the board, made the following observation in a December 1980 interview:

> By 1983, 217,000 rooms or 60 percent of the Holiday Inns hotel system will be new or extensively renovated. A major emphasis for company-owned hotels will be to move into destination and multiuser properties, such as airports, suburban, midtown, and downtown locations, which are expected to account for over 95 percent of all company-owned or -operated rooms.

Franchises

7   The 1,522 inns not operated by the company are owned by independent businesspeople called franchisees. The company carefully screened all applicants for franchises and placed a great deal of emphasis on the character, ability, and financial responsibility of the applicant, in addition to the appropriateness of the proposed location. Franchise

agreements, which were for a 20-year period, established standards for service and the quality of accommodations. The company trained franchise management personnel at Holiday Inn University near Memphis, Tennessee; made inspections of franchise operations three times a year; and provided detailed operational manuals, training films, and instructional aids for franchise personnel. During the initial period of 20 years, most franchises were terminated in certain circumstances by the franchisee. In the event of a franchisee's violation of the agreement, the company terminated the franchise. The company's policy in determining whether or not to renew a particular franchise agreement (after the initial 20 years) was in part to evaluate the overall desirability of retaining the franchisee's inn within the system.

8   Since Holiday Inns started franchising in 1955, 20-year renewal activity started becoming a regular issue by the late 1970s. Franchise expiration and renewal activity from 1977 through 1983 follow:

	Franchises expiring	Number renewed
1977	5	2
1978	6	2
1979	7	2
1980	34	32
1981	31	?
1982	41	?
1983	34	?

9   Commenting on the financial attractiveness of franchising, Holiday Inns' CFO Charles Solomonson said:

> [One of our] unique characteristic[s] is franchising. Using our hotel group as an example, with franchise fees normally tied to room revenues, this provides a "top line" inflation hedge. Our franchise revenues, which include both initial fees and ongoing royalty payments, totaled $63.6 million in 1980 and have grown at a very steady 18.2 percent compound rate since 1975.
>
> The outlook for continued franchise revenue growth is quite positive. Industry supply and demand trends in our segment are favorable, and our franchisees have aggressive development plans as well. In addition, starting in the mid-1980s through the end of the century, an average of about 100 franchises a year—or 6 to 7 percent of the currently existing franchise system—will come up for renewal. At renewal time the company not only requires that the units be refurbished to current standards, which helps upgrade the system, but in virtually all cases the new franchise fee will be well in excess of the old rate.

10   The fees required by newly issued or renewed franchise agreements have been increased from time to time. A comparison of requirements for new or renewed domestic franchise agreements is provided at the top of the next page.

Early 1980s	Mid-1980s
An initial payment of $5,000.	No initial payment.
A one-time fee of $150 per room ($20,000 minimum).	One-time fee of $300 per room ($30,000 minimum).
A royalty of 4 percent of gross sales paid monthly.	Same 4 percent royalty as in 1978.
Conversion of 2 percent of gross room sales for marketing and reservation services monthly.	Same conversion charge but with a minimum of 14 cents per room per night.

Multinational Operations

11 Foreseeing possible obstacles in the intensive expansion of hotels/motels in the United States, Holiday Inns, Inc., had been rapidly expanding hotel operations abroad. The company's international development strategy had been to build strong national chains within the country where it now operated, as well as to gradually expand into new markets. Holiday Inns, Inc., argued that this strategy differs from that of its competitors who had but one location in each major city overseas. At the same time, the company had emphasized multiuser, politically stable locations for company-owned hotels. For example, 18 of the 24 hotels in which the company had an ownership interest in 1980 were located in major European cities.

12 At the beginning of the 1980s the Holiday Inns system had 195 international locations in 55 countries (of which 161 were franchised) with well over 40,000 rooms. By 1981, the number of non–U.S. locations had increased to 226. International operations' performance information is provided below.

	International operations[*]		
	1979	1980	1981
Consolidated assets	$123,580	$134,117	$137,641
Consolidated equity	79,896	98,951	108,488
Revenues	129,698	143,244	129,219
Operating income	26,014	28,049	21,949

[*] In thousands of dollars.

13 International projects under way in 1981 nearly equaled domestic activity. By the end of 1981, Holiday Inns maintained an equity interest in only 18 international properties, as it sought to decrease its international asset exposure.

Key Operating Systems

14 Holiday Inns operated the Holidex reservation system, which linked over 17,000 terminals throughout the world, thus representing the largest reservation system in the hotel industry. The importance of a reservation system such as the Holidex network

cannot be overstated. Approximately 70 percent of all room-nights at Holiday Inns were sold through advance reservations. The company invested over $20 million in the second generation of this system, Holidex II. It was not only an information system, providing accounting and room inventory services, but it also provided a marketing data base as well as information services at the unit location.

15   In 1980, the new Holidex II network booked about 33 million room-nights, more than a third of all system reservations, and several times more than competing hotel chains. Nonetheless, the number of room-nights booked was down 50 percent from mid-1970 levels.

16   In concert with expanded Holidex II computer capabilities, Holiday Inns' operations management system (OMS) was developed to improve profits at the hotel level. Consisting of weekly department forecast, energy control, staff scheduling, inventory control, industrial engineering, and quality assurance, the system was fully implemented in company-owned or -operated properties by 1981. The program helped improve margins on a consistent basis, even where occupancies declined temporarily.

17   Another new internal program—Inn-level business planning—called for careful monitoring of trends in the local market environment, including product competitiveness, rates, opportunities, and competitive developments. This market-by-market monitoring enabled each hotel to stay abreast of, and react quickly to, changing competitive situations.

18   Another technological system on which Holiday Inns placed major future importance was its HI-NET Satellite Communications Network. The HI-NET system provides low-cost, in-room entertainment that is free to the guest, as well as the capability to hold nationwide teleconferences linking over 150 Holiday Inn facilities. As an example of the capabilities of the HI-NET system for teleconferencing, Holiday Inns, Inc., held a 1981 teleconference meeting for its employees that was aimed at increasing employee involvement and ultimately improving productivity in all of its businesses. They were able to communicate directly with approximately 15,000 employees of Holiday Inns, Harrah's, Perkins, and Delta at over 130 locations throughout the United States.

Competitive Posture

19   President and CEO Mike Rose offered the following summary of the hotel group's 1980s mission:

> The current mission of the hotel group is to [increase] Holiday Inns' leadership position in the broad midscale segments of the lodging industry. This mission will be achieved by producing superior consumer satisfaction through increased emphasis on the quality of our product and further capitalization on our significant distributional advantages over all other competitors. We also intend to [increase] our consumer recognition as the preferred brand in the lodging industry.

20   The Holiday Inns hotel system led the lodging industry in terms of number of rooms (see Exhibit 3) as well as customer preference (see Exhibit 4). The sustained leadership of the Holiday Inn brand in the broad midpriced market segment, which accounts for approximately two thirds of all travelers, was attributable to the hotel group's focus on customer satisfaction, according to corporate executives. These

---

Exhibit 3
Leading lodging firms by number of rooms, 1981 (in thousands)

Holiday Inns	308
Best Western	204
Sheraton	109
Ramada	98
Hilton	76

---

executives cite hotel operating systems, extensive training, and emphasis on value for price paid as key elements of this focus. Marketing efforts reinforce this focus. For example, in 1981, the company introduced a "No Excuses" room guarantee program for all U.S. hotels, which promised guests would be satisfied with their rooms or their room charge for the night's stay would be refunded. The Holiday Inns hotel system was the only hotel chain to offer guests such a guarantee.

21   During the period from 1979 to 1983, the hotel group planned to increase the number of company-owned rooms by 72,000 and sell 75,000 new franchise rooms. Riding the crest of steady occupancy growth, the hotel system offered nearly twice as many rooms as its nearest competitor and sold one out of every three hotel chain room-nights in 1979. In the face of mounting competition from both the budget and luxury segments of the lodging industry, Holiday Inns executives did not expect occupancy to drop due to price or service competition. As Exhibit 2 shows, occupancy of Holiday Inns properties declined for the third year in a row to 69.2 percent in 1981, down from 71.5 percent in 1980, and 73.8 percent in 1979. General economic weakness, a decline in family disposable income, and rapidly increasing airline fares were given as primary reasons. Single occupancy, an indicator of business travel, remained virtually unchanged in 1981. Business travel accounts for approximately 60 percent of Holiday Inn hotel room-nights sold. Multiple occupancy, which the company felt reflects personal travel, was down in each of these years. Room rates increased 10.8 percent in 1981, compared with 12.7 percent in 1980 and 17.4 percent in 1979 (see Exhibit 2).

22   Some industry forecasters predicted that demand for hotel accommodations would grow faster than supply into the 1990s, with the middle-priced segment projected to account for the majority of this growth. Other analysts warned of potential overbuilding as the industry became increasingly segmented. Commenting on growth potential in different industry segments, president and CEO Mike Rose offered the following:

Holiday Inn® hotels are ideally positioned in the moderate-price market segment to take advantage of the large projected demand growth within this segment. In simple terms, the lodging industry could be described in three major segments: the high-price or image segment, the moderate-price segment, and the low-price segment.

While we think the percentage growth of demand will be highest in the high-price or image segment, in absolute terms the demand for rooms in the moderate-

Exhibit 4
Hotel brand preference (percent)

	1979	1980	1981	1988 (projected)
Holiday Inns	40%	36%	38%	34%
Best Western	6	7	7	9
Hilton	6	5	6	7
Ramada	6	7	6	7
Sheraton	5	5	5	5
Days Inn	1	1	4	6
Hyatt	2	2	4	6
Mariott	2	2	3	6
Howard Johnson	3	3	2	2
Quality Inn	—	1	2	3
Motel 6 (and others)	—	1	2	12

price segment will grow three times faster than in either the high-price or low-price segments.

We are further encouraged that new room supply is being focused more and more at the high end of the market, and we can foresee an oversupply of hotel rooms in that segment during this decade. On the other hand, we think that most of our chain competitors in the moderate segment do not have the inherent strength to keep pace with the demand growth in the moderate-price segment, and that we will continue to [increase] our share of that segment during the next decade.

Our domestic parent company development will be predominantly in major metropolitan areas in locations where we serve multiple demand sources. For example, we would like to be in locations that serve both business and leisure travelers, that also serve small group meetings, and that serve people arriving by automobile and air.

23   While Holiday Inns sees enormous growth potential in the middle-priced segment, rumors were beginning to surface in early 1980 that Holiday Inns was considering entry (through acquiring existing chains and/or starting new ones) into both the high-priced and low-priced industry segments. The growth rates and profit margins reported by chains like Days Inns and La Quinta were twice those of Holiday Inns.

Transportation Group

24   The transportation group of Holiday Inns, Inc., consisted of two major units: Trailways (headquartered in Dallas, Texas), the second-largest intercity bus system, and Delta Steamship Lines. The transportation group accounted for 35 percent of Holiday Inns, Inc.'s revenue, with bus operations producing 22 percent and steamship operations producing 13 percent (see Exhibits 5 and 6).

Exhibit 5
Transportation group: Bus operations

Bus operating statistics

	1976	1977	1978	1985 (projected)
Bus operating revenues (000)	$ 226,568	$ 240,262	$ 254,495	$ 275,000
Bus-miles (000)	207,678	198,125	190,770	180,000
Number of intercity buses	2,312	2,203	2,158	2,100
Passenger-miles (000)	2,727,453	2,856,095	2,694,454	2,500,000
Bus occupancy (load factor)	36.4%	40.4%	39.5%	38%

Bus operations—financial performance ($ millions)

	1976	1977	1978
Passenger	$ 136.8	$ 141.9	$ 145.7
Charter	38.9	41.2	44.7
Express	44.9	51.3	58.8
Other	14.1	10.0	18.9
Total revenue	$ 234.7	$ 244.4	$ 268.1
Operating income	$ 15.4	$ 16.4	$ 19.7
Operating margin	6.5%	6.7%	7.4%
Capital expenditures	$ 13.1	$ 10.0	$ 21.4
Assets	165.5	171.3	177.0

Note: More current statistics are not available.

Exhibit 6
Transportation group: Steamship operations

Steamship operating statistics

	1979	1980	1981	1985 (projected)	Compound growth rates (percent) 5-year	10-year
Voyages completed	162	177	174	190	27.8%	11.6%
Tons of cargo (000)	2,635.2	3,183.6	3,264.2	4,000	29.1	15.3

Steamship operations—financial performance ($ millions)

	1979	1980	1981
Revenue	$278.1	$377.1	$413.2
Operating income	16.6	47.8	46.2
Operating margin	9.8%	20.1%	15.9%
Capital expenditures	1.4	5.7	6.4
Assets	233.5	268.4	258.0

25   Trailways' fundamental business was to provide intercity passenger service, charter bus service, and express package services. In 1979, the Trailways route system covered 70,000 miles, serving 5,000 cities and towns in 43 states.

26   J. Kevin Murphy, formerly president of Purolator Services, Inc., was president of the bus operations. Placing primary emphasis on new marketing approaches, Murphy streamlined the company's name from Continental Trailways to Trailways and adopted a sunburst logo. A new marketing program—Anywhere Program—was initiated. It allowed the traveler to go anywhere in the United States—from one origin city to a destination city—with unlimited stopovers for a low, fixed price. Advertising expenditures were increased on programs stressing the cost-saving aspects of bus travel as opposed to other transportation forms.

27   Greyhound (number one in the bus service industry) and Trailways began to experience increased competition from the newly deregulated airline industry for low-cost intercity travel. Travelers could often fly and arrive at a destination from 3 to 10 times faster for a fare only 15 to 25 percent above the cost of a bus ticket. Between 1974 and 1979, the number of scheduled passengers increased by 25 percent for airlines, while it declined over 32 percent for buses.

28   In an effort to combat discount fares offered by airlines on selected routes, the Trailways division announced a new series of low fares between major cities in the northeastern section of the United States. In addition to competing with the airlines, Trailways was trying to counteract Greyhound's discount offerings on interstate routes. These fares represented a reduction of 30 to 50 percent from regular fares and applied primarily to interstate trips averaging 775 miles (one way) or more. An article in *Fortune* concluded that Greyhound and Trailways' price war was hurting only each other's profitability, without producing any additional share of the long-haul business, which was dominated by the airlines at fares only 50 percent above the discount bus fares.

29   Trailways became the first intercity bus company to offer a discount to senior citizens, a group that made up 25 percent of its market. The idea was initiated as a result of a recommendation from Trailways' senior citizen advisory council. Holiday Inns corporate executives anticipated that Trailways' senior citizen and charter passengers would provide a convenient customer base for its hotel properties.

30   Two growing segments of bus services were charter operations and package express. Trailways' charter operations served 26 million passengers a year, representing 9 percent of the total charter market. During the last half of the 1970s, charter sales grew at a compounded annual rate of almost 13 percent.

31   Package express, the fastest-growing segment of the Trailways division, accounted for 22 percent of total revenues from bus operations. Package pickup and delivery were offered in more than 110 major U.S. cities. The package express and overnight delivery industry was growing at over 60 percent in the early 1980s. Federal Express, the industry leader, virtually created this industry and doubled its volume every six months between 1977 and 1981. The industry became very competitive, and telecommunication technology threatened to become a future basis for the overnight message service.

32   The company lobbied vigorously in favor of municipal ownership of bus terminals. Airplane terminals and other public transportation terminals (e.g., trains) are primarily

municipally owned. This would have transferred the cost of bus terminal maintenance from the company to the taxpayer—a key savings for Trailways. Unfortunately, this effort met with little success. The movement in the passenger transportation industry, as evidenced by deregulation of airlines, was toward decreased government involvement. Business analysts forecast continued hard times for the intercity bus industry, which was caught between rising energy, labor, and maintenance costs on the one hand and increasing price competition, particularly with airlines, on the other. Top management was beginning to seriously question the strategic fit of Trailways in Holiday Inns, Inc.'s mission and business portfolio.

33   Delta Steamship Lines was acquired by Holiday Inns, Inc., in the 1960s. Delta operated a fleet of 24 vessels between Gulf ports, Central America, South America, and Africa.

34   In June 1978, Delta reached an agreement with Prudential Lines, Inc., to acquire 13 vessels and add five new trade routes (from the East and West coasts of the United States) over the next two years at a cost in excess of $71.5 million (see Exhibit 7). Approximately half of the Prudential acquisition cost was financed using Delta's capital construction fund, and the balance came through Delta assuming low-interest, government-guaranteed mortgages on the vessels.

35   The Prudential acquisition returned Delta to passenger service, in which the line had had no involvement since 1968. All four combination passenger/cargo vessels acquired from Prudential have first-class accommodations for 100 passengers.

36   Of greater importance to Holiday Inns' steamship operation, the acquisition doubled the number of Delta's Latin and South American trade routes to Pacific U.S. ports.

37   In 1973, Delta introduced LASH (light aboard ship) cargo containers in its operations. The LASH containers (they are found in all of Delta's fleet) were filled before the arrival of a ship to improve the scheduling of the ship's time in port. For example, the average length of a typical South American voyage was reduced from 84 to 42 days by using LASH containers.

38   While Delta's revenue nearly doubled in 1978, operating income dropped significantly (see Exhibit 6). Captain J. W. Clark, president of the Delta operation, offered the following reasons:

> For one thing, it took longer to absorb the Prudential Lines, Inc., operations than originally thought. This was due to start-up costs connected with the acquisition, the transfer of vessels to new routes, higher-than-anticipated maintenance costs required to bring the new fleet up to Delta standards, and a delay in closing the transaction [that] reduced the revenue base over which expenses could be spread. Unsettled political and economic conditions also affected Delta's West Africa Trade.

39   Though faced with heavy foreign competition, Delta, the major U.S.-flag cargo carrier in its trade routes, anticipated increased market share through effective vessel scheduling, LASH technology, and beneficial government subsidies of U.S. marine transport operations.[1]

---

[1] Delta operated under differential subsidy agreements (expiring in 1995 and 1997) in which the U.S. Maritime Administration compensated Delta for portions of certain vessel operating expenses that are in excess of those incurred by its foreign competitors. The subsidy recorded in 1980, 1979, 1978, and 1977 amounted to $60,419,000; $52,429,000; $33,666,000; and $15,035,000, respectively.

manpower costs of ship transport?

Exhibit 7
Delta Steamship Line, Inc.'s trade routes

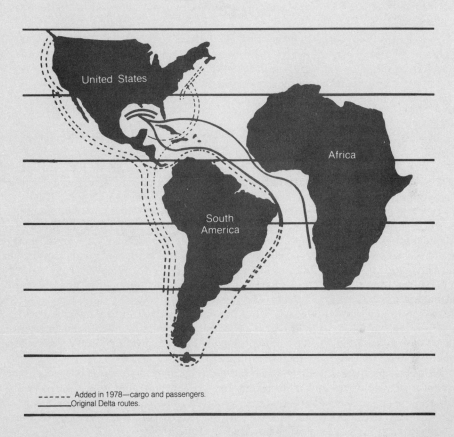

- - - - - Added in 1978—cargo and passengers.
————— Original Delta routes.

40   By 1980, Delta Steamship Lines, Inc.'s operating income almost tripled to a record $47.8 million on a 35.6 percent revenue increase. This dramatic improvement was accompanied by the installation of a new management team. Fifty percent of the subsidiary's top 28 positions were filled by people new to the company. This revitalized management successfully instituted a number of marketing and operational programs, which contributed greatly to the 1980 improvement. Cargo tonnage increased by 15.4 percent through fleet deployment to trade routes that best utilized each vessel's capabilities. Better scheduling permitted a 6.8 percent improvement in completed voyages. This increased the frequency of port calls, a factor important to shippers and their customers. Fifty percent more containers for better cargo handling and inexpensive hardware modifications allowed Delta to provide more container equipment to customers while reducing its unit costs through this expanded LASH technology as well as through favorable lease arrangements.

41   While Delta's performance improved dramatically, top management was seriously questioning its fit in Holiday Inns, Inc.'s hospitality-oriented portfolio for the next decade. Some managers were arguing that Delta should be divested. Others agreed with chairman of the board Winegardner's perspective, summarized in the following comment:

> We recognize that Delta might not fit Holiday Inns' long-term objective of being a hospitality company, although . . . its improved performance provides significant cash flow to fund investment in our hospitality businesses. As a result, Delta has earned an important position in our plans to maintain leadership in the hospitality industry.

Restaurant Group

42   On April 18, 1979, Holiday Inns, Inc., acquired Perkins Cake and Steak, Inc., a privately held restaurant chain headquartered in Minneapolis. The decision to enter the free-standing restaurant business reflected significant research on demographic trends as well as a corporate desire to build a broader earnings base. The 20-to-45-year-old age group will grow to over 50 percent of the U.S. population by 1990. This group eats out frequently—an average of five meals per week. The number of women in the work force was projected to exceed 60 percent in 1990. The number of single households was also steadily increasing. Both trends were associated with more eating out. According to Holiday Inns' research, food away from home is increasingly viewed as a necessary convenience.

43   Based on Holiday Inns' prepurchase market research, two thirds of Perkins' customers were found to be between the ages of 18 and 49 and to have annual household incomes in excess of $25,000. Demographically, the Perkins customer profile was similar in many respects to that of a Holiday Inn hotel guest.

44   Perkins was positioned in the marketplace as a family restaurant. It offered a broad menu at moderate prices and table service in "pleasant surroundings." Most Perkins restaurants were open 24 hours a day. A typical Perkins restaurant built since 1977 seats 172 people in a 5,000-square-foot structure. About one third of the restaurants in the Perkins system in 1980 were less than four years old.

45   There were 270 franchised units and 71 company-owned units when Holiday Inns bought the chain in early 1979. By the end of 1979, the number of franchised units remained unchanged, while 23 new company-owned units were added. Exhibit 8 highlights Perkins' activity between 1979 and 1981. Commenting on future emphasis for Perkins' growth, one major Holiday Inns executive offered the following in late 1981:

> It is our intent [that] Perkins [grows] primarily through the franchise system, with corporate stores filling in those major markets where we have already established a strong presence. Obviously, Perkins can never become a large part of Holiday Inns, Inc., with such mammoth businesses as the hotel and casino

Exhibit 8
Perkins operating data ($ millions)

	1979	1980	1981
Revenues	$81.8	$93.2	$96.4
Operating profit	10.1	4.3	6.5
Food and labor cost as percent of sales	54.6%	55.6%	56.7%
Number of stores:			
Corporate units	94	106	101
Franchise units	270	269	242
Total units	364	375	343

businesses, but we do think it is a vehicle for percentage growth and high return on assets employed.

It is our intention that Perkins will continue to grow using only its own cash flow, so that it will not be competitive with the hotel or casino businesses for capital resources.

46   Perkins' initial performance since being acquired was disappointing. The average customer count at company-owned restaurants dropped annually since the acquisition. This trend and the change in average guest checks are shown below as a percent of change from the previous year:

Average company-owned restaurant	Percent change from previous year			
	1979	1980	1981	1982
Change in average customer count	(14.9)%	(13.3)%	1.4%	9.0%
Change in average guest check	6.8	5.4	3.8	0.4

47   In general, there was no clear nationwide leader among family restaurant chains. In 1980, Perkins' system sales represented 10 percent of total sales generated by the five largest family restaurant chains. Perkins was fifth in sales in the family restaurant category in which it competed.

48   Overall, the restaurant industry was becoming increasingly competitive. The family restaurant market segment represented about one fourth of total U.S. restaurant sales (see Exhibit 9). Holiday Inns' management expected this segment to have continued growth during the 1980s, with chains expanding at the expense of independent operators.

Exhibit 9
Family restaurant industry: 1980s

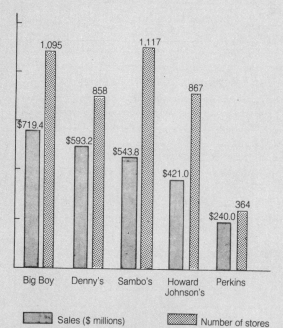

Diversified-menu family restaurant segment

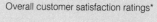

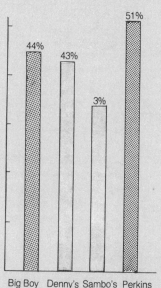

Overall customer satisfaction ratings*

* Percentage giving an "excellent" or "very good" rating.
Source: *Institutions Magazine.*

49   Perkins competed in the large middle market and differentiated itself from the competition, according to company sources, by focusing on consistent high quality, as opposed to focusing on low price. Holiday Inns' consumer research showed that Perkins' customers preferred a quality dining-out experience in terms of food, service, ambience, and decor. Guest checks at company-owned Perkins restaurants averaged 10 percent to 25 percent higher than typical competitors' checks.

50   Mike Rose, president and CEO, had the following comment in late 1981: "While Perkins has frankly been a bit of a disappointment to us at this stage, we do strongly believe that we can rebuild head counts, continue to control costs, and expand on a regional basis to obtain sufficient market penetration."

51   In response to corporate concerns, Perkins management adopted a back-to-basics philosophy in its approach to operations, especially in service and food preparation, in 1981. The clarity and effectiveness of Perkins' long-term strategy appeared very much in question as top management started planning for the next decade.

Gaming Group

52   In 1979, the board of directors of Holiday Inns, Inc., expanded corporate policy to explore potential opportunities for hotel/casino operations in any area where such operations were legal.[2] While the company stressed that this decision implied no firm commitment toward a new development, it did indeed recognize the fact that the expansion in this area represented a natural extension of its current hotel operations. Previously, corporate policy restricted the expansion of hotel/casino operations to the state of Nevada and areas external to the United States.

53   Immediately following this announcement, the company approved a proposal to construct and manage a $75 million hotel/casino in Atlantic City, New Jersey.

54   Gaming was one industry that was examined when the company began researching future growth opportunities in the hospitality industry in 1975. Initial investigation revealed that most successful casino operations included hotels, a business in which the company was an acknowledged leader. Casinos also have sizable food and beverage operations, an area where the Holiday Inns system averaged more than $1 billion in annual revenues. Preliminary studies also indicated that the Holiday Inn hotel customer exhibited demographic characteristics similar to those of gaming participants (see the accompanying table). Of greater importance to Holiday Inns, customer surveys indicated that the overwhelming majority of Holiday Inn hotel guests had no objection to the company's becoming involved in the gaming business.

Demographic comparison: Holiday Inn versus Las Vegas

	Las Vegas casino visitor	Holiday Inn guest
Age 21–50	66%	66%
Family income: over $30,000	73	69
Occupation: professional, manager, white-collar	40	37

55   Holiday Inns' research showed that 80 percent of adults approve of gambling, and 60 percent participate in some form, ranging from casino visits to fund-raising raffles. Their conclusion: Gaming was truly a national pastime and was viewed by the public as a leisure activity. Of the 11 million people who visited Las Vegas, the average guest spent about $200 in nongaming expenditures and budgeted $300 for gaming.

56   Traditionally thought of as the exclusive domain of Nevada, the opening of Atlantic City to casino operations has given gaming a whole new outlook, and casino revenues

---

[2] This decision, however, was reached over considerable internal management dissension. Several key managers questioned the inappropriateness of gambling relative to the founding philosophy and mission of Holiday Inns. As evidence of the degree of top-management polarity, this decision triggered the resignation of the company president and chief executive officer, L. M. Clymer. Clymer said his resignation was incited by personal and religious opposition to this company decision.

were expected to more than double to between $5 billion and $7.5 billion nationwide by 1985.

57   Holiday Inns' extensive research led to the conclusion that it "needed outside expertise in gaming and big-name entertainment contracting. Careful control of the large volumes of cash handled requires well-run operations and specialized procedures. Thus, if we [Holiday Inns] were to succeed, we would need seasoned management in place."

58   In 1979, Holiday Inns formed a joint venture company with Harrah's (of Nevada) to develop, build, and operate all future gaming facilities for both companies. In September 1979, a merger agreement was approved by both firms. Under the merger, Harrah's will maintain its identity as a wholly owned subsidiary and will be the gaming operations arm of Holiday Inns, Inc.

59   Commenting on the merger with Harrah's, a Holiday Inns executive said: "We could not have picked a better company than Harrah's, a leader in the hotel/casino and entertainment industry. The control measures developed by Harrah's are now the standards for the industry. They provide seasoned expertise in gaming and big-name entertainment contracting. Their growth record has been superior."

60   U.S. casino gaming industry revenues reached $3 billion in 1980, compared to $2.4 billion in 1979, a 25 percent increase despite the impact of the 1980 recession and escalating transportation costs. In 1980, Atlantic City nearly doubled its 1979 casino revenues, winning more than $600 million. Forecasts made in 1976 (when casino gaming was first legalized in New Jersey) predicted the Atlantic City market would not reach $800 million in gaming revenues annually until 1988. Many industry experts expected Atlantic City to gross over $2 billion in gaming revenues in 1985. Part of their prediction was based on Atlantic City's location—one day's drive from one fourth of the U.S. population.

61   Some analysts were less sure about Atlantic City's potential. They pointed out that many Atlantic City gamblers only stayed one day and came back more often rather than staying for an extended period in a hotel facility. Also, Atlantic City had been slow in gaining convention traffic and gambling junkets, partially because of a much more heavily regulated situation than in Nevada.

62   Through its entry into casino gaming operations, Holiday Inns, Inc., kept pace with the spectacular industry growth. With the November 23, 1980, opening of Harrah's Marina hotel/casino in Atlantic City, Holiday Inns, Inc., became the largest U.S. gaming concern, operating alone or in partnership the most slot machines, 5,656; most table games, 439; and most casino space, 188,200 square feet. Holiday Inns, Inc., was the only company with properties in all four major U.S. gaming centers (see Exhibit 10). Casino gaming accounted for 13 percent of Holiday Inns' revenues in 1980 and 22 percent in 1981 (see Exhibit 10).

63   Commenting on Holiday Inns' rapid success in casino gaming, Holiday Inns President and CEO Mike Rose offered management's view of the gaming future:

Harrah's management depth and the strength of its operating programs and systems place Holiday Inns, Inc., in an excellent position to capitalize on the future growth of gaming. The company is already the largest in terms of facilities and has begun to successfully establish a nationally recognized brand name. These accomplishments, together with innovative marketing and planning, will

Exhibit 10
U.S. gaming industry: 1981–1985

A. Largest U.S.
   gaming companies (1981)

(Casino square feet in thousands—1981)

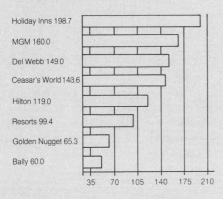

Holiday Inns 198.7

MGM 160.0

Del Webb 149.0

Ceasar's World 148.6

Hilton 119.0

Resorts 99.4

Golden Nugget 65.3

Bally 60.0

35   70   105   140   175   210

B. Gaming representation in major
   U.S. markets

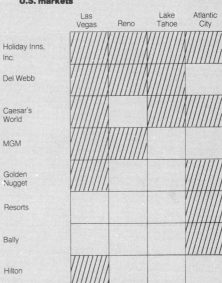

	Las Vegas	Reno	Lake Tahoe	Atlantic City
Holiday Inns, Inc.	▨	▨	▨	▨
Del Webb	▨	▨		▨
Caesar's World	▨		▨	▨
MGM	▨	▨		
Golden Nugget	▨	▨		▨
Resorts				▨
Bally				▨
Hilton	▨			

C. U.S. gaming revenues

($ billions)

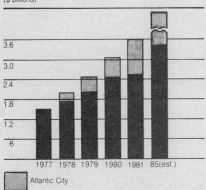

3.6

3.0

2.4

1.8

1.2

.6

1977   1978   1979   1980   1981   85(est.)

▨ Atlantic City

■ Nevada

D. Holiday Inns, Inc.: Gaming group
   market share by location (in percent of
   market gaming revenues—1981)

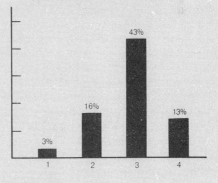

43%

16%

3%

13%

1   2   3   4

1. Las Vegas.
2. Reno.
3. Lake Tahoe.
4. Atlantic City

Source: Nevada Gaming Control Board and New Jersey Casino Control Commission.

put the company in the same leadership position in gaming that it enjoys in the lodging industry.

64   Indeed, numerous traditional competitors share the same view. Hilton Hotels Corp. and Hyatt Corporation had already entered the field and were doing quite well. Gerald E. Hollier, chief operating officer at Ramada Inns, echoed Holiday Inns' optimism in a 1980 interview:

> As the gaming industry expands rapidly, smaller companies will have difficulty keeping up with market growth. Even established companies that are doing well in Nevada, such as Del Webb, Caesar's World, and Summa, don't have as good a chance as the big companies because they lack the base [from which] to expand. In the long run, it's the big companies like Holiday Inns, Ramada Inns, and Hilton which will do best, because they have the muscle.

65   Only two major lodging competitors, Best Western and Days Inn, were not pursuing casino gaming. Best Western President Robert Hazard saw gaming as "an infatuation that could burst like a bubble," while Days Inn executives considered gaming outside the concept and corporate philosophy underlying Days Inn.

Financial Perspective

66   Exhibit 11 provides a corporatewide summary of selected financial results at Holiday Inns, Inc., since 1976.

67   Cash flow from operations was $291.8 million in 1981. This provided a sizable source of internally generated funds Holiday Inns, Inc., could use to support future expansion. Capital expenditures corporatewide were $170.9 million and $207.1 million in 1981 and 1980, respectively. The company had available at year-end 1981 $225 million of prime-related, intermediate-term credit facilities and $43 million in unused, short-term credit facilities. Only $30 million of the intermediate-term credit was utilized at the end of 1981. Holiday Inns, Inc.'s customers were generally required to pay for the company's products and services at the time they were provided. Consequently, high working capital levels were not necessary. Furthermore, the size and nature of the company's assets offered a number of ways to finance expansion, including fee ownership, leasing, joint ventures, management contracts, and franchising.

68   Corporate management had traditionally been very concerned about maintaining and improving return on shareholders' equity. Shareholders' equity rose by $64.4 million or 9.1 percent in 1981, which reflects Holiday Inns, Inc.'s net income less its dividend payments *and* the effect of a 2-million-share repurchase program. Dividends in 1981 increased for the 18th consecutive year. Return on average shareholders' equity increased to 18.5 percent in 1981, up from 16.1 percent in 1980, and exceeding near-term corporate objectives.

69   The ratio of long-term debt to invested capital at the end of 1981 was 41.9 percent, up slightly from 1980's 41.3 percent, but still considerably higher than pre-1980 levels (see Exhibit 11). Corporate management considered this debt ratio conservative in view of the company's asset base. Holiday Inns, Inc., engaged an independent firm in

Exhibit 11
Selected financial results: Holiday Inns, Inc. (corporatewide)

	1979	1980	1981	5-year compound growth rate*	10-year compound growth rate†
Operating results ($ millions)					
Revenues	$1,112.6	$1,533.8	$1,765.1	12.8%	10.3%
Operating income	169.3	238.1	290.8	22.7	11.5
Income before income taxes	125.1	166.6	196.2	25.0	11.2
Pretax margin (percent)	11.2%	10.9%	11.1%	—	—
Tax rate (percent)	43.0%	35.0%	30.0%	—	—
Income	$ 71.3	$ 108.3	$ 137.4	28.5	13.0
Discontinued operations	(15.4)	—	—		
Net income	$ 55.9	$ 108.3	$ 137.4	28.8%	13.7%
Common stock data					
Income per share	$1.76	$2.92	$3.66	23.6%	10.7%
Cost dividends declared per share	0.66	0.70	0.74	13.1	11.5
Book value per share	18.93	21.51	24.73	10.2	8.3
Price range of common	22⅞–15¼	33½–13¾	33¼–21⅛	—	—
Average number of common and outstanding (000)	31,704	39,278	39,449	5.2%	2.8%
Financial position ($ millions)					
Total assets	$1,227.3	$1,680.1	$1,815.4	13.6%	59.0%
Property and equipment (net)	737.1	1,147.7	1,323.3	14.3	10.4
Long-term debt	311.3	546.6	639.6	16.4	8.4
Shareholders' equity	624.5	708.0	772.4	10.6	8.6
Depreciation and amortization	56.3	74.6	87.3	9.2	n/a
Capital expenditures	133.4	207.1	170.9	19.5	
Current ratio	1.4	0.9	0.8	—	—
Performance measures (percent)					
Return on sales	6.4%	7.1%	7.8%	—	—
Return on average invested capital	7.1	10.6	12.0	—	—
Return on average equity	9.5	16.1	18.5	—	—
Long-term debt to invested capital	30.1	41.3	41.9	—	—

* Base 1976.
† Base 1971.

1981 to appraise the appreciated value of the company's tangible assets and certain contract rights. The study indicated a market value of $1.86 billion, or nearly 2.5 times the $.77 billion reported shareholders' equity shown on its 1981 balance sheet. Corporate management believed this information provided a clearer definition of the true financial condition of Holiday Inns, Inc., showing the value of the company's contract income streams as well as the "real" benefits from the appreciation of its substantial real estate assets.

70   Holiday Inns, Inc., had two convertible subordinate debenture issues as a part of its long-term debt. The first, an 8 percent issue for which the company was making sinking fund payments to 1985, was convertible into common stock at $35 per share. The 1981 value of this issue was $5.85 million. The second issue, a 9⅝ percent debenture with sinking fund payments scheduled between 1991 and 2005, was convertible into common stock at $20 per share. This issue represented a $144.2 million long-term debt on Holiday Inns' 1981 balance sheet. The company was considering calling the 9⅝ percent debentures for redemption in 1982 to lower the debt-to-capital ratio (removing $144.2 from debt into capital would lower the ratio to 32.3 percent). The stock price hovered around $22 per share toward the end of 1981.

For the Future

71   Mike Rose, president and CEO, offered the following corporate philosophy to guide Holiday Inns in the 1980s:

> We are operating our businesses under a very simple and straightforward management philosophy. We have shared this philosophy with the entire rank and file of our company, and I would like to share it with you because it says a lot about our future success. Our philosophy is:
>
> We are *a forward-looking, innovative industry leader with clearly defined goals, producing superior products, services, and consistently high return for our shareholders.*
>
> We will *maintain integrity in both our internal and external relationships, fostering respect for the individual and open, two-way communications.*
>
> We will *promote a climate of enthusiasm, teamwork, and challenge, which attracts, motivates, and retains superior personnel and rewards superior performance.*

72   Charles Barnette, director of corporate public relations, succinctly summarized the perspective adopted by Holiday Inns, Inc., for the future. He stated, "We want to focus business activities on markets and market segments where we can excel, achieve competitive advantage, and be the cost-effective leader."

73   Some of the specifics that emerge from Barnette's statement are: (1) maintain a corporate debt ratio of 35 percent of invested capital; (2) increase corporate return on investment capital (ROIC) to over 13 percent; (3) grow at a rate of 15 percent or more per year; (4) achieve a dividend payment representing 35 percent of net income. While these corporatewide objectives offer a realistic challenge, the future contribution of different business groups could vary considerably.

74   To summarize their optimism about the future, Kemmons Wilson, founder and then retiring chairman of the board, placed all corporate objectives for the future in a concise framework. He stated:

> Now it's time to embark on a new era of growth and to continue the very favorable trends for our shareholders that we've seen in the past 10 years. The outlook on tourism in this country and worldwide has never been better. We are truly becoming a unified world where people are traveling farther, more frequently, and for more reasons.
>
> Twenty-seven years ago I had a dream. It has been fulfilled. But even in my wildest dreams I could not see the changes that were ahead. I never dreamed that so many people would travel between countries. Or that people would choose to spend a weekend in their own hometown, or that people would begin to eat more meals away from home than at home, or that forms of acceptable entertainment would change so dramatically.
>
> Today we have a better picture of the future, and at Holiday Inns, Inc., I am proud to say we're anticipating change. In fact, we welcome it. And we're determined to be out in front in whatever markets we are able to serve.

75   "Whatever markets we are able to serve" may have a double meaning for Holiday Inns as it moves toward the 1990s. Is it a challenge for further diversification of this travel-related company or a call for urgent reexamination of what its mission and business strategies should be? Is Holiday Inns' diversified group of businesses inspired by Mr. Wilson's desire for a broadened earnings base consistent with the perspective articulated above by Charles Barnette and Mike Rose? Can each separate business achieve the "cost-effective leadership" position Barnette talks about, or is such an accomplishment possible for only a few Holiday Inns, Inc., businesses? Are Holiday Inns' stockholders better served by diverse businesses or by a concentrated focus in the company's major leadership areas—lodging and gaming? Which focus represents the company's best chance to meet its ambitious, corporatewide goals [see paragraph 73]? These questions and more faced Holiday Inns executives as they met to shape a strategic plan for the 1990s.

Chapter 1 Cohesion Case Illustration

Strategic Management and Holiday Inns, Inc.

Chapter 1 provided a broad introduction to strategic management. What role does strategic management play (or could it play) at Holiday Inns? Based on the material in Chapter 1, this question can be answered by addressing four issues:

1. Is Holiday Inns facing a strategic decision?
2. What is Holiday Inns' strategy?
3. What value would strategic management offer Holiday Inns?
4. What strategic management structure is appropriate at Holiday Inns?

Is Holiday Inns facing a strategic decision? Yes! Lower-cost air travel (due to deregulation of the airline industry) led to fundamental changes in the travel practices of the American public. In the early 1980s, the lodging industry also had the largest oversupply of rooms since the 1930s. These are but a few key factors that significantly affect Holiday Inns and point out the need for sound strategic decisions.

Other issues foretell a need for strategic decisions. Budget motels are expanding. This threatens the hotel business in Holiday Inns' midpriced segment, which is Holiday Inns, Inc.'s key revenue generator. Holiday Inns is trying to diversify, but the percentage breakdown of revenues shows little change since 1974. Why? Is Holiday Inns' management not seriously pushing diversification? Is the necessary expertise lacking? The recent move into casino gaming represents a potentially major philosophical change for the company, as evidenced by the resignation of President L. M. Clymer. Is this to be a sideline operation or a serious future commitment? What ramifications, in light of Clymer's resignation, does this have for Holiday Inns' top-management structure and cohesion? With Holiday Inns still dependent on hotels/motels for 55 percent of its revenue, is there still room for growth, or is the domestic (and international) market becoming saturated? With the departure of Kemmons Wilson, has Holiday Inns completed the evolution from an entrepreneurially run company to a professionally managed one? Clearly, Holiday Inns faces a number of the strategic issues described in Chapter 1.

What is Holiday Inns' strategy? Holiday Inns appears to be pursuing steady growth through gradual, concentric diversification into hospitality- and transportation-related businesses. Its business portfolio is still dominated by the

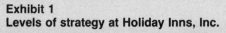

Exhibit 1
Levels of strategy at Holiday Inns, Inc.

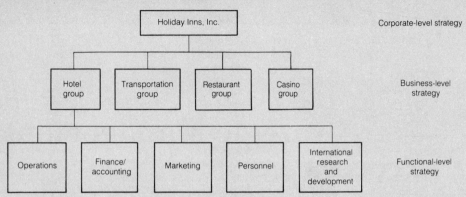

hotel division. But the transportation and other divisions now represent just under 50 percent of Holiday Inns' revenues. And the gaming industry is seen as a strong avenue for growth.

What value does strategic management offer Holiday Inns? With the numerous strategic issues facing Holiday Inns, systematic strategic management would appear essential for survival and prosperity. Holiday Inns' top management team is clearly interested in adopting a proactive rather than reactive strategic orientation. While its nonhotel divisions represent approximately 52 percent of Holiday Inns' revenue, this breakdown has not changed significantly since 1974, raising the question of whether its long-term strategy is just to supplement the hotel core or to actually reduce dependence on the traditional hotel side of its business.

Systematic strategic management clearly is needed to address this issue in looking to the 1990s. Holiday Inns' management also believes the need for strategic management is imperative, based on this comment in the 1981 annual report: "The strategic framework and management team of Holiday Inns, Inc., are in place, and we are well positioned for growth and accomplishment."

What strategic management structure is appropriate at Holiday Inns? Clearly, the multibusiness structure presented in Figure 1–1 is called for at Holiday Inns. It could be illustrated as shown in Exhibit 1.

2

The Strategic Management Process

Businesses vary in the processes they use to formulate and direct their strategic management activities. Sophisticated planning organizations, such as General Electric, Procter & Gamble, and IBM, have developed more detailed processes than similarly sized, less formal planners. Small businesses that rely on the strategy formulation skills and limited time of an entrepreneur typically exhibit very basic planning concerns when contrasted with larger firms in their industries. Understandably, firms with diverse operations due to their reliance on multiple products, markets, or technologies also tend to utilize more complex strategic management systems. However, despite differences in detail and degree of formalization, the basic components of the models used to analyze strategic management operations are very similar.[1]

Because of the similarity among general models of the strategic management process, it is possible to develop one eclectic model representative of the foremost thought in the area. Such a model was developed for this text and is

---

Portions of this chapter are from John A. Pearce II, "An Executive-Level Perspective on the Strategic Management Process," *California Management Review,* Spring 1982, pp. 39–48.

[1] Models by academics, typically developed from consulting experience and intended either for business or educational use, that reflect such similarity include those of Stevenson (1976), Rogers (1975), King and Cleland (1978), and numerous others. Models recommended for use by small businesses are almost identical to those recommended for larger firms, for example, those published by Gilmore (1973) and Steiner (1967). Finally, models that describe approaches for accomplishing strategic options contain elements similar to those included in general models; see, for example, Pryor (1964) on mergers and Steiner (1964) on diversification. The bibliography at the end of this chapter contains complete citations.

Figure 2–1
Strategic management model

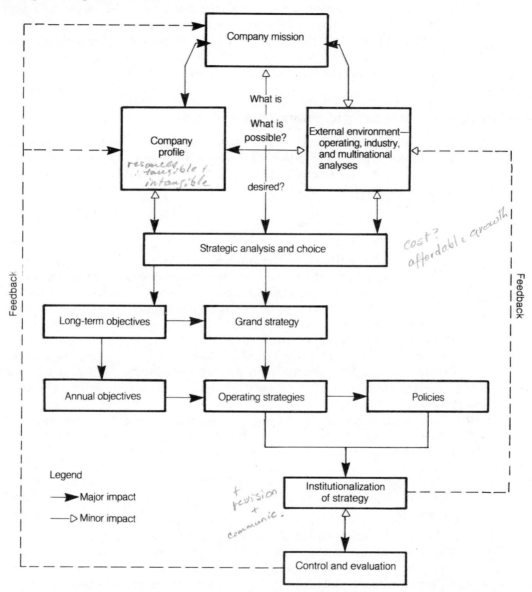

shown in Figure 2–1. This *strategic management model* serves three major functions. First, it provides a visual representation of the major components of the entire strategic management process. The model also shows how the components are related and how they are arranged in sequence throughout the process. Second, the model will serve as the outline for this text. After providing a general overview of the strategic management process in this chapter, the major components of the model will be used as the principal theme of subsequent chapters. Finally, the model is suggested for use in analyzing the case studies included in this text. In this context, the model enhances development of strategy formulation skills by guiding the analyst in a systematic and comprehensive study of each business situation.

Components of the Strategic Management Model

In this section the key components of the strategic management model will be defined and briefly described. Each will receive much greater attention in a later chapter. The intention here is simply to provide an introduction to the major concepts.

Company Mission

Answers why we are in business.

The mission of a business is the fundamental, unique purpose that sets it apart from other firms of its type and identifies the scope of its operations in product and market terms. The mission is a general, enduring statement of company intent. It embodies the business philosophy of strategic decision makers, implies the image the company seeks to project, reflects the firm's self-concept, and indicates the principal product or service areas and primary customer needs the company will attempt to satisfy. In short, the mission describes the product, market, and technological areas of emphasis for the business in a way that reflects the values and priorities of the strategic decision makers.

Because conceptualizing a company mission can be difficult, an excellent example is shown in Figure 2–2, the mission statement of Nicor, Inc., as abstracted from an annual report to its stockholders.

Company Profile

A firm's internal analysis determines its performance capabilities based on existing or accessible resources. From this analysis, a company profile is generated. At any designated point in time, the company profile depicts the quantity and quality of financial, human, and physical resources available to the firm. The profile also assesses the inherent strengths and weaknesses of the firm's management and organizational structure. Finally, it contrasts the historical successes of the firm and the traditional values and concerns of management with the firm's current capabilities in an attempt to identify the future capabilities of the business.

study history first

Figure 2–2
Mission statement of Nicor, Inc.

Preamble

We, the management of Nicor, Inc., here set forth our belief as to the purpose for which the company is established and the principles under which it should operate. We pledge our effort to the accomplishment of these purposes within these principles.

Basic purpose

The basic purpose of Nicor, Inc., is to perpetuate an investor-owned company engaging in various phases of the energy business, striving for balance among those phases so as to render needed satisfactory products and services and earn optimum, long-range profits. _which will support growth and stakeholder interests_

What we do

The principal business of the company, through its utility subsidiary, is the provision of energy through a pipe system to meet the needs of ultimate consumers. To accomplish its basic purpose, and to ensure its strength, the company will engage in other energy-related activities, directly or through subsidiaries or in participation with other persons, corporations, firms, or entities.

All activities of the company shall be consistent with its responsibilities to investors, customers, employees, and the public and its concern for the optimum development and utilization of natural resources and for environmental needs.

Where we do it

The company's operations shall be primarily in the United States, but no self-imposed or regulatory geographical limitations are placed upon the acquisition, development, processing, transportation, or storage of energy resources, or upon other energy-related ventures in which the company may engage. The company will engage in such activities in any location where, after careful review, it has determined that such activity is in the best interest of its stockholders.

Utility service will be offered in the territory of the company's utility subsidiary to the best of its ability, in accordance with the requirements of regulatory agencies and pursuant to the subsidiary's purposes and principles.

External Environment

leader as influencer

A firm's external environment consists of all the conditions and forces that affect its strategic options but are typically beyond the firm's control. The strategic management model shows the external environment as consisting of two interactive and interrelated segments: the operating environment and the remote environment.

The operating environment consists of the forces and conditions within a specific industry and a specific competitive operating situation, external to the firm, that influence the selection and attainment of alternative objective/ strategy combinations. Unlike changes in the remote environment, changes in the operating environment often result from strategic actions taken by the firm or its competitors, consumers, users, suppliers, and/or creditors. Thus, a consumer shift toward greater price consciousness, a loosening of local bank credit restrictions, a new entrant into the marketplace, the development of a substitute product, or the opening of a new wholesale outlet by a competitor are all likely to have direct and intentional positive or negative effects on a firm.

The remote environment refers to forces and conditions that originate beyond and usually irrespective of any single firm's immediate operating environment and provide the general economic, political, social, and technological framework within which competing organizations operate. For example, a company's strategic planners and managers may face spiraling inflation (economic), import restrictions on raw materials (political), demographic swings of population in the geographic areas they serve (social), or revolutionary technological innovations that make their production systems unexpectedly obsolete (technological).

Strategic Analysis and Choice

Simultaneous assessment of the external environment and company profile enables a firm to identify a range of possibly attractive interactive opportunities. These opportunities are *possible* avenues for investment. However, the full list must be screened through the criterion of the company mission before a set of possible and *desired* opportunities is generated. This process results in the selection of a *strategic choice*. It is meant to provide the combination of long-term objectives and grand strategy that will optimally position the firm in the external environment to achieve the company mission.

Consider the case when strategic managers feel that a firm is overly dependent on a single customer group, for example, a chain of record shops with principal customers 10 to 20 years old. The firm's interactive opportunities might include expanding the product line, heavily emphasizing related products, accepting the status quo, or selling out profitably to a competitor. While each of these options might be possible, a firm with a mission that stressed commitment to continued existence as a growth-oriented, autonomous organization might find that only the first two opportunities are desirable. In that case, these options would be evaluated on the basis of payoff and risk potential, compatibility with or capability for becoming the firm's competitive advantage, and other critical selection criteria.

A complicated subprocess is used to derive the strategic choice. Strategic analysis involves matching each of the possible and desirable interactive opportunities with reasonable long-term objectives and targets. In turn, these are matched with the most promising means—known as grand strategies—for achieving the desired results. Each of the sets of alternatives is then evaluated individually and comparatively to determine the single set or group of sets that is expected to best achieve the company mission. The chosen set (or sets) is known as the strategic choice.

Critical assessment of strategic alternatives initially involves developing criteria for comparing one set of alternatives with all others. As is the case in making any choice, a company's strategic selection involves evaluating alternatives that are rarely wholly acceptable or wholly unacceptable. The alternatives are therefore compared to determine which option will have the most favorable overall, long-run impact on a firm.

Among the criteria used in assessing strategic choice alternatives are strategic managers' attitudes toward risk, flexibility, stability, growth, profitability, and diversification. Other factors included in the decision-making process are volatility of the external environment, life-cycle stages of the evaluated products, and the company's current level of commitment to its organizational structure, access to needed resources, traditional competitive advantages, as well as the potential reaction of influential external or internal interest groups.

Long-Term Objectives — measurable

The results an organization seeks over a multiyear period are its *long-term objectives*.[2] Such objectives typically involve some or all of the following areas: profitability, return on investment, competitive position, technological leadership, productivity, employee relations, public responsibility, and employee development. To be of greatest value, each objective must be specific, measurable, achievable, and consistent with other objectives of the firm. Objectives are a statement of *what* is expected from pursuing a given set of business activities. Examples of common company objectives include the following: doubling of earnings per share within five years with increases in each intervening year; moving from third to second as a seller of commercial electrical fixtures in Oregon; and a decrease of 10 percent a year in undesirable employee turnover over the next five years.

Grand Strategy

The comprehensive, general plan of major actions through which a firm intends to achieve its long-term objectives in a dynamic environment is called the *grand strategy*. This *statement of means* indicates how the objectives or ends of business activity are to be achieved. Although every grand strategy is, in fact, a fairly unique package of long-term strategies, 12 basic approaches can be identified: concentration, market development, product development, innovation, horizontal integration, vertical integration, joint venture, concentric diversification, conglomerate diversification, retrenchment/turnaround, divestiture, and liquidation. Each of these grand strategies will be covered in detail in Chapter 9. Any of these grand, master, or business strategies are meant to guide the acquisition and allocation of resources over an extended period of time. Admittedly, no single grand strategy, or even several in combination, can describe in adequate detail the strategic actions a business will undertake over a long period. However, when a firm's strategic managers are committed to a fundamental approach for positioning the business in the competitive marketplace, it provides a galvanizing central focal point for subsequent decision making.

---

[2] Five years is the normal, but largely arbitrary, period of time identified as long term.

Some brief examples of grand strategies include Hewlett-Packard's technological innovation approach for capturing the high profit margins on new products, First Pennsylvania's retrenchment approach for avoiding bankruptcy despite $75 million in 1980 losses, and General Electric's concentric diversification approach allowing growth through acquisition of related business.

Annual Objectives

The results an organization seeks to achieve within a one-year period are *annual objectives*. Short-term or annual objectives involve areas similar to those entailed in long-term objectives. The differences between them stem principally from the greater specificity possible and necessary in short-term objectives. For example, a long-term objective of increasing companywide sales volume by 20 percent in five years might be translated into a 4 percent growth objective in year one. In addition, it is reasonable that the planning activities of all major functions or divisions of the firm should reflect this companywide, short-run objective. The research and development department might be expected to suggest one major addition to the product line each year, the finance department might set a complementary objective of obtaining the necessary $300,000 in funds for an immediate expansion of production facilities, and the marketing department might establish an objective of reducing turnover of sales representatives by 5 percent per year.

Functional Strategies

Within the general framework of the grand strategy, each distinctive business function or division needs a specific and integrative plan of action. Most strategic managers attempt to develop an operating strategy for each related set of annual objectives (for example, there will be a functional strategy to indicate how the marketing department's annual objectives will be achieved, one for the production department's objectives, and so on).

Operating strategies are detailed statements of the *means* that will be used to achieve objectives in the following year. The company's budgeting process is usually coordinated with the development of the operating strategies to ensure specificity, practicality, and accountability in the planning process.

Policies

Policies are directives designed to guide the thinking, decisions, and actions of managers and their subordinates in implementing the organization's strategy. Policies provide guidelines for establishing and controlling the ongoing operating processes of the firm consistent with the firm's strategic objectives. Policies are often referred to as *standard operating procedures* and serve to increase managerial effectiveness by standardizing many routine decisions and to limit the discretion of managers and subordinates in implementing operation strategies.

The following are examples of the nature and diversity of company policies:

A requirement that managers have purchase requests for items costing more than $500 cosigned by the controller.

The minimum equity position required for all new McDonald's franchises.

The standard formula used to calculate return on investment for the 43 strategic business units of General Electric.

A companywide decision that employees have their annual performance review on the anniversary of their hiring date.

Institutionalizing the Strategy *permeate*

Annual objectives, functional strategies, and specific policies provide important means of communicating what must be done to implement the overall strategy. By translating long-term intentions into short-term guides to action, they make the strategy operational. But the strategy must also be *institutionalized*— must permeate the very day-to-day life of the company—if it is to be effectively implemented.

Three organizational elements provide the fundamental, long-term means for institutionalizing the firm's strategy: (1) structure, (2) leadership, and (3) culture. Successful implementation requires effective management and integration of these three elements to ensure the strategy "takes hold" in the daily life of the firm.

Control and Evaluation

An implemented strategy must be monitored to determine the extent to which objectives are achieved. The process of formulating a strategy is largely subjective despite often extensive efforts at objectivity. Thus, the first substantial reality test of a strategy comes only after implementation. Strategic managers must watch for early signs of marketplace response to their strategies. Managers must also provide monitoring and controlling methods to ensure their strategic plan is followed.

Although early review and evaluation of the strategic process concentrates on market-responsive modifications, the underlying and ultimate test of a strategy is ability to achieve its end—the annual objectives, long-term objectives, and mission. In the final analysis, a firm is only successful when its strategy achieves designated objectives.

Strategic Management as a Process

A *process* is an identifiable flow of information through interrelated stages of analysis directed toward the achievement of an aim. Thus, the strategic management model in Figure 2–1 depicts a process. In the strategic management process, the flow of information involves historical, current, and forecast data on the business, its operations, and environment, which are evaluated in light of the values and priorities of influential individuals and groups—often called *stakeholders*—who are vitally interested in the actions of the business. The interrelated stages of the process are the 12 components discussed in the last section. Finally, the aim of the process is the formulation and implementation of strategies that result in long-term achievement of the company's mission and near-term achievement of objectives.

Viewing strategic management as a process has several important implications. First, a change in any component will affect several or all other components. Notice that the majority of arrows in the model point two ways, suggesting that the flow of information or impact is usually reciprocal. For example, forces in the external environment influence the nature of the mission designed by a company's strategic managers and stakeholders. The existence of a given company with a given mission in turn legitimizes the environmental forces and implicitly heightens competition in the firm's realm of operation. A specific example is a power company persuaded, in part by governmental incentives, that its mission statement should include a commitment to the development of energy alternatives. The firm might then promise to extend its R&D efforts in the area of coal liquification. Obviously, in this example, the external environment has affected the firm's definition of its mission, and the existence of the revised mission signals a competitive condition in the environment.

A second implication of strategic management as a process is that strategy formulation and implementation are sequential. The process begins with development or reevaluation of the company mission. This step is associated with, but essentially followed by, development of a company profile and assessment of the external environment. Then follow, in order: strategic choice, definition of long-term objectives, design of grand strategy, definition of short-term objectives, design of operating strategies, institutionalization of the strategy, and review and evaluation. However, the apparent rigidity of the process must be qualified.

First, the strategic posture of a firm may have to be reevaluated in terms of any of the principal factors that determine or affect company performance. Entry by a major new competitor, death of a prominent board member, replacement of the chief executive officer, or a downturn in market responsiveness are among the thousands of changes that can prompt reassessment of a company's strategic plan. However, no matter where the need for a reassessment originates, the strategic management process begins with the mission statement.

Second, not every component of the strategic management process deserves equal attention each time a planning activity takes place. Firms in an extremely stable environment may find that an in-depth assessment is not required every five years.[3] Often companies are satisfied with their original mission

---

[3] Formal strategic planning is not necessarily done on a rigid five-year schedule, although this is most common. Some planners advocate planning on an irregular time basis to keep the activity from being overly routine.

reiterative ?

statements even after decades of operation and thus need to spend only a minimal amount of time in addressing the subject. In addition, while formal strategic planning may be undertaken only every five years, objectives and strategies are usually updated each year, and rigorous reassessment of the initial stages of strategic planning is rarely undertaken at these points.

A third implication of strategic management as a process is the necessity of feedback from institutionalization, review, and evaluation to the early stages of the process. *Feedback* can be defined as postimplementation results collected as inputs for the enhancement of future decision making. Therefore, as indicated in Figure 2–1, strategic managers should attempt to assess the impact of implemented strategies on external environments. Thus, future planning can reflect any changes precipitated by strategic actions. Strategic managers should also carefully measure and analyze the impact of strategies on the need for possible modifications in the company mission.

A fourth and final implication of strategic management as a process is the need to view it as a dynamic system. *Dynamic* describes the constantly changing conditions that affect interrelated and interdependent strategic activities. Managers should recognize that components of the strategic process are constantly evolving, while formal planning artificially freezes the changing conditions and forces in a company's internal and external environments, much as an action photograph freezes the movement of a swimmer. In actuality, change is continuous, and thus the dynamic strategic planning process must be constantly monitored for significant changes in any components as a precaution against implementing an obsolete strategy.

Practical Limitations of the Model

It is important to understand the limitations of the strategic management model to gain an awareness of how the model can be properly used. This awareness will help ensure effective strategic management. Thus, in this section, three points will be stressed: the model is holistic, analytical, and nonpolitical.

Holistic

Users of the model believe strategic planning should be initiated by a company's top management. Thus, because of the broad perspective of these executives, the strategy-formulating process develops from general to specific. The business is first studied as a whole within the context of its competitive environment, then from the standpoint of individual functions or divisions, and eventually specific operational activities of the firm are involved in the process.

Some researchers have argued that in certain circumstances the holistic approach is inferior to a tactical approach in strategic planning.[4] With the tactical approach, strategic managers work "up" through the firm in their study of its potential. After obtaining an operational view of the firm's strengths and weaknesses, managers assess their firm's compatibility with its external environment.

The risk of using the holistic approach implicitly advocated in the strategic management model is that planning might be unrealistic because of the potential tendency to minimize the difficulties of implementation. The holistic approach can sometimes lead managers to gloss over details that may eventually be critical in making the firm's strategies operational.

limiting factors

On the other hand, the tactical approach poses far greater risks to strategic managers, first because planning may be inflexible. Managers risk emphasizing operational details and overstating the extent to which the firm is locked into the status quo. It is difficult to envision new interactive opportunities when initial planning activities stress narrow operational concerns. Second, the integration of planning activities is more difficult with the tactical approach. Because there is no overall planning framework, as is characteristic of the holistic method, the initial phases of planning are often disjointed, complicating development of a unified strategic plan. Third, and most damaging, the tactical approach leads to a concentration on the present rather than on the future, while strategic planning is specifically intended to be future oriented. With tactical planning, the emphasis is too often on improving current capabilities instead of on satisfying anticipated needs.

In the final analysis, the holistic approach of the strategic management model appears to be superior to tactical alternatives. However, users of the model should be alert to the shortcomings in planning that the strategic model fosters and should guard against them. Specifically, users of the model should continually monitor the data-gathering and implementation phases. In this context, it is important to remember that although middle- and lower-level managers seldom have a voice in the strategic choice process, they are a principal source of the operational data on which the ultimate decisions are largely based. Therefore, their advice and critiques should be actively sought and carefully considered in all phases of strategic management.

Analytic versus Prescriptive

A second major issue of concern in using the strategic management model is that it is analytical rather than prescriptive or procedural. The model generally describes the logical or analytical steps many businesses actually use in their strategic activities. However, it does not describe the procedures or routines necessary to carry out each step. Further, research has not proved that the model is *ideal*. In fact, while considerable evidence indicates that firms having

---

[4] For example, see George W. McKinney III, "An Experimental Study of Strategy Formulation Systems" (Ph.D. dissertation, Graduate School of Business, Stanford University, 1969).

formal strategic planning outperform nonplanners, somewhat different planning models were used by almost every business studied.[5] As a result, no model should be seen as providing a prescription for the way strategic planning should be done. Therefore, when the strategic management model is used it should be remembered that the model builders are recommending the general approach they believe will provide a sound basis for strategic planning, not a model they are certain will lead to the best results. It is important that users of the model be continually alert to the need for occasional additions or deletions. The model will be most valuable if it is treated as a dependable outline for construction of individualized planning systems.

Nonpolitical

The third major limitation of the model is that it is nonpolitical. A naive observer could therefore be misled into seeing strategic management as largely devoid of subjective assessments, biased interpretations, human error, self-serving voting by individual managers, intuitive decision making, favoritism, and other forms of political activity. In reality, most strategic management experts believe the opposite. Strategic management is a behavioral activity and, as such, is vulnerable to the same pitfalls as other "people" processes. It is truly a management process. People involved in all phases of strategy formulation and implementation must be skillfully organized, led, planned about, and controlled. For this reason, the behavioral implications of each phase of the strategic management process will be discussed extensively in this book. However, limitation of the strategic management model per se is that it presumes strategic planners are skilled managers who are sensitive to the people-related issues that continuously arise in every phase of the process.

The effects of political activity on the strategic management process are critical to its effective functioning and are a principal determinant of the plan's final composition. Effective strategic managers must be attentive to this aspect and attempt to skillfully manage the inevitable people-related concerns.

Evolutionary

The strategic management process undergoes continual assessment and subtle updating. While elements in the basic model rarely change, the relative emphasis each element receives varies with decision makers and the environments of their companies.

Strategy in Action 2–1 presents a recent update on the general trends in strategic management. In summarizing the responses of over 200 corporate

---

[5] See, for example, Ansoff et al. (1971), Burt (1978), Eastlock and McDonald (1970), Herold (1972), Karger and Malik (1975), Malik and Karger (1975), Rue and Fulmer (1972), Schoeffler et al. (1974), Thune and House (1970), and Wood and LaForge (1979), all listed in the bibliography in this chapter.

Strategy in Action 2–1
General Trends in Strategic Management

Item	Percent of respondents indicating		
	Increase	*No change*	*Decrease*
1. Overall emphasis on strategic planning systems.	81.2	7.7	11.1
2. Perceived usefulness of strategic planning.	82.0	10.2	7.8
3. Involvement of line managers in strategic planning activities.	75.2	21.4	3.4
4. Time spent by the chief executive in strategic planning.	78.7	17.8	3.5
5. Acceptance of the outputs of the strategic planning exercise by top management.	74.0	20.6	5.4
6. Perceived usefulness of annual planning.	53.9	38.7	7.4
7. Involvement of staff managers in the annual planning exercise.	52.9	39.3	7.8
8. Involvement of the board of directors in strategic planning.	51.4	47.0	1.6
9. Resources provided for strategic planning.	62.9	23.9	13.2
10. Consistency between strategic plans and budgets.	53.4	38.2	8.3
11. Use of annual plans in monthly performance review.	42.3	55.6	2.1
12. Overall satisfaction with the strategic planning system.	57.4	24.5	18.1
13. Number of planners (that is, those management personnel whose primary task is planning).	52.9	24.8	22.3
14. Attention to stakeholders other than stockholders.	32.8	63.0	4.2
15. Use of planning committees.	40.9	46.1	13.1
16. Attention to societal issues in planning.	33.2	59.8	7.0
17. The planning horizon (that is, the number of years considered in the strategic plan).	28.8	56.6	14.6
18. The distance between the CEO and the chief of planning.	13.3	45.1	41.5
19. Threats to the continuation of strategic planning.	12.0	47.0	41.0
20. Resistance to planning in general.	10.2	31.7	58.0

Source: Adapted from V. Ramanujam, J. C. Camillus, and N. Venkatraman, "Trends in Strategic Planning," in *Strategic Planning and Management Handbook,* ed. W. R. King and D. I. Cleland (New York: Van Nostrand Reinhold, 1987), p. 614.

executives, it shows an increasing emphasis on and appreciation for the value of strategic management activities throughout a company. It further provides evidence of increasing attention given by practicing managers to the needs for frequent and widespread involvement in the formulation and implementation phases of the strategic management process.

Finally, the report indicates that the potential negative consequences of instituting a vigorous strategic management process are overcome as managers and their firms gain knowledge, experience, skill, and understanding in how to design and manage their planning activities.

Summary

This chapter presented an overview of the strategic management process. The model provided will serve as the structure for understanding and integrating all of the major phases of strategy formulation and implementation. Although each of these phases is given extensive individual attention in subsequent chapters, it is important to acquire an early feeling for their nature.

The chapter stressed that the strategic management process centers around the belief that the mission of a firm can best be achieved through a systematic and comprehensive assessment of both a firm's resource capabilities and its external environment. Subsequent evaluation of the company's opportunities leads, in turn, to the choice of long-term objectives and grand strategies and, ultimately, to annual objectives and operating strategies, which must be implemented, monitored, and controlled.

The holistic approach of strategic management was preferable to a tactical one. However, three potential problems with the holistic method were discussed, as were the means by which their negative impact can be minimized.

Questions for Discussion

1. Think about the courses you have had in functional areas such as marketing, finance, production, personnel, and accounting. What is the importance of each of these areas to the strategic planning process?

2. Discuss with practicing business managers the strategic planning approaches used in their businesses. What are the similarities and differences between their models and the one in the text?

3. In what ways do you believe the strategic planning approach would differ in profit-oriented and not-for-profit organizations?

4. How do you explain the success of businesses that do not use a formal strategic planning process?

5. Think about your postgraduation job search as a strategic decision. How would the model be helpful to you in identifying and securing the most promising position?

6. Examine the collection of corporate annual reports in your school's library. Can you locate a report that includes a good mission statement? Does it exhibit the characteristics of a company mission described in this chapter?

Bibliography

Ansoff, H. Igor; R. Brandenberg; F. Portner; and R. Radosevich. *Acquisition Behavior of U.S. Manufacturing Firms, 1946–65.* Nashville, Tenn.: Vanderbilt University Press, 1971.

Burt, David. "Planning and Performance in Australian Retailing." *Long-Range Planning,* June 1978, pp. 62–66.

Eastlock, Joseph, Jr., and Philip McDonald. "CEO's Role in Corporate Growth." *Harvard Business Review,* May–June 1970, pp. 150–63.

Gilmore, Frank. "Formulating Strategy in Smaller Companies." *Harvard Business Review,* May–June 1971, pp. 75–85.

Glueck, William F. *Business Policy and Strategic Management.* 3rd ed. New York: McGraw-Hill, 1980.

Herold, David. "Long-Range Planning and Organizational Performance: A Cross Validation Study." *Academy of Management Review,* March 1972, pp. 91–102.

Karger, Delmar, and Zafar Malik. "Long-Range Planning and Organizational Performance." *Long-Range Planning,* December 1975, pp. 60–64.

King, William R., and David I. Cleland. *Strategic Planning and Policy.* New York: Van Nostrand Reinhold, 1978.

Malik, Zafar, and Delmar Karger. "Does Long-Range Planning Improve Company Performance?" *Management Review,* September 1975, pp. 27–31.

McKinney, George W., III. "An Experimental Study of Strategy Formulation Systems." Ph.D. dissertation, Graduate School of Business, Stanford University, 1969.

Pearce, John A., II. "An Executive-Level Perspective on the Strategic Management Process." *California Management Review,* Spring 1982, pp. 39–48.

Pryor, Millard H., Jr. "Anatomy of a Merger." *Michigan Business Review,* July 1964, pp. 28–34.

Rogers, David C. D. *Essentials of Business Policy.* New York: Harper & Row, 1975.

Rue, Leslie, and Robert Fulmer. "Is Long-Range Planning Profitable?" *Academy of Management Proceedings,* 1972.

Schoeffler, Sidney; Robert D. Buzzell; and Donald F. Heany. "Impact of Strategic Planning on Profit Performance." *Harvard Business Review,* March–April 1974, pp. 137–45.

Stagner, Ross. "Corporate Decision Making." *Journal of Applied Psychology,* February 1969, pp. 1–13.

Steiner, George A. "Why and How to Diversify." *California Management Review,* Summer 1964, pp. 11–18.

————. "Approaches to Long-Range Planning for Small Business." *California Management Review,* Fall 1967, pp. 3–16.

Stevenson, Howard H. "Defining Corporate Strengths and Weaknesses." *Sloan Management Review,* Spring 1976, pp. 51–68.

Thune, Stanley, and Robert House. "Where Long-Range Planning Pays Off." *Business Horizons,* August 1970, pp. 81–87.

Wood, D. Robley, Jr., and R. Lawrence LaForge. "The Impact of Comprehensive Planning on Financial Performance." *Academy of Management Journal* 22, no. 3 (1979), pp. 516–26.

Chapter 2 Cohesion Case Illustration

Strategic Management Framework for Holiday Inns, Inc.

Chapter 2 presented a framework for the strategic management process. How should it be applied at Holiday Inns, Inc.?

Holiday Inns, Inc., is a multibusiness firm. As such, it must have an overall corporate-level strategy for dealing with decisions involving its portfolio of businesses and for guiding strategic decisions made by key managers within each business group. In addition, *each* business group must formulate and implement a business-level strategy to guide resource deployment and pursuit of opportunity consistent with overall corporate objectives.

The purpose of Chapter 2 was to introduce a logical process for developing and implementing a strategy. Each component was briefly discussed in this chapter; the remaining 11 chapters will deal with each component in greater detail. Thus, the objective at this point is to broadly apply the strategic management paradigm to Holiday Inns, Inc.

As assistant to the president, how would one approach strategy development at Holiday Inns? (Illustrations of two possibilities are provided based on the material in Chapter 2.)

Looking to the 1990s, Holiday Inns must first address its corporate-level strategy. Exhibit 1 shows how to go about this. Strategy at this level is a critical issue for Holiday Inns. What should the company mission be? Is the company a travel business or a hospitality business? How does the current portfolio of business groups fit this overall mission? What do the trends in the competitive environment(s) suggest for each group and for the overall mission? What alternative portfolios are available? Which is best? What guidelines must be given to business groups to ensure that their strategy is consistent with and supportive of the corporate strategy chosen? These are some of the issues that must be addressed in designing the corporate-level side of strategic management for Holiday Inns.

Strategies generated for Holiday Inns must also deal with the formulation and implementation of business-level strategy for each business group. Exhibit 2 shows how one might apply the material in Chapter 2 to organize the strategic management of each business group. The mission of the hotel group may be quite different than that of the transportation group or the casino group. Each group has its own strengths and weaknesses. Their respective competitive environments present different opportunities and threats. Alternative strategies, generated through comparison of internal capacity and environmental

Exhibit 1
Corporate-level strategic management process

```
                    ┌─────────────────────────────────┐
                    │         Company mission          │
                    ├─────────────────────────────────┤
                    │ HI has traditionally sought to   │
                    │ provide moderately priced,       │
                    │ quality services as a part of    │
                    │ the travel industry.             │
                    │ Management interchanges          │
                    │ "hospitality" and "travel," with │
                    │ its bus and steamships           │
                    │ operations suggesting emphasis   │
                    │ on the latter.                   │
                    └─────────────────────────────────┘
```

Company profile: Business portfolio	Environmental analysis industry attractiveness
HI has four basic businesses: hotels transportation, restaurants, and casinos. Hotels provide the core business activity, and shipping and transportation are sizable, but are they maturing? Restaurants and casinos are new areas to HI, with minimal revenue contribution to date.	What are the key trends (energy, competition, customer characteristics and habits, costs of capital, etc.) influencing each of these businesses' competitive environments? What market share do the businesses hold in each? What are barriers to entry and exit? How does each of the business groups environments compare vis-a-vis opportunities and threats?

Strategic analysis

How does the *current* business portfolio fit the company mission? Are we in the right business? What optional portfolios, or emphases in portfolios, do we have? What acquisitions, divestitures, joint ventures, or investments could enhance our company mission? What risks and gains are associated with each option?

Strategic choice

Which set of businesses is most consistent with our company mission and allows for the best use of corporate resources? Which set is most consistent with environmental trends and presents an acceptable level of risk? Which set is most synergistic allowing for the best use of our distinctive competencies? What are the long-term objectives for the company?

Operationalizing and institutionalizing the strategy

How will corporate-level resources be allocated among the various business groups? What are basic strategic guidelines for each business group? Have key corporate policies been communicated? Does our structure support the strategy? Do we have the right managers in the right positions? Is the corporate culture compatible with the strategy?

Control and evaluation of corporate-level strategy

What are the strategic success factors? Are budgetary, schedule, and reward systems in place to guide and control business-level managers in the desired execution? Are interim objectives being met? Are trigger points and contingency plans available if corporate-level performance falls below or above projected levels? Is desired synergy between business groups working out?

Exhibit 2
Business-level strategic management process

Company mission: HI's business groups

Hotel group: A strong hospitality focus providing moderately priced, quality food and lodging services to the traveling public.
Restaurant group: Build a national, freestanding restaurant business via franchise and company-owned Perkins restaurants.
Casino gaming: Build an HI presence in this hospitality-related market. Use Harrah's to build a leadership position in gaming markets by providing high-quality service at a high perceived value.

Company profile: internal analysis of each business group

What are distinct competencies within each of the businesses? What are the critical weaknesses? Identify both in light of the industry sectors and competitors the businesses face.

Environmental assessment for each business group

What are key external factors facing or influencing each business? Who are their competitors? What changes/trends are occurring that present major impacts on each business's future operations?

Strategic analysis

For each business group, what broad strategy options are suggested by comparing the respective environmental/internal analyses? How do they fit with the current mission? What are the risks and gains associated with each alternative? How compatible are alternatives for each business group, with corporate-level strategy and objectives?

Strategy choice

For each business group, which strategy offers the desired risk level and uses the business's key resource strengths to best exploit environmental opportunities? Is each chosen strategy within each business's realistic capacity to support? Are the choices compatible with corporate strategy and portfolio objectives?

Long-term objectives

For each business group, what are the objectives the strategy is meant to achieve (market shares, sales, ROI, social responsibility)? What is the time frame for accomplishment?

Grand strategy

For each business group, provide a clear, consistent, comprehensive statement of the business's long-term strategy. Ensure agreement with corporate management understanding and commitment from business's management.

Annual objectives

For each business group, what should these initial functional actions accomplish in the next year? What targets and timing are critical to insure the strategy is on track?

Functional strategies

For each business group, what critical actions must be taken in marketing, finance, operations, and personnel to initiate the grand strategy?

Policies

What specific policies need to be changed to be consistent with the new strategy? What new policies are essential to communicating and implementing the new strategy?

Institutionalizing the strategy

For each business group, is the current organization structure appropriate for the chosen strategy? Should it be adjusted or redesigned? Do we have the right managers in the critical assignments? Do the values and norms of managers and employees create a culture that "fits" the strategy?

Control and evaluation of strategy

For each business group, have key targets and milestones been set? Is an effective information system in place to provide timely feedback? Do we have trigger points and contingency plans for rapid adjustments in strategy or actions? For example, have we pre-planned responses if systemwide occupancy rates run 10 percent below or above current projections over the next six months? Are budgets prepared and communicated to enhance control? Have we scheduled the use of time-constrained and sequential physical and human resources? Is the reward system consistent with desired actions?

opportunities, must be evaluated for each business group. And for each business group, a strategy that stakes out the desired competitive position must be chosen, implemented, and controlled. This must also be consistent with the role of the business group as expressed in the corporate-level strategy.

The interactive nature of the strategic management process should also be apparent in Exhibits 1 and 2. If the content of one component of the model changes, then the other components will change as well.

STRATEGIC MANAGEMENT MODEL

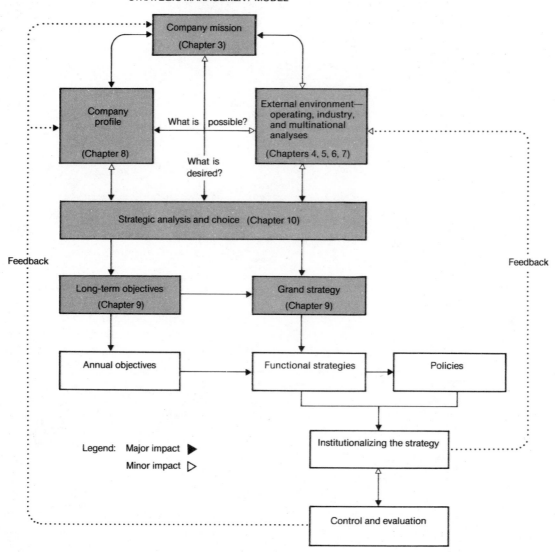

PART TWO

Strategy Formulation

Strategy formulation is designed to guide executives in defining the business their company is in, the aims it seeks, and the means it will use to accomplish these aims. Strategy formulation involves an improved approach to traditional long-range planning. As discussed in the following eight chapters, strategy formulation combines a future-oriented perspective with concern for a firm's internal and external environments in developing its competitive plan of action.

The process of strategy formulation begins with a definition of the company mission, as discussed in Chapter 3. In this chapter the purpose of business will be defined to reflect the values of a wide variety of interested parties.

Chapter 4 deals with the principal factors in a firm's external environment that must be assessed by strategic managers so that they can anticipate and take advantage of future business conditions. A recently popular approach to the strategic study of a firm's industry is the focal point of Chapter 5. This chapter systematically outlines and describes a five-force method of conducting a competitive industry analysis.

Chapter 6 describes the key differences between domestic and multinational firms in terms of the ways they impact on strategic planning and success. Special attention is given to the new vision of itself that a corporation must create when it multinationalizes, as is communicated in a revised mission statement.

Chapter 7 focuses on environmental forecasting—approaches currently used by strategic managers in assessing and anticipating changes in the external environment.

Chapter 8 shows how businesses evaluate their internal strengths and weaknesses to produce a company profile. Such profiles are used by strategic managers to target the competitive advantages they can emphasize and the competitive disadvantages they should correct or minimize.

In Chapter 9 attention turns to the types of long-range objectives set by strategic managers and to the qualities these objectives must have to provide a basis for direction and evaluation. The 12 grand strategies that companies use as broadly defined approaches for achieving long-range objectives are also highlighted.

Detailed comprehensive approaches to evaluation of strategic opportunities and to the final strategic decision are the focus of Chapter 10. The chapter deals with comparing strategic alternatives in a way that allows selection of the best available option for a firm, measured by potential for satisfying the company purpose.

Defining the Company Mission

What Is a Company Mission?

Whether developing a new business or reformulating direction for an ongoing company, the basic goals, characteristics, and philosophies that will shape a firm's strategic posture must be determined. This *company mission* will guide future executive action. Thus, the company mission is defined as the fundamental, unique purpose that sets a business apart from other firms of its type and identifies the scope of its operations in product and market terms. As discussed in Chapter 2, the mission is a broadly framed but enduring statement of company intent. It embodies the business philosophy of strategic decision makers; implies the image the company seeks to project; reflects the firm's self-concept; indicates the principal product or service areas and primary customer needs the company will attempt to satisfy. In short, the mission describes the product, market, and technological areas of emphasis for the business. And it does so in a way that reflects the values and priorities of strategic decision makers.

Strategy in Action 3–1 presents an example of a good mission statement that incorporates major features and provides a broad framework. The statement is from an internal communication of the Zale Corporation, a company

Note: Portions of this chapter are adopted from John A. Pearce II, "The Company Mission as a Strategic Tool," *Sloan Management Review,* Spring 1982, pp. 15–24.

Strategy in Action 3–1
Zale Corporation—Summary Statement of Corporation Mission

Our business is specialty retailing. Retailing is a people-oriented business. We recognize that our business existence and continued success is dependent on how well we meet our responsibilities to several critically important groups of people.

Our first responsibility is to our customers. Without them we would have no reason for being. We strive to appeal to a broad spectrum of consumers, catering in a professional manner to their needs. Our concept of value to the customer includes a wide selection of quality merchandise, competitively priced and delivered with courtesy and professionalism.

Our ultimate responsibility is to our shareholders. Our goal is to earn an optimum return on invested capital through steady profit growth and prudent, aggressive asset management. The attainment of this financial goal, coupled with a record of sound management, represents our approach toward influencing the value placed on our common stock in the market.

We feel a deep, personal responsibility to our employees. As an equal opportunity employer we seek to create and maintain an environment where every employee is provided the opportunity to develop to his or her maximum potential. We expect to reward employees commensurate with their contribution to the success of the company.

We are committed to honesty and integrity in all relationships with suppliers of goods and services. We are demanding but fair. We evaluate our suppliers on the basis of quality, price, and service.

We recognize community involvement as an important obligation and as a viable business objective. Support of worthwhile community projects in areas where we operate generally accrues to the health and well-being of the community. This makes the community a better place for our employees to live and a better place for us to operate.

We believe in the free enterprise system and in the American democratic form of government under which this superior economic system has been permitted to flourish. We feel an incumbent responsibility to ensure that our business operates at a reasonable profit. Profit provides opportunity for growth and job security. We believe growth is necessary to provide opportunities on an ever-increasing scale for our people. Therefore, we are dedicated to profitable growth—growth as a company and growth as individuals.

with annual sales of $1 billion from four major lines: jewelry ($700 million), sporting goods, footwear, and drugs. Zale is best known for its 769 jewelry stores and enjoys operating profits of approximately $130 million per year.

The Need for an Explicit Mission

Defining the company mission is time consuming, tedious, and not required by any external body. The mission contains few specific directives, only broadly outlined or implied objectives and strategies. Characteristically, it is a statement of attitude, outlook, and orientation rather than of details and measurable targets.

What then is a company mission designed to accomplish? King and Cleland provide seven good answers:

1. To ensure unanimity of purpose within the organization.
2. To provide a basis for motivating the use of the organization's resources.
3. To develop a basis, or standard, for allocating organizational resources.
4. To establish a general tone or organizational climate, for example, to suggest a businesslike operation.
5. To serve as a focal point for those who can identify with the organization's purpose and direction, and to deter those who cannot from participating further in the organization's activities.
6. To facilitate the translation of objectives and goals into a work structure involving the assignment of tasks to responsible elements within the organization.
7. To specify organizational purposes and the translation of these purposes into goals in such a way that cost, time, and performance parameters can be assessed and controlled.[1]

Formulating a Mission

The process of defining the mission for a specific business can perhaps be best understood by thinking about a firm at its inception. The typical business organization begins with the beliefs, desires, and aspirations of a single entrepreneur. The sense of mission for such an owner-manager is usually based on several fundamental elements:

1. Belief that the *product* or *service* can provide benefits at least equal to its price.
2. Belief that the product or service can satisfy a *customer need* currently not met adequately for specific market segments.

---

[1] W. R. King and D. I. Cleland, *Strategic Planning and Policy* (New York: Van Nostrand Reinhold, 1978), p. 124.

3. Belief that the *technology* to be used in production will provide a product or service that is cost and quality competitive.

4. Belief that with hard work and the support of others the business can do better than just *survive,* it can *grow* and be *profitable.*

5. Belief that the *management philosophy* of the business will result in a favorable *public image* and will provide financial and psychological rewards for those willing to invest their labor and money in helping the firm to succeed.

6. Belief that the entrepreneur's *self-concept* of the business can be communicated to and adopted by employees and stockholders.

As the business grows or is forced by competitive pressures to alter its product/market/technology, redefining the company mission may be necessary. If so, the revised mission statement will reflect the same set of elements as the original. It will state the basic type of product or service to be offered, the primary markets or customer groups to be served, the technology to be used in production or delivery; the fundamental concern for survival through growth and profitability; the managerial philosophy of the firm; the public image sought; and the self-concept those affiliated with it should have of the firm. These components will be discussed in detail in this chapter. The examples shown in Strategy in Action 3–2 provide insights as to the way the components are actually handled by some major corporations.

Strategy in Action 3–2
Identifying Mission Statement Components: A Compilation of Excerpts from Actual Corporate Mission Statements

1.	Customer/ market	We believe our first responsibility is to the doctors, nurses, and patients, to mothers and all others who use our products and services. (Johnson & Johnson)
		To anticipate and meet market needs of farmers, ranchers, and rural communities within North America. (CENEX)
2.	Product/ service	AMAX's principal products are molybdenum, coal, iron ore, copper, lead, zinc, petroleum and natural gas, potash, phosphates, nickel, tungsten, silver, gold, and magnesium. (AMAX)

Continued on Page 77

Strategy in Action 3–2 *(concluded)*

3.	Geographic domain	We are dedicated to the total success of Corning Glass Works as a worldwide competitor. (Corning Glass)
4.	Technology	Control Data is in the business of applying microelectronics and computer technology in two general areas: computer-related hardware; and computing-enhancing services, which include computation, information, education, and finance. (Control Data)
		The common technology in these areas relates to discrete particle coatings. (NASHUA)
5.	Concern for survival	In this respect, the company will conduct its operations prudently, and will provide the profits and growth which will assure Hoover's ultimate success. (Hoover Universal)
6.	Philosophy	We are committed to improve health care throughout the world. (Baxter Travenol)
		We believe human development to be the worthiest of the goals of civilization and independence to be the superior condition for nuturing growth in the capabilities of people. (Sun Company)
7.	Self-concept	Hoover Universal is a diversified, multi-industry corporation with strong manufacturing capabilities, entrepreneurial policies, and individual business unit autonomy. (Hoover Universal)
8.	Concern for public image	We are responsible to the communities in which we live and work and to the world community as well. (Johnson & Johnson)
		Also, we must be responsive to the broader concerns of the public including especially the general desire for improvement in the quality of life, equal opportunity for all, and the constructive use of natural resources. (Sun Company)

Source: J. A. Pearce II and F. R. David, "Corporate Mission Statements: The Bottom Line," *Academy of Management Executive* 1, no. 2 (May 1987), pp. 109–16.

Basic Product or Service; Primary Market; Principal Technology

Three components of a mission statement are indispensable: specification of the basic product or service, primary market, and principal technology for production or delivery. The three components are discussed under one heading because only in combination do they describe the business activity of the company. A good example of these three mission components is to be found in the business plan of ITT Barton, a division of ITT. Under the heading of business mission and area served, the company presents the following information:

The unit's mission is to serve industry and government with quality instruments used for the primary measurement, analysis, and local control of fluid flow, level, pressure, temperature, and fluid properties. This instrumentation includes flow meters, electronic readouts, indicators, recorders, switches, liquid level systems, analytical instruments such as titrators, integrators, controllers, transmitters, and various instruments for the measurement of fluid properties (density, viscosity, gravity) used for process variable sensing, data collection, control, and transmission. The unit's mission includes fundamental loop-closing control and display devices, when economically justified, but excludes broadline central control room instrumentation, systems design, and turnkey responsibility.

Markets served include instrumentation for oil and gas production, gas transportation, chemical and petrochemical processing, cryogenics, power generation, aerospace, government and marine, as well as other instrument and equipment manufacturers.

This segment of the mission statement clearly indicates to all readers—from company employees to casual observers—the basic products, primary markets, and principal technologies of ITT Barton, and it was accomplished in only 129 words.

Often a company's most referenced public statement of selected products and markets is presented in "silver bullet" form in the mission statement; for example, "Dayton-Hudson Corporation is a diversified retailing company whose business is to serve the American consumer through the retailing of fashion-oriented quality merchandise."[2] Such a statement serves as an abstract of company direction and is particularly helpful to outsiders who value condensed overviews.

Company Goals: Survival, Growth, Profitability

Three economic goals guide the strategic direction of almost every viable business organization. Whether or not they are explicitly stated, a company mission statement reflects the firm's intention to secure its *survival* through sustained *growth* and *profitability*.

Unless a firm is able to survive, it will be incapable of satisfying any of its stakeholders' aims. Unfortunately, like growth and profitability, survival is such an assumed goal that it is often neglected as a principal criterion in strategic decision making. When this happens, the firm often focuses on short-term aims at the expense of the long run. Concerns for expediency, a quick fix, or a bargain displace the need for assessing long-term impact. Too often the result is near-term economic failure owing to a lack of resource synergy and sound business practice. For example, Consolidated Foods, makers of Shasta soft drinks and L'Eggs hosiery, sought growth in the 1960s through the acquisition of bargain businesses. However, the erratic sales patterns of their diverse holdings forced the firm to divest itself of more than four dozen of the companies in the late 1970s. The resulting stabilization cost Consolidated Foods millions of dollars and hampered its growth.

Profitability is the mainstay goal of a business organization. No matter how it is measured or defined, profit over the long term is the clearest indication of a firm's ability to satisfy the principal claims and desires of employees

---

[2] See W. Ouchi, *Theory Z* (Reading, Mass.: Addison-Wesley Publishing, 1981). Ouchi presents more complete mission statements of three of the companies discussed in this chapter: Dayton-Hudson, Hewlett-Packard, and Intel.

and stockholders. The key phrase in the sentence is "over the long term." Obviously, basing decisions on a short-term concern for profitability would lead to a strategic myopia. A firm might overlook the enduring concerns of customers, suppliers, creditors, ecologists, and regulatory agents. In the short term the results may produce profit, but over time the financial consequences are likely to be detrimental.

The following excerpt from the Hewlett-Packard Company's statement of corporate objectives (i.e., mission) ably expresses the importance of an orientation toward long-term profit:

> Objective: To achieve sufficient profit to finance our company growth and to provide the resources we need to achieve our other corporate objectives.
>
> In our economic system, the profit we generate from our operations is the ultimate source of the funds we need to prosper and grow. It is the one absolutely essential measure of our corporate performance over the long term. Only if we continue to meet our profit objective can we achieve our other corporate objectives.

A firm's growth is inextricably tied to its survival and profitability. In this context, the meaning of growth must be broadly defined. While growth in market share has been shown by the product impact market studies (PIMS) to be correlated with firm profitability, other important forms of growth do exist. For example, growth in the number of markets served, in the variety of products offered, and in the technologies used to provide goods or services frequently leads to improvements in the company's competitive ability. Growth means change, and proactive change is a necessity in a dynamic business environment. Hewlett-Packard's mission statement provides an excellent example of corporate regard for growth:

> Objective: To let our growth be limited only by our profits and our ability to develop and produce technical products that satisfy real customer needs.
>
> We do not believe that large size is important for its own sake; however, for at least two basic reasons continuous growth is essential for us to achieve our other objectives.
>
> In the first place, we serve a rapidly growing and expanding segment of our technological society. To remain static would be to lose ground. We cannot maintain a position of strength and leadership in our field without growth.
>
> In the second place, growth is important in order to attract and hold high-caliber people. These individuals will align their future only with a company that offers them considerable opportunity for personal progress. Opportunities are greater and more challenging in a growing company.

The issue of growth raises a concern about the definition of a company mission. How can a business specify product, market, and technology sufficiently to provide direction without delimiting unanticipated strategic options? How can a company define its mission so opportunistic diversification can be considered while at the same time maintaining parameters that guide growth decisions? Perhaps such questions are best addressed when a firm outlines its mission conditions under which it might depart from ongoing operations. The growth philosophy of Dayton-Hudson shows this approach:

> The stability and quality of the corporation's financial performance will be developed through the profitable execution of our existing businesses, as well as through the acquisition or development of new businesses. Our growth priorities, in order, are as follows:
>
> 1. Development of the profitable market preeminence of existing companies in existing markets through new store development or new strategies within existing stores;
> 2. Expansion of our companies to feasible new markets;
> 3. Acquisition of other retailing companies that are strategically and financially compatible with Dayton-Hudson;
> 4. Internal development of new retailing strategies.
>
> Capital allocations to fund the expansion of existing operating companies will be based on each company's return on investment, in relationship to its return-on-investment (ROI) objective and its consistency in earnings growth, and on its management capability to perform up to forecasts contained in capital requests.
>
> Expansion via acquisition or new venture will occur when the opportunity promises an acceptable rate of long-term growth and profitability, acceptable degree of risk, and compatibility with the corporation's long-term strategy.

Company Philosophy

The statement of a company's philosophy, often called a company creed, usually accompanies or appears as part of the mission. It reflects or explicitly states basic beliefs, values, aspirations, and philosophical priorities. In turn, strategic decision makers are committed to emphasizing these in managing the firm. Fortunately, company philosophies vary little from one firm to another. Thus, owners and managers implicitly accept a general, unwritten, yet pervasive code of behavior. Through this code, actions in a business setting are governed and largely self-regulated. Unfortunately, statements of philosophy are so similiar and are so full of platitudes that they look and read more like public relations statements than the commitment to values they are meant to be.

Despite similarities in these philosophies, strategic managers' intentions in developing them do not warrant cynicism. In most cases managers attempt, often successfully, to provide a distinctive and accurate picture of the firm's managerial outlook. One such valuable statement is that of Zale Corporation, whose company mission was presented earlier in this chapter. As shown in Strategy in Action 3–3, Zale has subdivided its statement of management's operating philosophy into four key areas: marketing and customer service, management tasks, human resources, and finance and control. These subdivisions allow more refinement than the mission statement itself. As a result, Zale has established especially clear directions for company decision making and action.

Strategy in Action 3–3
Zale Corporation—Operating Philosophy

1. Marketing and customer service.
   a. We require that the entire organization be continuously customer oriented. Our future success is dependent on meeting the customers' needs better than our competition.
   b. We expect to maintain a marketing concept and distribution capability to identify changing trends and emerging markets and effectively promote our products.
   c. We strive to provide our customers with continuous offerings of quality merchandise, competitively priced—stressing value and service.
   d. We plan to constantly maintain our facilities as modern, attractive, clean, and orderly stores that are pleasing and exciting places for customers to shop.

2. Management tasks.
   a. We require profitable results from operations—activity does not necessarily equate with accomplishment—results must be measurable.
   b. We recognize there are always better ways to perform many functions. Continuous improvement in operating capability is a daily objective of the entire organization.
   c. We expect all managers to demonstrate capabilities to plan objectives, delegate responsibilities, motivate people, control operations, and achieve results measured against planned objectives.
   d. We must promote a spirit of teamwork. To succeed, a complex business such as ours requires good communication, clearly understood policies, effective controls and, above all, a dedication to "make it happen."
   e. We are highly competitive and dedicated to succeeding. However, as a human organization we will make mistakes. We must openly acknowledge our mistakes, learn from them, and take corrective action.

3. Human resources.
   a. We must develop and maintain a competent, highly motivated, results-oriented organization.
   b. We seek to attract, develop, and motivate people who demonstrate professional competence, courage, and integrity in performing their jobs.
   c. We strive to identify individuals who are outstanding performers,

Continued on Page 82

Strategy in Action 3–3 *(concluded)*

provide them with continuous challenges, and search for new, effective ways to compensate them—utilizing significant incentives.

d. Promotion from within is our goal. We must have the best talent available and, from time to time, will have to reach outside to meet our ever-improving standards. We heartily endorse and support development programs to prepare individuals for increased responsibility. In like manner, we must promptly advise those who are not geared to the pace, in order that they make the necessary adjustments without delay.

4. Finance and control.

a. We will maintain a sound financial plan that provides capital for growth of the business and provides optimum return for our stockholders.

b. We must develop and maintain a system of controls that highlights potential significant failures early for positive corrective action.

The mission statement of the Dayton-Hudson Corporation is at least equally specific in detailing the firm's management philosophy, as shown in Strategy in Action 3–4. Perhaps most noteworthy is the delineation of responsibility at both the corporate and business levels. In many ways, the statement could serve as a prototype for the three-tiered approach to strategic management. This new approach argues that the mission statement must address strategic concerns at the corporate, business, and functional levels of the organization. To this end, Dayton-Hudson's management philosophy is a balance of operating autonomy and flexibility on the one hand, and corporate input and direction on the other.

Public Image

Particularly for the growing firm involved in a redefinition of its company mission, public image is important. Both present and potential customers attribute certain qualities to a particular business. Gerber and Johnson & Johnson make safe products; Cross Pen makes high-quality writing instruments; Aigner Etienne makes stylish but affordable leather products; Corvettes are power machines; and Izod Lacoste is for the preppy look. Thus, mission statements often reflect public anticipations, making achieving the firm's goals a more likely consequence. Gerber's mission should not open the possibility for diversification into pesticides, nor Cross Pen's into 39-cent brand-named disposables.

On the other hand, a negative public image often prompts firms to re-emphasize the beneficial aspects reflected in their mission. For example, as a result of what it saw as a disturbing trend in public opinion, Dow Chemical

Strategy in Action 3–4
Management Philosophy of Dayton-Hudson Corporation

The corporation will:
  Set standards for return on investment (ROI) and earnings growth.
  Approve strategic plans.
  Allocate capital.
  Approve goals.
  Monitor, measure, and audit results.
  Reward performance.
  Allocate management resources.
The operating companies will be accorded the freedom and responsibility:
  To manage their own business.
  To develop strategic plans and goals that will optimize their growth.
  To develop an organization that can ensure consistency of results and
    optimum growth.
  To operate their businesses consistent with the corporation's statement of
    philosophy.
The corporate staff will provide only those services that are:
  Essential to the protection of the corporation.
  Needed for the growth of the corporation.
  Wanted by operating companies and that provide a significant advantage
    in quality or cost.
The corporation will insist on:
  Uniform accounting practices by type of business.
  Prompt disclosure of operating results.
  A systematic approach to training and developing people.
  Adherence to appropriately high standards of business conduct and civic
    responsibility in accordance with the corporation's statement of
    philosophy.

undertook an aggressive promotional campaign to fortify its credibility, particularly among "employees and those who live and work in [their] plant communities." Dow's approach was described in its 1980 annual report:

All around the world today, Dow people are speaking up. People who care deeply about their company, what it stands for, and how it is viewed by others. People who are immensely proud of their company's performance, yet realistic enough to realize it is the public's perception of that performance that counts in the long run.

A firm's concern for its public image is seldom addressed in an intermittent fashion. While public agitation often stimulates greater response, a corporation is concerned about its image even when public concern is not expressed. The following excerpt from the mission statement of Intel Corporation is an example of this attitude:

> We are sensitive to our *image with our customers and the business community*. Commitments to customers are considered sacred, and we are upset with ourselves when we do not meet our commitments. We strive to demonstrate to the business world on a continuing basis that we are credible in describing the state of the corporation, and that we are well organized and in complete control of all things that determine the numbers.

Company Self-Concept

A major determinant of any company's continued success is the extent to which it can relate functionally to the external environment. Finding its place in a competitive situation requires the firm to realistically evaluate its own strengths and weaknesses as a competitor. This idea—that the firm must know itself—is the essence of the company's self-concept. This notion per se is not commonly integrated into theories of strategic management; however, scholars have appreciated its importance to an individual: "Man has struggled to understand himself, for how he thinks of himself will influence both what he chooses to do and what he expects from life. Knowing his identity connects him both with his past and the potentiality of his future."[3]

There is a direct parallel between this view of the importance of an individual's self-concept and the self-concept of a business. Fundamentally, the need for each to know the self is crucial. The ability of a firm or an individual to survive in a dynamic and highly competitive environment would be severely limited if the impact on others and of others is not understood.

In some senses, then, the organization takes on a personality of its own. Hall stated that much behavior in organizations is organizationally based, that is, a business acts on its members in other than individual and interacting ways.[4] Thus businesses are entities that act with a personality transcending those of particular company members. As such, the firm can be seen as setting decision-making parameters, based on aims different than and distinct from the individual aims of its members. The effects of organizational considerations are pervasive.

---

[3] J. Kelly, *Organizational Behavior* (Homewood, Ill.: Richard D. Irwin, 1974), p. 258.

[4] R. H. Hall, *Organization—Structure and Process* (Englewood Cliffs, N.J.: Prentice-Hall, 1972), p. 11.

Organizations do have policies, do and do not condone violence, and may or may not greet you with a smile. They also manufacture goods, administer policies, and protect the citizenry. These are organizational actions and involve properties of organizations, not individuals. They are carried out by individuals, even in the case of computer-produced letters, which are programmed by individuals—but the genesis of the actions remains in the organization.[5]

The actual role of the corporate self-concept has been summarized as follows:

1. The corporate self-concept is based on management perception of the way others (society) will respond to the corporation.
2. The corporate self-concept will function to direct the behavior of people employed by the company.
3. The actual response of others to the company will in part determine the corporate self-concept.
4. The self-concept is incorporated in statements of corporate mission to be explicitly communicated to individuals inside and outside the company, that is, to be actualized.[6]

A second look at the company mission of the Zale Corporation in Strategy in Action 3–1 reveals much about the business's self-concept. The strategic decision makers see the firm as socially responsive, prudent, and fiercely independent.

Characteristically, descriptions of self-concept per se do not appear in company mission statements. Yet, strong impressions of a firm's self-image are often evident. An example from Intel Corporation is given in Strategy in Action 3–5.

The Claimant Approach to Company Responsibility

In defining or redefining the company mission, strategic managers must recognize and acknowledge the legitimate claims of other stakeholders of the firm. These include both investors and employees as well as outsiders affected by the company's actions. Such outsiders commonly include customers, suppliers, governments, unions, competitors, local communities, and the general public. Each of these interest groups has justifiable reasons to expect, and often to demand, the company to act in a responsible manner in satisfying their claims. Generalizing, stockholders claim appropriate returns on their investment; employees seek broadly defined job satisfaction; customers want what they pay for; suppliers seek dependable buyers; governments want adherence to legis-

---

[5] Ibid., p. 13.

[6] E. J. Kelley, *Marketing Planning and Competitive Strategy* (Englewood Cliffs, N.J.: Prentice-Hall, 1972), p. 55.

Good!

Strategy in Action 3–5
Abstract of Intel's Mission-Related Information

Management Style. Intel is a company of individuals, each with his or her own personality and characteristics.

Management is *self-critical*. The leaders must be capable of recognizing and accepting their mistakes and learning from them.

✓ Open *(constructive) confrontation is encouraged* at all levels of the corporation and is viewed as a method of problem solving and conflict resolution.

✓ Decision by *consensus* is the rule. Decisions once made are supported. Position in the organization is not the basis for quality of ideas.

✓ A *highly communicative, open management* is part of the style.

✓ A high degree of *organizational skills and discipline* are demanded.

✓ *Management must be ethical.* Managing by telling the truth and treating all employees equitably has established credibility that is ethical.

Work Ethic/Environment

It is a general objective of Intel to line up individual work assignments with career objectives.

We strive to provide an *opportunity for rapid development.*

Intel is a *results-oriented* company. The focus is on *substance* versus form, *quality* versus quantity.

We believe in the principle that *hard work, high productivity* is something to be proud of.

✗ The concept of *assumed responsibility* is accepted. (If a task needs to be done, assume you have the responsibility to get it done.)

Commitments are long term; if career problems occur at some point, reassignment is a better alternative than termination.

✓ We desire to have *all employees involved and participative* in their relationship with Intel.

---

lation; unions seek benefits for members in proportion to contributions to company success; competitors want fair competition; local communities want companies to be responsible citizens; and the general public seeks some improvement in the quality of life resulting from the firm's existence.

However, when a business attempts to define its mission to incorporate

Claimant
= stakeholder.

the interests of these groups, broad generalizations are insufficient. Thus, four steps need to be taken:

?
,

1. Identification of claimants.
2. Understanding of specific claims vis-à-vis the company.
3. Reconciliation of claims and assigning them priorities.
4. Coordination of claims with other elements of the mission.

Identification.   The left-hand column of Figure 3–1 lists the commonly encountered claimants, to which the executive officer group is often added. Obviously though, every business faces a slightly different set of claimants, who vary in number, size, influence, and importance. In defining a mission, strategic managers must identify all claimant groups and weight their relative ability to affect firm success.

Understanding.   The concerns of principal claimants tend to center around the generalities in the right-hand column of Figure 3–1. However, strategic decision makers should understand the specific demands of each group. Then strategic managers will be better able to both appreciate these concerns and initiate clearly defined actions.

Reconciliation and Priorities.   Unfortunately, the concerns of various claimants often conflict. For example, the claims of governments and the general public tend to limit profitability, which is the central concern of most creditors and stockholders. Thus, claims must be reconciled. To achieve a unified approach managers must define a mission that resolves the competing, conflicting, and contradictory claims. For objectives and strategies to be internally consistent and precisely focused, mission statements must display a single-minded, though multidimensional, approach to business aims.

There are hundreds, if not thousands, of claims on any business—high wages, pure air, job security, product quality, community service, taxes, occupational health and safety (OSHA) and equal opportunity (EEOC) regulations, product variety, wide markets, career opportunities, company growth, investment security, high ROI, and many, many more. Although most, if not all, of these claims are desirable ends, they cannot be pursued with equal emphasis. Claims must be assigned priorities that reflect the relative attention the firm will give to each. Such emphasis is reflected by the criteria used in strategic decision making; by the company's allocation of human, financial, and physical resources; and by the long-term objectives and strategies developed for the firm.

Coordination with Other Elements.   Demands of claimant groups for responsible action by a company constitute only one set of inputs to the mission. Managerial operating philosophies and determination of the product-market

Figure 3-1
A claimant view of company responsibility

Claimant	Nature of the claim
Stockholders	Participation in distribution of profits, additional stock offerings, assets on liquidation; vote of stock; inspection of company books; transfer of stock; election of board of directors; and such additional rights as established in the contract with the corporation.
Creditors	Legal proportion of interest payments due and return of principal from the investment. Security of pledged assets; relative priority in event of liquidation. Subsume in some management and owner prerogatives if certain conditions exist within the company (such as default of interest payments).
Employees	Economic, social, and psychological satisfaction in the place of employment. Freedom from arbitrary and capricious behavior on the part of company officials. Share in fringe benefits, freedom to join union and participate in collective bargaining, individual freedom in offering up their services through an employment contract. Adequate working conditions.
Customers	Service provided with the product; technical data to use the product; suitable warranties; spare parts to support the product during customer use; R&D leading to product improvement; facilitation of consumer credit.
Suppliers	Continuing source of business; timely consummation of trade credit obligations; professional relationship in contracting for, purchasing, and receiving goods and services.
Governments	Taxes (income, property, etc.), fair competition, and adherence to the letter and intent of public policy dealing with the requirements of fair and free competition. Legal obligation of businessmen (and business organizations); adherence to antitrust laws.
Unions	Recognition as the negotiating agent for employees. Opportunity to perpetuate the union as a participant in the business organization.
Competitors	Norms established by society and the industry for competitive conduct. Business statesmanship on the part of peers.
Local communities	Place of productive and healthful employment in the community. Participation of company officials in community affairs, regular employment, fair play, purchase of reasonable portion of products of the local community, interest in and support of local government, support of cultural and charity projects.
The general public	Participation in and contribution to society as a whole; creative communications between governmental and business units designed for reciprocal understanding; bear fair proportion of the burden of government and society. Fair price for products and advancement of state-of-the-art technology which the product line involves.

Source: From William R. King and David I. Cleland, *Strategic Planning and Policy.* © 1978 by Litton Educational Publishing Inc., p. 153. Reprinted by permission of Van Nostrand Reinhold Company.

offering are the other principal components considered. The latter factors essentially pose a reality test the accepted claims must pass. The key question is: How can the company satisfy claimants and simultaneously optimize its success in the marketplace?

Social Responsibility

The various claimants on a company can be divided into two categories, as indicated by Figure 3-2. Insiders are individuals and groups who are stockholders or are employed by the firm. Outsiders are all other individuals or groups

Figure 3–2
Inputs to the development of the company mission

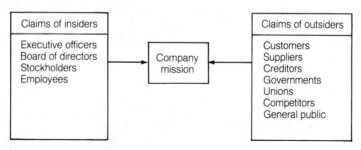

affected by the actions of the firm. This extremely large and often amorphous set of outsiders makes the general claim that the company be socially responsible.

Questions of social responsibility are perhaps the thorniest of all issues faced in defining a company mission. The claimant approach offers the clearest perspective on the problem. Broadly stated, outsiders often demand that the claims of insiders be subordinated to the greater good of the society, that is, to the greater good of the outsiders. They believe such issues as elimination of solid and liquid wastes, pollution, and conservation of natural resources should be principal considerations in strategic decision making. Also broadly stated, insiders tend to believe that the competing claims of the outsiders should be balanced against each other in a way that protects the company mission. For example, the consumers' need for a product must be balanced against the water pollution resulting from production, if the company cannot totally afford to eliminate the pollution and remain profitable. Additionally, some insiders argue that the claims of society, as activated by government regulation, provide tax money that is more than sufficient to eliminate unwanted business by-products, such as water pollution, if this is truly the wish of the general public.

The issues are numerous and complex, and the problems are contingent on the situation. Thus, rigid rules of conduct are not possible. Each business must decide on its approach in trying to meet its perceived social responsibility. Different approaches will reflect differences in competitive position, industry, country, environmental and ecological pressure, and a host of other factors. In other words, they will reflect both situational factors and differing priorities in the acknowledgment of claims.

Despite differences in approaches, most American companies now try to assure outsiders that they attempt to conduct business in a socially responsible manner. Many firms, including Abt Associates, Eastern Gas and Fuel Associates, and the Bank of America, have gone to the effort of conducting and publishing annual social audits. For example, the social audit of Eastern Gas and Fuel, as published in its 1981 annual report, is given in Strategy in

Action 3–6. These social audits attempt to evaluate the business from the perspective of social responsibility. They are often conducted for the firm by private consultants, who offer minimally biased evaluations on what are inherently highly subjective issues.

Strategy in Action 3–6
Social Audit of Eastern Gas and Fuel, 1981

Beyond Financial Concerns

Managing for profit is a common objective of all business, the cornerstone of the free enterprise system. However, business style varies widely. Eastern's philosophy is based on the premise that its performance objectives can be achieved in a manner that is responsive to the needs of Eastern's people—its shareholders, customers, employees, and the general public.

Corporate performance must be in line with shareholder expectations to justify their continued financial support. Service to Eastern's many customers must not be compromised. The selection and development of a highly skilled and motivated work force is essential. The work environment must be safe, healthy, and provide ample opportunity for self-improvement. The needs of the communities in which Eastern has a presence must also be addressed.

In striving to meet all of these objectives, Eastern has established proper business conduct as a top priority.

A.   Health and Safety

	Incidence rate per 100 full-time workers*					
	Number of fatalities		Disabling injuries and illnesses		All injuries and illnesses	
	1981	1980	1981	1980	1981	1980
Coal	1	3	5.9	7.7	6.8	8.6
Coke	0	0	9.3	24.0	60.7	24.4
Gas	0	0	5.7	5.3	6.6	5.8
Marine	0	0	8.0	7.7	13.6	14.0
Total corporate	1	3	6.5	7.4	8.9	9.9

* The incidence rates represent Number of work-related injuries and illnesses × 200,000 (100 employees working 40 hours per week, 50 weeks per year) ÷ Total hours worked by employees.

Continued on Page 91

Strategy in Action 3–6 *(concluded)*

B. Charitable Giving

	Total charitable giving	
	1981	*1980*
Total contributions (000)	$770.3	$679.0
Percent of pretax income*	1.0%	1.0%
Dollar per employee	$ 82.83	$ 73.01
Cost per share, after income tax	1.8¢	1.6¢

* Five-year average pretax income.

C. Minority Employment

	Minority employment levels (December 31)			
	1981		*1978*	
	Number	*Percent of total*	*Number*	*Percent of total*
Officers and managers	35	2.6%	29	2.0%
Professional and technical	36	5.0	37	4.6
Clerical	94	10.2	89	9.6
Skilled	613	13.6	441	9.3
Unskilled	187	9.0	324	16.2
Total Eastern	965	10.0%	920	9.3%

D. Pensions

	Annual cost of pensions and welfare plans ($000)	
	1981	*1980*
Company-administered plans for salaried, nonunion, and certain union employees	$ 9,413	$ 8,991
Other union retirement and welfare plans	30,086	27,684
Total cost	$29,509	$36,675

Many other firms periodically report to both insiders and outsiders on their progress to reach self-set social goals. Primarily through their annual reports, companies such as Diamond Shamrock discuss their efforts and achievements in social responsibility. Strategy in Action 3–7 provides the 1980 Diamond Shamrock report.

Strategy in Action 3–7
Social Responsibility Report of Diamond Shamrock
(Excerpts from the 1980 Annual Report)

Concern for the safety and well-being of our employees and those communities in which we operate is an integral part of Diamond Shamrock's management philosophy. These concerns are translated into company policies, procedures, and programs, from planning and research to the production, sale, and distribution of our products.

Safety, Health, and the Environment

It is the policy of Diamond Shamrock to manufacture and market our products with care, exercising regard for potential hazards involved in their use and handling by our employees, customers, and the public in general.

During 1980, Diamond Shamrock improved its plant safety record for the 10th consecutive year. Thirty plants and facilities operated without a lost-time accident. Companywide, lost-time injuries were reduced 21 percent from 1979.

The company's highly trained staff of environmental specialists continues to establish an admirable record of meeting or exceeding standards established by local, state, and national regulatory agencies. Diamond Shamrock invested more than $19 million in new and replacement environmental equipment during 1980.

Diamond Shamrock administered 4,626 extensive physical examinations to employees in 1980 at no cost to [the employees]. These served as an integral part of Diamond Shamrock's computer-operated health and environmental surveillance system (COHESS). Developed at a cost of more than $2 million, COHESS is designed to compare workplace exposure, employee characteristics, and the results of physical examinations to help ensure that our industrial hygiene programs are effective and to identify unknown risks as quickly as possible. The company has made the program available to other corporations at reasonable cost.

In addition to our worker health and environmental control programs, Diamond Shamrock invested more than $4.1 million during 1980 to determine the potential health and environmental effects of our products and to communicate that information to employees and customers. The company not only participates actively in industrywide studies of its products but, through multidisciplinary functions, conducts extensive in-house toxicological and environmental studies through its research center and its health and environmental affairs department.

Continued on Page 93

Strategy in Action 3–7 *(concluded)*

Human Resources

Company-sponsored employee development spending exceeded $800,000 in 1980, with more than 1,500 individuals attending Diamond Shamrock training programs. These continuing programs have resulted in improved job performance and have assisted employees in achieving individual career goals.

Diamond Shamrock actively pursues equal opportunity, without regard to religion, race, or sex. In addition, the company participates in and supports programs for the handicapped, Vietnam era veterans, women, and minority students.

Diamond Shamrock's compensation and benefit programs are designed not only to be competitive with [those of] the best of our peer companies but to provide an environment that fosters and gives recognition to excellence. Individual employee compensation is based on performance measured against job goals mutually selected by employee and supervisor.

Public Affairs

Diamond Shamrock maintains a responsive attitude to the needs of those communities in which we operate and considers this an important management responsibility. Several community relations programs assisted us in addressing these concerns during 1980.

The company invested $1,289,005 in philanthropic funds to support public, nonprofit organizations addressing needs of critical importance to the company, our employees, shareholders, and individual communities in 1980, a 26 percent increase from 1979. Plans call for $1,409,000 in philanthropic spending in 1981.

Diamond Shamrock encourages its employees to become involved in community affairs. Through our Citizen-of-the-Year program, inaugurated in 1980, the company provides recognition for those employees who unselfishly invest personal time and [funds] for the betterment of their communities. Last year, 40 employees were recognized for their outstanding service to others.

Diamond Shamrock management also plays an important role in other local, state, and national affairs through advice and counsel offered to planning and zoning commissions, cooperation with various regulatory agencies, testimony before congressional review and policymaking committees, and regional task forces addressing significant social challenges.

Guidelines for a Socially Responsible Firm

After decades of debate on the topic of social responsibility, an individual firm still must struggle to determine the orientation reflected in its mission statement. However, public debate and business concern have led to a jelling of perspectives. One excellent summary of guidelines for a socially responsible firm, consistent with the claimant approach, was provided by Sawyer:

1. The purpose of the business is to make a profit; its managers should strive for the optimal profit that can be achieved over the long run.

2. No true profits can be claimed until business costs are paid. This includes all social costs, as determined by detailed analysis of the social balance between the firm and society.

3. If there are social costs in areas where no objective standards for correction yet exist, managers should generate corrective standards. These standards should be based on managers' judgment of what ought to exist and should simultaneously encourage individual involvement of firm members in developing necessary social standards.

4. Where competitive pressure or economic necessity precludes socially responsible action, the business should recognize that its operation is depleting social capital and, therefore, represents a loss. It should attempt to restore profitable operation through either better management, if the problem is internal, or by advocating corrective legislation, if society is suffering as a result of the way that the rules for business competition have been made.[7]

Summary

Defining a company mission is one of the most easily slighted tasks in strategic management. Emphasizing operational aspects of long-range management activities comes much more easily for most executives. But the critical role of the company mission as the basis of orchestrating managerial action is repeatedly demonstrated by failing firms whose short-run actions are ultimately found to be counterproductive to their long-run purpose.

The principal value of a mission statement is its specification of the ultimate aims of the firm. A company gains a heightened sense of purpose when its managers address the issues of: "What business are we in?" "What customer do we serve?" "Why does this organization exist?" Yet managers can undermine the potential contribution of the company mission when they accept platitudes or ambiguous generalizations in response to these questions. It is not enough to say that Lever Brothers is in the business of "making anything that cleans anything," or that Polaroid is committed to businesses that deal with "the interaction of light and matter." Rather, a firm must clearly articulate its long-term intentions. In this way, its goals can serve as a basis for shared expectations, planning, and performance evaluation.

When a mission statement is developed from this perspective, it provides managers with a unity of direction that transcends individual, parochial, and temporary needs. It promotes a sense of shared expectations among all levels

---

[7] G. E. Sawyer, *Business and Society: Managing Corporate Social Impact* (Boston: Houghton Mifflin, 1979), p. 401.

and generations of employees. It consolidates values over time and across individuals and interest groups. It projects a sense of worth and intent that can be identified and assimilated by company outsiders, that is, customers, suppliers, competitors, local committees, and the general public. Finally, it affirms the company's commitment to responsible action in symbiosis with the firm's needs to preserve and protect the essential claims of insiders— sustained survival, growth, and profitability.

Questions for Discussion

1. Reread the mission statement of the Zale Corporation in Strategy in Action 3–1. List five insights into the company you feel you gained as a result of knowing its mission.

2. Locate the mission statement of a company not mentioned in the chapter. Where did you find it? Was it presented as a consolidated statement or were you forced to assemble it yourself from various publications of the firm? How many elements of a mission statement outlined in this chapter did you find discussed or revealed in your company's mission?

3. Prepare a one- or two-page, typewritten mission statement for your school of business or for a company selected by your instructor.

4. List five potentially vulnerable areas for a business without a stated company mission.

5. The social audit shown in Strategy in Action 3–6 included only a few of the possible indicators of a firm's social responsibility performance. Name five additional potentially valuable indicators and describe how company performance in each could be measured.

6. Define the term *social responsibility*. Find an example of a company action that was legal but not socially responsible. Defend your example on the basis of your definition.

Bibliography

Ackoff, R. L. *A Concept of Corporate Planning.* New York: Wiley-Interscience, 1970.

Andrews, K. R. *The Concept of Corporate Strategy.* Homewood, Ill.: Dow Jones-Irwin, 1971.

Ansoff, H. I. *Corporate Strategy.* New York: McGraw-Hill, 1965.

Bender, M. "The Organizational Shrink." *New York Times,* March 5, 1972, p. 3.

Beresford, D., and S. Cowen. "Surveying Social Responsibility Disclosure in Annual Reports." *Business,* March–April 1979, pp. 15–20.

Cleland, D. I., and W. R. King. *Management: A System Approach.* New York: McGraw-Hill, 1972.

"Florida Developer to Refund $17 Million to Buyers." *New York Times,* September 14, 1974.

Hall, R. H. *Organization—Structure and Process.* Englewood Cliffs, N.J.: Prentice-Hall, 1972.

Harrison, R. "Understanding Your Organization's Character." *Harvard Business Review,* May–June 1972, pp. 119–28.

Kelley, E. J. *Marketing Planning and Competitive Strategy.* Englewood Cliffs, N.J.: Prentice-Hall, 1972.

Kelley, J. *Organizational Behavior.* Homewood, Ill.: Richard D. Irwin, 1974.

King, W. R., and D. I. Cleland. *Strategic Planning and Policy.* New York: Van Nostrand Reinhold, 1978.

Ouchi, W. *Theory Z.* Reading, Mass.: Addison-Wesley Publishing, 1981.

Pearce, J. A., II, and F. R. David. "Corporate Mission Statements: The Bottom Line." *Academy of Management Executive* 1, no. 2 (May 1987), pp. 109–16.

Pearce, J. A., II; R. B. Robinson, Jr.; and K. Roth. "The Company Mission as a Guide to Strategic Action." In *Strategic Planning and Management Handbook,* ed. W. R. King and D. I. Cleland. New York: Van Nostrand Reinhold, 1987.

Rogers, C. R. *Client-Centered Therapy.* New York: Houghton Mifflin, 1965.

Sawyer, G. E. *Business and Society: Managing Corporate Social Impact.* Boston: Houghton Mifflin, 1979.

Chapter 3 Cohesion Case Illustration

The Company Mission at Holiday Inns, Inc.

Chapter 3 described what is necessary for a good mission statement and why such a statement is needed. This Cohesion Case Illustration will first present mission statements of Holiday Inns, Inc., at the corporate and business levels. Afterward, a brief evaluation of the mission statements will be provided, as well as an examination of how these must be readdressed in the strategic management process at Holiday Inns, Inc. (See Exhibit 1.)

Several observations can be made about Holiday Inns' mission statements. The corporate statement gives a clear overview of products and services offered, primary customer attributes, fundamental concerns, and basic management philosophy. This statement emphasizes the hospitality side of the enterprise when identifying its technology for providing goods and services. This may reflect a lack of in-depth consideration of how parts of the product and transportation businesses fit into the overall corporate mission. With this exception, the business group missions otherwise adequately identify the product/market scope of each unit's operations and fit within the umbrella of the corporate mission.

While these mission statements appear adequate and useful, an underlying mission-related issue must be considered while moving through the strategic management process at Holiday Inns. That issue involves the fundamental purpose of defining company mission: "What businesses are (or should) Holiday Inns be in?" From its beginning until the early 1970s, Holiday Inns was in one business—full-service lodging facilities. Seeking a broader earnings base, Kemmons Wilson and senior management redefined the company as a travel- and transportation-related business. This definition is strongly reflected in the current corporate mission statement. That definition led to the Trailways and Delta Steamship acquisitions, and freestanding restaurants.

The company mission should provide long-term direction, but that does not mean the mission should be cast in stone. As the strategic management model in Chapter 2 indicated, the mission must be reconsidered in light of environmental analysis, the company profile, and the evaluation of alternative strategies. Thus, the underlying, mission-related issue of whether Holiday Inns should be in a travel- and transportation-related business, a travel-related business, or a hospitality-related business cannot be resolved until strategists begin to evaluate alternative strategies.

Exhibit 1
Holiday Inns, Inc., mission statements

Corporate mission

Holiday Inns, Inc. is a diversified, international corporation providing services in the lodging, food service, entertainment, and transportation industries. Hotel operations consist of both company-managed and franchised Holiday Inn hotels. Transportation operations include Trailways, Inc., the nation's second largest intercity busline, and Delta Steamship Lines, Inc., a major U.S.-flag shipping company. Freestanding restaurant operations include the Perkins Cake 'n Steak chain. Various product operations market institutional furnishings, design services, equipment, and supplies.

We are a forward-looking, innovative industry leader with clearly defined goals, producing superior products, services, and consistently high returns for our stockholders.

We are committed to leadership in marketing our products and services to the traveling and leisure-time public. Internal growth of our operations will continue to be emphasized. We are also closely monitoring changes in consumer needs and lifestyles so that we can develop or acquire new services to satisfy emerging trends. Pursuing these opportunities will supplement the growth that we anticipate from our existing lines of business.

Five basic tenets form our corporate philosophy. They are:
1. Maintain high ethical standards.
2. Provide above-average growth in earnings.
3. Improve our return on invested capital (ROIC).
4. Maintain a strong balance sheet through prudent financial management.
5. People are our greatest asset. We will promote a climate of enthusiasm, teamwork, and challenge which attracts, motivates, and retains superior personnel and rewards superior performance.

Hotel group mission

The hotel group is committed to maintaining and expanding HI's leadership position in the lodging industry by staying ahead of its competitors in responding to the ever-changing needs of the traveling consumer. Through our company-owned and extensive franchise network, HI will offer moderately priced, full-service facilities in a manner that gives the customer the best price/value in the industry, provides for a superior return on stockholders' equity, and meets our social responsibilities to the communities in which we operate.

Restaurant group mission

The restaurant group is designed to provide a broader earnings base while transferring known skills—franchising, food service, freestanding locations in a brand new network—to the mid-priced restaurant industry. Through company-owned and extensive franchising, this group will grow the newly acquired Perkins chain to a national leadership position and also look for other restaurant acquisitions.

Transportation group mission

To provide a solid, profitable base for corporate diversification into travel-related areas, *Trailways*. To position HI as a market leader in providing innovative solutions to transportation (bus) industry problems through quality terminal facilities, better equipment utilization and reversing the industry decline in passenger miles, *Delta Steamships*; Delta is committed to becoming the leading U.S.-flag cargo carrier between U.S. ports and the growing markets of South America, West Africa, and the Caribbean through cost-effective management practices and state-of-the-art technology in cargo vessels.

New developments group mission

To build a broader base for future corporate earnings through diversification into hospitality-related businesses with exceptional growth potential. The customer profiles as well as the necessary operating expertise of these businesses should overlap HI's core capabilities in the food and lodging area. Primary focus in the near future should be on the casino/hotel business.

Note: This mission was prominent in 1977-78. By 1980-81, HI's gaming operations had become a *business group* with its own distinct mission—see paragraph 62.* This early mission statement is retained here to give you an example of a "new development" mission statement.

*Numbers refer to paragraphs in the Cohesion Case at the end of Chapter 1.

Assessing the External Environment

A host of external and often largely uncontrollable factors influence a firm's choice of direction and action and, ultimately, its organizational structure and internal processes. These factors, which constitute the *external environment,* can be divided into two interrelated subcategories: those in the *remote* environment and those in the more immediate *operating* environment.[1] The aim of this chapter is to describe the complexities and necessities involved in formulating strategies that optimize a firm's opportunities in a highly competitive market within the overall business environment. Figure 4–1 suggests the interrelationship between the firm and the remote and operating environments.

Remote Environment

The remote environment is composed of a set of forces that originate beyond and usually irrespective of any single firm's operating situation—that is, political, economic, social, technological, and industry factors. It presents opportunities, threats, and constraints for the firm, while the organization rarely exerts any meaningful reciprocal influence. For example, when the economy slows and recession is threatening, an individual housing contractor is likely to

---

[1] Many authors refer to the operating environment as the *task* or *competitive* environment.

Figure 4–1
The firm's external environment

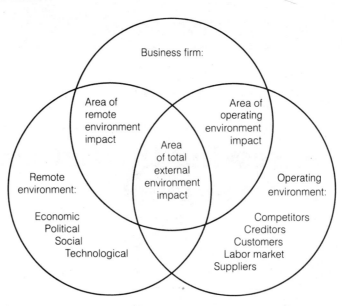

suffer a decline in business consistent with an industrywide decrease in construction starts. Yet that same contractor would be unable to reverse the negative economic trend even though it might be successful in stimulating local building activity. As a second example, political forces were operative in the trade agreements that resulted in improved relations between America and China in the mid-1970s. These agreements provided opportunities for individual U.S. electronics manufacturers to broaden their international bases of operation.

As a further example, Strategy in Action 4–1 describes the major conclusion of one firm in its pre-1984 assessment of the remote environment.

Economic Considerations

Economic considerations refer to the nature and direction of the economy in which the business operates. Because consumption patterns are affected by the relative affluence of various market segments, each firm must understand economic trends in the segments that affect its industry. On both national and international levels, a firm must consider the general availability of credit, the level of disposable income, and the propensity of people to spend. Prime interest rates, rates of inflation, and growth trends of the gross national product are additional economic factors that must be carefully considered in strategic planning.

Strategy in Action 4–1
External Factors Affecting the 1984 Strategy of Eastern Air Lines

Before determining its 1984 strategy, Eastern Air Lines conducted an assessment of its remote external environment. The following are the six major conclusions reached by Eastern's strategic planners:

The economic recovery is expected to continue.
　GNP: +4.5%

Fuel prices should be stable.

The industry outlook is good:

Domestic passenger-miles:	+10.5%
Domestic yield:	+ 6.0%

New, low-cost carriers will continue to exert pressure on prices.
　People Express, for example, is expected to take delivery of 18 B-727-200s
　　by April 1984 and to more than double its capacity.

Extensive discounting of daytime fares will continue to limit our ability to
　establish night coach fare differentials and to increase night coach flying.

Schedule restrictions related to the PATCO (air controllers) strike are being
　removed. Slot restrictions at all but four airports will be removed by the
　end of 1983. Removal of restrictions at Denver and Los Angeles and an
　increase to at least prestrike levels at La Guardia and O'Hare are expected
　during the first quarter of 1984. (Quotas at La Guardia and O'Hare were
　in effect prior to the strike and may be retained.)

　　　Until recently, the potential economic impact of international forces appeared to be severely restricted and was largely discounted. However, the emergence of new international power brokers has changed the focus of economic environmental forecasting. Three prominent examples of these new influences are the European Economic Community (EEC), the Organization of Petroleum Exporting Countries (OPEC), and coalitions of lesser-developed countries (LDC).

　　　The EEC or Common Market was established by the Treaty of Rome in 1957, and its members include most Western European countries. Its purposes are elimination of quotas and establishment of a tariff-free trade area for industrial products. This unique example of intra-European cooperation has helped member countries compete more effectively in international markets.

Following the EEC precedent of economic cooperation, the United States, Canada, Japan, the EEC, and other countries conducted multilateral trade negotiations in 1979 to establish rules for international trade and conduct. The outcome of those negotiations had a profound, yet differential, effect on almost every aspect of business activity in the United States.

OPEC is among the most powerful international economic forces in existence today in terms of its impact on the United States. This cartel includes most major world suppliers of oil and gas, and its drastic increases in the price of energy supplied not only impeded U.S. recovery from the recession of the early 1970s but also fueled inflationary fires the world over. The U.S. automobile industry was particularly affected through an increase in user costs and the legislated redesign of engine sizes and performance standards.

Third World and Fourth World countries have recently assumed a greater role in international commerce, as a source of both threats and opportunities. Following the success of OPEC, these less developed countries have found it economically beneficial to directly confront the established powers. Since 1974, producers of primary commodities in the LDCs have formed or greatly strengthened their trade organizations to enforce higher prices and achieve larger real incomes for their members. On the other hand, developing countries offer U.S. firms huge new markets for foodstuffs and capital machinery.

Even countries not desiring or unable to form cartels exhibit the new aggressive attitude.

> The intense nationalism of the developing countries, with nearly three fourths of the world's population, represents perhaps the greatest challenge our industrialized society and multinational corporations will face in the next two decades. As one Third World expert puts it, "the vastly unequal relationship between the rich and poor nations is fast becoming the central issue of our time."[2]

Each of these international forces has the capacity to affect the U.S. business community's economic well-being—for better or worse, for richer or poorer. Consequently, companies must try to forecast major repercussions of actions taken in both the domestic and international economic arenas. Such forecasts are a critical part of the strategic management process.

Social Considerations

Social considerations involve the beliefs, values, attitudes, opinions, and lifestyles of those in a firm's external environment, as developed from their cultural,

---

[2] Richard Steade, "Multinational Corporations and the Changing World Economic Order," *California Management Review,* Winter 1978, p. 5.

ecological, demographic, religious, educational, and ethnic conditioning. As social attitudes change, so does demand for various clothing styles, books, leisure activities, and other products and services. As is true of other forces in the remote external environment, social forces are dynamic with constant change resulting from individuals' efforts to control and adapt to environmental factors to satisfy their desires and needs.

1.   One of the most profound social changes in recent years is the large number of women entering the labor market. Not only have women affected the hiring and compensation policies and resource capabilities of firms employing them, they have also created or greatly expanded demand for a wide range of products and services necessitated by their absence from the home. Businesses that correctly anticipated or quickly reacted to this social change have profited by offering such products and services as convenience foods, microwave ovens, and day-care centers.

2.   A second accelerating social change is consumer and employee interest in quality-of-life issues, even at the expense of greater affluence. Evidence of this change is seen in recent contract negotiations in that added to the traditional demand for increased salaries have been worker preferences for such benefits as sabbaticals, flexible hours or four-day workweeks, lump-sum vacation plans, and opportunities for advanced training.

3   A third important change in the social environment is the shift in national age distribution. Changing social values and increased acceptance of improved birth control methods have resulted in a rise in the mean age of the U.S. population from 27.9 in 1970 to an expected 34.9 years by the end of the 20th century. This trend will have an increasingly unfavorable impact on most producers of predominantly youth-oriented goods and will necessitate a shift in long-range marketing strategies. For example, producers of hair- and skin-care preparations have already begun to adjust research and development to reflect anticipated changes in the types of products demanded. One company that has recognized the potential impact is Procter & Gamble, as discussed in Strategy in Action 4–2.

A consequence of the changing population distribution is sharply increased demands from a growing senior citizen population. Constrained by fixed incomes, the elderly have demanded that arbitrary and rigid policies on retirement age be modified. They have successfully lobbied for tax exemptions and increases in social security benefits. Such changes have significantly altered the opportunity-risk equations of many firms—often much to the benefit of those businesses that anticipated the social impacts.

Translating social change into forecasts of business effects is a difficult process at best. Nevertheless, informed estimates of the impact of such alterations as geographic shifts in populations and changing work values, ethics, and religious orientation can only help a strategizing firm in its attempts to prosper.

Strategy in Action 4–2
Procter & Gamble

Procter & Gamble announced a new product on August 7, 1979, symbolizing a revolutionary era at the big Cincinnati company. The product was a medicinal cream for the treatment of skin lesions. Procter & Gamble had just begun a grand invasion of new markets, many of which were institutional and commercial fields well outside of its traditional haven in the nation's supermarkets. The first phalanx of these new products from P&G involved fanning out into such fields as prescription drugs, synthetic foods and food ingredients, and supplies for hospitals and nursing homes. Others, destined for the soft-drink and agriculture-chemicals markets, were laying in wait. These nonsupermarket offerings were forecast to account for as much as 20 percent of the company's business by the mid-1980s.

The broad intent of this strategy was clear. With birthrates declining and population growth leveling off, the demographic trends that fueled P&G's ascent over the decades of the 1960s and 1970s were reversing. Given this shift, the company decided to look elsewhere to continue expanding at its previous rate.

The diversification drive also involved huge, unexplored risks. In many of its new fields, such as drugs and chemicals, the company had to take on formidable competitors that were not much impressed by P&G's recognized preeminence in packaged goods. Although the company boasted an unequaled marketing network for consumer products, many rivals doubted its ability to sell to institutions, doctors, and pharmacists.

Still, P&G had clearly decided that the competitive risks did not outweigh the potential rewards of its new product campaign, nor did they eclipse the company's need to find new avenues of growth.

Based on the article "P&G's New New-Product Onslaught," from the October 1, 1979, issue of *Business Week*.

Political Considerations

The direction and stability of political factors is a major consideration for managers in formulating company strategy. Political considerations define the legal and otherwise governing parameters in which the firm must or may wish to operate. Political constraints are placed on each company through fair-trade decisions, antitrust laws, tax programs, minimum wage legislation, pollution and pricing policies, administrative jawboning, and many other actions aimed at protecting the consumer and the environment. These laws, practices, and regulations are most commonly restrictive, and as a result, they tend to reduce a firm's potential profits. However, other political actions are designed to benefit and protect a company. Examples include patent laws, government subsidies, and product research grants. Thus, political forces are both a limitation and a benefit to the firms they influence.

Political activity may also have a significant impact on three additional governmental functions influencing a firm's remote environment.

Supplier Function.   Government decisions regarding creation and accessibility of private businesses to government-owned natural resources and national stockpiles of agricultural products will profoundly affect the viability of some firms' strategies.

Customer Function.   Government demand for products and services can create, sustain, enhance, or eliminate many market opportunities. For example, in the same way that the Kennedy administration's emphasis on landing a man on the moon spawned the demand for literally thousands of new products in the 1960s, the Carter administration's emphasis on developing synthetic fuels temporarily created a similar demand for new skills, technologies, and products in the 1980s. And the Reagan administration's priority on a strategic defense initiative ("Star Wars" defense) sharply accelerated the development of laser technologies.

Competitor Function.   The government can operate as an almost unbeatable competitor in the marketplace. Thus, knowledge of its strategies gained through assessment of the remote environment can help a firm to avoid unfavorable confrontation with government as a competitor. For example, forecasts that government will increase the number of nuclear power plants or communication facilities might simultaneously serve as a retreat signal to direct private competitors and as an invitation to private producers of services or associated activities.

Businesses are greatly affected by government decisions, as shown in Strategy in Action 4–3. Thus, continual assessment of government strategizing will help individual firms to develop complementary plans that anticipate and optimize environmental opportunities.

Technological Considerations

The final set of considerations in the remote environment involves technological advancements. To avoid obsolescence and promote innovation, a firm must be aware of technological changes that might influence its industry. Creative technological adaptations can affect planning in that new products may be suggested or existing ones improved; manufacturing and marketing techniques may also be improved.

Strategy in Action 4–3
A Major Threat in the CPA Firm's Environment

"These are our own ideas and opinions, our private notes," says Robert Hermann, a tax manager with the accounting firm of Deloitte Haskins & Sells. "They are none of the IRS's business."

The Internal Revenue Service disagrees, however, and the result is a bitter controversy.

The notes in question are those in which auditors spell out any doubts they have about a client's tax position. Accountants have always considered these confidential. But now, they say, recent IRS aggressiveness in seeking these papers has undermined their relationships with their corporate clients and has threatened to damage the quality of financial reports.

Says William Raby, a partner in Touche Ross & Co., "We've seen a drying up of the willingness of clients to discuss or even show data to their auditors. And the bottom line is that it isn't leading to good financial reporting."

When preparing and auditing financial statements, accountants include a reserve for taxes that might be payable if the IRS investigates. A company may take an investment tax credit, for instance, although it realizes that the IRS could disagree. [The company's] memos, and those of its auditors, would spell out the arguments on each side.

But the tax credit would likely be just one of many such items, and the IRS typically sees only the grand total reserve. If [the IRS] had access to the internal documents, it could see a breakdown of all the uncertain areas.

"It's a trail to the sensitive issues on the tax return," says William T. Holloran, a New York City lawyer and accountant. He says accountants try to dream up the worst possible scenarios, but "if the IRS sees that you wondered about something, they may just say 'Gee, there must be something wrong with it.'"

An IRS official takes a different view: "We feel that the information might throw light on the correctness of a taxpayer return." He says the memos are necessary because corporations usually are more open with accountants than with the government, "and we can't stay with a company for an unlimited period of time" ferreting out information. "The tax system shouldn't be viewed as a game of hide and seek. If we can get the papers, we can make a determination [of tax liability] much quicker, and not waste the taxpayers' money."

Most experts say that the only answer may rest with the IRS. "We can only hope that the IRS won't go bananas in this area," says Holloran. "On a normal audit, they have to show restraint."

A technological innovation can have a sudden and dramatic effect on the environment of a firm. A breakthrough may spawn sophisticated new markets and products or significantly shorten the anticipated life of a manufacturing facility. Thus, all firms, and most particularly those in turbulent growth industries, must strive for an understanding both of the present state of technological advancement affecting their products and services and of probable future innovations. This quasi science of attempting to foresee advancements and estimate their probable impact on an organization's operations is known as *technological forecasting*.

Technological forecasting can help protect and improve the profitability of firms in growing industries. It alerts strategic managers to both impending challenges and promising opportunities. As examples: (1) advances in xerography were a key to Xerox's success but caused major difficulties for carbon paper manufacturers; and (2) the perfection of transistors changed the nature of competition in the radio and television industry, helping giants like RCA while seriously weakening smaller firms with resource commitments that required products to continue to be based on vacuum tubes.

The key to beneficial forecasting of technological advancement lies in accurately predicting future capabilities and probable future impacts. A comprehensive analysis of the effect of technological change involves study of the expected impact of new technologies on the remote environment, on the competitive business situation, and on the business–society interface. In recent years, forecasting in the last area has warranted particular attention. For example, as a consequence of increased concern over the environment, businesses must carefully investigate the probable effect of technological advances on quality-of-life factors, such as ecology, aesthetics, and public safety.

Operating Environment

The operating environment involves factors in the immediate competitive situation that provide many of the challenges a particular firm faces in attempting to attract or acquire needed resources or in striving to profitably market its goods and services. Among the most prominent of these factors are a firm's competitive position, customer profile, reputation among suppliers and creditors, and accessible labor market. The operating environment, also called the competitive or task environment, differs from the remote environment in that it is typically subject to much more influence or control by the firm. Thus, when they consider conditions in the operating environment, businesses can be much more proactive (as opposed to reactive) in strategic planning than they are when dealing with remote factors.

Competitive Position

By assessing its competitive position, a business improves its chances of designing strategies that optimize environmental opportunities.

Development of competitor profiles enables a firm to more accurately forecast both its short- and long-term growth and profit potentials. Although the exact criteria used in constructing a competitor's profile are largely determined by situational factors in the environment, the following are often included:

1. Market share.
2. Breadth of product line.
3. Effectiveness of sales distribution.
4. Proprietary and key-account advantages.
5. Price competitiveness.
6. Advertising and promotion effectiveness.
7. Location and age of facility.
8. Capacity and productivity.
9. Experience.
10. Raw material costs.
11. Financial position.
12. Relative product quality.
13. R&D advantages/position.
14. Caliber of personnel.
15. General image.[3]

Once appropriate criteria have been selected, they are subjectively weighted to reflect their relative importance to a firm's success. Next, the competitor being evaluated is rated on the criteria. The rankings are multiplied by the weightings, and the resulting weighted scores are summed to yield a numerical profile of the competing business, as shown in Figure 4–2.

The type of competitor profile suggested is limited by the subjectivity of the criteria selection, weighting, and evaluation approaches employed. Nevertheless, this process is of considerable value in helping a business to explicitly define its perception of its competitive position. Comparing profiles of the firm and its competitors can further aid managers in identifying specific factors that might make a competitor vulnerable to alternative strategies the firm might choose to implement.

Customer Profiles

Perhaps the most valuable result of analyzing the operating environment is an understanding of the composition of a firm's customers. In developing a profile of present and prospective customers, managers are better able to plan the strategic operations of the firm, anticipate changes in the size of

---

[3] These items were selected from a competitive position assessment matrix proposed by Charles W. Hofer and Dan Schendel, *Strategy Formulation: Analytical Concepts* (St. Paul, Minn.: West Publishing, 1978), p. 76.

Figure 4–2
Competitor profile

Key success factors	Weight	Rating†	Weighted score
Market share	.30	4	1.20
Price competitiveness	.20	3	.60
Facilities location	.20	5	1.00
Raw materials cost	.10	3	.30
Caliber of personnel	.20	1	.30
	1.00*		3.30

* The total of the weights must always equal 1.00.

† The rating scale suggested is as follows: very strong competitive position (5 points), strong (4), average (3), weak (2), very weak (1).

markets, and allocate resources supporting forecast shifts in demand patterns. Four principal types of information are useful in constructing a customer profile: geographic, demographic, psychographic, and buyer behavior, as illustrated in Figure 4–3.

Geographic.   It is important to define the geographic area from which customers do or could come. Almost every product or service has some quality that makes it variably attractive to buyers from specific locations. Obviously, a successful regional manufacturer of snow skis in Wisconsin should think twice about investing in a wholesale distribution center in South Carolina. On the other hand, advertising by a major Myrtle Beach (South Carolina) hotel in the Milwaukee *Sun-Times* could significantly expand the hotel's geographically defined customer market.

Demographic.   Demographic variables are most commonly used for differentiating groups of customers. The term refers to descriptive characteristics that can be used to identify present or potential customers. Demographic information (such as sex, age, marital status, income, and occupation) is comparatively easy to collect, quantify, and use in strategic forecasting, and it is the minimum data used as the basis of a customer profile.

Psychographic.   Customer personality and lifestyle are often better predictors of purchasing behavior than geographic or demographic variables. In such situations, a psychographic study of customers is an important component of the total profile. Recent soft-drink advertising campaigns by Pepsi-Cola ("the Pepsi generation"), Coca-Cola ("catch the wave"), and 7UP ("America's turning 7UP") reflect strategic management's attention not only to demographics but also to the psychographic characteristics of their largest customer segment—physically active, group-oriented nonprofessionals.

Figure 4–3
Customer profile considerations

Type of information	Typical breakdowns
Geographic	
Region	Pacific; Mountain; West North Central; West South Central; East North Central; East South Central; South Atlantic; Middle Atlantic; New England
County size	A, B, C, D
City or SMSA size*	Under 5,000; 5,000–19,999; 20,000–49,999; 50,000–99,999; 100,000–249,999; 250,000–499,999; 500,000–999,999; 1,000,000–3,999,999; 4 million or over
Density	Urban, suburban, rural
Climate	Northern, Southern
Demographic	
Age	Under 6, 6–11, 12–17, 18–34, 35–49, 50–64, 65+
Sex	Male/female
Family size	1–2, 3–4, 5+ persons
Family life cycle	Young, single; young, married, no children; young, married, youngest child under 6; young, married, youngest child 6 or over; older, married, with children; older, married, no children under 18; older, single; other
Income	Under $5,000; $5,000–$10,000; etc.
Occupation	Professional and technical; managers, officials, and proprietors; clerical, sales; craft workers, supervisors; operatives; farmers; retired; students, homemakers; unemployed
Education	Grade school or less, some high school, graduated from high school, some college, graduated from college
Religion	Catholic, Protestant, Jewish, other
Race	Caucasian, Negro, Oriental, other
Nationality	American, British, French, German, Eastern European, Scandinavian, Italian, Spanish, Latin American, Middle Eastern, Japanese, and so on
Social class	Lower-lower, upper-lower, lower-middle, middle-middle, upper-middle, lower-upper, upper-upper
Psychographic	
Compulsiveness	Compulsive/noncompulsive
Gregariousness	Extrovert/introvert
Autonomy	Dependent/independent
Conservatism	Conservative/liberal/radical
Authoritarianism	Authoritarian/democratic
Leadership	Leader/follower
Ambitiousness	High achiever/low achiever
Buyer behavior	
Usage rate	Nonuser, light user, medium user, heavy user
Readiness stage	Unaware, aware, interested, intending to try, trier, regular buyer
Benefits sought	Economy, status, dependability
End use	Varies with the product
Brand loyalty	None, light, strong
Marketing-factor sensibility	Quality, price, service, advertising, sales promotion

* SMSA stands for standard metropolitan statistical area.

Source: Adapted from Philip Kotler, *Marketing Management* (Englewood Cliffs, N.J.: Prentice-Hall, 1972), p. 170.

Buyer Behavior.   Buyer behavior data can also be used in constructing a customer profile. This includes a multifaceted set of factors used to explain or predict some aspect of customers' behavior with regard to a product or service. As shown in Figure 4–3, information on buyer behavior (such as usage rate, benefits sought, and brand loyalty) can significantly aid in designing more accurate and profitably targeted strategies.

Suppliers and Creditors: Sources of Resources

Dependable relationships between a business firm and its suppliers and creditors are essential to the company's long-term survival and growth. A firm regularly relies on its suppliers for financial support, services, materials, and equipment. In addition, a business is occasionally forced to make special requests of its creditors and suppliers for such favors as quick delivery, liberal credit terms, or broken-lot orders. Particularly at these times, it is essential for a business to have an ongoing relationship with its suppliers and creditors.

In addition to the strength of a firm's relationships with suppliers and creditors, several other factors should be considered in assessing this aspect of the operating environment. With regard to its competitive position with suppliers, a firm should address the following questions:

1. Are suppliers' prices competitive? Do suppliers offer attractive quantity discounts? How costly are their shipping charges?
2. Are vendors competitive in terms of production standards? In terms of deficiency rates?
3. Are suppliers' abilities, reputation, and services competitive?
4. Are suppliers reciprocally dependent on the firm?

With regard to its position with its creditors, the following questions are among the most important for the strategizing firm:

1. Is stock fairly valued and willingly accepted as collateral?
2. Do potential creditors perceive the firm as having an acceptable record of past payment? A strong working capital position? Little or no leverage?
3. Are creditors' current loan terms compatible with the firm's profitability objectives?
4. Are creditors able to extend the necessary line of credit?

Answers to these and related questions help a business forecast availability of the resources it will need to implement and sustain its competitive strategies. Because quantity, quality, price, and accessibility of financial, human, and material resources are rarely ideal, assessment of suppliers and creditors is critical to an accurate evaluation of the firm's operating environment.

Personnel: Nature of the Labor Market

The ability to attract and hold capable employees is a prerequisite for a firm's success. However, the nature of a business's operating environment most often influences personnel recruitment and selection alternatives. Three factors most affect a firm's access to needed personnel: reputation as an employer, local employment rates, and ready availability of needed knowledge and skills.

Reputation. A business's reputation within its operating environment is a major element in its long-term ability to satisfy personnel needs. A firm seen as permanent in the community, at least competitive in its compensation package, and concerned with employee welfare, as well as respected for its product or service and appreciated for its overall contribution to general welfare, is more likely to attract and retain valuable employees than is a rival firm that either exhibits fewer of these qualities or emphasizes one factor to the detriment of others.

Employment Rates. Depending principally on the stage of growth of a business community, the readily available supply of skilled and experienced personnel may vary considerably. A new manufacturing firm seeking skilled employees in a vigorous and established industrialized community obviously faces a more difficult problem than would the same firm if it were to locate in an economically depressed area where other similar firms had recently cut back operations.

Availability. Some people's skills are so specialized that they may be forced to relocate to secure appropriate jobs and the impressive compensations their skills commonly command. Examples include oil drillers, experienced chefs, technical specialists, and industry executives. A firm seeking to hire such an individual is said to have broad labor market boundaries; that is, the geographic area within which the firm might reasonably expect to attract qualified candidates is quite large. On the other hand, an individual with more common skills would be less likely to relocate from considerable distance to achieve modest economic or career advancement. Thus, the labor market boundaries are fairly limited for such occupational groups as unskilled laborers, clerical personnel, and retail clerks.

Emphasis on Environmental Factors

This chapter has described the remote environment as encompassing four components—economic, political, social, and technological—and the operating environment five factors— competitors, creditors, customers, labor markets, and suppliers. While these descriptions are generally accurate, they may give the false impression that the components and factors are easily identified, mutually exclusive, and equally applicable in all situations. In fact, forces in the external environment are so dynamic and interactive that the impact of any single element cannot be wholly disassociated from the impact of other elements. For example, are increases in OPEC oil prices the result of economic, political, social, or technological changes? Or, are a manufacturer's surprisingly good relations with suppliers a result of competitors', customers', creditors', or the supplier's own activities? The answer to both questions is probably that a number of forces in the external environment have combined to create the situation. Such is the case in most studies of the environment.

Strategic managers are frequently frustrated in their attempts to anticipate the environment's changing influences. Different external elements affect different strategies at different times and with varying strengths. The only certainty is that the impact of the remote and operating environment will be uncertain until a strategy is implemented. This disconcerting reality leads many managers, particularly in comparatively less powerful, smaller firms, to minimize long-term planning, which requires a commitment of resources. Instead, they favor more flexibility, allowing managers to adapt to new pressures from the environment. While such a decision has considerable merit for many firms, there is an associated trade-off: namely, that absence of a strong resource and psychological commitment to a proactive strategy effectively bars the firm from assuming a leadership role in its competitive environment.

There is a final difficulty in assessing the probable impact of remote and operating environments on the effectiveness of alternative strategies. This involves collecting information that can be analyzed to disclose predictable effects. Except in rare instances, it is virtually impossible for any single firm to anticipate the consequences of a change in the environment, for example, the precise effect on alternative strategies of a 2 percent increase in the national inflation rate, a 1 percent decrease in statewide unemployment, or the entry of a new competitor in a regional market.

However, there is a real advantage in assessing the potential impact of changes in the external environment. In this way, decision makers are better able to narrow the range of available alternatives and eliminate options that are clearly inconsistent with forecast opportunities. Environmental assessment seldom identifies the best strategy, but it characteristically leads to the elimination of all but the most promising alternatives.

Designing Opportunistic Strategies

The process of designing business strategies is multifaceted, complex, and often principally dependent on fairly subjective and intuitive impact assessments (see Strategy in Action 4–4 for an example). The process is multifaceted because the decision maker must investigate independent and interactive influences from both the remote and operating environments. Such studies must

Strategy in Action 4–4
A Coal Industry Perspective

For the coal industry, 1979 was a bleak year. Spare capacity was as high as 20 percent, or 150 million tons. Miners were out of work, and mines were closing. Coal profits were off by more than 50 percent.

However, one segment of the industry appeared on the verge of remarkable gains—coal companies owned by oil companies. Eleven oil companies owned 25 percent of all the coal in the country in 1979, and had the future of coal in their grip. Moreover, oil companies planned to increase their 22 percent production share in 1979 to 50 percent by 1985.

In the past, during periods of slack demand, it was common for small mines to close; when prices firmed up, the mines reopened. In 1978, however, the growing cost and complexity of federal regulations made many such comebacks too expensive for small mines. Approximately 1,000 companies had left the coal business since the mid-1960s—about half of them since 1977.

But if costly regulation and a slack market spelled trouble to the small mines, their impact on big companies was just the opposite. "What oil companies contribute to their coal subsidiaries is staying power," said Hiram E. Bond, president of ARCO Coal Company. In fact, there was little evidence that the industry's slump in 1978 slowed big oil's plan for coal. Most of the country's top oil companies had major coal expansion programs under way. Increasingly, oil company money, technology, and management skills set the pace for coal's growth.

One reason the oil companies were banking on coal was a firmly held belief that utilities, the major coal consumers, had little choice about the fuel they burned in new plants—it had to be coal. The companies also believed coal would be a major beneficiary of the problems of nuclear energy.

There were some problems. These included environmental laws, such as the Clean Air Act, and reclamation regulations. In addition, new leasing regulations for federal coal mines slowed the industry's growth. Skyrocketing transportation costs were also a factor. However, the most troubling industry problem was another touchy political issue—the growing tide of sentiment against the oil industry could lead to antitrust action against energy conglomerates.

Based on the article "The Oil Majors Bet on Coal," from the September 24, 1979, issue of *Business Week*.

be conducted to prepare any systematic or comprehensive strategic decision. The process is complex because environmental forces have both individual and interactive effects on business generally and variable effects on a given business depending on the unique situation. Finally, most strategies are developed from fairly subjective and intuitive assessments of information gathered on the environment. Limited objectivity is an understandable consequence in that historical trends alone cannot be used to accurately predict future events, given constant changes in competitive external environments.

Designing a strategy to optimize opportunities identified by assessing the business environment is a difficult task:

> It usually means questioning old methods, exploring unfamiliar environmental waters, facing up to an objective evaluation of strengths and weaknesses, forcing important changes on people in the firm and [on] organizational arrangements, and taking high risks with the firm's capital. Moreover, it has to be done in a world of rapid change, and it has to be done continuously.[4]

As a result of the multifaceted, complex, and subjective nature of corporate strategy formulation, strategic managers should give special emphasis to four major design recommendations when developing their firm's plans: issue selection, data collection, conducting environmental impact studies, and planning for flexibility.

Issue Selection

An initial task is to determine the issues most likely to be critical to the success of the strategy. The identification of these issues will help to focus and prioritize data collection efforts.

In a recent study involving more than 200 company executives, the respondents were asked to identify key planning issues in terms of their recently increasing importance to strategic success. As shown in Strategy in Action 4–5, competitive domestic trends, customer or end-user preferences, and technological trends were the issues they selected.

Data Selection

Managers gather much of the forecasting information used to design strategies in the regular pursuit of business activities, for example, reading business and government publications, discussing competitive conditions with sales managers and clients, and serving on community councils and committees. However, such personal data collection is subject to considerable bias in interpretation, and its validity is often difficult to document and verify. Therefore, it is beneficial to systematically collect pertinent data from public sources. Such data are readily available, inexpensive, and, in general, comparatively reliable. Public data sources include annual reports, business literature indexes, business periodicals and reference services, government publications, trade publications, stockbroker reports, and many others. While all of these

---

[4] George A. Steiner, *Top-Management Planning* (New York: Macmillan, 1969), pp. 238–39.

Strategy in Action 4–5
Key Planning Issues

Issue	Percent of respondents indicating		
	Increase	*No change*	*Decrease*
✓ 1. Competitive (domestic) trends	83.6	13.5	2.9
2. Customer or end-user preferences	69.0	29.1	2.0
✓ 3. Technological trends	71.4	25.6	3.0
4. Diversification opportunities	61.7	30.3	8.0
5. Worldwide or global competition	59.4	34.4	6.3
6. Internal capabilities	55.4	40.2	4.4
7. Joint venture opportunities	56.6	36.7	6.6
8. Qualitative data	55.9	38.1	5.9
9. General economic and business conditions	46.4	47.3	6.3
10. Regulatory issues	42.8	51.2	6.0
11. Supplier trends	26.0	69.1	5.0
12. Reasons for past failures	27.6	62.3	10.1
13. Quantitative data	36.8	40.7	22.5
14. Past performance	27.3	51.2	21.5

Source: Adapted from V. Ramanujam, J. C. Camillus, and N. Venkatraman, "Trends in Strategic Planning," in *Strategic Planning and Management Handbook,* ed. W. R. King and D. I. Cleland (New York: Van Nostrand Reinhold, 1987), p. 615.

sources may be examined to detect general environmental trends, managers must carefully select from among them when constructing a strategic data base. Relevance, importance, manageability, accessibility, variability, and cost must be considered in selecting or generating data to be used.

Impact Studies

The nature and magnitude of the predicted impact of new strategic action is a second important consideration in designing opportunistic strategies. After forecasting data is selected, a business must conduct impact studies to determine the overall consequences of implementing available alternative strategies. In the process, the firm will transform environmental data into situation-specific environmental information. A typical impact study involves a system view in assessing probable effects on the firm's strengths and weaknesses, operating environment, competitive position, and likelihood of achieving corporate objectives, grand strategies, and mission. Although impact studies are predominately subjective and intuitive, businesses attempt to develop objective estimates whenever possible. Firms increasingly employ such techniques as exponential smoothing, time trends, and adaptive forecasting to increase the objectivity of data analysis.

Flexibility

A third important consideration in the design of strategies is the need to incorporate flexibility. Because forecasting environmental conditions is uncertain, decision makers enhance their chances of profitability if they strive for an optimal level of flexibility in their strategic plans. Several approaches to increasing such flexibility can be suggested:

1. State a strategy in general terms so that those implementing it have some discretion in terms of their unique situations.
2. Review strategies frequently.
3. Treat strategies as rules with exceptions so that an aspect of a strategy can be violated if such action can be justified.
4. Keep options open.

While flexibility in a strategic plan will lessen the plan's benefits by increasing costs, shortening planning and action horizons, and increasing internal uncertainty, an overly rigid stance in support of a particular strategy can be devastating to a firm faced with unexpected environmental turbulence.

Summary

The external environment of a business consists of two interrelated sets of variables that play a principal role in determining the opportunities, threats, and constraints a firm faces. Variables originating beyond and usually irrespective of any single firm's operating situation (political, economic, social, and technological forces) form the remote environment. Variables influencing a firm's immediate competitive situation (competitive position, customer profiles, suppliers and creditors, and the accessible labor market) constitute the operating environment. These two sets of forces provide many of the challenges faced by a particular firm attempting to attract or acquire needed resources and striving to profitably market its goods and services. Environmental assessment is more complicated for MNCs because multinationals must evaluate several environments simultaneously.

Designing corporate strategies that will enable a firm to effectively interact with a dynamic external environment is multifaceted, complex, and often principally dependent on fairly subjective and intuitive assessments. Nevertheless, assessments of a firm's external environment can provide a valuable planning base, especially when three major recommendations are followed:

1. Environmental data should be collected for a meaningful range of factors. The personal perceptions of strategic managers should be combined with data from public sources.
2. Impact studies should be undertaken to convert the data into relevant information used in determining the overall consequences for the firm of implementing the available alternative strategies.
3. Flexibility should be incorporated in the strategy to allow for unexpected variations from the environmental forecasts.

Thus, designing opportunistic strategies is based on the conviction that a company able to anticipate future business conditions will improve its performance and profitability. Despite the uncertainty and dynamic nature of the business environment, an assessment process that narrows, if not precisely defines, future expectations is of substantial value to strategic managers.

Questions for Discussion

1. Briefly describe two important recent changes in the remote external environment of U.S. business in each of the following areas:
   a. Economic.
   b. Political.
   c. Social.
   d. Technological.
2. Describe two major anticipated environmental changes that you forecast as having a major impact on the wholesale food industry in the next 10 years.
3. Develop a competitor profile for your college and the one geographically closest to it. Next, prepare a brief strategic plan to improve the competitive position of the weaker of the two schools.
4. Assume a competitively priced synthetic fuel is invented that could supply 25 percent of U.S. energy needs within 20 years. In what major ways might the external environment of U.S. business be changed?
5. With the help of your instructor, identify a local business that has enjoyed great growth in recent years. To what degree and in what ways do you think this firm's success resulted from taking advantage of favorable conditions in its external remote and operating environments?

Bibliography

Capon, N.; J. Farley, Jr.; and J. Hulbert. "International Diffusion of Corporate and Strategic Planning Practices." *Columbia Journal of World Business,* Fall 1980, pp. 5–13.

Channon, D. F., and M. Jalland. *Multinational Strategic Planning.* New York: AMACOM, 1978.

Conover, Horbart H. "Meeting the New Social Concerns." *Management World,* May 1977, pp. 25–27.

Contractor, F. J. "The Role of Licensing in International Strategy." *Columbia Journal of World Business,* Winter 1981, pp. 73–83.

Cox, Joan G. "Planning for Technological Innovation." *Long-Range Planning,* December 1977, pp. 40–44.

Davidson, W. H. *Global Strategic Management.* New York: John Wiley & Sons, 1982.

Dymsza, W. A. *Multinational Business Strategy.* New York: McGraw-Hill, 1972.

Fayerweather, J., and A. Kapoor. *Strategy and Negotiation for the International Corporation.* Cambridge, Mass.: Ballinger, 1976.

Gerstenfeld, Arthur. "Technological Forecasting." *Journal of Business* 44 (1971), pp. 10–18.

Healey, Dennis F. "Environmental Pressures and Marketing in the 1970s." *Long-Range Planning,* June 1975, pp. 41–45.

Hout, T.; M. Porter; and E. Rudden. "How Global Companies Win Out." *Harvard Business Review,* September–October 1982, pp. 98–108.

Kiser, J. W. "Tapping Eastern Bloc Technology." *Harvard Business Review,* March–April 1982, pp. 85–93.

Neubauer, F. Fredrick, and Norman B. Solomon. "Managerial Approach to Environmental Assessment." *Long-Range Planning,* April 1977, pp. 13–20.

Perry, P. T. "Mechanisms for Environmental Scanning." *Long-Range Planning,* June 1977, pp. 2–9.

Pfeffer, Jeffery, and Gerald Salancik. *The External Control of Organizations.* New York: Harper & Row, 1978.

Preble, John. "Corporate Use of Environmental Scanning." *University of Michigan Business Review,* September 1978, pp. 12–17.

Ronstadt, R., and R. Kramer. "Getting the Most out of Innovation Abroad." *Harvard Business Review,* March–April 1982, pp. 94–99.

Sadler, Philip. "Management and the Social Environment." *Long-Range Planning,* April 1975, pp. 18–26.

Steade, Richard. "Multinational Corporations and the Changing World Economic Order." *California Management Review,* Winter 1978, pp. 5–12.

Steiner, George A. *Top-Management Planning.* New York: Macmillan, 1969.

Turner, Robert C. "Should You Take Business Forecasting Seriously?" *Business Horizons,* April 1978, pp. 64–72.

Watson, C. M. "Counter Competition Abroad to Protect Home Markets." *Harvard Business Review,* January–February 1982, pp. 40–42.

Chapter 4 Cohesion Case Illustration

Environmental Assessment at Holiday Inns, Inc.

Environmental assessment at Holiday Inns, Inc., must first involve evaluation of the remote and operating environments of each business group. Afterward, these evaluations would be synthesized to determine the environmental situation facing the overall corporate enterprise. This Cohesion Case Illustration will briefly analyze the remote and operating environments of the key business groups using a tabular format. To aid in this analysis, a scale from +10 to −10 will be used to identify the degree to which each environmental factor represents an opportunity or threat in the business's environment.

Comparing the remote environments in Exhibit 1, Holiday Inns' most favorable opportunities appear in the three hospitality-related businesses: hotels, restaurants, and casinos. Social factors in the remote environment are strongly favorable for all three businesses. The remote environment presents a moderate opportunity for the steamship operation but is inconsequential for the products group. The major remote environment threats appear in relation to the Trailways bus operation.

Exhibit 2 examines the operating environments of each business group. The operating environments presenting the greatest opportunity are those of the hotel and casino groups. The similarity of their competitive advantages (existing or potential) and favorable opportunities suggest strong synergy between the two groups from a corporate perspective. The operating environment of freestanding restaurants appears favorable, with several dimensions suggesting limited but clearly exploitable opportunities. Delta Steamship encounters selectively favorable opportunities, while Trailways' operating environment presents several formidable threats.

From a corporate perspective, the remote and operating environment analyses identify factors suggesting that the greatest opportunities exist in hospitality-related businesses, and the most pressing threats face the Trailways bus operation.

Exhibit 1
Assessment of remote environment factors

Business	Economy	Political	Social	Technology
Hotels	Reduced vacation travel during recessions/energy costs (21,22) (−4)	Political stability of international locations (11) (−2)	Increasing leisure time/older population/single travelers and smaller families/baby boom now 25–40 years old (42) (+8)	Electronic and computer technology in reservations and control systems/satellite communication/labor-saving technologies (14,17) (+6)
Trailways	Less travel during recession but bus is a low-priced alternative means of transportation (27,28) (+1)	Safety regulations/no government ownership of terminals/deregulation of airline industry (−5)	All of the factors in above hotel block applicable here, though considerably less beneficial (42) (−2)	Labor-saving and cost-saving technology only minimal benefits, other transportation areas more affected (32) (−3)
Delta Steamship	Recession can hurt exports and imports/energy costs (−3)	Emergence of Third World markets/U.S. subsidies of U.S.-flag carriers and low-interest loans (+5)	Increasing concern for U.S. international trade effectiveness (38) (+1)	Labor-saving (LASH) and energy-saving technologies (37) (+3)
Freestanding restaurants	Recessions generally have a limited impact on family restaurants/energy costs less severe (+2)	Legal challenges to franchising (−1)	Increasing pattern of eating out/baby boom now 25–40/number of single-member households rising/women in work force (42) (+8)	Labor-saving and energy-saving improvements/food preparation technology (+4)
Casino gaming	Recessionary impact on leisure travel/energy costs (60) (−2)	Regulation of casino gambling/limited legal gaming markets (62) (−2)	All the factors mentioned in the hotel block above/increasing social acceptance of gaming (42,54,55) (+8)	Similar to hotel above though with less impact (+3)

Note: Italicized numbers in parentheses at the end of the comments refer to paragraph numbers in the Cohesion Case at the end of Chapter 1. Each comment is based on the information provided in the paragraphs identified in italics.

Exhibit 2
Assessment of operating environment factors

Business	Competition	Customers	Labor	Creditors	Suppliers
Hotel group	Substantial increase in the number of budget-chain competitors/no immediate threat to HI's leadership position but gap is narrowing, especially with budget-conscious traveler (21) (+3)	1 out of 6 American travelers stayed at HIs in 1978/research shows HI to be the preference of 40 percent of traveling public—high but declining since 1975/ages 24–49 with +$20,000 incomes most frequent guest/increasing number of single travelers and women travelers (25 percent in 1979)/steady demand for HI franchise, with over 60 percent of new franchise locations sought by current franchisees (21) (+6)	Adequate labor supply, although HI's labor-sensitive operating margins hurt by minimum wage increases (+2)	Strong capital structure, undervalued real estate and leadership position make credit readily available (66) (+5)	Gasoline cost for customers is rising, which begins to curtail travel (−2)
Trailways	Powerful competition from Greyhound on price, facilities, size, etc./increasing competition from other transportation sectors, such as airlines, trains, and package delivery services/intensive price-cost squeeze (27,28) (−6)	Customer profile quite different than typical HI guest, especially in income/limited gains in passenger miles since 1975/no strong customer loyalty (26) (−2)	Labor cost rising though some labor-saving technology improvements (−1)	Weak capital structure in highly competitive industry lessens available credit (−2)	Energy costs, especially fuel, rising significantly (−3)

Exhibit 2 (concluded)

Delta Steamship	Stiff competition from foreign cargo vessels in all routes/LASH technology improving relative position/major U.S.-flag carrier (37,39) (+2)	Primarily agriculture and manufacturing importers and exporters at both ends of route structure/strong in Gulf ports area (36) (+2)	Severely dependent on independent longshore workers/decreasing labor intensity via LASH technology (37,40) (−2)	Legislation access to U.S. government low-interest loans and cost subsidies (39) (+5)	Energy costs, especially fuel, rising significantly (−3)
Freestanding restaurants	Stiff competition from several nationwide chains, but Perkins' position in northern United States rather strong/expanding primary demand, which negates, to some extent, competitive impact/opportunities for additional acquisition (48,49) (+1)	Customer's profile quite similar to typical HI guest/family-oriented image/good brand identity in current geographic locations/trend of increased outside dining and more single households quite favorable/substantial franchise network and interest (43) (+5)	Nonskilled labor positions/labor intensive/adequate supply, though profit margins sensitive to minimum wage (+1)	Adequate capital structure and operating history for outside credit/HI corporate resources (66) (+2)	Rising energy costs in operating units and in food products (−2)
Casino gaming	Growing competition in each of the four legalized gambling markets in United States/but no dominant competitor overall/rapidly growing primary demand related to increased leisure time and aging population (62) (+5)	Customer profile very similar to typical HI guest/HI name, image, and reputation should prove quite beneficial/changing population demographics—baby boom age, single households, increasing leisure time—are strongly favorable (54) (+8)	Temporary labor shortages but benefit by HI link in hotel, food, and lodging side/rising labor costs (54) (−2)	Impressive profit potential but too early to tell/HI corporate resources (55,56) (+1)	Fuel-sensitive business and energy-intensive facilities (−3)

Note: Italicized numbers in parentheses at the end of the comments refer to paragraph numbers in the Cohesion Case at the end of Chapter 1.

5

Industry Analysis

Foreword

Harvard Professor Michael E. Porter's book *Competitive Strategy* propelled the concept of industry analysis into the foreground of strategic thought and business planning. The cornerstone of the book is the following article from the *Harvard Business Review* in which Porter emphasized five forces that shape industry competition. His well-defined analytical framework helps strategic managers to understand industry dynamics and to correctly anticipate the impact of remote factors on a firm's operating environment.

The Authors

Overview

The nature and degree of competition in an industry hinge on five forces: the threat of new entrants, the bargaining power of customers, the bargaining power of suppliers, the threat of substitute products or services (where applicable), and the jockeying among current contestants. To establish a strategic agenda for dealing with these contending currents and to grow despite them, a company must understand how they work in its industry and how they affect the company in its particular situation. This chapter will detail how these forces operate and suggest ways of adjusting to them, and, where possible, of taking advantage of them.

How Competitive Forces Shape Strategy

The essence of strategy formulation is coping with competition. Yet it is easy to view competition too narrowly and too pessimistically. While one sometimes hears executives complaining to the contrary, intense competition in an industry is neither coincidence nor bad luck.

Moreover, in the fight for market share, competition is not manifested only in the other players. Rather, competition in an industry is rooted in its underlying economics, and competitive forces exist that go well beyond the established combatants in a particular industry. Customers, suppliers, potential entrants, and substitute products are all competitors that may be more or less prominent or active depending on the industry.

The state of competition in an industry depends on five basic forces, which are diagrammed in Figure 5–1. The collective strength of these forces determines the ultimate profit potential of an industry. It ranges from intense in industries like tires, metal cans, and steel, where no company earns spectacular returns on investment, to mild in industries like oil-field services and equipment, soft drinks, and toiletries, where there is room for quite high returns.

In the economists' "perfectly competitive" industry, jockeying for position is unbridled and entry to the industry very easy. This kind of industry structure, of course, offers the worst prospect for long-run profitability. The weaker the forces collectively, however, the greater the opportunity for superior performance.

Whatever their collective strength, the corporate strategist's goal is to find a position in the industry where his or her company can best defend itself against these forces or can influence them in its favor. The collective strength of the forces may be painfully apparent to all the antagonists; but to cope with them, the strategist must delve below the surface and analyze the sources of competition. For example, what makes the industry vulnerable to entry? What determines the bargaining power of suppliers?

Knowledge of these underlying sources of competitive pressure provides the groundwork for a strategic agenda of action. They highlight the critical strengths and weaknesses of the company, animate the positioning of the company in its industry, clarify the areas where strategic changes may yield the greatest payoff, and highlight the places where industry trends promise to hold the greatest significance as either opportunities or threats.

Understanding these sources also proves to be of help in considering areas for diversification.

Figure 5–1
Forces driving industry competition

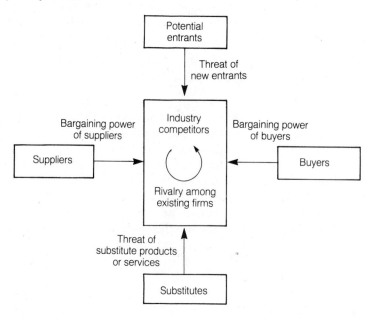

Contending Forces

The strongest competitive force or forces determine the profitability of an industry and so are of greatest importance in strategy formulation. For example, even a company with a strong position in an industry unthreatened by potential entrants will earn low returns if it faces a superior or a lower-cost substitute product—as the leading manufacturers of vacuum tubes and coffee percolators have learned to their sorrow. In such a situation, coping with the substitute product becomes the number one strategic priority.

Different forces take on prominence, of course, in shaping competition in each industry. In the ocean-going tanker industry the key force is probably the buyers (the major oil companies), while in tires it is powerful OEM buyers coupled with tough competitors. In the steel industry the key forces are foreign competitors and substitute materials.

Every industry has an underlying structure, or a set of fundamental economic and technical characteristics, that gives rise to these competitive forces. The strategist, wanting to position his company to cope best with its industry environment or to influence that environment in the company's favor, must learn what makes the environment tick.

This view of competition pertains equally to industries dealing in services and to those selling products. To avoid monotony in this article, I refer to both products and services as "products." The same general principles apply to all types of business.

A few characteristics are critical to the strength of each competitive force. They will be discussed in this section.

Threat of Entry

New entrants to an industry bring new capacity, the desire to gain market share, and often substantial resources. Companies diversifying through acquisition into the industry from other markets often leverage their resources to cause a shape-up, as Philip Morris did with Miller beer.

The seriousness of the threat of entry depends on the barriers present and on the reaction from existing competitors that the entrant can expect. If barriers to entry are high and a newcomer can expect sharp retaliation from the entrenched competitors, obviously he will not pose a serious threat of entering.

There are six major sources of barriers to entry:

1. Economies of Scale.   These economies deter entry by forcing the aspirant either to come in on a large scale or to accept a cost disadvantage. Scale economies in production, research, marketing, and service are probably the key barriers to entry in the mainframe computer industry, as Xerox and GE sadly discovered. Economies of scale can also act as hurdles in distribution, utilization of the sales force, financing, and nearly any other part of a business.

2. Product Differentiation.   Brand identification creates a barrier by forcing entrants to spend heavily to overcome customer loyalty. Advertising, customer service, being first in the industry, and product differences are among the factors fostering brand identification. It is perhaps the most important entry barrier in soft drinks, over-the-counter drugs, cosmetics, investment banking, and public accounting. To create high fences around their business, brewers couple brand identification with economies of scale in production, distribution, and marketing.

3. Capital Requirements.   The need to invest large financial resources in order to compete creates a barrier to entry, particularly if the capital is required for unrecoverable expenditures in up-front advertising or R&D. Capital is necessary not only for fixed facilities but also for customer credit, inventories, and absorbing start-up losses. While major corporations have the financial resources to invade almost any industry, the huge capital requirements in certain fields, such as computer manufacturing and mineral extraction, limit the pool of likely entrants.

4. Cost Disadvantages Independent of Size. Entrenched companies may have cost advantages not available to potential rivals, no matter what their size and attainable economies of scale. These advantages can stem from the effects of the learning curve (and of its first cousin, the experience curve), proprietary technology, access to the best raw materials sources, assets purchased at preinflation prices, government subsidies, or favorable locations. Sometimes cost advantages are legally enforceable, as they are through patents. (For an analysis of the much-discussed experience curve as a barrier to entry, see Strategy in Action 5–1.)

Strategy in Action 5–1
The Experience Curve as an Entry Barrier

In recent years, the experience curve has become widely discussed as a key element of industry structure. According to this concept, unit costs in many manufacturing industries (some dogmatic adherents say in all manufacturing industries) as well as in some service industries decline with "experience," or a particular company's cumulative volume of production. (The experience curve, which encompasses many factors, is a broader concept than the better-known learning curve, which refers to the efficiency achieved over a period of time by workers through much repetition.)

The causes of the decline in unit costs are a combination of elements, including economies of scale, the learning curve for labor, and capital–labor substitution. The cost decline creates a barrier to entry because new competitors with no "experience" face higher costs than established ones, particularly the producer with the largest market share, and have difficulty catching up with the entrenched competitors.

Adherents of the experience curve concept stress the importance of achieving market leadership to maximize this barrier to entry, and they recommend aggressive action to achieve it, such as price cutting in anticipation of falling costs in order to build volume. For the combatant that cannot achieve a healthy market share, the prescription is usually, "Get out."

Is the experience curve an entry barrier on which strategies should be built? The answer is: not in every industry. In fact, in some industries, building a strategy on the experience curve can be potentially disastrous. That costs decline with experience in some industries is not news to corporate executives. The

Continued on Page 129

Strategy in Action 5–1 *(concluded)*

significance of the experience curve for strategy depends on what factors are causing the decline.

A new entrant may well be more efficient than the more experienced competitors; if it has built the newest plant, it will face no disadvantage in having to catch up. The strategic prescription, "You must have the largest, most efficient plant," is a lot different from "You must produce the greatest cumulative output of the item to get your costs down."

Whether a drop in costs with cumulative (not absolute) volume erects an entry barrier also depends on the sources of the decline. If costs go down because of technical advances known generally in the industry or because of the development of improved equipment that can be copied or purchased from equipment suppliers, the experience curve is not an entry barrier at all—in fact, new or less experienced competitors may actually enjoy a cost advantage over the leaders. Free of the legacy of heavy past investments, the newcomer or less experienced competitor can purchase or copy the newest and lowest-cost equipment and technology.

If, however, experience can be kept proprietary, the leaders will maintain a cost advantage. But new entrants may require less experience to reduce their costs than the leaders needed. All this suggests that the experience curve can be a shaky entry barrier on which to build a strategy.

While space does not permit a complete treatment here, I want to mention a few other crucial elements in determining the appropriateness of a strategy built on the entry barrier provided by the experience curve:

The height of the barrier depends on how important costs are to competition compared with other areas like marketing, selling, and innovation.

The barrier can be nullified by product or process innovations leading to a substantially new technology and thereby creating an entirely new experience curve. New entrants can leapfrog the industry leaders and alight on the new experience curve, to which those leaders may be poorly positioned to jump.

If more than one strong company is building its strategy on the experience curve, the consequences can be nearly fatal. By the time only one rival is left pursuing such a strategy, industry growth may have stopped and the prospects of reaping the spoils of victory long since evaporated.

5. Access to Distribution Channels.   The new boy on the block must, of course, secure distribution of his product or service. A new food product, for example, must displace others from the supermarket shelf via price breaks, promotions, intense selling efforts, or some other means. The more limited the wholesale or retail channels are and the more that existing competitors have these tied up, obviously the tougher that entry into the industry will be. Sometimes this barrier is so high that, to surmount it, a new contestant must create its own distribution channels, as Timex did in the watch industry in the 1950s.

6.   Government Policy.   The government can limit or even foreclose entry to industries with such controls as license requirements and limits on access to raw materials. Regulated industries like trucking, liquor retailing, and freight forwarding are noticeable examples; more subtle government restrictions operate in fields like ski-area development and coal mining. The government also can play a major indirect role by affecting entry barriers through controls such as air and water pollution standards and safety regulations.

The potential rival's expectations about the reaction of existing competitors also will influence its decision on whether to enter. The company is likely to have second thoughts if incumbents have previously lashed out at new entrants or if:

The incumbents possess substantial resources to fight back, including excess cash and unused borrowing power, productive capacity, or clout with distribution channels and customers.

The incumbents seem likely to cut prices because of a desire to keep market shares or because of industrywide excess capacity.

Industry growth is slow, affecting its ability to absorb the new arrival and probably causing the financial performance of all the parties involved to decline.

Changing Conditions.   From a strategic standpoint there are two important additional points to note about the threat of entry.

First, it changes, of course, as these conditions change. The expiration of Polaroid's basic patents on instant photography, for instance, greatly reduced its absolute cost entry barrier built by proprietary technology. It is not surprising that Kodak plunged into the market. Product differentiation in printing has all but disappeared. Conversely, in the auto industry economies of scale increased enormously with post–World War II automation and vertical integration—virtually stopping successful new entry.

Second, strategic decisions involving a large segment of an industry can have a major impact on the conditions determining the threat of entry. For example, the actions of many U.S. wine producers in the 1960s to step up product introductions, raise advertising levels, and expand distribution nationally surely strengthened the entry roadblocks by raising economies of scale and making access to distribution channels more difficult. Similarly, decisions by members of the recreational vehicle industry to vertically integrate in order to lower costs have greatly increased the economies of scale and raised the capital costs barriers.

Powerful Suppliers and Buyers

Suppliers can exert bargaining power on participants in an industry by raising prices or reducing the quality of purchased goods and services. Powerful suppliers can thereby squeeze profitability out of an industry unable to recover cost increases in its own prices. By raising their prices, soft-drink concentrate producers have contributed to the erosion of profitability of bottling companies because the bottlers, facing intense competition from powdered mixes, fruit drinks, and other beverages, have limited freedom to raise their prices accordingly. Customers likewise can force down prices, demand higher quality or more service, and play competitors off against each other—all at the expense of industry profits.

The power of each important supplier or buyer group depends on a number of characteristics of its market situation and on the relative importance of its sales or purchases to the industry compared with its overall business.

A *supplier* group is powerful if:

It is dominated by a few companies and is more concentrated than the industry it sells to.

Its product is unique or at least differentiated, or if it has built up switching costs. Switching costs are fixed costs buyers face in changing suppliers. These arise because, among other things, a buyer's product specifications tie it to particular suppliers, it has invested heavily in specialized ancillary equipment or in learning how to operate a supplier's equipment (as in computer software), or its production lines are connected to the supplier's manufacturing facilities (as in some manufacture of beverage containers).

It is not obliged to contend with other products for sale to the industry. For instance, the competition between the steel companies and the aluminum companies to sell to the can industry checks the power of each supplier.

It poses a credible threat of integrating forward into the industry's business. This provides a check against the industry's ability to improve the terms on which it purchases.

The industry is not an important customer of the supplier group. If the industry is an important customer, suppliers' fortunes will be closely tied to the industry, and they will want to protect the industry through reasonable pricing and assistance in activities like R&D and lobbying.

A *buyer* group is powerful if:

It is concentrated or purchases in large volumes. Large-volume buyers are particularly potent forces if heavy fixed costs characterize the industry—as they do in metal containers, corn refining, and bulk chemicals, for example—which raise the stakes to keep capacity filled.

The products it purchases from the industry are standard or undifferentiated. The buyers, sure that they can always find alternative suppliers, may play one company against another, as they do in aluminum extrusion.

The products it purchases from the industry form a component of its product and represent a significant fraction of its cost. The buyers are likely to shop for a favorable price and purchase selectively. Where the product sold by the industry in question is a small fraction of buyers' costs, buyers are usually much less price sensitive.

It earns low profits, which create great incentive to lower its purchasing costs. Highly profitable buyers, however, are generally less price sensitive (that is, of course, if the item does not represent a large fraction of their costs).

The industry's product is unimportant to the quality of the buyers' products or services. Where the quality of the buyers' products is very much affected by the industry's product, buyers are generally less price sensitive. Industries in which this situation obtains include oil-field equipment, where a malfunction can lead to large losses; and enclosures for electronic medical and test instruments, where the quality of the enclosure can influence the user's impression about the quality of the equipment inside.

The industry's product does not save the buyer money. Where the industry's product or service can pay for itself many times over, the buyer is rarely price sensitive; rather, he is interested in quality. This is true in services like investment banking and public accounting, where errors in judgment can be costly and embarrassing, and in businesses like the logging of oil wells, where an accurate survey can save thousands of dollars in drilling costs.

The buyers pose a credible threat of integrating backward to make the industry's product. The Big Three auto producers and major buyers of cars have often used the threat of self-manufacture as a bargaining lever. But sometimes an industry engenders a threat to buyers that its members may integrate forward.

Most of these sources of buyer power can be attributed to consumers as a group as well as to industrial and commercial buyers; only a modification of the frame of reference is necessary. Consumers tend to be more price sensitive if they are purchasing products that are undifferentiated, expensive relative to their incomes, and of a sort where quality is not particularly important.

The buying power of retailers is determined by the same rules, with one important addition. Retailers can gain significant bargaining power over manufacturers when they can influence consumers' purchasing decisions, as they do in audio components, jewelry, appliances, sporting goods, and other goods.

Strategic Action.   A company's choice of suppliers to buy from or buyer groups to sell to should be viewed as a crucial strategic decision. A company can improve its strategic posture by finding suppliers or buyers who possess the least power to influence it adversely.

Most common is the situation of a company being able to choose whom it will sell to—in other words, buyer selection. Rarely do all the buyer groups a company sells to enjoy equal power. Even if a company sells to a single industry, segments usually exist within that industry that exercise less power (and that are therefore less price sensitive) than others. For example, the replacement market for most products is less price sensitive than the overall market.

As a rule, a company can sell to powerful buyers and still come away with above-average profitability only if it is a low-cost producer in its industry or if its product enjoys some unusual, if not unique, features. In supplying large customers with electric motors, Emerson Electric earns high returns because its low cost position permits the company to meet or undercut competitors' prices.

If the company lacks a low cost position or a unique product, selling to everyone is self-defeating because the more sales it achieves, the more vulnerable it becomes. The company may have to muster the courage to turn away business and sell only to less potent customers.

Buyer selection has been a key to the success of National Can and Crown, Cork and Seal. They focus on the segments of the can industry where they can create product differentiation, minimize the threat of backward integration, and otherwise mitigate the awesome power of their customers. Of course, some industries do not enjoy the luxury of selecting "good" buyers.

As the factors creating supplier and buyer power change with time or as a result of a company's strategic decisions, naturally the power of these groups rises or declines. In the ready-to-wear clothing industry, as the buyers (department stores and clothing stores) have become more concentrated and control has passed to large chains, the industry has come under increasing pressure and suffered falling margins. The industry has been unable to differentiate its product or engender switching costs that lock in its buyers enough to neutralize these trends.

Substitute Products

By placing a ceiling on prices it can charge, substitute products or services limit the potential of an industry. Unless it can upgrade the quality of the product or differentiate it somehow (as via marketing), the industry will suffer in earnings and possibly in growth.

Manifestly, the more attractive the price–performance trade-off offered by substitute products, the firmer the lid placed on the industry's profit potential. Sugar producers confronted with the large-scale commercialization of high-fructose corn syrup, a sugar substitute, are learning this lesson today.

Substitutes not only limit profits in normal times, they also reduce the bonanza an industry can reap in boom times. In 1978 the producers of fiberglass insulation enjoyed unprecedented demand as a result of high energy costs and severe winter weather. But the industry's ability to raise prices was tempered by the plethora of insulation substitutes, including cellulose, rock wool, and styrofoam. These substitutes are bound to become an even stronger force once the current round of plant additions by fiberglass insulation producers has boosted capacity enough to meet demand (and then some).

Substitute products that deserve the most attention strategically are those that (a) are subject to trends improving their price–performance trade-off with the industry's product or (b) are produced by industries earning high profits. Substitutes often come rapidly into play if some development increases competition in their industries and causes price reduction or performance improvement.

Jockeying for Position

Rivalry among existing competitors takes the familiar form of jockeying for position—using tactics like price competition, product introduction, and advertising slugfests. Intense rivalry is related to the presence of a number of factors:

Competitors are numerous or are roughly equal in size and power. In many U.S. industries in recent years foreign contenders, of course, have become part of the competitive picture.

Industry growth is slow, precipitating fights for market share that involve expansion-minded members.

The product or service lacks differentiation or switching costs, which lock in buyers and protect one combatant from raids on its customers by another.

Fixed costs are high or the product is perishable, creating strong temptation to cut prices. Many basic materials businesses, like paper and aluminum, suffer from this problem when demand slackens.

Capacity is normally augmented in large increments. Such additions, as in the chlorine and vinyl chloride businesses, disrupt the industry's supply-demand balance and often lead to periods of overcapacity and price cutting.

Exit barriers are high. Exit barriers, like very specialized assets or management's loyalty to a particular business, keep companies competing even though they may be earning low or even negative returns on investment. Excess capacity remains functioning, and the profitability of the healthy competitors suffers as the sick ones hang on. If the entire industry suffers from overcapacity, it may seek government help—particularly if foreign competition is present.

The rivals are diverse in strategies, origins, and "personalities." They have different ideas about how to compete and continually run head-on into each other in the process.

As an industry matures, its growth rate changes, resulting in declining profits and (often) a shakeout. In the booming recreational vehicle industry of the early 1970s, nearly every producer did well; but slow growth since then has eliminated the high returns, except for the strongest members, not to mention many of the weaker companies. The same profit story has been played out in industry after industry—snowmobiles, aerosol packaging, and sports equipment are just a few examples.

An acquisition can introduce a very different personality to an industry, as has been the case with Black & Decker's takeover of McCullough, the producer of chain saws. Technological innovation can boost the level of fixed costs in the production process, as it did in the shift from batch to continuous-line photo finishing in the 1960s.

While a company must live with many of these factors—because they are built into industry economics—it may have some latitude for improving matters through strategic shifts. For example, it may try to raise buyer's switching costs or increase product differentiation. A focus on selling efforts in the fastest-growing segments of the industry or on market areas with the lowest fixed costs can reduce the impact of industry rivalry. If it is feasible, a company can try to avoid confrontation with competitors having high exit barriers and can thus sidestep involvement in bitter price cutting.

Formulation of Strategy

Once the corporate strategist has assessed the forces affecting competition in his industry and their underlying causes, he can identify his company's strengths and weaknesses. The crucial strengths and weaknesses from a strategic standpoint are the company's posture vis-à-vis the underlying causes of each force. Where does it stand against substitutes? Against the sources of entry barriers?

Then the strategist can devise a plan of action that may include (1) positioning the company so that its capabilities provide the best defense against the competitive force; and/or (2) influencing the balance of the forces through strategic moves, thereby improving the company's position; and/or (3) anticipating shifts in the factors underlying the forces and responding to them, with the hope of exploiting change by choosing a strategy appropriate for the new competitive balance before opponents recognize it. Each strategic approach will now be considered in turn.

Positioning the Company

The first approach takes the structure of the industry as given and matches the company's strengths and weaknesses to it. Strategy can be viewed as building defenses against the competitive forces or as finding positions in the industry where the forces are weakest.

Knowledge of the company's capabilities and of the causes of the competitive forces will highlight the areas where the company should confront competition and where to avoid it. If the company is a low-cost producer, it may choose to confront powerful buyers while it takes care to sell them only products not vulnerable to competition from substitutes.

The success of Dr Pepper in the soft-drink industry illustrates the coupling of realistic knowledge of corporate strengths with sound industry analysis to yield a superior strategy. Coca-Cola and Pepsi-Cola dominate Dr Pepper's industry, where many small concentrate producers compete for a piece of the action. Dr Pepper chose a strategy of avoiding the largest-selling drink segment, maintaining a narrow flavor line, forgoing the development of a captive bottler network, and marketing heavily. The company positioned itself so as to be least vulnerable to its competitive forces while it exploited its small size.

In the $11.5 billion soft-drink industry, barriers to entry in the form of brand identification, large-scale marketing, and access to a bottler network are enormous. Rather than accept the formidable costs and scale economies in having its own bottler network—that, following the lead of the Big Two and of 7UP—Dr Pepper took advantage of the different flavor of its drink to "piggyback" on Coke and Pepsi bottlers who wanted a full line to sell to customers. Dr Pepper coped with the power of these buyers through extraordinary service and other efforts to distinguish its treatment of them from that of Coke and Pepsi.

Many small companies in the soft-drink business offer cola drinks that thrust them into head-to-head competition against the majors. Dr Pepper, however, maximized product differentiation by maintaining a narrow line of beverages built around an unusual flavor.

Finally, Dr Pepper met Coke and Pepsi with an advertising onslaught emphasizing the alleged uniqueness of its single flavor. This campaign built strong brand identification and great customer loyalty. Helping its efforts was the fact that Dr Pepper's formula involved lower raw materials cost, which gave the company an absolute cost advantage over its major competitors.

There are no economies of scale in soft-drink concentrate production, so Dr Pepper could prosper despite its small share of the business (6 percent). Thus, Dr Pepper confronted competition in marketing but avoided it in product line and in distribution. This artful positioning combined with good implementation has led to an enviable record in earnings and in the stock market.

Influencing the Balance

When dealing with the forces that drive industry competition, a company can devise a strategy that takes the offensive. This posture is designed to do more than merely cope with the forces themselves; it is meant to alter their causes.

Innovations in marketing can raise brand identification or otherwise differentiate the product. Capital investments in large-scale facilities or vertical integration affect entry barriers. The balance of forces is partly a result of external factors and partly in the company's control.

Exploiting Industry Change

Industry evolution is important strategically because evolution, of course, brings with it changes in the sources of competition. In the familiar product life-cycle pattern, for example, growth rates change, product differentiation is said to decline as the business becomes more mature, and the companies tend to integrate vertically.

These trends are not so important in themselves; what is critical is whether they affect the sources of competition. Consider vertical integration. In the maturing minicomputer industry, extensive vertical integration, both in manufacturing and in software development, is taking place. This very significant trend is greatly raising economies of scale as well as the amount of capital necessary to compete in the industry. This in turn is raising barriers to entry and may drive some smaller competitors out of the industry once growth levels off.

Obviously, the trends carrying the highest priority from a strategic standpoint are those that affect the most important sources of competition in the industry and those that elevate new causes to the forefront. In contract aerosol packaging, for example, the trend toward less product differentiation is now dominant. It has increased buyers' power, lowered the barriers to entry, and intensified competition.

The framework for analyzing competition can also be used to predict the eventual profitability of an industry. In long-range planning the task is to examine each competitive force, forecast the magnitude of each underlying cause, and then construct a composite picture of the likely profit potential of the industry.

The outcome of such an exercise may differ a great deal from the existing industry structure. Today, for example, the solar heating business is populated by dozens and perhaps hundreds of companies, none with a major market position. Entry is easy, and competitors are battling to establish solar heating as a superior substitute for conventional methods.

The potential of this industry will depend largely on the shape of future barriers to entry, the improvement of the industry's position relative to substitutes, the ultimate intensity of competition, and the power captured by buyers and suppliers. These characteristics will in turn be influenced by such factors as the establishment of brand identities, significant economies of scale or experience curves in equipment manufacture wrought by technological change, the ultimate capital costs to compete, and the extent of overhead in production facilities.

The framework for analyzing industry competition has direct benefits in setting diversification strategy. It provides a road map for answering the extremely difficult question inherent in diversification decisions: "What is the potential of this business?" Combining the framework with judgment in its application, a company may be able to spot an industry with a good future before this good future is reflected in the prices of acquisition candidates.

Multifaceted Rivalry

Corporate managers have directed a great deal of attention to defining their businesses as a crucial step in strategy formulation. Numerous authorities have stressed the need to look beyond product to function in defining a business, beyond national boundaries to potential international competition, and beyond the ranks of one's competitors today to those that may become competitors tomorrow. As a result of these urgings, the proper definition of a company's industry or industries has become an endlessly debated subject.

One motive behind this debate is the desire to exploit new markets. Another, perhaps more important, motive is the fear of overlooking latent sources of competition that someday may threaten the industry. Many managers concentrate so single-mindedly on their direct antagonists in the fight for market share that they fail to realize that they are also competing with their customers and their suppliers for bargaining power. Meanwhile, they also neglect to keep a wary eye out for new entrants to the contest or fail to recognize the subtle threat of substitute products.

The key to growth—even survival—is to stake out a position that is less vulnerable to attack from head-to-head opponents, whether established or new, and less vulnerable to erosion from the direction of buyers, suppliers, and substitute goods. Establishing such a position can take many forms—solidifying relationships with favorable customers, differentiating the product either substantively or psychologically through marketing, integrating forward or backward, or establishing technological leadership.

Questions for Discussion

1. Choose a specific industry and, relying solely on your impressions, evaluate the impact of the five forces that drive competition in that industry.
2. Repeat your analysis in question 1 but this time refer to published sources to provide more objective information on which to base your conclusions. (Hint: The appendix to Chapter 7 provides a helpful list of sources.)

3. Choose an industry in which you would like to compete. Use the five-forces method of analysis to explain why that industry is attractive to you.

4. Many businesses neglect industry analysis. When does this hurt them; when does it not?

5. The model below depicts industry forces analysis as a funnel that focuses on remote-factor analysis as a means of better understanding the impact of factors in the operating environment. Do you agree with this model? If not, how would you improve it?

6. Who in an organization should be responsible for industry analysis? Suppose there is no strategic planning department.

Bibliography

Caves, R. E., and M. E. Porter. "From Entry Barriers to Mobility Barriers: Conjectural Decisions and Contrived Deterrence to New Competition." *Quarterly Journal of Economics* 91 (1976), pp. 421–34.

Elzinga, K. G. "The Restructuring of the U.S. Brewing Industry." *Industrial Organization Review* 1 (1973), pp. 101–14.

Koch, J. V. "Industry Market Structure and Industry Price-Cost Margins." *Industrial Organization Review* 2 (1974), pp. 186–93.

Porter, M. E. "The Structure within Industries' and Companies' Performance." *Review of Economics and Statistics* 61 (1979), pp. 214–27.

Scherer, F. M. *Industrial Market Structure and Economic Performance.* 2nd ed. Skokie, Ill.: Rand McNally, 1980.

Weber, J. A. "Market Structure Profile Analysis and Strategic Growth Opportunities." *California Management Review* 20 (1977), pp. 34–46.

Chapter 5 Cohesion Case Illustration

Industry Analysis at Holiday Inns, Inc.

Industry analysis is a useful aid to the strategic management process at Holiday Inns, Inc. Each of Holiday Inns' business units must understand how the five basic competitive forces work in their industries and how they affect the business in its particular situation. In doing this, strategists are better prepared to establish an agenda for dealing with these contending forces. One business group—hotels—will be used to illustrate industry analysis at Holiday Inns, Inc. The technique is also necessary for the strategic management of each of Holiday Inns' remaining groups. Readers are encouraged to apply industry analysis to one or more of the other business groups.

Exhibit 1 is a diagram of basic forces driving competition in the lodging industry. It is useful to assess these forces to understand their relative influence on the lodging industry and ultimately to provide a basis for charting Holiday Inns' strategic course.

Threats of/Barriers to Entry. The lodging industry has created several strong barriers to entry. *Economies of scale* have been built via the existence of large, franchised networks for each of the major chains. This allows cost sharing in marketing, research, training, and technological services (like reservation systems). Interestingly, these networks have also facilitated the emergence of *product differentiation* as a barrier to entry. Brand identity and customer loyalty, particularly for firms like Holiday Inns, has been strongly established within the lodging industry. *Capital requirements,* particularly when the need for a network of locations is so important, is a substantial barrier to entry. Franchising has been one way to overcome this barrier, although the proliferation of franchises has lessened the viability of this strategy for newcomers to the industry. *Knowledge* of how to operate in the industry has become increasingly important as operating complexity increases. This in turn is becoming an entry barrier. *Access to distribution channels,* particularly in the sense of controlling prime locations (such as proximity to airports, downtown business centers, resorts, etc.) can create a substantial barrier to entry in several specific locations.

While entry barriers are increasing in this industry, the 1970s witnessed several entrants that overcame the barriers, particularly in the budget segment of the industry (e.g., Days Inn, La Quinta). Numerous individual investors aided this entrance as franchises. In the 1980s there appear to be potentially

Exhibit 1
Forces driving lodging-industry competition

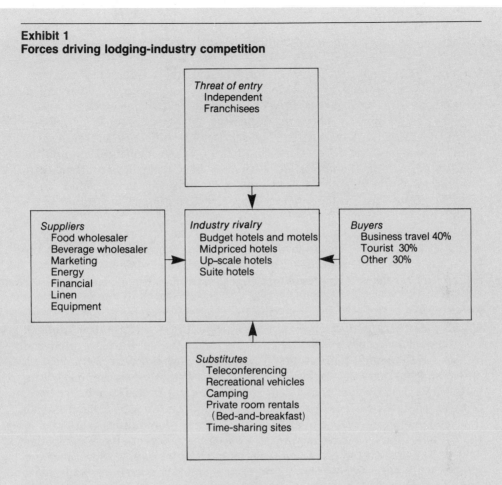

successful entrance strategies in the high-priced end of the industry. Predominantly located in large cities or resort locations, these "destination" entrants are successfully building positions in the industry by offering elaborate, expensive service to a narrow clientele.

Suppliers.   Typical *suppliers* to the lodging industry include equipment manufacturers, linen suppliers, food and beverage wholesalers, energy sources, financial suppliers and "people" resources. Generally, these suppliers are rather fragmented and do not offer unique products. Overall, there is very little threat of forward integration. Labor sources are generally not unionized, and the skill level required for entry positions is minimal. Training is provided by the industry. Finally, the lodging industry is usually an important, steady customer for most products and services offered by these suppliers. Therefore, the lodging industry is generally quite powerful relative to its suppliers.

Buyers.   The lodging industry is relatively powerful in relation to its *buyers*. First, buyers are primarily individuals, relatively small groups, and organizations—there is limited *concentration* of buying power. In some ways the service offered—bed, shower, TV, phone, food and beverage—can be seen as undifferentiated. Realistically, however, lodging services *are differentiated* by level of service, location of facilities, marketing efforts, brand identification, and the capacity of facilities (banquets, etc.). There is very little threat of backward integration. While buyers are fragmented, buyer power has manifest itself to some extent via the emergence of greater industry segmentation. To a sizable buyer segment—family businesses, salespeople on fixed allowances, families on limited budgets—lodging accommodations can represent a significant part of their "cost." Standard accommodation, not excess quality, is the key to the needs of these groups. Their "collective" power has led to the emergence of numerous chains providing budget accommodations.

Substitutes.   The services deserving the greatest strategic attention as potential *substitute products* are improving their price–performance trade-off with current lodging services, particularly when the services are produced by industries earning high profits. Teleconferencing and telecommunication are examples of this type of emerging potential substitute. Business and government employees, a major component of the lodging industry's customer base, have frequent travel needs (e.g., to attend meetings, call on people, demonstrate products). As satellite-based teleconferencing and telecommunications technology become steadily less expensive, they represent potentially cost-effective alternatives to travel and lodging services in some situations. Several major lodging firms, most notably Holiday Inns, have made significant commitments to expanding their teleconferencing capability so that this threat actually becomes a service advantage for their lodging network.

Competitive Rivalry.   Several factors are associated with intense *rivalry among competitors* in the lodging industry. Competitors have become numerous in virtually every segment of the lodging industry. While Holiday Inns is still recognized as the industry leader and has the largest number of rooms, other competitors have grown much more rapidly in the last 10 years. For example, Best Western actually has more locations in its system than does Holiday Inns.

Industry growth has slowed, particularly during the recession of 1981–82. Yet expansion-minded competitors are quite active, which should rapidly precipitate major market-share fights. The services offered, while somewhat differentiated, generally do not involve "switching costs" that tie buyers to one particular competitor.

Fixed costs (debt service and overhead) are high in the lodging industry, and the product ("one room-night") is *very* perishable in that it cannot be retained in inventory if it is not rented. This could create a strong temptation to cut prices if the capacity of lodging facilities expands too fast. Exit barriers can intensify the problem—who wants to buy a poorly performing motel? Industry participants have increasingly built their properties to purposely plan for office or condominum conversion so that exit options are greater.

The five-forces method of analysis suggests industry rivalry is the critical force shaping industry competition. Teleconferencing is emerging as the most important *potential* substitute. Neither suppliers nor buyers are very powerful, and barriers to entry are generally high. Increasing segmentation of buyers has increased industry rivalry and in some ways allowed selected entrants to successfully overcome entry barriers.

6

Evaluating the Multinational Environment

Strategic Considerations for Multinational Firms

Special complications confront a firm involved in international operations. Multinational corporations (MNCs) headquartered in one country with subsidiaries in others experience difficulties understandably associated with operating in two or more distinctly different competitive arenas.

Awareness of the strategic opportunities and threats posed and faced by MNCs is important to planners in almost every domestic U.S. industry. Among U.S.-headquartered corporations that receive more than 50 percent of their annual profits from foreign operations are Citicorp, the Coca-Cola Company, Exxon Corporation, the Gillette Company, IBM, Otis Elevator, and Texas Instruments. In fact, according to 1983 statistics, the 100 largest U.S. multinationals earned an average of 37 percent of their operating profits abroad. Equally impressive is the impact of foreign-based multinationals that operate in the United States. Their direct "foreign investment" in America now exceeds $70 billion, with Japanese, West German, and French firms leading the way. The extent of this foreign influence is evident in Strategy in Action 6–1.

Understanding the myriad and sometimes subtle nuances of competing in international markets or against multinational firms is rapidly becoming a prerequisite competency for strategic managers. Therefore, this section will focus on the nature, outlook, and operations of MNCs.

Strategy in Action 6–1
Multinational Corporation Ownership Test

In this test, you go down the alphabet and pick out the products that are foreign owned.

A Airwick, Alka-Seltzer antacid, Aim toothpaste.
B Baskin Robbins ice cream, Bactine antiseptic, Ball Park Franks.
C Certain-Teed, Capitol records, Castrol oils.
D Deer Park sparking water, Dove soap, Dunlop tires.
E ENO antacids, Eureka vacuum cleaners, Ehler spices.
F Four Roses whisky, French's mustard, First Love dolls.
G Good Humor ice cream, Garrard turntables, Grand Trunk Railroad.
H Humpty Dumpty magazine, Hires Root Beer, Hills Brothers coffee.
I Imperial margarine, Instant potato mix, Indian Head textiles.
J Juvena cosmetics, Jaeger sportswear, Jade cosmetics.
K Knox gelatine, Kool cigarettes, Keebler cookies.
L Libby's fruits and vegetables, *Look* magazine, Lifebuoy soap.
M Magnavox, Massey-Ferguson tractors, Mr. Coffee.
N Norelco appliances, Nescafé coffee, New Yorker Hotel.
O Ovaltine drink mix, One-a-Day vitamins.
P Panasonic, Pop Shoppes, Pepsodent toothpaste.
Q Nestlé Quik chocolate mix, Quasar television sets, Quadra-Bar sedatives.
R Ray-O-Vac batteries, Rinso, Rona Barret's gossip magazines.
S Scripto pens, Seven Seas salad dressings, Slazenger tennis balls.
T Tetley tea, Tic Tac Breath fresheners, Taster's Choice instant coffee.
U Underwood typewriters, Urise antiseptics, Ultra Tears eye lotion.
V Valium tranquilizers, Vogue pipe tobacco, Vim detergent.
W Wish-Bone salad dressings, Wisk detergent, White Motor trucks.
X Xam clock radios, Xylocaine salves, Xylee plastics.
Y Yardley cosmetics, Yale locks, Yashica cameras.
Z Zesta crackers, Zig-Zag cigarette papers, Zestatabs vitamins.

Answer: All of the companies (A through Z) are foreign owned.

Development of an MNC

The evolution of a multinational company often entails progressively involved strategies. The first strategy entails export–import activity but minimal effect on existing management orientation or product lines. The second levels involves foreign licensing and technology transfer but still little change in management or operation. The third level of strategy is characterized by direct investment in overseas operations, including manufacturing plants. This level requires large capital outlays as well as management effort in the development of international skills. At this point, domestic operations continue to dominate company policy, but the firm is commonly categorized as a true MNC. The most involved strategy is indicated by a substantial increase in foreign investment, with foreign assets comprising a significant portion of total assets. The company begins to emerge as a global enterprise with world approaches to production, sales, finance, and control.

While some firms downplay their multinational nature—so as never to appear distracted from their domestic operations—others highlight their international intentions. For example, General Electric's formal statement of mission and business philosophy includes the following commitment:

> To carry on a diversified, growing, and profitable worldwide manufacturing business in electrical apparatus, appliances, and supplies, and in related materials, products, systems, and services for industry, commerce, agriculture, government, the community, and the home.

A similar worldwide orientation is evident at IBM, which operates in 125 countries, conducts business in 30 languages and more than 100 currencies, and has 23 major manufacturing facilities in 14 different countries.

Why Companies Internationalize

The past 30 years has seen a dramatic decline in the technological advantage once enjoyed by the United States. In the late 1950s, over 80 percent of the world's major innovations were first introduced in the United States. By 1965 this figure had declined to 55 percent, and the decline continues today. On the other hand, France has made impressive advances in electric traction, nuclear power, and aviation. West Germany is a proclaimed leader in chemicals and pharmaceuticals, precision and heavy machinery, heavy electrical goods, metallurgy, and surface transport equipment. Japan leads in optics, solid-state physics, engineering, chemistry, and process metallurgy. Eastern Europe and the Soviet Union, the so-called COMECON (Council for Mutual Economic Assistance) countries, generate 30 percent of annual worldwide patent applications. However, the United States can regain some of its lost competitive advantages. Through internationalization U.S. firms can often reap benefits from emerging industries and evolutionary technologies developed abroad.

Multinational development makes sense as a competitive weapon in many situations. Direct penetration of foreign markets can drain vital cash flows from a foreign competitor's domestic operations. The resulting lost opportunities, reduced income, and limited production can impair the competitor's ability to invade U.S. markets. A case in point is the strategic action of IBM, which moved to establish a position of strength in the Japanese mainframe computer industry before two key competitors, Fiyitsue and Hitachi, could gain dominance. Once it had achieved an influential market share, IBM worked to deny its Japanese competitors the vital cash and production experience they needed to invade the U.S. market.[1]

Considerations prior to Internationalization

To begin their internationalizing activities, businesses are advised to take four steps:[2]

Scan the International Situation.   Scanning includes reading journals and patent reports and checking other printed sources—as well as meeting people at scientific–technical conferences and/or in-house seminars.

Make Connections with Academia and Research Organizations.   Enterprises active in overseas R&D often pursue work-related projects with foreign academics and sometimes form consulting agreements with faculty members.

Increase the Company's International Visibility.   Common methods of attracting attention include participation in technological trade fairs, circulation of brochures illustrating company products and inventions, and hiring technology–acquisition consultants.

Undertake Cooperative Research Projects.   Some multinational enterprises engage in joint research projects to broaden their contacts, reduce expenses, diminish the risk for each partner, or forestall entry of a competitor into the market.

In a similar vein, external and internal assessments may be conducted before a firm enters international markets.[3] External assessment involves

---

[1] C. M. Watson, "Counter Competition Abroad to Protect Home Markets," *Harvard Business Review*, January–February 1982, p. 40.

[2] R. Ronstadt and R. Kramer, "Getting the Most out of Innovation Abroad," *Harvard Business Review*, March–April 1982, pp. 94–99.

[3] J. Fayweather and A. Kapoor, *Strategy and Negotiation for the International Corporation* (Cambridge, Mass.: Ballinger, 1976).

careful examination of critical international environmental features with particular attention to the status of the host nation in such areas as economic progress, political control, and nationalism. Expansion of industrial facilities, balance of payments, and improvements in technological capabilities over the past decade should provide some idea of the host nation's economic progress. Political status can be gauged by the host nation's power in and impact on international affairs.

Internal assessment involves identification of the basic strong points of a company's present operations. These strengths are particularly important in international operations because they are often the elements valued most by the host nation and thus offer significant bargaining leverage. Both resource strengths and global capabilities must be analyzed. The resources to be examined in particular include technical and managerial skills, capital, labor, and raw materials. The global capability components include assessing the effectiveness of proposed product delivery and financial management systems.

A firm that gives serious consideration to internal and external assessment is Business International Corporation, which recommends that seven broad categories of factors be considered. As shown in Strategy in Action 6–2, these

Strategy in Action 6–2
Checklist of Factors to Consider in Choosing a Foreign Manufacturing Site

The following considerations were drawn from an 88-point checklist developed by Business International Corporation.

Economic factors:
1. Size of GNP and projected rate of growth.
2. Foreign exchange position.
3. Size of market for the company's products; rate of growth.
4. Current or prospective membership in a customs union.

Political factors:
5. Form and stability of government.
6. Attitude toward private and foreign investment by government, customers, and competition.
7. Practice of favored versus neutral treatment for state industries.
8. Degree of antiforeign discrimination.

Continued on Page 149

Strategy in Action 6–2 *(concluded)*

Geographic factors:

9. Efficiency of transport (railways, waterways, highways).
10. Proximity of site to export markets.
11. Availability of local raw materials.
12. Availability of power, water, gas.

Labor factors:

13. Availability of managerial, technical, and office personnel able to speak the language of the parent company.
14. Degree of skill and discipline at all levels.
15. Presence or absence of militant or Communist-dominated unions.
16. Degree and nature of labor voice in management.

Tax factors:

17. Tax rate trends (corporate and personal income, capital, withholding, turnover, excise, payroll, capital gains, customs, and other indirect and local taxes).
18. Joint tax treaties with home country and others.
19. Duty and tax drawbacks when imported goods are exported.
20. Availability of tariff protection.

Capital source factors:

21. Cost of local borrowing.
22. Local availability of convertible currencies.
23. Modern banking systems.
24. Government credit aids to new businesses.

Business factors:

25. State of marketing and distribution system.
26. Normal profit margins in the company's industry.
27. Competitive situation in the firm's industry; do cartels exist?
28. Availability of amenities for expatriate executives and families.

categories include economic, political, geographic, labor, tax, capital source, and business factors.

Complexity of the Multinational Environment

Multinational strategic planning is more complex than such purely domestic planning. There are at least five contributing factors:

1. The multinational faces multiple political, economic, legal, social, and cultural environments as well as various rates of change within each of them.

2. Interactions between the national and foreign environments are complex because of national sovereignty issues and widely differing economic and social conditions.
3. Geographical separation, cultural and national differences, and variations in business practices all tend to make communication between headquarters and the overseas affiliates difficult.
4. Multinationals face extreme competition because of differences in industry structures.
5. Multinationals are confronted by various international organizations, such as the European Economic Community, the European Free Trade Area, and the Latin American Free Trade Area, that restrict a firm's selection of its competitive strategies.

Indications of how these factors contribute to increased complexity in strategic planning and management are provided in Figure 6–1.

Control Problems for the Multinational Firm

An inherent complicating factor for many international firms is that financial policies of the multinational are typically designed to further the goals of the parent company with a minimum of attention paid to the goals of the host countries. This built-in bias creates conflict between the different parts of the organization, between the whole organization and its home and host countries, and between the home and host countries themselves. The conflict is accentuated by various schemes used to shift earnings from one country to another to avoid taxes, minimize risk, or achieve other objectives.

Different financial environments also make normal standards of company behavior concerning disposition of earnings, sources of finance, and the structure of capital more problematic. Thus, the performance of multinational divisions becomes increasingly difficult to measure.

In addition, important differences in measurement and control systems often exist. Fundamental to the concept of planning is a well-conceived, future-oriented approach to decision making based on accepted procedures and methods of analysis. Consistent approaches to planning throughout an organization are needed for effective review and evaluation by corporate headquarters. Such planning is complicated by differences in accounting conventions among countries, by attitudes about work measurement, and by different government requirements for disclosure of information.

Although such problems are more an aspect of the multinational environment than they are consequences of poor management, the problems are often most effectively reduced through increased attention to strategic management. Such planning aids in coordinating and integrating the company's future direction, objectives, and policies around the world. It enables the company to

Figure 6–1
Differences between U.S. and multinational operations that affect strategic management

Factor	U.S. operations	International operations
Language	English used almost universally	Local language must be used in many situations
Culture	Relatively homogeneous	Quite diverse, both between countries and within a country
Politics	Stable and relatively unimportant	Often volatile and of decisive importance
Economy	Relatively uniform	Wide variations among countries and between regions within countries
Government interference	Minimal and reasonably predictable	Extensive and subject to rapid change
Labor	Skilled labor available	Skilled labor often scarce, requiring training or redesign of production methods
Financing	Well-developed financial markets	Poorly developed financial markets. Capital flows subject to government control
Market research	Data easy to collect	Data difficult and expensive to collect
Advertising	Many media available; few restrictions	Media limited; many restrictions; low literacy rates rule out print media in some countries
Money	U.S. dollar used universally	Must change from one currency to another; changing exchange rates and government restrictions are problems
Transportation/ communication	Among the best in the world	Often inadequate
Control	Always a problem. Centralized control will work	A worse problem. Centralized control won't work. Must walk a tightrope between overcentralizing and losing control through too much decentralizing
Contracts	Once signed, are binding on both parties, even if one party makes a bad deal	Can be avoided and renegotiated if one party becomes dissatisfied
Labor relations	Collective bargaining; can lay off workers easily	Often cannot lay off workers; may have mandatory worker participation in management; workers may seek change through political process rather than collective bargaining
Trade barriers	Nonexistent	Extensive and very important

Source: R. G. Murdick, R. C. Moor, R. H. Eckhouse, and T. W. Zimmerer, *Business Policy: A Framework for Analysis,* 4th ed. (Columbus, Ohio: Grid, 1984), p. 275.

anticipate and better prepare for change. It facilitates the creation of programs to deal with worldwide developments. Finally, it helps the management of overseas affiliates become more actively involved in setting goals and in developing means to more effectively utilize the enterprise's total resources.

Multinational Strategic Planning

It should be evident from the previous sections that, as a company begins competing in the international marketplace, strategic decisions become increasingly complex and multidimensional. A manager cannot view the international operations as a set of independent decisions.[4] Rather, a manager is faced with trade-off decisions considering multiple products, country environments, resource sourcing options, corporate and subsidiary capabilities, and strategic options.[5]

Two recent trends, the globalization of industries and the increased activism of stakeholders, further add to this complexity of strategic planning for the multinational firm.[6] *Globalization* refers to a strategy of approaching worldwide markets with a standardized product. Such markets are most commonly created by end-consumers preferring a lower-priced, standardized product over higher-priced, customized products and by multinational corporations using their worldwide operations to compete in local markets.[7] *Stakeholder activism* refers to demands placed on the company by each foreign environment, principally foreign governments. This section provides a basic framework in which to analyze and better understand strategic decisions in this complex environment.

Multidomestic Industries and Global Industries

Michael E. Porter has developed a framework to view the basic strategic alternatives of a firm competing internationally.[8] The starting point of the analysis is understanding the industry or industries in which the firm competes. International industries can be characterized along a continuum from multidomestic to global.

Multidomestic Industries.   A multidomestic industry is one in which the competition within the industry is essentially segmented from country to country. Thus, although multinational corporations are involved in the industry, competition in a country occurs independent of competition in other countries. Examples of such industries include retailing, insurance, and consumer finance.

---

[4] Yoram Wind and Susan Douglas, "International Portfolio Analysis and Strategy: The Challenge of the 80s," *Journal of International Business Studies,* Fall 1981, pp. 69–82.

[5] Thomas H. Naylor, "The International Strategy Matrix," *Columbia Journal of World Business,* Summer 1985, pp. 11–19.

[6] Balaj S. Chakravarthy and Howard V. Perlmutter, "Strategic Planning for a Global Business," *Columbia Journal of World Business,* Summer 1985, pp. 3–10.

[7] Theodore Levitt, "The Globalization of Markets," *Harvard Business Review,* September–October 1982, p. 92; and T. Hout, M. E. Porter, and E. Rudden, "How Global Companies Win Out," *Harvard Business Review,* September–October 1982, pp. 98–108.

[8] Michael E. Porter, "Changing Patterns of International Competition," *California Management Review* 28, no. 2 (Winter 1986), pp. 9–40.

In a multidomestic industry, the subsidiaries of an MNC should be managed as distinct entities; that is, each subsidiary should be rather autonomous, having independent decision-making authority to respond to local market conditions. Thus, in a multidomestic industry, an international strategy actually becomes the sum of the strategies developed by subsidiaries operating in different countries. The primary distinctions between a domestic firm and the multinational firm competing in a multidomestic industry are decisions related to what countries the company competes in and to how it conducts business abroad.

Factors determining the degree to which a market is multidomestic include:[9]

The need for customized products to meet the tastes or preferences of local customers.

A very fragmented industry with many competitors in each national market.

The lack of economies of scale in the functional activities of the business.

Distribution channels unique in each country.

A low technological dependence of each subsidiary on R&D provided by corporation.

Global Industries.   A global industry is one in which competition within the industry crosses national borders. A firm's strategic moves in one country can be significantly affected by its competitive position in another country. In fact, competition occurs on a world basis. Examples of global industries include commercial aircraft, automobiles, mainframe computers, and electronic consumer equipment.

In such industries, a multinational firm must link its subsidiaries together, maximizing its capabilities through a worldwide strategy. This necessitates a higher degree of centralized decision making in corporate headquarters so that trade-off decisions across subsidiaries can be made. Factors influencing the creation of global markets include:[10]

The presence of economies of scale in functional activities of the business.

A high level of R&D expenditures on products that require more than one market to recover development costs.

Predominantly multinational companies in the industry, who expect the same consistent product and service across markets.

Homogeneous product needs, which reduce the requirement of customizing the product for each market.

A small group of global competitors in the industry.

A low level of trade and foreign direct investment regulation.

[9] Yves Doz and C. K. Prahalad, "Patterns of Strategic Control within Multinational Corporations," *Journal of International Business Studies,* Fall 1984, pp. 55–72.

[10] Gary Harvel and C. K. Prahalad, "Managing Strategic Responsibility in the MNC," *Strategic Management Journal* 4 (1983), pp. 341–51.

The Multinational Challenge

Although industries can be characterized by the global–multidomestic distinction, few "pure" cases of either exist. Thus, a multinational competing in a global industry must, to some degree, also be responsive to local market conditions. Similarly, the multinational firm competing in a multidomestic industry cannot totally ignore opportunities to utilize intracorporate resources in competitive positioning. The question then becomes one of deciding which corporate functional activities should be performed where and what degree of coordination should exist between them.

Location and Coordination of Functional Activities.   Typical functional activities of a business include purchases of input resources, operations, research and development, marketing and sales, and after-sale service. A multinational corporation has a wide range of possible location options for each of these activities and must decide which set of activities will be performed in how many and which locations. A multinational corporation may desire each location to perform each activity, or it may have the activity centered in one location to serve the organization worldwide. For example, research and development may be centralized in one facility to serve the entire organization.

The multinational corporation must also decide the degree to which these activities are to be coordinated with each other across different countries. Coordination can be extremely low, allowing each location to perform each activity autonomously. Conversely, coordination can be extremely high, with the activities in different locations tightly linked together. For example, the Coca-Cola Company tightly coordinates R&D and marketing worldwide to offer a standardized brand name, concentrate formula, market positioning, and advertising theme. However, manufacturing is more adaptive to each location, with the artificial sweetener and packaging differing across countries.[11]

Location and Coordination Issues.   Figure 6–2 presents some of the issues related to the critical dimensions of location and coordination in international strategic planning. It also shows the different functional activities performed by the organization for each dimension. Given that a firm has a wide array of location and coordination options, Figure 6–2 highlights the different issues that address these basic options. For example, for the service activity, a company must decide where after-sale service should be performed throughout the world and the extent to which the service should be standardized.

Addressing these issues for a particular firm depends on the nature of the industry and the type of international strategy pursued by the firm. As dis-

---

[11] John A. Quelch and Edward J. Hoff, "Customizing Global Marketing," *Harvard Business Review,* May–June 1986, pp. 59–68.

Figure 6–2
Location and coordination issues by functional activity

Functional activity	Location issues	Coordination issues
Operations	Location of production facilities for components	Networking of international plants
Marketing	Product line selection	Commonality of brand name worldwide
	Country (market) selection	Coordination of sales to multinational accounts
		Similarity of channels and product positioning worldwide
		Coordination of pricing in different countries
Service	Location of service organization	Similarity of service standards and procedures worldwide
Research and development	Number and location of R&D centers	Interchange among dispersed R&D centers
		Developing products responsive to market needs in many countries
		Sequence of product introductions around the world
Purchasing	Location of the purchasing function	Managing suppliers located in different countries
		Transferring market knowledge
		Coordinating purchases of common items

Source: Adapted from Michael E. Porter, "Changing Patterns of International Competition," *California Management Review* 28, no. 2 (Winter 1986), pp. 9–40.

cussed earlier, the industry can be characterized along a continuum between multidomestic at one extreme and global at the other. In a multidomestic industry, competition occurs within each country; consequently, little coordination of functional activities across countries may be necessary. However, as the industry becomes increasingly global, the firm must begin to coordinate an increasing number of functional activities in order to effectively compete across countries.

International Strategy Options. Figure 6–3 presents the basic international strategies derived from considering the location and coordination dimensions. If the firm is operating in a multidomestic industry, choosing a country-centered strategy implies low coordination of functional activities and geographical dispersion of organization activities. This allows each subsidiary to closely monitor the local market conditions it faces and the freedom to respond competitively.

A high coordination and geographical concentration of the multinational's activities results from choosing a pure global strategy. Although some activities, such as after-sale service, may need to be located in each market, the activities need to be tightly controlled so that standardized performance occurs

---

Figure 6–3
International strategy options

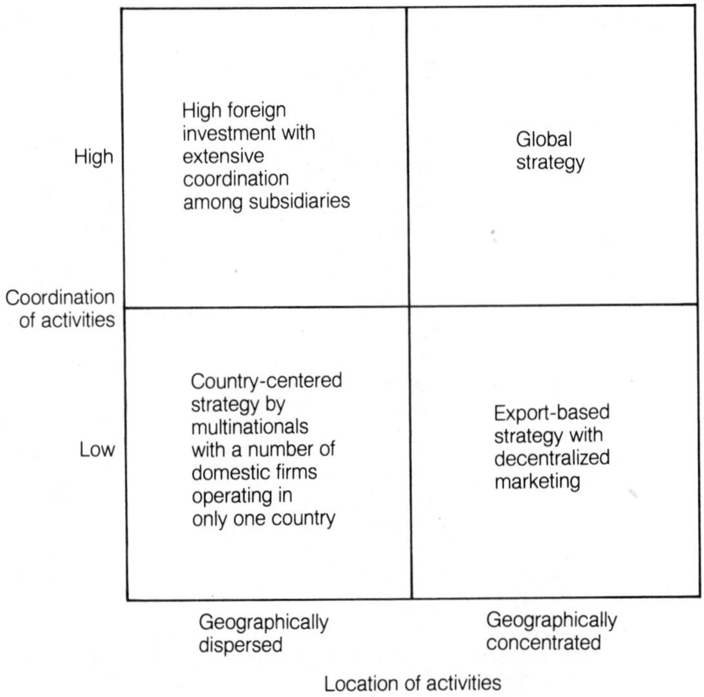

		Geographically dispersed	Geographically concentrated
Coordination of activities	High	High foreign investment with extensive coordination among subsidiaries	Global strategy
	Low	Country-centered strategy by multinationals with a number of domestic firms operating in only one country	Export-based strategy with decentralized marketing

Location of activities

Source: Adapted from Michael E. Porter, "Changing Patterns of International Competition," *California Management Review* 28, no. 2 (Winter 1986), pp. 9–40.

worldwide. For example, IBM expects the same high level of marketing support and service for its customers, regardless of their location.

The final two types of strategies are a high foreign investment with extensive coordination among subsidiaries and an export-based strategy with decentralized marketing. These two strategies can represent the choice to remain at a particular stage, such as an exporter, or they can represent transition strategies as a multinational moves to a global strategy.

Multinationalization of the Corporate Mission[12]

Few strategic decisions bring about a more radical departure from the existing direction and operations of a company than the decision to expand internationally. Multinationalization subjects a company to a radically redefined and challenging set of environmentally determined opportunities, constraints, and risks. To prevent the company's direction from being dictated by these external

---

[12] The material in this section is taken from John A. Pearce II and Kendall Roth, "Multinationalization of the Corporate Mission," *Advanced Management Journal,* in press.

factors, top management must reassess the corporation's fundamental purpose, philosophy, and strategic intentions prior to multinationalization, thus ensuring that these basic values will continue as decision criteria in proactive planning.

Caterpillar Tractor's 1986 decline in market share and profitability highlight the purpose and need for multinationalization of a mission statement. Caterpillar's reversal can be primarily attributed to the strength of the U.S. dollar, in that the strong dollar made Caterpillar's products relatively more expensive in a global market. However, the impact of the dollar on Caterpillar's operations was anticipated and considered in declaring its long-term commitments. As shown in Strategy in Action 6–3, Caterpillar's corporate mission states that:

1. Subsidiaries should be located wherever in the world it is most economically advantageous to do so from a long-term standpoint.
2. Facility operations should be planned with the long term in mind in order to minimize the impact of sudden changes in the local work force and economy.

Adherence to these commitments helped synchronize the strategic and tactical decisions Caterpillar made in addressing the problems associated with the current currency imbalance. In the absence of such guidelines, Caterpillar actions could have possibly included:

Relocating facilities to gain short-term competitive production advantages.

Shifting production schedules radically throughout global operations regardless of the resultant impact on host country environments.

These actions would have redistributed production to weak-currency production locations, thereby enhancing Caterpillar's competitive pricing capabilities. However, they were not consistent with the more compelling motivations of the mission statement, which were to promulgate Caterpillar's commitment to high-quality products, stable operations, and corporate social responsibility. Consequently, irrespective of environmental aberrations, Caterpillar's mission provided for the corporation's broader, long-term strategic consistency.

The development of the corporate mission progresses through stages during the life of a company. At a company's inception and early stages of development, the mission is often the proprietary knowledge of the entrepreneur, who alone understands why the company exists and what purposes it serves—and this may be sufficient. As the company grows, it reaches a stage at which more formal mechanisms are required to coordinate increasingly complex and diverse organizational units. At this stage the mission statement needs to be made explicit so that it can be precisely communicated to organizational claimants.

For the remainder of this chapter, we will focus on a third developmental stage, at which the nature or character of the corporate mission is altered to encourage and encompass multinational expansion. A second-stage mission statement is usually designed with a domestic perspective, which does not recognize the added dimensions inherent in multinationalization. Thus, we will now look at the content of the domestic mission statement to determine appropriate modifications for a multinational corporation (MNC) that can help to ensure the resultant mission statement will continue to provide the necessary framework for strategic decision processes.

Strategy in Action 6–3
Mission Statement of Caterpillar Tractor Company

Business Purpose

The overall purpose of Caterpillar is to enhance the long-term interests of those who own the business—the shareholders.

This in no way diminishes the strong and legitimate claims of employees, dealers, customers, suppliers, governments, and others whose interests touch upon our own—nor, indeed, of the public at large. Nor is this to assert that profit should be maximized in any short-term framework of months, or even years, at the expense of other valid considerations.

Rather, it is to say we attempt to take a long-range view of things. We believe we can best serve the interests of shareholders and the long-term profitability of the enterprise by fair, honest, and intelligent actions with respect to all our constituencies.

With this in mind, our business aims are as follows:

1. Maintain corporate real growth at a rate not less than in the past, remain financially strong, and maximize long-term return on common stock equity.
2. Follow product and sourcing strategies that best utilize Caterpillar's strengths and resources . . . and that are consistent with users' needs and world economic, political, and social conditions.
3. Provide customers a total value—in terms of product quality and product support—that will maximize profit on their investment, as compared with competitive alternatives.
4. Work with suppliers, and those who sell our products, in upgrading their capabilities—to the end that each is the best available when judged by appropriate criteria.
5. Make wise and efficient use of energy and natural resources, and seek substitutes for those in critically short supply.
6. Remember that management is an acquired skill, not an intuitive art—and work continuously at improving the practice of management by objectives and judgment by results.

Continued on Page 159

Strategy in Action 6–3 *(concluded)*

7. Enhance our reputation for quality by pursuing excellence in all we do—in the belief that such is not only the best way to operate this business but also a key to personal satisfaction and happiness.

8. Improve our pursuit of goals, principles, and philosophies contained in this document.

Corporate Facilities

Caterpillar prefers to locate facilities wherever in the world it is most economically advantageous to do so, from a long-term standpoint.

Decisions as to location of facilities will, of course, consider such conventional factors as proximity to sources of supply, transportation, and sales opportunities; possibilities for volume production and resulting economies of scale; and availability of energy sources and a trained or trainable work force. Also considered will be political and fiscal stability, demonstrated governmental attitudes, industrial development plans, and other factors normally included in defining the local investment or business "climate."

We desire to provide functional, safe, attractive, efficient facilities that are harmonious with national modes. They are to be compatible with local environmental considerations, complement public planning, and reflect Caterpillar's commitment to conserve energy and other scarce resources.

Facility operations should be planned with the long term in mind, in order to minimize the impact of sudden change on the local work force and economy.

Source: Excerpted from "A Code of Worldwide Business Conduct and Operating Principles," Caterpillar Tractor Company.

The MNC Mission Statement

Expanding across national borders to secure new market or production opportunities may be initially viewed as consistent with a company's growth objectives as outlined in its existing mission statement. However, as multinationalization occurs, the direction of a company is inherently altered. For example, as a company expands overseas, its operations are physically relocated in foreign operating environments. Since strategic decisions are made in the context of some perception or understanding of the environment, information from new sources will be absorbed into planning processes as the environment becomes pluralistic, with revised corporate directions as a probable and desirable result. Thus, prior to the reconsideration of the corporate strategic choice, top management must reassess the mission statement and institute changes as required so that the appropriate environmental information is defined, collected, analyzed, and integrated into existing data bases.

Management must also provide a mission statement that continues to serve as a basis for evaluating strategic alternatives as this additional information is incorporated into the organization's system of decision-making processes.

Consider one component of the Zale Corporation's mission statement from this perspective:

> Our ultimate responsibilities are to our shareholders. Our goal is to earn an optimum return on invested capital through steady profit growth and prudent, aggressive asset management. The attainment of this financial goal, coupled with a record of sound management, represents our approach toward influencing the value placed upon our common stock in the market.

From a U.S. perspective this financial component seems quite reasonable. However, it could be unacceptable in a global context where financial goals are frequently divergent. Research has shown that financial goals are of differing importance in various countries.[13] Executives from France, Japan, and the Netherlands have displayed a clear preference for maximizing growth in after-tax earnings. Norwegian executives place a higher priority on maximizing earnings before interest and taxes. In contrast, the maximization of stockholder wealth has received little acclaim in any of these four countries. Thus, a mission statement specifying that a firm's ultimate responsibility is to its stockholders may or may not be appropriate as the basis for the company's financial operating philosophy when viewed from a global perspective. This illustrates the critical need for reviewing and revising the corporate mission prior to international expansion so that the mission statement maintains its relevance by overarching divergent situations and environmental factors.

Components of the Corporate Mission Revisited

Because multinationalization mandates change in strategic decision making, corporate direction, and strategic alternatives, the content of each mission component must be revised to incorporate multinational contingencies. The additional strategic capabilities that will result from internationalizing operations must continue to be encompassed by the corporate mission statement. Therefore, each basic component needs to be analyzed in light of specific considerations that serve to multinationalize the corporate mission.

Product or Service, Market, and Technology. The mission statement defines the basic market need the company aims to satisfy. The essence of this definition is likely to remain intact in the MNC context in that the company has acquired competencies domestically that can be exploited as competitive advantages when transferred internationally. However, confronted with a multiplicity of contexts, some degree of prioritization and redefining the primary market and customer is necessary.

The MNC could define a global market, which would necessitate standardization in product and company responses, or it could pursue a "marketing concept" orientation by focusing on each national market's particular or unique de-

---

[13] A. Stonehill, T. Beekhuisen, R. Wright, L. Remmers, N. Toy, P. Pares, A. Shapiro, D. Egan, and T. Bates, "Financial Goals and Debt Ratio Determinants: A Survey of Practice in Five Countries," *Financial Management,* Autumn 1975, pp. 27–40.

mands. Thus, the mission statement must provide a basis for strategic decision making in this trade-off situation. For example, Hewlett-Packard's statement includes the directive that "HP customers must feel that they are dealing with one company with common policies and services," implying a standardized approach designed to provide comparable service to all customers. In contrast, Holiday Inns, Inc.'s corporate mission reflects the marketing concept "Basic to almost everything Holiday Inns, Inc. does is its interaction with its market, the consumer, and its consistent capacity to provide what the consumer wants, when, and where it is needed."

Subsequent to defining the company's target market, the mission statement should suggest the corresponding internal mechanisms required to support this definition. For example, if a company defines a global market, the mission statement may establish centralized corporate functions and activities that promote standardization. Illustrative of this example, the mission statement of Drew Chemical Corporation (shown in Strategy in Action 6–4) establishes three industry-defined divisions and one international division, which represents and supports the others. Thus, the international market is viewed as a standardized extension of the domestic divisions. To support this view, the mission statement creates economies of scale and product standardization across the industry division by specifying centralized research, production, and administrative operations to support the marketing organizations.

Company Goals: Survival, Growth, and Profitability. The mission statement includes the company's intention to secure its future through growth and profitability. In the United States, growth and profitability are considered essentials for survival. Similarly, in environments relatively supportive of the free enterprise system, these priorities are widely acceptable. However, following international expansion, the firm may operate in economies not unequivocally committed to the profit motive. A host country may view social welfare and development goals as taking precedence over free market capitalism. For example, in Third World countries, employment and income distribution goals often take precedence over rapid economic growth.

Opposition to profit goals may also come from a nonphilosophical perspective; that is, even in environments that accept the profit motive, MNC profits are often viewed as having a unidirectional flow. At the extreme, the multinational is seen as a tool for exploiting the host country exclusively for the benefit of the parent's home country. Profits are the evidence of perceived corporate atrocities. Thus, in a multinational context, a corporate commitment to profits may not only fail to help secure survival, it may even increase the risk of failure.

Therefore, an MNC mission statement must reflect the firm's intention to secure its survival through dimensions that extend beyond growth and profitability. An MNC must develop a corporate philosophy that expresses the need for a bidirectional flow of benefits among the firm and its multiple environments. Such a view is expressed deftly by Gulf & Western Americas Corpora-

Strategy in Action 6–4
Drew Chemical Corporation Mission Statement

The Drew Chemical Corporation is a service-oriented chemical company that consists of four basic marketing organizations. Drew's assets are in people—not land, plant, or equipment.

Each of the operations is primarily concerned with the beneficiation of the world's most basic resource—water—through the use of performance.

The Water and Waste Treatment Division markets chemicals, equipment, and services for boiler and cooling water treatment and for use in waste disposal plants.

The Marine Division markets chemicals, equipment, and services for marine boilers and maintenance products and fuel oil additives for use aboard ships.

The Specialty Chemicals Division markets process additives and chemical specialties for the pulp and paper, paint and latex, textile, and chemical industries.

International Operations consist of 12 wholly owned subsidiaries. Eight subsidiaries are essentially sales agents for the Marine Division and licensees of the Water and Treatment and Specialty Chemicals Divisions. Drew Ameroid International is a tax shelter for Marine business outside of the United States. The other three subsidiaries function quite independently of the parent company, drawing on it mainly for technical support.

.The marketing organizations are supported by centralized research, production, and administrative operations.

tion: "We believe that in a developing country, revenue is inseparable from mandatory social responsibility and that a company is an integral part of the local and national community in which its activities are based."[14] This statement illustrates a corporate attitude that acknowledges the intention of MNC contributions to the host country yet clearly maintains a commitment to firm profitability.

In a broader context, a company's mission must recognize not only economic dimensions but also an effectiveness dimension—where effectiveness is the ability to meet the desires of all major organizational claimants. This implies that effectiveness is in part an external standard, relative to and defined by each MNC context. Therefore, an MNC must identify which coalitions in each environment determine these external standards or, more important, the spe-

---

[14] See O. Williams, "Who Cast the First Stone?" *Harvard Business Review,* September–October 1984, pp. 151–61.

cific coalitions on which the MNC depends for its existence and prosperity. The organization must then include as an essential part of its corporate mission a "legitimization" element so as to proactively create and sustain this coalition support, thereby securing the organization's survival. For example, management of Caterpillar Tractor Company has stated:

> We affirm that Caterpillar investment must be compatible with social and economic priorities of host countries, and with local customs, tradition, and sovereignty. We intend to conduct our business in a way that will earn acceptance and respect for Caterpillar, and allay concerns by host country governments and others about multinational corporations.

The growth dimension of the mission statement continues to be closely tied to survival and profitability even in the MNC context. Multinationalization creates geographical dispersion of corporate resources and operations. This implies that strategic decision makers are no longer located exclusively at corporate headquarters, nor are they as easily and readily accessible to participate in collective decision-making processes. Therefore, some mechanism is required for recording the commitment to a unifying purpose, by which the cohesiveness of the organization is to be maintained. The mission statement can provide this basis for unification, tying together decision makers' perspectives with a common guiding thread of understanding and purpose.

Company Philosophy.   While an inclusive and detailed corporate philosophy may go unstated, the implicit understanding of the domestic environment results in a general uniformity of corporate values and behavior within the domestic setting. Few events that occur domestically will directly challenge a company to self-examine its espoused or actual philosophy to ensure that it is both properly formulated and implemented. Multinationalization is, however, clearly such an event. A corporate philosophy developed from a singular perspective cannot be assumed to maintain its relevance in variant cultures. Corporate values and beliefs are primarily culturally defined, reflecting the general philosophical perspective of the society in which the company operates. Thus, when a company extends into another social structure, it encounters a new set of accepted corporate values and preferences, which must be assimilated and incorporated into its own.

The critical concern for the MNC is to decide which values and philosophical needs will be given top priority, considering that multiple cultures are involved. The MNC has the basic choice of adopting a company philosophy for each operating environment or of defining an overarching, supranational corporate philosophy. Although each subsidiary must verify that its philosophy is not in direct conflict with existing cultural norms, the preferable choice for the MNC is usually the latter approach—striving to define an acceptable overall corporate philosophy not contingent on specific environments. The communication capabilities of modern society seldom allow exclusively subsidiary-defined corporate philosophies. For example, numerous U.S. multinational corporations have been subject to considerable criticism from U.S. special interest groups regarding the policies of their South African, Namibian, and Dominican Republic subsidiaries. The allegation of corporate social responsibility violations has, in general, not been instigated, motivated, or defined by coalitions within the host countries. Rather, values and beliefs regarding working standards and conditions have been directly transferred to each country by external coalitions from the United States, such as the Interfaith Center on Corporate Responsibility. Thus, though corporate philosophical preferences, values, and beliefs can be tailored to each host country, they cannot be fundamentally redefined because of the capability of concerned interest groups to selectively match or mismatch potentially conflicting positions. The result is a significantly enlarged external conscience to which the corporations must respond. Consequently, when expressing a corporate value system, the MNC's accountability to this collective conscience must be recognized in its entirety.

The mission statement must also provide for operationalizing the corporate philosophy to serve as a basis for strategic decision making and operational activities. The acquisition of corporate resources as well as their allocation and utilization must be consistent with the corporate value objectives. This necessitates a formal mechanism to assess contemplated corporate actions and ensure that value preferences will be implemented. For example, in responding to world criticism regarding the use of its infant formula, Nestlé established an independent audit committee to monitor its market practices and its compliance with the international code of the World Health Organization regarding infant formula marketing activities. Unfortunately, the committee was viewed by some critics as merely a public relations ploy. This criticism may have been avoided had the corporate philosophy provided for the committee prior to the infant formula crisis. Nevertheless, a committee is an example of a mechanism for monitoring the operationalization of the corporate philosophy on an ongoing basis.

Self-Concept. The multinationalized self-concept is dependent on management's understanding and evaluation of the company's strengths and weaknesses as a competitor in each of its operating arenas. The firm's ability to survive in multiple dynamic and highly competitive environments is severely limited if strategic decision makers do not understand the impact the company has or could have on the environment and vice versa. They are, in fact, partially responsible for determining the environment to which they must subsequently respond; that is, a company may engage in actions to proactively select and impact its environments, or it may decide to take a reactive stance in which it responds and adapts to environmental changes once their impact is known with greater certainty. Activities by which management may proactively manage the environment include:

Developing leadership and innovation in products, marketing, and technology.

Securing monopolistic market or distribution positions.

Co-opting key environmental-determining coalitions.

Participating in environmental-determining political processes.

Joint venturing with environmental-determining coalitions.

Selecting particular portions of the environment to engage in competitively.

The mission statement must convey the overall corporate intentions and strategic orientation toward a proactive versus reactive choice. Subsidiaries cannot be allowed to determine their own environmental posture if the MNC is to fully capitalize on the potential advantages inherent in internationalized operations.

Public Image.   Domestically, the public image is often shaped from a marketing viewpoint. The firm's public image is considered a marketing tool that is managed with the objective of customer acceptance of the firm's product in the market. Although this dimension remains a critical consideration in the multinational environment, it msut be properly balanced with concern for organizational claimants other than the customer. The multinational firm is a major user of national resources and a major force in the socialization processes of many countries. Thus, the MNC must manage its image with respect to this larger context by clearly conveying its intentions to recognize the additional internal and external claimants resulting from multinationalization. The following excerpt from Hewlett-Packard's mission statement exemplifies this broadened public image: "As a corporation operating in many different communities throughout the world, we must assure ourselves that each of these communities is better for our presence. . . . Each community has its particular set of social problems. Our company must help to solve these problems." Through this statement, Hewlett-Packard conveys to the public an image of responsiveness to claimants throughout the world.

Summary

Managers need to recognize that different types of industry-based competition exist and that these differences are linked to an understanding of the strategic planning options available to a multinational corporation. Specifically, managers must identify their industry along the global versus multidomestic continuum and then consider the implications for their firm. This is the first step in developing a multinational strategy.

Global and multidomestic industries necessitate distinctive strategic emphasis as a result of the location and coordination of the corporation's functional activities. Consequently, once the industry is understood, managers must pursue a strategy consistent with the industry and supported through the functional activities. Specifically, managers must emphasize increased coordination and concentration of functional activities as the competition in the industry becomes global in nature.

The appendix at the end of this chapter lists many of the environmental components with which multinational companies must contend. This list is useful both in trying to comprehend the breadth of issues operating in the multinational environment and in evaluating the strategies of MNCs to determine their thoroughness.

As a starting point for international expansion, management needs to review and revise the corporate mission statement. A mission statement developed from a domestic perspective is often thought to continue encompassing and directing multinational activities. However, as multinational operations fundamentally alter corporate direction and strategic capabilities, the guiding purpose of the firm must be reclarified through multinationalization of the mission statement.

The multinationalized mission statement expresses the ultimate aim of the firm and provides a unity of direction that transcends both divergent managerial perspectives and geographically dispersed strategic decision makers. It provides a basis for strategic decision-making processes, particularly in situations where strategic alternatives may appear to conflict. It promotes the shared corporate values and commitments that extend beyond a single culture and can be identified and assimilated by internal and external organizational claimants. Finally, it asserts the legitimacy of the organization with respect to support coalitions in each of its operating environments, which is essential for the company to ensure and protect its survival.

Questions for Discussion

1. How does environmental analysis at the domestic level differ from a multinational analysis?

2. Which factors complicate environmental analysis at the multinational level? Which factors are making such analysis easier?

3. Do you agree with the suggestion that soon all industries will need to evaluate global environments?

4. Which industries operate almost devoid of international competition? Which inherent immunities do they enjoy?

5. Which components of a mission statement are most critical to revise when a corporation develops multinationally?

6. Obviously, multinationalization forces many changes in addition to those a corporation makes in its mission statement. Using the chapter appendix as a guide, develop a scheme for classifying the additional changes that should be considered.

Bibliography

Chakravarthy, Balaj S., and Howard V. Perlmutter. "Strategic Planning for a Global Business." *Columbia Journal of World Business,* Summer 1985, pp. 3–10.

Doz, Yves, and C. K. Prahalad. "Patterns of Strategic Control within Multinational Corporations." *Journal of International Business Studies,* Fall 1984, pp. 55–72.

Fayweather, J., and A. Kapoor. *Strategy and Negotiation for the International Corporation.* Cambridge, Mass.: Ballinger, 1976.

Harvel, Gary, and C. K. Prahalad. "Managing Strategic Responsibility in the MNC." *Strategic Management Journal* 4 (1983), pp. 341–51.

Hout, T.; M. E. Porter; and E. Rudden. "How Global Companies Win Out." *Harvard Business Review,* September–October 1982, pp. 98–108.

Levitt, Theodore. "The Globalization of Markets." *Harvard Business Review,* September–October 1982, p. 92.

Naylor, Thomas H. "The International Strategy Matrix." *Columbia Journal of World Business,* Summer 1985, pp. 11–19.

Pearce, John A., II, and Kendall Roth. "Multinationalization of the Corporate Mission." Advanced Management Journal, in press.

Porter, Michael E. "Changing Patterns of International Competition." *California Management Review 28,* no. 2 (Winter 1986), pp. 9–40.

Quelch, John A., and Edward J. Hoff. "Customizing Global Marketing." *Harvard Business Review,* May–June 1986, pp. 59–68.

Ronstadt, R., and R. Kramer. "Getting the Most out of Innovation Abroad." *Harvard Business Review,* March–April 1982, pp. 94–99.

Stonehill, A.; T. Beekhuisen; R. Wright; L. Remmers; N. Toy; P. Pares; A. Shapiro; D. Egan; and T. Bates. "Financial Goals and Debt Ratio Determinants: A Survey of Practice in Five Countries." *Financial Management,* Autumn 1975, pp. 27–40.

Watson, C. M. "Counter Competition Abroad to Protect Home Markets." *Harvard Business Review,* January–February 1982, p. 40.

Williams, O. "Who Cast the First Stone?" *Harvard Business Review,* September–October 1984, pp. 151–61.

Wind, Yoram, and Susan Douglas. "International Portfolio Analysis and Strategy: The Challenge of the 80s." *Journal of International Business Studies,* Fall 1981, pp. 69–82.

Appendix

Components of the Multinational Environment

Multinational companies must operate within an environment that has numerous components. These components include:

I. Government, laws, regulations and policies of home country (United States, for example).
  A. Monetary and fiscal policies and their effect on price trends, interest rates, economic growth, and stability.
  B. Balance-of-payment policies.
    1. Mandatory controls on direct investment.
    2. Interest equalization tax and other policies.
  C. Commercial policies, especially tariffs, quantitative import restrictions, and voluntary import controls.
  D. Export controls and other restrictions on trade with Eastern European and other Communist nations.
  E. Tax policies and their impact on overseas business.
  F. Antitrust regulations, their administration, and their impact on international business.

Source: W. A. Dymsza, *Multinational Business Strategy* (New York: McGraw-Hill, 1972), pp. 83–85.

      G. Investment guarantees, investment surveys, and other programs to encourage private investments in less developed countries.

      H. Export–import and governmental export expansion programs.

      I. Other changes in government policy that affect international business.

II. Key political and legal parameters in foreign countries and their projection.

      A. Type of political and economic system, political philosophy, national ideology.

      B. Major political parties, their philosophies, and their policies.

      C. Stability of the government.

          1. Changes in political parties.

          2. Changes in governments.

      D. Assessment of nationalism and its possible impact on political environment and legislation.

      E. Assessment of political vulnerability.

          1. Possibilities of expropriation.

          2. Unfavorable and discriminatory national legislation and tax laws.

          3. Labor laws and problems.

      F. Favorable political aspects.

          1. Tax and other concessions to encourage foreign investments.

          2. Credit and other guarantees.

      G. Differences in legal system and commercial law.

      H. Jurisdiction in legal disputes.

      I. Antitrust laws and rules of competition.

      J. Arbitration clauses and their enforcement.

      K. Protection of patents, trademarks, brand names, and other industrial property rights.

III. Key economic parameters and their projection.

      A. Population and its distribution by age groups, density, annual percentage increase, percentage of working age, percentage of total in agriculture, percentage in urban centers.

      B. Level of economic development and industrialization.

      C. Gross national product, gross domestic product, or national income in real terms and also on per capita basis in recent years and projections over future planning period.

      D. Distribution of personal income.

      E. Measures of price stability and inflation, wholesale price index, consumer price index, other price indexes.

      F. Supply of labor, wage rates.

      G. Balance-of-payments equilibrium or disequilibrium, level of international monetary reserves, and balance-of-payments policies.

H. Trends in exchange rates, currency stability, evaluation of possibility of depreciation of currency.

I. Tariffs, quantitative restrictions, export controls, border taxes, exchange controls, state trading, and other entry barriers to foreign trade.

J. Monetary, fiscal, and tax policies.

K. Exchange controls and other restrictions on capital movements, repatriation of capital, and remission of earnings.

IV. Business system and structure.

A. Prevailing business philosophy: mixed capitalism, planned economy, state socialism.

B. Major types of industry and economic activities.

C. Numbers, size, and types of firms, including legal forms of business.

D. Organization: proprietorships, partnerships, limited companies, corporations, cooperatives, state enterprises.

E. Local ownership patterns: public and privately held corporations, family-owned enterprises.

F. Domestic and foreign patterns of ownership in major industries.

G. Business managers available: their education, training, experience, career patterns, attitudes, and reputations.

H. Business associations and chambers of commerce and their influence.

I. Business codes, both formal and informal.

J. Marketing institutions: distributors, agents, wholesalers, retailers, advertising agencies, advertising media, marketing research and other consultants.

K. Financial and other business institutions: commercial and investment banks, other financial institutions, capital markets, money markets, foreign exchange dealers, insurance firms, engineering companies.

L. Managerial processes and practices with respect to planning, administration, operations, accounting, budgeting, control.

V. Social and cultural parameters and their projections.

A. Literacy and educational levels.

B. Business, economic, technical, and other specialized education available.

C. Language and cultural characteristics.

D. Class structure and mobility.

E. Religious, racial, and national characteristics.

F. Degree of urbanization and rural–urban shifts.

G. Strength of nationalistic sentiment.

H. Rate of social change.

I. Impact of nationalism on social and institutional change.

Chapter 6 Cohesion Case Illustration

The Multinational Environment of Holiday Inns, Inc.

Each of Holiday Inns, Inc.'s business groups could easily find itself facing international considerations associated with various strategic options that group managers might choose. The two groups with significant international involvement are the hotel group and the transportation (Delta Steamships) group. These two groups are used below to selectively illustrate issues associated with evaluating the multinational environment.

Differences between U.S. Operations and International Operations

Hotels are service businesses designed to meet the lodging, food, and entertainment needs of travelers and local customers. The service is highly personalized and takes place in each hotel location on a one-to-one basis.

Language, cultural, economic, political, and transportation/communication considerations vary from country to country. This variability makes it difficult for a hotel chain built on a guarantee of "no surprises" or differences in standards from place to place to ensure consistency and control across multinational locations. Holiday Inns established a separate international division, which is subdivided globally to facilitate recognition of such differences and to accommodate them in profitable ways at individual locations covering over 55 countries worldwide.

Delta Steamships confronts a wide array of differences when comparing its international markets (Latin America, South America, and Africa) with domestic ones. Port operations are more strongly controlled in each international setting. Government involvement often includes ownership of key competitors, control of loading facilities and dockworkers, and heavy taxation of Delta's revenue derived in that port.

Multidomestic Industries versus Global Industries

The worldwide lodging industry is steadily evolving from what was once a multidomestic industry to an increasingly global industry. With the speed of intercontinental travel, communication, and increased commerce, lodging services are increasingly open to nondomestic-based competition. And the concentration on heavy demand for lodging services in large, truly international cities worldwide has created fewer market differences for operating major hotels.

The ocean shipping business has been closer to a global industry for some time. Countries active in shipping and exporting for centuries have spawned sizable shipping enterprises that are knowledgeable and positioned to operate in all the major ports of the world.

Location and Coordination: Multinational Strategic Options

Figure 6–3 (presented earlier in Chapter 6) portrayed basic differences in the options available to multinational firms. These differences arise from the demands necessary to coordinate activities of the business and the location requirements to provide the firm's activities. Holiday Inns' hotel group and its Delta Steamship business are located on Figure 6–3 as follows:

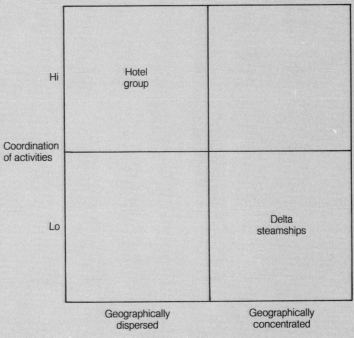

Following Figure 6–3's guidelines, Holiday Inns' multinational hotel business would face high foreign investment (each lodging facility must be built and run on foreign soil) and require extensive coordination (reservations, standards, and financial). The steamship business is much the opposite. It could follow an "export-based" strategy, meaning its main location could remain U.S. based while it emphasized decentralized marketing. The "decentralized marketing" suggests that Delta Steamship would need to market its transportation services within each port/country it serves.

Both suggestions emanating from Figure 6–3 are consistent with the international setting and options considered by these two business groups. The hotel business was concerned with the high foreign investment required to operate in foreign cities with non-U.S. governments. In addition to a heavy reliance on franchising, hotel group executives were considering moving extensively toward providing the Holiday Inn name and extended management services to foreign investors who would own the hotel facility rather than having any company-owned properties.

The steamship operation was more difficult to deal with. Extensive subsidy by foreign (host) governments to their respective merchant marine fleets was becoming increasingly impossible for Delta to compete with—even considering the new LASH technology.

CHAPTER

7

Environmental Forecasting

Importance of Forecasting

Change was rapid in the 1970s and early 1980s, with even greater changes and challenges forecast as the 80s come to a close. The crucial responsibility for managers will be ensuring their firm's capacity for survival. This will be done by anticipating and adapting to environmental changes in ways that provide new opportunities for growth and profitability. The impact of changes in the remote industry and task environments must be understood and predicted.

Even large firms in established industries will be actively involved in transitions. The $5.5 billion loss in the U.S. auto industry during 1980 and 1981 shows what can happen when firms fail to place a priority on environmental forecasting. The preceding decade saw a 20 percent penetration of the U.S. new car market by foreign competition; the oil embargo in 1973; rapidly climbing fuel prices; and uncertain future supplies of crude oil. Yet the long-term implications of these predictable factors on future auto sales were largely ignored by U.S. automakers. Because it was not open to changes in technology, Detroit was left without viable, fuel-efficient, quality-made alternatives for the American market. On the other hand, the Japanese anticipated the future need for fuel efficiency, quality, and service through careful market research

Note: Portions of this chapter are adopted from John A. Pearce II and Richard B. Robinson, Jr., "Environmental Forecasting: Key to Strategic Management," *Business,* July–September 1983, pp. 3–12.

and environmental forecasting. As a result, the Japanese gained additional market share at Detroit's expense. However, in the early 1980s, American automakers spent $80 billion on product and capital-investment strategies meant to recapture their lost market share. They realized that success in strategic decisions rests not solely on dollar amounts but also on anticipation of and preparation for the future.

Accurate forecasting of changing elements in the environment is an essential part of strategic management. One specific example is the case of National Intergroup described in Strategy in Action 7–1.

Strategy in Action 7–1
National Intergroup

In 1982 National Steel's sales dropped 26 percent to $3 billion, while the previous year's $86 million profit disintegrated into a massive $463 million loss. But long before the company reached this abyss, Chairman Howard M. Love, perplexed by the historically poor returns on steel, began to take a "cold, ungilded look" at every aspect of the company. This three-year analysis asked why the company's management did not perform better and culminated with the adoption of a new name that does not mention steel: National Intergroup Inc. (NII).

As the 1980s began National seemed mired, and its efforts to change were fizzling. Attempts to establish then-unproved quality circles at its Weirton, West Virginia, steel mill foundered because middle management—not labor—was unresponsive. With the help of Responsive Organizations, an Arlington, Virginia, consulting firm, National's top management came to realize that its managers lacked commonly held goals. To remedy that, 250 executives were involved for over a year in meetings meant to seek a consensus on the company's mission and to outline its financial, marketing, personnel, and social goals.

The company also set up task forces to study its strategic planning process and the system by which one unit, such as coal, charged another unit, such as steel, for its products. But the discussions "all began running up against a stone wall," said John A. McCreary, NII's vice president for human resources. The barrier, "an inappropriate organizational structure," focused too much on steel production.

So in 1982 the corporation was restructured into six autonomous business groups—steel, financial services, aluminum, distribution, energy, and diversified

Continued on Page 175

Strategy in Action 7–1 *(concluded)*

business. Each was a profit center with its own group president, and the new corporate name reflected this change.

National's studies showed that its two biggest markets—autos and cans—were irrevocably reducing their use of steel. "The size of the steel company we have now matches the markets we want to participate in," said Love. Future capital investment could be concentrated on improving smaller plants. Consequently, Love believed, "we'll be significantly more profitable with less tons." In early 1983 National showed this was no idle boast: It reported an operating profit of $2 for each ton of steel it produced, while other major steel makers lost from $17 to $32 per ton. The company's mills were running at 82 percent of capacity, while industry as a whole was sputtering along at 56 percent.

National's balance sheet was in much better shape than it had been in the previous year. As of June 30, 1983, the company had $74 million in cash, three times its holdings at year-end. Long-term debt was knocked down to $600 million by September 30, 1983, or 36 percent of capitalization versus 41 percent the previous year, and its stock had more than doubled in price in the same year. "They've got their act together," said John C. Tumazos, an industry analyst with Oppenheimer & Company, who in 1982 listed National as one of the steel industry's financially weakest companies.

Source: Adapted from *Business Week,* September 26, 1983, p. 82.

Forecasting the business environment for the second half of the 1980s has led some firms, such as Sears, Roebuck, to expand. From 1980 to 1985, Sears opened new financial centers in 250 retail stores.

Other corporations have forecast a need for massive retrenchment. One such firm is the Weyerhauser Company, which laid off 2,000 employees in 1982 to streamline its cost of doing business. Still other companies have cut back in one area of operations to underwrite growth in another. In 1984 General Electric decided to close 10 plants and reduce its work force by 1,600 employees while simultaneously making a commitment to spend $250 million by 1986 to upgrade its facilities.

These and many other examples indicate that strategic managers need to develop skill in predicting significant environmental changes. To aid in the search for future opportunities and constraints, the following steps should be taken:

1. Select those environmental variables that are critical to the firm.
2. Select the sources of significant environmental information.
3. Evaluate forecasting approaches or techniques.
4. Integrate forecast results into the strategic management process.
5. Monitor the critical aspects of managing forecasts.

Select Critical Environmental Variables

Management experts have argued that the most important cause of the turbulent business environment is the change in population structure and dynamics. This change, in turn, produces other major changes in the economic, social, and political environments.

Historically, population shifts tended to occur over 40- to 50-year periods and, therefore, had little relevance to business decisions. However, during the second half of the 20th century, population changes have become radical, erratic, contradictory, and therefore of great importance.

For example, the U.S. baby boom between 1945 and the mid-1960s has had and will have a dramatic impact on all parts of society—from maternity wards and schools to the labor force and the marketplace. This population bulge is facing heavy competition for jobs, promotions, and housing, despite a highest-ever education level. Compounding this dilemma are the heightened demands of women and racial minorities. The lack of high-status jobs to fit the expectations of this large, educated labor force poses a potential for major social and economic changes. In addition, these workers encounter an increasingly aging labor force that finds it difficult to give up status, power, and employment when retirement programs are either not financially attractive or not available at the traditional age of 65. (See Figure 7–1 for comparative population growth projections.)

Obviously, the demands of these groups will have important effects on social and political changes in terms of lifestyle, consumption patterns, and political decisions. In economic terms, the size and potential affluence of these groups suggest increasing markets for housing, consumer products, and leisure goods and services.

Interestingly, the same shifts in population, life expectancy, and education have occurred in many developed nations. However, developing nations face the opposite population configurations. Although birthrates have declined, survival rates, because of medical improvements, have created a large population of people reaching adulthood in the 1980s. Jobs and food are expected to be in short supply. Therefore, many developing countries will face severe social and political instability unless they can find appropriate work for their surplus labor.[1]

The rates of population increase can obviously be of great importance, as indicated by the contrasting effects forecast above. If a growing population has sufficient purchasing power, new markets will be developed to satisfy their needs. However, too much growth in a country with a limited amount

---

[1] Peter M. Drucker, *Managing in Turbulent Times* (New York: Harper & Row, 1980), suggests that the practice of production sharing between developed and developing nations can be the economic integration needed by both groups of countries. Production sharing will include bringing together the abundant labor resources of the developing countries with the management, technology, educated people, markets, and purchasing power of the developed countries.

Figure 7–1
Population growth by age group (millions)

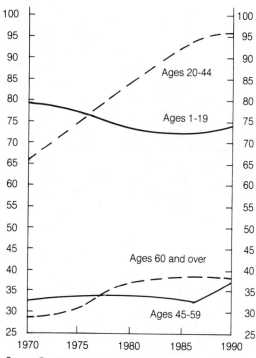

Source: Bureau of the Census, U.S. Department of Commerce,
1980.

or a drastic inequity in distribution of resources may result in major social
and political upheavals and may pose substantial risks for businesses.

If forecasting were as simple as predicting population trends, strategic managers would only need to examine census data to predict future markets.
But economic interpretations are more complex. Migration rates; mobility
trends; birth, marriage, and death rates; and racial, ethnic, and religious
structures complicate population statistics. In addition, resource development
and its political use in this interdependent world further confuse the problem—
as evidenced by the actions of some of the oil states (e.g., Saudi Arabia, Iraq,
Libya, and Kuwait). Changes in political situations, technology, or culture
add further complications.

Domestically, the turbulence is no less severe. Continually changing products and services, changing competitors, uncertain government priorities, rapid
social change, and major technological innovations all add to the complexity
of planning for the future. To grow, be profitable, at times even to survive in

this turbulent world, a firm needs sensitivity, commitment, and skill in recognizing and predicting those variables that will most profoundly affect its future.

Who Selects the Key Variables? Although executives or committees in charge of planning may assist in obtaining forecast data, responsibility for environmental forecasting usually lies with top management. This is the case at the Sun (oil) Company, where responsibility for the long-range future of the corporation is assigned to the chairman and vice chairman of the board of directors. One key duty of the vice chairman is environmental assessment. In this context, *environment* refers not to air, water, and land but rather to the general business setting created by the economic, technological, political, and social forces in which Sun plans to operate.

The environmental assessment group consists of Sun's chief economist, a specialist in technological assessment, and a public issues consultant—all reporting to the vice president of environmental assessment. The chief economist evaluates and forecasts the state of the economy; the technological assessment specialist covers technology and science; and the public issues consultant concentrates on politics and society.[2]

However, headquarters' capability and proficiency may be limited in analyzing political, economic, and social variables around the world. Therefore, on-the-spot personnel, outside consultants, or company task forces may be assigned to assist in forecasting.

What Variables Should Be Selected? A list of key variables that will have make-or-break consequences for the firm must be developed. Some may have been crucial in the past, and others may appear to be important in the future. This list can be kept to manageable size by limiting key variables in the following ways:

1. Include all variables that would have a significant impact although their probability of occurrence is low (e.g., trucking deregulation). Also include highly probable variables regardless of impact (e.g., a minimal price increase by a major supplier). Delete others with little impact and low probabilities.
2. Disregard major disasters, such as nuclear war.
3. Aggregate when possible into gross variables (e.g., a bank loan is based more on the dependability of a company's cash flow than on the flow's component sources).
4. If the value of one variable is based on the value of the other, separate the dependent variable for future planning.[3]

---

[2] Eric Weiss, "Future Public Opinion of Business," *Management Review*, March 1978, p. 9.

[3] Robert E. Linneman and John D. Kennell, "Shirt-Sleeve Approach to Long-Range Plans," *Harvard Business Review*, March–April 1977, p. 145.

Limits of money, time, and skill in forecasting prevent a firm from predicting many variables in the environment. The task of predicting even a dozen variables is substantial. Often firms try to select a set of key variables by analyzing the environmental factors in the industry that are most likely to force sharp growth or decline in the marketplace. For the furniture, appliance, and textiles industries, housing starts are significant. Housing, in turn, is greatly affected by high interest rates.

Figure 7–2 identifies some of the key issues that may have critical impacts

---

Figure 7–2
Strategic forecasting issues

Key issues in the remote environment

Economy

Purchasing power depends on current income, savings, prices, and credit availability. The economic trends to be forecast often attempt to answer the following questions.

What are the probable future directions of the economies in the corporation's regional, national, and international markets? What changes in economic growth, inflation, interest rates, capital availability, credit availability, and consumer purchasing power can be expected?

What income differences can be expected between the wealthy upper-middle class, working class, and underclass in various regions?

What shifts in relative demand for different categories of goods and services can be expected?

Example.   The record-setting high interest rates of 1980 and 1981 resulted in a general economic washout in the United States. Industries that depend on long- and short-term credit for their sales, such as housing and automobiles, were most severely affected. Despite the possibility that higher interest rates would be used to curtail the increasing inflation, little effort was made by loan institutions to develop innovative loan programs, such as variable-interest loans.

Society

In the rapidly changing social environment of the highly interdependent spaceship earth, businesses feel great pressure to respond to the expectations of society more effectively.

What effect do changes in social values and attitudes regarding childbearing, marriage, lifestyle, work, ethics, sex roles, racial equality, education, retirement, energy, pollution, and so on have on the firm's development? What effect will population changes have on major social and political expectations—at home and abroad? What constraints or opportunities will develop? What pressure groups will increase in power?

Example.   The declining birthrate of the United States is a threat to some industries producing children's food, toys, clothes, and furniture. However, forecasting by trend extrapolation of birthrates in the late 1950s was so inaccurate that it created a severe threat to such firms as the Gerber Company. The six firms that survived or prospered into the 1980s were those that learned to recognize sociocultural value changes and to incorporate such changes in their strategic forecasts.

Politics

Although political forecasts are usually based on "soft" data, as compared to hard—attitudes and opinions—the impact of political issues and trends, as shown below, is frequently as important as economic or technological variables.

What changes in government policy can be expected regarding industry cooperation, antitrust activities, foreign trade, taxation, depreciation, environmental protection, deregulation, defense, foreign trade barriers, and other governing parameters? What success will a new administration have in achieving its stated goals? What effect will that success have on the firm?

Example.   After the 1980 presidential election, major forecast adjustments were made to reflect the Reagan administration's new priorities in military defense, private sector growth, and reduced government spending.

Figure 7–2 *(continued)*

✓ Will specific international climates be hostile or favorable? Is there a tendency toward instability, corruption, or violence? What is the level of political risk in each foreign market? What other political or legal constraints or support can be expected in international business (e.g., trade barriers, equity requirements, nationalism, patent protection)?

> *Example.* Despite the low political risk involved, several major U.S. firms discovered the importance of in-depth environmental forecasting when investing in Canada. Although aware of the Quebec separatist movement, ITT Rayonier dismissed its potential effect on construction of a $120-million pulp mill. ITT's use of English-speaking supervisors, supervisor conflict with the separatists, a power struggle between two labor federations, and a shortage of skilled labor more than doubled the construction cost to $250 million. Asbestos Corporation of America was also surprised when the province of Quebec nationalized its asbestos mines. Both firms underestimated the significance of growing nationalism.

Technology

Technological innovations can give the firm a special competitive advantage. Without continued product or service improvement, profitability and survival are often jeopardized.

> What is the current state of the art? How will it change? What pertinent new products or services are likely to become technically feasible in the foreseeable future? What is the future impact of technological breakthroughs in related product areas? How will they interface with other remote considerations, such as economic issues, social values, public safety, regulations, and court interpretations?

> *Example.* Recent applications to telephone interconnections of sophisticated computer technology (such as PBX units) have developed an entire new industry seen as a first step toward the integrated electronic office of the future. In addition, decisions by the Federal Communications Commission curtailed previous monopolistic practices of AT&T that excluded the use of equipment from other than AT&T sources. The result has been the spin-off from AT&T of a marketing-oriented unit that will compete head on with firms seeking to relate computers to communication systems. Among the announced competitors are Xerox, IBM, Exxon, Volkswagen, ROLM Corporation, Northern Telecom, Mitel Corporation, and Nippon Electric Company.

Industry

At any given time in its life cycle, certain underlying forces in an industry operate to broadly define the potential for a company's success.

> What is the degree of integration of major competitors? What is the industry's average percentage utilization of production capacity? What is the industry's vulnerability to new or substitute products? What, and how great, are the barriers to entry? What is the number and concentration of suppliers? What is the nature of the industry's customer base?

> *Example.* Head Ski began with a concentration strategy targeted at the high-quality/high-price niche of the snow ski market. With a quickly achieved 50 percent market share, the company faced only four major competitors. However, industry competition had changed dramatically. Head had diversified into new product markets, such as ski clothing, accessories, and archery equipment. It had also diversified geographically into Europe. Competitors had buttressed their resource bases through mergers with conglomerates such as Beatrice Foods. Head Ski followed suit when it was acquired by AMF. Thus, in just five years, the competitive industry composition had shifted from nondiversified, relatively small, single-industry businesses to large, multinational, multi-industry, diversified conglomerates.

Key issues in the operating environment

Competitive position

How probable is the entrance of important new competitors into the industry? Will they offer substitute or competing products? What strategic moves are expected by existing rivals—inside and outside the United States? What competitive advantage is necessary in selected foreign markets? What will be the competitors' priorities and their ability to change? Is their behavior predictable?

> *Example.* Employing a penetration strategy similar to that used in the auto, steel, shipbuilding, and television markets, Japanese medical electronics makers are gaining a niche with low-cost, stripped-down versions of competitors' equipment. American firms, like General Electric, dismissed the Japanese strategy by insisting that users of medical electronic equipment are concerned not with price but quality. However, as in past entry strategies, the Japanese researched the needs of

Figure 7–2 (concluded)

the market. They then began development of a three-dimensional scanner-monitor, which was a major technical breakthrough and may eventually give them a competitive edge in the marketplace.

Customer profiles and market changes

What is and will be considered as needed value by our customers? Is market research done, or do managers talk to each other to discover what the customer wants? Which customer needs are not being met by existing products? Why? Are R&D activities under way to develop means for fulfilling these needs? What is their status? What marketing and distribution channels should be used?

Example.   The Japanese research future customer needs and wants by interviewing those who own products of their major competitor, thereby identifying desired improvements. As an example, in the 1970s Japanese researchers identified Volkswagen's shortcomings by interviewing owners in the United States. They then designed Toyotas and Datsuns accordingly and consequently overcame the Beetle's dominance in the United States.

What demographic and population changes can be anticipated? What do they portend for the size of the market and sales potential? What new market segment or product might develop as a result of these changes? What will be our customer groups' buying power?

Example.   Because 95 percent of its $3.5 billion in revenues are generated from soft drinks and other beverages, Coca-Cola has become concerned about the aging of the prime soft drink population, 13- to 24-year-olds. Because Coke can identify the key population variables that will have make-or-break consequences for its product lines, it can more accurately forecast future market potential. As a result, Coke has decided to pursue the aging population bulge in the United States by diversifying into wines. By further expanding internationally with its soft drink products, Coke is also tapping growing youth markets in foreign countries.

Suppliers and creditors

What is the likelihood of major cost increases because of dwindling supplies of a needed natural resource? Will sources of supply, especially of energy, be reliable? Are there reasons to expect major changes in cost and availability of inputs as a result of money, people, or subassembly problems? Which suppliers and creditors can be expected to respond to special emergency requests?

Example.   As short-term interest rates skyrocketed to 20 percent in late 1979, hundreds of small firms fell into the marginal or money-losing categories. Officers of their banks often became alarmed and called in the loans. The resulting squeeze forced many of these businesses into bankruptcy.

Labor market

Are potential employees with desired skills and abilities available in the geographic areas involved? Are colleges and vocational–technical schools located near plant or store sites to aid in meeting training needs? Are labor relations in the industry conducive to expanding needs for employees?

Example.   The 1950s and 1960s were periods of business expansion into the southern states, where labor was plentiful and unions were comparatively weak. In the 1970s and 1980s, northern states regained a measure of attractiveness because they were able to offer unemployed or underemployed skilled workers and attractively priced industrial sites.

on a firm's future success. Examples of the importance of a few of these variables are also presented.

Select Sources of Significant Environmental Information

Before forecasting can begin in a formal way, appropriate sources of environmental information should be identified. Casual gathering of strategic information is part of the normal course of executive actions—reading, interactions, and meetings—but is subject to bias and must be balanced with alternative viewpoints. Although *The Wall Street Journal, Business Week, Fortune, Harvard Business Review, Forbes,* and other popular trade and scholarly journals are important sources of forecasting information, formal, deliberate, and structured searches are desirable. The appendix to this chapter lists published sources that can be used in forecasting. A review of these will help strategic managers identify sources that can help meet specific forecasting needs. If the firm can afford the time and expense, primary data should also be gathered in such areas as market factors, technological changes, and competitive and supplier strategies.

Evaluate Forecasting Techniques

Debate exists over the accuracy of quantitative versus qualitative approaches to forecasting (see Figure 7–3), with most research supporting quantitative models. However, the difference in predictions made using each type of approach is often minimal. Additionally, subjective or judgmental approaches may often be the only practical method of forecasting political, legal, social, and technological trends in the remote external environment. The same is true of several factors in the task environment, especially customer and competitive considerations.

Ultimately, the choice of technique depends not on the environmental factor under review but on such considerations as the nature of the forecast decision, the amount and accuracy of available information, the accuracy required, the time available, the importance of the forecast, the cost, and the competence and interpersonal relationships of the managers and forecasters involved.[4] Frequently, assessment of these factors leads to the selection of a combination of quantitative and qualitative techniques, thereby strengthening the accuracy of the ultimate forecast.

Techniques Available

Economic Forecasts.   At one time, only forecasts of economic variables were used in strategic management. These forecasts were primarily concerned with remote factors, such as general economic conditions, disposable personal income, the consumer price index, wage rates, and productivity. Derived from government and private sources, the economic forecasts served as the framework for industry and company forecasts. The latter forecasts dealt with task-environment concerns, such as sales, market share, and other pertinent economic trends.

---

[4] Steven C. Wheelwright and Darral G. Clarke, "Corporate Forecasting: Promise and Reality," *Harvard Business Review*, November–December 1976, p. 42.

Figure 7–3
Popular approaches to forecasting

Technique*	Short description†	Cost	Popularity‡	Complexity	Association with life-cycle stage§
Quantitative					
Causal					
Econometric models	Simultaneous systems of multiple regression equations	High	High	High	Steady state
Single and multiple regression	Variations in dependent variables are explained by variations in the independent one(s)	High/Medium	High	Medium	Steady state
Time series	Linear, exponential, S-curve, or other types of projections	Medium	High	Medium	Steady state
Trend extrapolation	Forecasts are obtained by linear or exponential smoothing or averaging of past actual values	Medium	High	Medium	Steady state
Qualitative or judgmental					
Sales force estimate‖	A bottom-up approach aggregating salespersons' forecasts	Low	High	Low	All stages
Juries of executive opinion	Marketing, production, finance, and purchasing executives jointly prepare forecasts	Low	High	Low	Product development
Customer surveys; market research	Learning about intentions of potential customers or plans of businesses	Medium	Medium	Medium	Market testing and early introduction
Scenario	Forecasters imagine the impacts of anticipated conditions	Low	Medium	Low	All stages
Delphi method	Experts are guided toward a consensus	Low	Medium	Medium	Product development
Brainstorming	Idea generation in a noncritical group situation	Low	Medium	Medium	Product development

* Only techniques discussed in this chapter are listed.

† Adapted in part from S. C. Wheelwright and S. Makridakis, *Forecasting Methods for Management*, 3rd ed. (New York: John Wiley & Sons, 1980), pp. 34–35.

‡ Adapted in part from S. C. Wheelwright and D. C. Clark, "Corporate Forecasting: Promise and Reality," *Harvard Business Review*, November–December 1976.

§ Adapted in part from J. C. Chambers, J. K. Mullick, and D. D. Smith, "How to Choose the Right Forecasting Technique," *Harvard Business Review*, July–August 1971. The associations shown are "most common," but most techniques can be used at most stages.

‖ For details see N. C. Mohn and L. C. Sartorius, "Sales Forecasting: A Manager's Primer," *Business*, May–June 1981 and July–August 1981.

Econometric Models.   With the advent of sophisticated computers, the government and some wealthy companies contracted with private consulting firms to develop "causal models," especially those involving *econometrics*. These models utilize complex simultaneous regression equations to relate economic occurrences to areas of corporate activity. They are especially useful when information is available on causal relationships and when large changes are anticipated. During the relatively stable decade of the 1960s and on into the 1970s, econometrics became one of the nation's fastest-growing industries. However, since early in 1979 the big three econometric firms—Data Resources (McGraw-Hill), Chase Econometrics (Chase Manhattan Bank), and Wharton Econometric Forecasting Associates (Ziff-Davis Publishing)—have fallen on hard times. The explosion of oil prices, inflation, and the growing interdependence of the world economy have created problems beyond the inherent limits of econometric models. And despite enormous technological resources, these models still depend on the judgment of the model builders. Recently, that judgment has not been dependable.[5]

Two more widely used and less expensive approaches to forecasting are *time series models* and *judgmental models*. Time series models attempt to identify patterns based on combinations of historical trend, seasonal, and cyclical factors. This technique assumes the past is a prologue to the future. Time series techniques, such as exponential smoothing and linear projections, are relatively simple, well known, inexpensive, and accurate.

Of the time series models, *trend analysis* is the most frequently used. This model assumes the future will be a continuation of the past, following some long-range trend. If sufficient historical data, such as annual sales, are readily available, a trend analysis can be done quickly and inexpensively.

In the trend analysis depicted in Figure 7–4, concern should focus on long-term trends, such as Trend C, which represents 10 years of fluctuating sales. Trend A, where three excellent years were used in the trend analysis, is too optimistic. Similarly, the four bad years depicted in Trend B represent a much too pessimistic outlook.

The major limitation of trend analysis is the assumption that all relevant conditions will remain relatively constant in the future. Sudden changes in the conditions upset the trend prediction.

Judgmental models are useful when historical data are not available or when they are hard to use. Examples of judgmental or qualitative approaches are *sales force estimates* and *juries of executive opinion*. Sales force estimates consolidate salespeople's opinions of customer intentions and opinions regarding specific products. These can be relevant if customers respond honestly and remain consistent in their intentions. Juries of executive opinion combine estimates made by executives from marketing, production, finance, and pur-

---

[5] "Where the Big Econometric Models Go Wrong," *Business Week,* March 30, 1981, pp. 70–73.

Figure 7–4
Interpretations in trend analysis

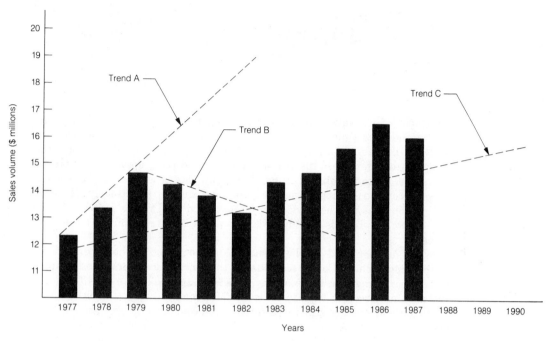

chasing and then average their views. No elaborate math or statistics are required.

Customer surveys may involve personal interviews or telephone questionnaires. The questions must be well stated and easily understood. Respondents are a random sample of the relevant population. Surveys can provide valuable in-depth information. They are often difficult to construct and time-consuming to administer, but many market research firms use such surveys. One strong advocate of judgmental approaches is a senior partner of Lord, Abbett Investment, as is discussed in Strategy in Action 7–2.

Social Forecasts.   Relying only on economic indicators for strategic forecasting neglects many important social trends that can have a profound impact. Some firms have recognized this and forecast social issues as part of their environmental scanning to identify social trends and underlying attitudes. Social forecasting is very complex. Recent efforts have involved analyzing such major social areas as population, housing, social security and welfare, health and nutrition, education and training, income, and wealth and expenditures.

Strategy in Action 7–2
Lord, Abbett Investment

Development of investment strategies usually involves sophisticated econometric and mathematical models to forecast future investment values. However, John M. McCarthy, senior partner of Lord, Abbett Investment, a $3.6 billion investment company, has developed his own qualitative forecasting approach. As president of its $1.7 billion Affiliated Fund, McCarthy uses a subjective approach that examines events for tangible signs of pending changes in the economy. He believes that if you wait for the obvious to be discussed on TV, the process of solving the economic problem is already under way and it is too late to invest for important gains.

While numbers and graphs are sometimes combined in the jury of executive opinion approach, McCarthy feels that by the time the numbers of the key indicators reflect changes in the economy, it is too late to aid investment strategies. Instead, his forecasts tend to focus on fundamental changes such as interest rates, government investment incentives, and consumer trends. Among McCarthy's specific forecasts were a drop in interest rates in 1981, a probable return to the bond market, and a depressed consumer goods market until the mid-80s. He believes that President Reagan's savings and investment incentives will break the American habit of borrow and spend. Company and personal investment strategies will need to be fine-tuned, as these and other forecasts do or do not become reality.

Generally, McCarthy looks for the mainly unpopular investments. Often these are undervalued. An illustration of his unique but commonsense approach resulted in investment strategies of purchasing stocks that declined in price while interest rates climbed in 1980. Interest-sensitive issues, such as AT&T, utilities, and banks, account for about 18 percent of Affiliated's current portfolio.

Although this conservative strategy caused Lord, Abbett's growth rate to be below the averages of the Dow Jones Industrial Average and Standard & Poor's 500 during the brief bull market in 1980, McCarthy has focused on long-term results. This forecasting approach and investment strategy enabled Affiliated to grow 173.1 percent compared to 105.5 percent for the Dow during the period January 1975 through September 1980.

Lord, Abbett follows the same forecast method and investment strategy in managing its $1.5 billion of pension fund money.

A variety of approaches is used in social forecasting, including time series analysis and the judgmental techniques described earlier. However, a fourth approach, called *scenario development,* is probably the most popular of all techniques. Scenarios are imagined stories that integrate objective and subjective parts of other forecasts. They are designed to help managers anticipate changes. Because scenarios can be presented in an easily understood form, they have gained popularity in social forecast situations. Scenarios can be developed by the following process:

1. Prepare the background by assessing the overall social environment under investigation (such as social legislation).
2. Select critical indicators and search for future events that may affect the key trends (e.g., growing distrust of business).
3. Analyze reasons for past behavior for each trend (e.g., perceived disregard for air and water quality).
4. Forecast each indicator in at least three scenarios, showing the least favorable environment, the likely environment, and the most favorable environment.
5. Write the scenario from the viewpoint of someone in the future and describe conditions then and how they developed.
6. Condense the scenario for each trend to a few paragraphs.

Figure 7–5 presents an example of a "most likely" scenario for the future of business-government relations on social issues. Scenarios prepare strategic managers for alternative possibilities if certain trends continue, thus enabling them to develop contingency plans.

Political Forecasts.   Some strategic planners want to treat political forecasts with the same seriousness and consideration given to economic forecasts. They believe shifts toward or against a broad range of political factors—such as the size of government budgets, tariffs, tax rates, defense spending, the growth of regulatory bodies, and the extent of business leader participation in government planning—can have profound effects on business success.

Political forecasts for foreign countries are also important. Political risks increase the threat to businesses in any way dependent on international subsidiaries or suppliers for customers or critical resources. Increasing world interdependence makes it imperative for firms of all sizes to consider the international political implications of their strategies.

Because of the billions of U.S. dollars lost in the 1970s as a result of revolutions, nationalization, and other manifestations of political instability, multinational firms and consultants have developed a variety of approaches to international forecast. Some of the better known are listed on the following page.

Figure 7–5
Scenario on the future of business–government regulations: Social issues

The government–corporate relationship in the 1978–1987 period continued to develop along patterns established in previous decades, with no major discontinuities or radical surprises. The most far-reaching and substantial change occurred late in the period when Congress enlarged the planning authority of its budget office, setting 5- and 10-year national manpower, natural resource, and other economic goals. This legislation primarily affected federal fiscal policies and contained no authority to compel action on the part of the private sector to meet the indicated goals.

Nevertheless, following the lead of West Germany, the federal government did offer some incentives to companies that acted to meet certain national objectives—for example, locating new industrial facilities in certain areas for social reasons (such as environmental or employment reasons). During the decade, the government made a commitment to guaranteed jobs rather than guaranteed income.

In the environmental arena, economic incentives and penalties became the government's major tools for compliance. Effluent charges were established to internalize the costs of pollution. Other tax incentives and loans were made available to companies for the installation of pollution-control equipment. Congress also legislated a time limit for legal actions to block a construction project on environmental grounds.

In other regulatory areas, the government moved selectively, increasing requirements on some industries while reducing controls on others. For example, while moving to deregulate much of the air transport business, Congress at the same time passed a full-disclosure labeling act for prepared foods that requires the listing of all ingredients and the percentage of each ingredient. Congress also set a rule requiring that every proposal for new regulation be accompanied by a regulatory impact statement detailing the probable effects of the proposal on the economy.

Turning down proposals for federal chartering of corporations, Congress nevertheless acted to influence the internal governance of large corporations: it passed a full-disclosure law concerning most corporate activities and established a limit on the number of inside directors permitted to serve on the boards of directors. Legislation established due process and protection for whistle blowers (employees who report legal violations). The government placed stringent safeguards on corporate data banks containing information about employees and customers.

In the domain of social legislation affecting business, the minimum wage was indexed to the cost of living, and Congress passed a comprehensive national health plan in which employers pay a significant portion.

Source: James O'Toole, "What's Ahead for Business–Government Relationships," *Harvard Business Review,* March–April 1979, p. 100.

Haner's Business Environmental Risk Index, which monitors 15 economic and political variables in 42 countries.

✓ Frost & Sullivan's World Political Risks Forecasts, which predicts the likelihood of various catastrophes befalling an individual company.

Probe International's custom reports for specific companies, which examine broad social trends.

✓ Arthur D. Little's (ADL) developmental forecasts, which examine a country's progress from the Stone Age to the computer age.[6]

Of all the approaches, ADL's forecasting techniques may be the most ambitious and sophisticated. With computer assistance, they follow the progress of each country by looking at five criteria: social development, technological advancement, abundance of natural resources, level of domestic tranquility, and type of political system. When a country's development in any one of

---

[6] Niles Howard, "Doing Business in Unstable Countries," *Dun's Review,* March 1980, pp. 49–55.

these areas gets too far ahead of the others, tension builds and violence often follows. Using this system, political turbulence was forecast in Iran as early as 1972. ADL foresees that uneven development will likely produce similar turmoil in 20 other countries, such as Peru, Chile, Malaysia, and the Philippines. ADL believes the world is highly predictable if one asks the right questions. Unfortunately, too many executives fail to use the same logic in analyzing political affairs that they use in other strategic areas. Political analysis should be routinely incorporated into economic analyses. Ford, General Motors, Pepsi, Singer, Du Pont, and United Technologies are among the many companies that follow ADL's advice.

Technological Forecasts. Such rapidly developed and revolutionary technological innovations as lasers, nuclear energy, satellites and other communication devices, desalination of water, electric cars, and miracle drugs have prompted many firms to invest in technological forecasts. Knowledge of probable technological development helps strategic managers prepare their firms to benefit from change. To make technological forecasts, all of the previously described techniques, except econometrics, can be used. However, uncertainty of information favors use of scenarios and two additional forecasting approaches: brainstorming and the Delphi technique.

Brainstorming is used to help a group generate new ideas and forecasts. With this technique, analysis or criticism of contributions made by participants is postponed so that creative thinking is not stifled or restricted. Because there are no interruptions, group members are encouraged to offer original ideas and build on the innovative thoughts of other participants. The most promising ideas generated by this means are thoroughly evaluated at a later time.

The *Delphi* method involves a systematic procedure for obtaining a consensus from a group of experts. The procedure includes:

1. A detailed survey of expert opinion, usually obtained through a mail questionnaire.
2. Anonymous evaluation of the responses by the experts involved.
3. One or more revisions of answers until convergence is achieved.

The Delphi technique, although expensive and time-consuming, can also be successful for social and political forecasting.

Integrate Forecast Results into the Strategic Management Process

Once the techniques are selected and the forecasts made, the results must be tied into the strategic management process. For example, the economic forecast must be related to analyses of the industry, suppliers, the competition,

Figure 7–6
Task and remote environment impact matrix

Remote environments	Task environments			
	Key customer trends	**Key competitor trends**	**Key supplier trends**	**Key labor market trends**
Economic	*Example:* Trends in inflation and unemployment rates		*Example:* Annual domestic oil demand and worldwide sulfur demand through 1987	
Social	*Example:* Increasing numbers of single-parent homes			*Example:* Increasing education level of U.S. population
Political	*Example:* Increasing numbers of punitive damage awards in product liability cases		*Example:* Possibility of Arab oil boycotts	
Technological		*Example:* Increasing use of superchips and computer-based instrumentation for synthesizing genes	*Example:* Use of Cobalt 60 gamma irradiation to extend shelf life of perishables	
Industry		*Example:* Disenchantment with vertical integration; increases in large horizontal mergers		*Example:* Increasing availability of mature workers with experience in "smokestack" industries

and key resources. Figure 7–6 presents a format for displaying interrelationships between forecast remote environment variables and the influential task environment variables. The resulting predictions become part of the assumed environment in formulating strategy.

It is critical that strategic decision makers understand the assumptions on which environmental forecasts are based. An example is the experience of Itel, a computer-leasing firm. In 1978, Itel was able to lease 200 plug-in computers made by Advanced Systems and by Hitachi largely because IBM was unable to deliver its newest systems. Consequently, Itel made a bullish sales forecast for 1979, that it would place 430 of its systems—despite the rumor that IBM would launch a new line of aggressively priced systems in the first quarter of that year. Even Itel's competitors felt that customers would hold off their purchasing decisions until IBM made the announcement. However, Itel signed long-term purchase contracts with its suppliers and increased its marketing staff by 80 percent. This forecasting mistake and the failure to examine sales forecasts in relationship to actions of competitors and suppliers was nearly disastrous. Itel slipped close to bankruptcy within less than a year.

Forecasting external events enables a firm to identify the probable requirements for future success, to formulate or reformulate its basic mission, and to design strategies to achieve goals and objectives. If the forecast identifies any gaps or inconsistencies between the firm's desired position and its present position, strategic managers can respond with plans and actions.

Dealing with the uncertainty of the future is a major function of the strategic manager. The forecasting task requires systematic information gathering coupled with the ability to utilize a variety of forecasting approaches. A high level of intuitive insight is also needed to integrate risks and opportunities in formulating strategy. However, intentional or unintentional delays or lack of understanding of certain issues may prevent an organization from using insights gained in assessing the impact of broader environmental trends. Consistent sensitivity and constant openness to new and better approaches and opportunities are therefore essential.

Monitor the Critical Aspects of Managing Forecasts

Although almost all aspects of forecasting can be considered critical in specific situations, three aspects stand out over the lifetime of a business.

The first is identification of factors that deserve forecasting. Although literally hundreds of different factors might affect a firm, often a few factors of immediate concern (such as sales forecasts and competitive trends) are most important. Unfortunately, seldom are enough time and resources available for complete understanding of all environmental factors that might be critical to the success of a strategy. Therefore, executives must depend on their collective experience and perception of what is important in identifying factors worthy of the expense of forecasting.

The second critical aspect is whether reputable, cost-efficient sources are available outside the firm that can expand the company's forecasting database. Strategic managers should locate federal and state governments, trade and industry associations, and other groups or individuals that can provide data forecasts at reasonable costs.

The third critical aspect of forecast management arises with the decision to handle forecasting tasks in-house. Given the great credence often accorded formally developed forecasts—despite the inherent uncertainty of the data base—the selection of forecasting techniques is indeed critical. A firm beginning its forecasting efforts is well advised to start with less technical methods, such as sales force estimates and the jury of executive opinion, rather than highly sophisticated forecasting techniques, such as econometrics. With added experience and understanding, the firm can add approaches that require greater analytical sophistication. In this way, managers learn to cope with the inherent weaknesses as well as the variable strengths of forecasting techniques.

Summary

Environmental forecasting starts with identification of factors external to the firm that might provide critical opportunities or pose threats in the future. Both quantitative and qualitative strategic forecasting techniques are used to project the long-range direction and impact of these critical remote- and task environment factors. The strengths and weaknesses of the various techniques must be understood in evaluating and selecting the most appropriate forecasting approaches for the firm. Employing more than one technique is usually advised to balance the potential bias or errors individual techniques involve.

Critical aspects in the management of forecasting include the selection of key factors to forecast, the selection of forecast sources outside the firm, the selection of forecasting activities to be done in-house, and understanding between developers and users of the environmental forecasts.

Questions for Discussion

1. Identify five anticipated changes in the remote environment that you believe will affect major industries in the United States over the next decade. What forecasting techniques could be used to assess the probable impact of these changes?

2. Construct a matrix with forecasting techniques on the horizontal axis and at least five qualities of forecasting techniques across the vertical axis. Next, indicate the relative strengths and weaknesses of each technique.

3. Develop three *heuristics* (rules of thumb) to guide strategic managers in using forecasting.

4. Develop a two-page, typewritten forecast of a variable that you believe will affect the prosperity of your business school over the next 10 years.

5. Using prominent business journals, find two examples of firms that either profited or suffered from environmental forecasts.

6. Describe the background, skills, and abilities of the individual you would hire as the environmental forecaster for your $500-million-in-annual-sales firm. How would the qualifications differ for a smaller or larger business?

Bibliography

Drucker, P. M. *Managing in Turbulent Times*. New York: Harper & Row, 1980.

Fahey, L., and W. R. King. "Environmental Scanning for Corporate Planning." *Business Horizons,* August 1977, pp. 61–71.

Howard, Niles. "Doing Business in Unstable Countries." *Dun's Review,* March 1980, pp. 49–55.

Kast, F. "Scanning the Future Environment: Social Indications." *California Management Review,* Fall 1980, pp. 22–32.

La Bell, D., and O. J. Krasner. "Selecting Environmental Forecasting Techniques from Business Planning Requirements." *Academy of Management Review,* July 1977, pp. 373–83.

Linneman, R. E. *Shirt-Sleeve Approach to Long-Range Planning: For the Smaller, Growing Corporation*. Englewood Cliffs, N.J.: Prentice-Hall, 1980.

Linneman, R. E., and J. D. Kennell. "Shirt-Sleeve Approach to Long-Range Plans." *Harvard Business Review,* March–April 1977, pp. 141–50.

Madridakis, S., and S. Wheelwright. "Forecasting: Issues and Challenges for Marketing Management." *Journal of Marketing,* October 1977, pp. 24–38.

————, eds. *Forecasting*. New York: North Holland Publishing, 1979.

Weiss, E. "Future Public Opinion of Business." *Management Review,* March 1978, pp. 8–15.

Wheelwright, S. C., and D. G. Clarke. "Corporate Forecasting: Promise and Reality." *Harvard Business Review,* November–December 1976, pp. 40–64.

"Where the Big Econometric Models Go Wrong." *Business Week,* March 30, 1981, pp. 70–73.

Appendix

Sources for Remote Environmental and Operating Forecasts

Remote Environment

A. Economic considerations.
   1. *Predicasts* (most complete and up-to-date review of forecasts).
   2. National Bureau of Economic Research.
   3. *Handbook of Basic Economic Statistics*.
   4. *Statistical Abstract of the United States* (also includes industrial, social, and political statistics).
   5. Publications by the Department of Commerce agencies:
      a. Office of Business Economics (e.g., *Survey of Business*).
      b. Bureau of Economic Analysis (e.g., *Business Conditions Digest*).

Sources: Adapted with numerous additions from C. R. Goeldner and L. M. Kirks, "Business Facts: Where to Find Them," *MSU Business Topics,* Summer 1976, pp. 23–76, reprinted by permission of the publisher; Division of Research, Graduate School of Business Administration, MSU: F. E. deCarbonnel and R. G. Donance, "Information Source for Planning Decisions," *California Management Review,* Summer 1973, pp. 42–53; and A. B. Nun, R. C. Lenz, Jr., H. W. Landford, and M. J. Cleary, "Data Sources for Trend Extrapolation in Technological Forecasting," *Long-Range Planning,* February 1972, pp. 72–76.

      c. Bureau of the Census (e.g., *Survey of Manufacturers* and various reports of population, housing, and industries).

      d. Business and Defense Service Administration (e.g., *United States Industrial Outlook*).

  6. Securities and Exchange Commission (various quarterly reports on plant and equipment, financial reports, working capital of corporations).

  7. The Conference Board.

  8. *Survey of Buying Power.*

  9. *Marketing Economic Guide.*

10. *Industrial Arts Index.*

11. U.S. and national chambers of commerce.

12. American Manufacturers Association.

13. *Federal Reserve Bulletin.*

14. *Economic Indicators,* annual report.

15. *Kiplinger Newsletter.*

16. International economic sources:

      a. *Worldcasts.*

      b. Master key index for business international publications.

      c. Department of Commerce.

        (1) Overseas business reports.

        (2) Industry and Trade Administration.

        (3) Bureau of the Census—*Guide to Foreign Trade Statistics.*

17. Business Periodicals Index.

B. Social considerations.

  1. Public opinion polls.

  2. Surveys such as *Social Indicators* and *Social Reporting,* the annals of the American Academy of Political and Social Sciences.

  3. Current controls: Social and behavioral sciences.

  4. Abstract services and indexes for articles in sociological, psychological, and political journals.

  5. Indexes for *The Wall Street Journal, New York Times,* and other newspapers.

  6. Bureau of the Census reports on population, housing, manufacturers, selected services, construction, retail trade, wholesale trade, and enterprise statistics.

  7. Various reports from groups such as the Brookings Institution and the Ford Foundation.

  8. World Bank Atlas (population growth and GNP data).

  9. World Bank–World Development Report.

C. Political considerations.

  1. *Public Affairs Information Services Bulletin.*

  2. CIS Index (Congressional Information Index).

  3. Business periodicals.

    4. Funk & Scott (regulations by product breakdown).
    5. Weekly compilation of presidential documents.
    6. *Monthly Catalog of Government Publications*.
    7. *Federal Register* (daily announcements of pending regulations).
    8. *Code of Federal Regulations* (final listing of regulations).
    9. Business International Master Key Index (regulations, tariffs).
    10. Various state publications.
    11. Various information services (Bureau of National Affairs, Commerce Clearing House, Prentice-Hall).

D. Technological considerations.
    1. *Applied Science and Technology Index*.
    2. *Statistical Abstract of the United States*.
    3. Scientific and Technical Information Service.
    4. University reports, congressional reports.
    5. Department of Defense and military purchasing publishers.
    6. Trade journals and industrial reports.
    7. Industry contacts, professional meetings.
    8. Computer-assisted information searches.
    9. National Science Foundation annual report.
    10. *Research and Development Directory* patent records.

E. Industry considerations.
    1. *Concentration Ratios in Manufacturing* (U.S. Bureau of the Census).
    2. *Input-Output Survey* (productivity ratios).
    3. *Monthly Labor Review* (productivity ratios).
    4. *Quarterly Failure Report* (Dun & Bradstreet).
    5. *Federal Reserve Bulletin* (capacity utilization).
    6. *Report on Industrial Concentration and Product Diversification in the 1,000 Largest Manufacturing Companies* (Federal Trade Commission).
    7. Industry trade publications.
    8. Bureau of Economic Analysis, U.S. Department of Commerce (specialization ratios).

Operating Environment

A. Competition and supplier considerations.
    1. Target Group Index.
    2. U.S. Industrial Outlook.
    3. Robert Morris annual statement studies.
    4. Troy, Leo Almanac of Business & Industrial Financial Ratios.
    5. Census of Enterprise Statistics.
    6. Securities and Exchange Commission (10-K reports).
    7. Annual reports of specific companies.

8. *Fortune 500 Directory, The Wall Street Journal, Barron's, Forbes, Dun's Review.*
9. Investment services and directories: Moody's, Dun & Bradstreet, Standard & Poor's, Starch Marketing, Funk & Scott Index.
10. Trade association surveys.
11. Industry surveys.
12. Market research surveys.
13. *County Business Patterns.*
14. *County and City Data Book.*
15. Industry contacts, professional meetings, salespeople.
16. *NFIB Quarterly Economic Report for Small Business.*

B. Customer profile.
1. *Statistical Abstract of the United States,* first source of statistics.
2. *Statistical Sources* by Paul Wasserman (a subject guide to data—both domestic and international).
3. *American Statistics Index* (Congressional Information Service Guide to statistical publications of U.S. government—monthly).
4. Office of the Department of Commerce.
   a. Bureau of the Census reports on population, housing, and industries.
   b. *U.S. Census of Manufacturers* (statistics by industry, area, and products).
   c. *Survey of Current Business* (analysis of business trends, especially February and July issues).
5. Market research studies (*A Basic Bibliography on Market Review,* compiled by Robert Ferber et al., American Marketing Association).
6. *Current Sources of Marketing Information: A Bibliography of Primary Marketing Data* by Gunther & Goldstein, AMA.
7. *Guide to Consumer Markets,* The Conference Board (provides statistical information with demographic, social, and economic data—annual).
8. *Survey of Buying Power.*
9. *Predicasts* (abstracts of publishing forecasts of all industries, detailed products, and end-use data).
10. *Predicasts Basebook* (historical data from 1960 to present, covering subjects ranging from population and GNP to specific products and services; series are coded by Standard Industrial Classifications).
11. *Market Guide* (individual market surveys of over 1,500 U.S. and Canadian cities; data includes population, location, trade area, banks, principal industries, colleges and universities, department and chain stores, newspapers, retail outlets, and sales).
12. *County and City Data Book* (includes bank deposits, birth and death rates, business firms, education, employment, income of families, manufacturers, population, savings, wholesale and retail trade).

13. *Yearbook of International Trade Statistics* (UN).
14. *Yearbook of National Accounts Statistics* (UN).
15. *Statistical Yearbook* (UN—covers population, national income, agricultural and industrial production, energy, external trade and transport).
16. *Statistics of (Continents): Sources for Market Research* (includes separate books on Africa, America, Europe).

C. Key natural resources.
   1. *Minerals Yearbook, Geological Survey* (Bureau of Mines, Department of the Interior).
   2. *Agricultural Abstract* (U.S. Department of Agriculture).
   3. Statistics of electric utilities and gas pipeline companies (Federal Power Commission).
   4. Publications of various institutions: American Petroleum Institute, U.S. Atomic Energy Commission, Coal Mining Institute of America, American Steel Institute, and Brookings Institution.

Chapter 7 Cohesion Case Illustration

Environmental Forecasting at Holiday Inns, Inc.

Holiday Inns, Inc., uses several of the forecasting techniques discussed in Chapter 7 to project changes in its remote and operating environments that are of major importance to the firm's future strategic position. The greatest emphasis, even at the corporate level, is on environmental forecasting for hospitality-related factors. The primary environmental variables emphasized include the following factors:

1. Customer.
2. Social.
3. Technological.
4. Competition.

Exhibit 1 summarizes some of the forecasting techniques in terms of their focus relative to these key environmental factors.

To help understand these forecasts and how they might be useful, a few items particularly relevant to the hotel business in Exhibit 1 are illustrated below.

In better managing properties on a weekly basis to ensure operating margins are maintained, projected occupancy cycles based on historical trends can be quite helpful from the corporate level (planning cash flows) to the individual hotel level (budgeting and scheduling). Exhibit 2 shows systemwide occupancy projections for 1982 relative to actual 1981 levels. The widely fluctuating, yet historically consistent, pattern can clearly accommodate weekly scheduling and budgeting of resources.

Trend analysis, surveys, and judgmental scenarios about changing customer profiles and social characteristics constitute the major forecasting emphasis at Holiday Inns. Using these techniques, the following forecasts have been made about customer and social characteristics:

> Fewer and later marriages mean that HI's customer base has
> broadened to include a greater concentration of single persons, couples,
> and businesspeople with greater freedom to travel (42).[1]

---

[1] Numbers in parentheses refer to the appropriate paragraphs in the Cohesion Case at the end of Chapter 1.

Exhibit 1
Environmental forecasting at Holiday Inns, Inc.

Main environmental factors	Forecasting techniques		
	Trend analysis	*Surveys*	*Judgment/ scenarios*
Customers	Changing demographic profile Specific HI guest characteristics Historical occupancy rate cycles	Changing consumer preferences Perceptions and brand recognition of HI	Future travel patterns and destination areas
Social	Baby boom generation Household composition Women's changing role Use of leisure time	(little use)	Worldwide status of the travel industry
Technology	Energy-saving technology, especially in terms of automobile and hotel operation Gas prices and impact on vacation travel	(little use)	Future travel modes Computer usage in property management Communication, especially satellite, developments
Competition	Size and growth of competitors Location emphasis (regions? type of location?), key price/ value available from competition	Level of consumer name recognition Consumer image and brand preference	Which competitors represent key threats to aspects of HI operations

The demographic characteristics of the typical hotel, restaurant, and casino guest are virtually identical: age 24 to 49, income over $30,000, with a preference for reliable and quality service instead of the lowest price (42, 55).

In three out of four instances, HI guests were male, but the trend to more women travelers is steadily growing (42, 75).

The movement of the baby boom generation through the prime traveling age (25 to 45) over the next 15 years suggests unprecedented growth opportunity in the hospitality business (42, 75).

There are predictions that by the end of the century, as larger numbers of

Exhibit 2
Company-owned properties monthly domestic occupancy comparison,
1982 versus 1981 (percent)

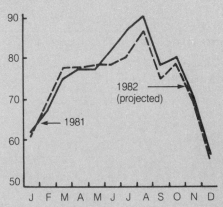

people pursue business and travel, the travel industry will have become the world's largest (74).

Using similar techniques regarding competition and technology, Holiday Inns, Inc., has developed such forecasts as:

Holiday Inn hotels will remain the brand preference of over one third of the traveling public through the 1990s (21).

Hospitality facilities located in multiuser locations will dominate industry growth and development in the 1990s (22).

Even with gasoline at $2 a gallon, highway driving habits will not change appreciably.

About 80 percent of U.S. adults approve of gambling, and 60 percent participate in some form. Gaming is fast becoming a national pastime and is viewed by the public as a leisure activity (55).

Most countries served by Delta Steamship are undergoing continued development and industrial expansion. This thrust provides a market for imports of high-value goods—of which U.S. industry is a major supplier (33, 34).

Are these forecasts accurate? Most seem plausible, although some have been previously questioned. At Best Western International, for example, a 17 percent cutback in auto travel if gas prices hit $2 a gallon is predicted. This view is shared by the American Petroleum Institute.

Holiday Inns executives disagree. They offer the following summary of their forecasts relative to the hospitality core of HI's business for the 1990s:

The decade of the 1990s offers excellent potential for the hospitality industry. Business analysts see continued growth for travel through the end of the century.

While temporary gasoline shortages have been a short-term negative factor in our operations twice in the past six years, we remain quite optimistic about gasoline availability for our customers. We expect occasional brief shortages, but by and large, we believe adequate supplies will be available.

Our optimism is fostered by a significantly more efficient car fleet and rising energy prices. The 1988 auto fleet is 55 percent more fuel efficient than its 1978 counterpart. In 1990, the average car will travel 27.5 miles per gallon of gas, a 37.5 percent increase over 1980. As gasoline prices rise, we believe the consumer will be more selective. Conservation is already becoming the rule, and needless intracity travel is being curtailed. Our research tells us that our customers will continue to use their automobiles for intercity travel and vacations. Thus, we believe we are strongly positioned for the coming decade, especially as demand for our facilities will continue to outgrow supply.

Our research shows us that the hospitality business is a good business and will remain so for as far as we can see. We look forward to the future and see continued growth, development, and profitability.

Two interesting factors that may receive increased attention at Holiday Inns for future forecasts are economic and political aspects. In the economic area, the 1981 recession was associated with poor performance years in Holiday Inns' hotel, restaurant, casino gambling, and transportation businesses. Although traditionally seen as somewhat "recession proof," these businesses are proving sensitive to economic cycles. Politically, as Holiday Inns concentrates on internal development, it will become more sensitive to such political factors as the situation in other countries and in terms of such concerns as currency exchange, regulation (of shipping, for example), and ownership restrictions.

8

The Company Profile: Internal Analysis of the Firm

Formulation of an effective strategy is based on a clear definition of company mission, an accurate appraisal of the external environment, and a thorough internal analysis of the firm. For a strategy to succeed, at least three ingredients are critical. First, the strategy must be *consistent* with conditions in the competitive environment. Specifically, it must take advantage of existing and/or projected opportunities and minimize the impact of major threats. Second, the strategy must place *realistic* requirements on the firm's internal resources and capabilities. In other words, pursuit of market opportunities must be based on key internal strengths and not only on the existence of such opportunity. Finally, the strategy must be *carefully executed*. The focus of this chapter is on the second ingredient for strategic success: realistic analysis of the firm's internal capabilities.

Internal analysis is difficult and challenging. An internal analysis that leads to a realistic company profile frequently involves trade-offs, value judgments, and educated guesses as well as objective, standardized analysis. Unfortunately, this dichotomy can lead managers to slight internal analysis by emphasizing personal opinion. But systematic internal analysis leading to an objective company profile is essential in the development of a realistic, effective strategy.

Internal analysis must identify the strategically important strengths and weaknesses on which a firm should ultimately base its strategy. Ideally, this purpose can be achieved by first identifying key internal factors (e.g., distribution channels, cash flow, locations, technology, and organizational structure) and second by evaluating these factors. In actual practice, the process is neither linear nor simple.[1] The steps tend to overlap, and managers in different positions and levels approach internal analysis in different ways. One major study found that managers even use different criteria for evaluating apparent strengths and potential weaknesses.[2] These findings will be examined in more detail later in this chapter.

While the process of internal analysis in most firms is not necessarily systematic, it is nonetheless recognized as a critical ingredient in strategy development. If only on an intuitive basis, managers develop judgments about what the firm does particularly well—its key strengths or distinct competencies. And based on the match between these strengths and defined or projected market opportunities, the firm ultimately charts its strategic course.

The Value of Systematic Internal Assessment

Before the components of internal analysis are discussed in greater detail, the impact of systematic internal analysis will be illustrated. The experiences of business firms, both large and small, suggest that thorough internal assessment is critical in developing a successful business strategy. Regardless of the favorable opportunities in the environment, a strategy must be based on a thorough consideration of internal strengths and weaknesses of the firm if such opportunities are to be maximized. Kalso Earth ® Shoes and Apple Computer Company illustrate the value of systematic internal analysis in shaping future strategies (see Figure 8–1).

Kalso Earth ® Shoes was a U.S. company that recently began making shoes based on the patented "negative-heel" design developed in Denmark by Ann Kalso. Earth ® Shoes were manufactured in Massachusetts and retailed by independent franchises throughout the United States.

Kalso Earth ® Shoes faced an impressive opportunity in the demand for its shoes among posture-conscious young professionals. Kalso's pursuit of this opportunity took precedence over *objective* internal analysis of production logistics, financial capacities, and dealer organization. The firm's single, large production facility in Massachusetts encountered difficulty in managing production runs and distribution to a nationwide network of small, franchised outlets. Each outlet ordered directly from the factory. Frequently, styles requested by outlets differed because of local market preferences. Therefore, the Kalso plant was constantly faced with the trade-off between small, inefficient production runs or, by holding orders until efficient runs were feasible, a slow response

---

[1] Howard H. Stevenson, "Defining Corporate Strengths and Weaknesses," *Sloan Management Review,* Spring 1976, pp. 51–68.

[2] Ibid., p. 65.

Figure 8–1
Kalso Earth® Shoe Company

Meet Anne Kalso . . .

We walk in a tough world. A world made of steel and concrete. A world without sympathy for our feet!

That's why Anne Kalso invented Earth® Shoes. They're designed to create underfoot the same natural terrain that existed before the earth was paved.

Patterned in the form of a healthy footprint in soft earth, the Earth® Shoe promises unsurpassed comfort and a new way of walking.

During her studies and experiments, Anne Kalso observed that by flexing the foot or lowering the heel, one could achieve a physical feeling similar to that attained in the Lotus or Buddah position of Yoga. Her further observations of foot imprints in sand, confirmed to her that nature intended people to walk with the weight of their bodies sunk low into the heels.

about the EARTH®
natural heel shoe.

Wearing the EARTH® Shoe, you will experience a completely new way of walking that might take some getting used to. Initially, you may feel off-balance because of the natural heel. This is normal so don't be alarmed. Young people adapt very quickly, older people take a little longer. . .

In effect, you are walking barefoot on the beach . . . or across summer fields . . . wherever you go. Because walking in EARTH® Shoes is a form of exercise, some may at first experience stiffness in the calves or thighs; some may find our unique arch may take getting used to; so moderate wear is advised in the beginning.

The uniquely contoured sole will allow you to walk in a gentle rolling motion. This helps to develop a more natural, graceful walk. There is no reason why you cannot interchange the use of other shoes with the EARTH® Shoes.

The human foot carries the entire weight load of our bodies and as we walk, this weight is constantly shifting.

The first point of contact, the heel **❶**, takes the brunt of the load which then shifts to the outside of the foot **❷**, and then across the metatarsal area to the ball **❸**, and finally onto the large toe **❹** from which we spring into our next step.

The EARTH® Shoe is specifically designed to accommodate the shifting of weight load on our feet with the greatest ease and comfort.

Another feature of the EARTH® Shoe is the unique arch support.

Style 110 is the classic walking shoe. Our most popular all-around casual shoe. Available in sizes 6½ - 11 for women, and 7 - 11½ for men. Colors are Almond (medium brown) and Syrup (light tan).

Style 150 is a rugged, moccasin-toe oxford featuring an attractive closed-stitched design. Available in sizes 6½ - 11 for women, and 7 - 11½ for men. Colors are Almond and Sand Suede.

to consumer demand. Each outlet was an autonomous distributor/retailer linked directly to the Massachusetts production facility.

Kalso's financial structure presented additional difficulties. The company sought to finance increasing demand through short-term borrowing and the leveraging available through franchising. Kalso management wanted to maintain tight control over ownership of the firm, which they considered critical to maintaining the quality associated with its patented, negative-heel design. The popularity of its product and demand for franchises increased, but Kalso's pressed financial structure could not support such rapid growth.

As a result of Kalso's production logistics, distribution system, and emphasis on short-term debt, Kalso became overextended and failed. This happened even as the demand for its negative-heel design was escalating. Kalso Earth ® Shoes' strategy, even given an enviable market opportunity, was not based on a systematic objective analysis of its internal strengths and weaknesses.

IBM's meteoric rise in the personal computer market during the early 1980s raised significant challenges for Apple Computer Company. While it pioneered the personal computer industry, Apple saw its market share rapidly descend. Apple had grown rapidly, employing almost 5,000 people by the mid-1980s. These people were divided into product-centered divisions, with significant autonomy and a zealous independence reflecting the entrepreneurial personality of the company's youthful cofounder, Steven Jobs. Apple personnel succeeded in persuading Jobs to run a full-page ad in *The Wall Street Journal* when IBM brought out its IBM PC, welcoming IBM into the personal computer industry. Apple personnel were confident that their ingenuity, spirit, unique and growing product lines, and strong educational market position would keep them toe to toe with IBM.

By 1985, Apple found itself reeling from a series of heavy quarterly losses. Its two early attempts to attract business customers with the Apple III and Lisa computers had failed, and Macintosh (the product on which the company bet its future) shipments were running only 10,000 per month versus Apple's 80,000-per-month capacity to make the machine. John Sculley (see Figure 8–2), after replacing Jobs as chairman of Apple, sought to realistically identify internal key strengths around which Apple could rebuild its competitive position. Sculley saw four—its Macintosh computer, its desktop publishing software and peripherals to go with the Macintosh, its user-friendly product capabilities, and its strong position in the educational market. Sculley devised a careful strategy centered on these four strengths. Over 50,000 Macintosh publishing systems were sold in 1986 alone, and by 1988 Macintosh had become the de facto industry standard in news graphics and desktop publishing. This success, and its lock in the educational market, allowed Sculley to personally lead a marketing effort targeted toward large, personal service companies and technology-driven companies to make them aware of the user-friendly attributes of the product. Finally, he totally reorganized and centralized the company around functions rather than the old product-based fiefdoms, which eliminated

Figure 8–2

20 percent of Apple's overhead and provided greater consistency in the focus of Apple's marketing efforts. By 1988, Apple's sales were growing at twice the rate of the PC industry, and profit margins were triple those of the mid-1980s.

Apple faced a major threat to its survival as a serious player in the personal computer business. Its strategy was based on attributes representing emotionally charged feelings among executives and founders rather than on objectively assessed strengths and weaknesses. Its new chairman, John Sculley, focused objectively and intensely on rather limited internal strengths as a basis for Apple's subsequent strategy. And, just as some industry watchers were writing Apple's obituary as a serious player in the industry, Apple has reemerged as a major factor in both business and educational sectors of the personal computer industry.

Systematic internal analysis is particularly essential in small business firms. Small firms are continually faced with limited resources and markets. At the same time, these firms are flexible and capable of making specialized, uniquely catered responses to selected market needs. To effectively channel their limited resources in directions that maximize these limited market opportunities, small firms must frequently make objective internal analyses.

Given these brief illustrations of the value of systematic internal analysis, it is appropriate to examine the process in more detail.

Developing the Company Profile

A company profile is the determination of a firm's strategic competencies and weaknesses. This is accomplished by identifying and then evaluating strategic internal factors.

What are strategic internal factors? Where do they originate? How do we decide which are truly strategic factors that must be carefully evaluated? These questions might be raised by managers in identifying and evaluating key internal factors as strengths or weaknesses on which to base the firm's future strategy.

Identification of Strategic Internal Factors

A Function Approach.   Strategic internal factors are a firm's basic capabilities, limitations, and characteristics. Figure 8–3 lists typical factors, some of which would be the focus of internal analysis in most business firms. This list of factors is broken down along functional lines.

Firms are not likely to consider all of the factors in Figure 8–3 as potential strengths or weaknesses. To develop or revise a strategy, managers would rather identify the few factors on which success will most likely depend. Equally important, reliance on different internal factors will vary by industry, market segment, product life cycle, and the firm's current position. Managers are looking for what Chester Barnard calls "the strategic factors," those internal capabilities that appear most critical for success in a particular competitive area.[3] For example, strategic factors for firms in the oil industry will be quite different from those of firms in the construction or hospitality industries. Strategic factors can also vary between firms within the same industry. In the mechanical writing industry, for example, the strategies of BIC and Cross, both successful, are based on different internal strengths: BIC's on its strengths in mass production, extensive advertising, and mass distribution channels; Cross's on high quality, image, and selective distribution channels.

Strategists examine past performance to isolate key internal contributors to favorable (or unfavorable) results. What did we do well, or poorly, in marketing, operations, and financial management that had a major influence on past results? Was the sales force effectively organized? Were we in the right channels of distribution? Did we have the financial resources to support the past strategy? The same examination and questions can be applied to a firm's current situation, with particular emphasis on changes in the importance of key dimensions over time. For example, heavy advertising along with mass production and mass distribution were strategic internal factors in BIC's initial

---

[3] Chester Barnard, *Functions of the Executive* (Cambridge, Mass.: Harvard University Press, 1939), chap. 14.

Figure 8–3
Key internal factors: Potential strengths and weaknesses

Marketing

Firm's products/services; breadth of product line.
Concentration of sales in a few products or to a few customers.
Ability to gather needed information about markets.
Market share or submarket shares.
Product/service mix and expansion potential: life cycle of key products; profit/sales balance in product/service.
Channels of distribution: number, coverage, and control.
Effective sales organization; knowledge of customer needs.
Product/service image, reputation, and quality.
Imaginative, efficient, and effective sales promotion and advertising.
Pricing strategy and pricing flexibility.
Procedures for digesting market feedback and developing new products, services, or markets.
After-sale service and follow-up.
Goodwill/brand loyalty.

Finance and accounting

Ability to raise short-term capital.
Ability to raise long-term capital: debt/equity.
Corporate-level resources (multibusiness firm).
Cost of capital relative to industry and competitors.
Tax considerations.
Relations with owners, investors, and stockholders.
Leverage position: capacity to utilize alternative financial strategies, such as lease or sale and leaseback.
Cost of entry and barriers to entry.
Price–earnings ratio.
Working capital; flexibility of capital structure.
Effective cost control; ability to reduce cost.
Financial size.
Efficient and effective accounting system for cost, budget, and profit planning.

Production/operations/technical

Raw materials cost and availability; supplier relationships.
Inventory control systems; inventory turnover.
Location of facilities; layout and utilization of facilities.
Economies of scale.
Technical efficiency of facilities and utilization of capacity.
Effective use of subcontracting.
Degree of vertical integration; value added and profit margin.
Efficiency and cost/benefit of equipment.
Effective operation control procedures: design, scheduling, purchasing, quality control, and efficiency.
Costs and technological competencies relative to industry and competitors.
Research and development/technology/innovation.
Patents, trademarks, and similar legal protection.

Personnel

Management personnel.
Employees' skill and morale.
Labor relations costs compared to industry and competition.

Figure 8–3 *(concluded)*

Efficient and effective personnel policies.
Effective use of incentives to motivate performance.
Ability to level peaks and valleys of employment.
Employee turnover and absenteeism.
Specialized skills.
Experience.

Organization of general management

Organizational structure.
Firm's image and prestige.
Firm's record for achieving objectives.
Organization of communication system.
Overall organizational control system (effectiveness and utilization).
Organizational climate; culture.
Use of systematic procedures and techniques in decision making.
Top-management skill, capabilities, and interest.
Strategic planning system.
Intraorganizational synergy (multibusiness firms).

strategy for ballpoint pens and disposable lighters. With the product life cycle fast reaching maturity, BIC has currently determined that cost-conscious mass production is a strategic factor, while heavy advertising is not.

Analysis of past trends in sales, costs, and profitability is of major importance in identifying strategic internal factors. And this identification should be based on a clear picture of the nature of the firm's sales. An anatomy of past trends broken down by product lines, channels of distribution, key customers or types of customers, geographic region, and sales approach should be developed in detail. A similar anatomy should focus on costs and profitability. Detailed investigation of the firm's performance history helps isolate internal factors influencing sales, costs, profitability, or their interrelationships. These factors are of major importance to future strategy decisions. For example, one firm may find that 83 percent of its sales result from 25 percent of its products. Another firm may find that 30 percent of its products (or services) contribute 78 percent of its profitability. To understand such results, a firm may determine that certain key internal factors (e.g., experience in particular distribution channels, pricing policies, warehouse location, technology) deserve major attention in formulating future strategy.

Identifying strategic factors also requires an external focus. When a strategist isolates key internal factors through analysis of past and present performance, industry conditions/trends and comparisons with competitors also provide insight. BIC's identification of mass production and advertising as key internal factors is based as much on analysis of industry and competitive characteristics as on past performance of BIC itself. Changing industry conditions can lead to the need to reexamine internal strengths and weaknesses

Strategy in Action 8–1
Merrill Lynch's Strategic Internal Factors: Are They Strengths or Weaknesses?

As deregulation melds together the once-segmented financial service industries, Merrill Lynch faces increasing direct competition from Sears Roebuck, American Express, Citicorp, and other formidable companies outside the securities industry. While Merrill Lynch has proved itself the equal of anyone in innovating financial products and services, in the way it delivers them to consumers, in its compensation methods, and in its corporate culture, Merrill Lynch remains quintessentially a brokerage house.

Merrill Lynch's attempt to strike a balance between old Wall Street and the emergence of one-stop financial shopping has trapped it in a truly nasty dilemma. The company's greatest strength—its retail system of 431 branch offices and 8,763 brokers—may have become its greatest weakness. By funneling nearly all of its growing number of financial products through its brokers, Merrill Lynch generates huge sales volume. But because its brokers get a cut of all they sell, this approach is very expensive. And its inflexibility makes Merrill Lynch vulnerable at a time when discount brokering and other low-cost distribution methods are gaining market share.

But any attempt to tamper with Merrill Lynch's retail sales organization is perilous because the broker—not the company—typically commands customer loyalty. "My customers are my blanket," said one veteran Merrill Lynch broker. "I can just pick them up and walk away." Merrill Lynch has gingerly begun to walk a fine line between remaking its vaunted broker system and destroying it. The company has raised its performance standards for brokers and is beginning to weed out the laggards. It has also begun the delicate task of converting the broker into a financial adviser at the hub of a network of salaried sales assistants and professionals who specialize in insurance, lending, and tax matters.

Some veteran brokers are disillusioned by the trend toward one-stop financial shopping, while the performance crackdown stirs resentment among the newcomers. "Merrill Lynch is losing touch with its distribution system," claims a senior executive of a major Wall Street firm. "It's become a case of the home office proposing and the field disposing." The erosion of Merrill Lynch's legendary morale has made it easier for his company to lure away brokers, he says.

Merrill's vice president for human resources insists that the turnover rate among Merrill Lynch's sales force is "trending sideways at an acceptable level" and that most of those brokers who do leave are not top performers. Still, Merrill

Continued on Page 211

Strategy in Action 8–1 (*concluded*)

Lynch was one of the first firms to sue former brokers who allegedly violated pledges not to take their customers with them to other firms.

Especially at a time of internal tension, Merrill Lynch's monolithic retail distribution system is a cumbersome way of serving an unsettled market. Discount brokers, which do not pay commissions to their brokers, tripled their share of equity trading volume to 24 percent by the mid-1980s.

Meanwhile, many full-service brokers are expanding their branch systems at a furious pace. "The name of the game in the financial services industry is distribution," said James Settel, a senior vice president at Prudential Bache. "The more good distribution points you have, the better are your chances of picking up all the marbles."

Dean Witter Reynolds Inc., now part of Sears Roebuck & Company, plans to nearly double its branches and to increase its corps of brokers from 4,900 to 11,000 by 1991. About 280 of the offices will be in Sears stores.

Roger Birk, Merrill Lynch board chairman, recognized the difficulty in first identifying and acting on the brokerage firm's strengths and weaknesses in the changing financial services industry. Birk seems undaunted. "Who ever said it would be easy? It's not," he says. "This is a tough business—a very difficult business to manage."

Source: Based on the article "Merrill Lynch's Big Dilemma," from the January 6, 1984, issue of *Business Week*.

in light of newly emerging determinants of success in the industry. Strategy in Action 8–1 illustrates a strategic shift in Merrill Lynch's internal strengths and weaknesses based on changing determinants of success in the financial services industry. Furthermore, strategic internal factors are often chosen for in-depth evaluation because firms are contemplating expansion of products or markets, diversification, and so forth. Clearly, scrutinizing the industry under consideration and current competitors is a key means of identifying strategic factors if a firm is evaluating its capability to move into unfamiliar markets.

The "Value Chain" Approach.   Diagnosing a company's key strengths and weaknesses requires the adoption of a disaggregated view of the firm. Examining the firm across distinct functional areas, as suggested above and in Figure 8–3, is one way to disaggregate the firm for internal analysis purposes. Another way to disaggregate the firm is to use a framework called the "value chain." Developed by Michael Porter in his book *Competitive Advantage,* a value chain is a systematic way of viewing the series of activities a firm performs to provide a product to its customers. Figure 8–4 diagrams a typical value chain. The value chain disaggregates a firm into its strategically relevant activities in order to understand the behavior of the firm's cost and its existing or

Figure 8–4
The value chain

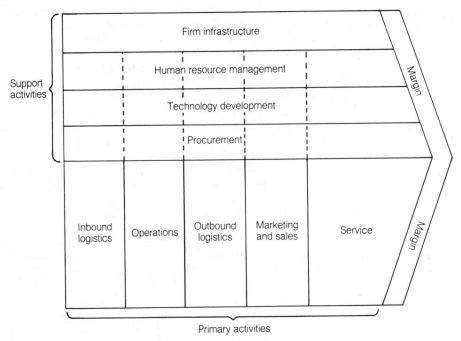

potential sources of differentiation. A firm gains competitive advantage by performing these strategically important activities—what we have called *key internal factors*—more cheaply or better than its competitors.

Every firm can be viewed (disaggregated) as a collection of value activities that are performed to design, produce, market, deliver, and support its product.

As portrayed in Figure 8–4, these activities can be grouped into nine basic categories for virtually any firm at the business unit level. Within each category of activity, a firm typically performs a number of discrete activities that may represent key strengths or weaknesses for the firm. Service activities, for example, may include such discrete activities as installation, repair, parts distribution, and upgrading—any of which could be a major source of competitive advantage or disadvantage. Through the systematic identification of these discrete activities, managers using the value chain approach can target potential strengths and weaknesses for further evaluation.

The basic categories of activities can be grouped into two broad types. *Primary* activities are those involved in the physical creation of the firm's product or service, its delivery and marketing to the buyer, and its after-sale support. Overarching each of these are *support* activities, which provide inputs or infrastructure allowing the primary activities to take place on an ongoing basis.

Identifying Primary Activities.   Identifying primary value activities requires the isolation of activities that are technologically and strategically distinct. Each of the five basic categories of primary activities is divisible into several distinct activities, such as the following:

Inbound Logistics: Activities associated with receiving, storing, and disseminating inputs to the product, such as material handling, warehousing, inventory control, vehicle scheduling, and returns to suppliers.

Operations: Activities associated with transforming inputs into the final product form, such as machining, packaging, assembly, equipment maintenance, testing, printing, and facility operations.

Outbound Logistics: Activities associated with collecting, storing, and physically distributing the product to buyers, such as finished goods warehousing, material handling, delivery vehicle operation, order processing, and scheduling.

Marketing and Sales: Activities associated with providing a means by which buyers can purchase the product and inducing them to do so, such as advertising, promotion, sales force, quoting, channel selection, channel relations, and pricing.

Service: Activities associated with providing service to enhance or maintain the value of the product, such as installation, repair, training, parts supply, and product adjustment.[4]

The primary activities most deserving of further analysis depend on the particular industry. For example, Holiday Inns may be much more concerned about operations activities—it provides its service instantaneously at each location—and marketing/sales activities than it is about outbound logistics. For a distributor, such as the food distributor PYA, inbound and outbound logistics are the most critical areas. After-sale service is becoming increasingly critical to automotive dealerships. Yet, in any firm, all the primary activities are present to some degree and deserve attention in a systematic internal analysis.

Identifying Support Activities.   Support value activities arise in one of four categories and can be identified or disaggregated by isolating technologically or strategically distinct activities. Often overlooked as sources of competitive advantage, these four areas can typically be distinguished as follows:

Procurement: Activities involved in obtaining purchased inputs, whether raw materials, purchased services, machinery, or so on. Procurement stretches

---

[4] Michael E. Porter, *Competitive Advantage* (New York: Free Press, 1985), pp. 39–40.

across the entire value chain because it supports every activity—every activity uses purchased inputs of some kind. Many discrete procurement activities are typically performed within a firm, often by different people.

Technology Development: Activities involved in designing the product as well as in creating and improving the way the various activities in the value chain are performed. We tend to think of technology in terms of the product or manufacturing process. In fact, every activity a firm performs involves a technology or technologies, which may be mundane or sophisticated, and a firm has a stock of know-how for performing each activity. Technology development typically involves a variety of discrete activities, some performed outside the R&D department.

Human Resource Management: Activities necessary to ensure the recruiting, training, and development of personnel. Every activity involves human resources, and thus human resource management activities cut across the entire chain.

Firm Infrastructure: Such activities as general management, accounting, legal, finance, strategic planning, and all others decoupled from specific primary or support activities but essential to the entire chain's operation.[5]

Using the Value Chain in Internal Analysis.   The value chain provides a useful approach to guide a systematic internal analysis of the firm's existing or potential strengths and weaknesses. By systematically disaggregating a firm into its distinct value activities across the nine activity categories, the strategist has identified key internal factors for further examination as potential sources of competitive advantage.

Whether using the value chain, an examination of functional areas, or both approaches, the strategist's next step in a systematic internal analysis is to compare the firm's status with meaningful standards to determine which value activities are strengths or weaknesses. Four sources of meaningful standards used to evaluate internal factors and value activities are discussed in the next section.

Evaluation of Strategic Internal Factors

Identification and evaluation of key internal factors have been separated for discussion, but in practice they are not separate, distinct steps. The objective of internal analysis is a careful determination of a firm's strategic strengths

---

[5] Michael Porter, "Changing Patterns of International Competition," *California Management Review* 28, no. 2 (1986), p. 14.

and weaknesses. An internal analysis that generates a long list of resources and capabilities has provided little to help in strategy formulation. Instead, internal analysis must identify and evaluate a limited number of strengths and weaknesses relative to the opportunities targeted in the firm's current and future competitive environment.

What are potential strengths and weaknesses? A factor is considered a strength if it is a distinct competency or competitive advantage. It is more than merely what the firm has the competence to do. It is something the firm does (or has the future capacity to do) particularly well relative to abilities of existing or potential competitors. A distinctive competence (strength) is important because it gives an organization a comparative advantage in the marketplace. For example, Kalso Earth ® Shoes' product image and patented design were two distinct competencies for that firm.

A factor is considered a weakness if it is something the firm does poorly or doesn't have the capacity to do although key rivals have the capacity. Centralized production facilities and lack of capital resources were major weaknesses for Kalso Earth ® Shoes in trying to compete with other shoe manufacturers on a nationwide basis. Scripto's outdated production facilities and lack of financial resources to support mass advertising were major weaknesses. The firm's management had to weigh these factors in deciding to challenge BIC in the ball-point segment of the writing implement industry.

How should strategists evaluate key internal factors and value activities as strengths or weaknesses? There are four basic perspectives: (1) comparison with the firm's past performance, (2) stage of product/market evolution, (3) comparison with competitors, and (4) comparison with key success factors in the firm's industry.

Comparison with Past Capabilities and Performance.   Strategists use the historical experience of the firm as a basis for evaluating internal factors. Managers are most familiar with their firm, its internal capabilities and problems, because they have been immersed over time in managing the firm's financial, marketing, production, and R&D activities. Not surprisingly, a manager's assessment of whether certain internal factors—such as production facilities, sales organization, financial capacity, control systems, and key personnel—are strengths or weaknesses will be strongly influenced by his or her internal experience. In the capital-intensive airline industry, for example, debt capacity is a strategic internal factor. Delta Airlines has a debt/equity ratio of less than 0.6, which is comparable to its past debt/equity ratio. Delta views this as a continued strength, representing significant flexibility to support Delta managers in deciding to invest in facilities or equipment. Yet Piedmont managers also view their 1.5 debt/equity ratio as a growing strength because it is down 100 percent from its 3.0 level in the early 1980s.

While historical experience can provide a relevant evaluation framework, strategists must avoid tunnel vision. Texaco management, for example, had long considered its large number of service stations (27,000 in 1980) a key strength. This strength (along with other perceived strengths) had "worked so well for so long [at Texaco] that even the thought of changing them was heretical to management."[6] But Shell, with just over 6,280 service stations, sold slightly more gasoline than Texaco.[7] Clearly, using only historical experience as a basis for identifying strengths and weaknesses can prove dangerously inaccurate.

Stages in Product/Market Evolution.　The requirements for success in product/market segments evolve and change over time. As a result, strategists can use these changing patterns associated with different stages in product/ market evolution as a framework for identifying and evaluating the firm's strengths and weaknesses.

Figure 8–5 depicts four general stages of product/market evolution and the typical changes in functional capabilities often associated with business success at each stage. The early development of a product/market, for example, entails minimal growth in sales, major R&D emphasis, rapid technological change in the product, operating losses, and a need for sufficient resources or slack to support a temporarily unprofitable operation. Success at this stage may be associated with technical skill with being first in new markets or with having a marketing advantage that creates widespread awareness. Radio Shack's initial success with its TRS-80 home computer was based in part on its ability to gain widespread exposure and acceptance in the ill-defined home computer market via the large number of existing Radio Shack outlets throughout the country.

The strengths necessary for success change in the growth stage. Rapid growth brings new competitors into the market. Such factors as brand recognition, product/market differentiation, and the financial resources to support both heavy marketing expenses and the effect of price competition on cash flow can be key strengths at this stage. IBM entered the personal computer market in the growth stage and was able to rapidly become the market leader with a strategy based on key strengths in brand awareness and the financial resources to support consumer advertising.

As the product/market moves through a "shakeout" phase and into the maturity stage, market growth continues but at a decreasing rate. The number of market segments begins to expand, while technological change in product design slows considerably. The result is usually more intense competition, and promotional or pricing advantages or differentiation become key internal

---

[6] "Texaco: Restoring Luster to the Star," *Business Week,* December 22, 1980, p. 54; and "Inside the Shell Oil Company," *Newsweek,* June 15, 1981, p. 74.

[7] "Texaco," p. 60.

Figure 8–5
Sources of distinctive competence at different stages of product/market evolution

Growth rate <0

Unit sales

Market growth rate = Population growth rate

Profits (dollars)

Takeoff

Functional area	Introduction	Growth	Maturity	Decline
Marketing	Resources/skill to create widespread awareness and find acceptance from customers; advantageous access to distribution	Ability to establish brand recognition; find niche; reduce price; solidify strong distribution relations and develop new channels	Skill in aggressively promoting products to new markets and holding existing markets; pricing flexibility; skills in differentiating products and holding customer loyalty	Cost-effective means of efficient access to selected channels and markets; strong customer loyalty or dependence; strong company image
Production/operations	Ability to expand capacity effectively; limit number of designs; develop standards	Ability to add product variants; centralize production or otherwise lower costs; improve product quality; seasonal subcontracting capacity	Improve product and reduce costs; ability to share or reduce capacity; advantageous supplier relationships; subcontracting	Ability to prune product line; cost advantage in production, location, or distribution; simplified inventory control; subcontracting or long production runs
Finance	Resources to support high net cash overflow and initial losses; ability to use leverage effectively	Ability to finance rapid expansion; still have net cash outflows but increasing profits; resources to support product improvements	Ability to generate and redistribute increasing net cash inflows; effective cost control systems	Ability to reuse or liquidate unneeded equipment; advantage in cost of facilities; control system accuracy; streamlined management control
Personnel	Flexibility in staffing and training new management; existence of employee with key skills in new products or markets	Existence and ability to add skilled personnel; motivated and loyal work force	Ability to cost effectively reduce work force; increase efficiency	Capacity to reduce and reallocate personnel; cost advantage
Engineering and research and development	Ability to make engineering changes; have technical bugs in product and process resolved	Skill in quality and new feature development; state developing successor product	Reduce costs; develop variants to differentiate products	Support other growth areas or apply to unique customer needs
Key functional area and strategy focus	Engineering; market penetration	Sales; consumer loyalty; market share	Production efficiency; successor products	Finance; maximum investment recovery

Source: Adapted from Peter Doyle, "The Realities of the Product Life Cycle," *Quarterly Review of Marketing,* Summer 1976, pp. 1–6; Harold Fox, "A Framework for Functional Coordination," *Atlantic Economic Review,* November–December 1973; Charles W. Hofer, *Conceptual Constructs for Formulating Corporate and Business Strategy* (Boston: Intercollegiate Case Clearing House, 1977), p. 7; Philip Kotler, *Marketing Management* (Englewood Cliffs, N.J.: Prentice-Hall, 1988); and Charles Wasson, *Dynamic Competitive Strategy and Product Life Cycles* (Austin, Tex.: Austin Press, 1978).

strengths. Technological change in process design becomes intense as the many competitors seek to provide the product in the most efficient manner. Where R&D was critical in the development stage, efficient production has now become crucial to a business's continued success in the broader market segments. Chrysler has found efficiency a key strength in the maturing auto industry.

When products/markets move toward a saturation/decline stage, strengths and weaknesses center on cost advantages, superior supplier or customer relationships, and financial control. Competitive advantage can exist at this stage, at least temporarily, if a firm serves gradually shrinking markets that competitors are choosing to leave. Strategy in Action 8–2 describes Radio Shack's efforts to reexamine its strengths and weaknesses in the rapidly maturing consumer electronics market.

Figure 8–5 is a rather simple model of the stages of product/market evolution. These stages can and do vary. But it is important to realize, especially as illustrated in the preceding discussion, that the relative importance of various determinants of success differs across stages of product/market evolution. Thus, stage of evolution must be considered in internal analysis. Figure 8–5 suggests different dimensions that are particularly deserving of in-depth consideration when developing a company profile.

Comparison with Competitors. A major focus in determining a firm's strengths and weaknesses is comparison with existing (and potential) competitors. Firms in the same industry often have different marketing skills, financial resources, operating facilities and locations, technical know-how, brand image, levels of integration, managerial talent, and so on. These different internal capabilities can become relative strengths (or weaknesses) depending on the strategy the firm chooses. In choosing strategy, a manager should compare the company's key internal capabilities with those of its rivals, thereby isolating key strengths or weaknesses.

In the major home appliance industry, for example, Sears and General Electric are major rivals. Sears' major strength is its retail network. For GE, distribution—through independent franchised dealers—has traditionally been a relative weakness. With the financial resources to support modernized mass production, GE has maintained both cost and technological advantages over its rivals, particularly Sears. This major strength for GE is a relative weakness for Sears, which depends solely on subcontracting to produce its Kenmore brand appliances. On the other hand, maintenance and repair service are important in the appliance industry. Historically, Sears has strength in this area because it maintains a fully staffed service component and spreads the costs over numerous departments at each retail location. GE, on the other hand, has had to depend on regional service centers and local contracting with independent service firms by its local, independent dealers.

In ultimately developing a strategy, distribution network, technological capabilities, operating costs, and service facilities are a few of the internal factors Sears and GE must consider. To ascertain whether their internal capabilities on these and other factors are strengths or weaknesses, comparison to key competitors can prove useful. Significant favorable differences (existing or expected) are potential cornerstones of the firm's strategy. Likewise, through comparison to major competitors, a firm may avoid strategic commitments it cannot competitively support.

Success Factors in the Industry. Industry analysis involves identifying factors associated with successful participation in a given industry. As was

Strategy in Action 8–2
Internal Analysis at Radio Shack

After almost completely missing the VCR boom of the mid-1980s and also seeing its share of the personal computer market erode from 19 percent in the early 1980s to 8.6 percent by 1985, Radio Shack (Tandy) executives decided serious internal analysis was necessary if the highly successful electronics retailer was to regain its prominence in that industry. Radio Shack had been a profitable, resourceful retailer of electrical equipment (such as antenna wires, radios, electronic parts, telephones, stereos, CB radios, and radar) that entered the personal computer market at its infancy, taking prime advantage of its 6,800 locations in the United States and Canada. Executives arrived at the following assessment after six months of thorough analysis:

Strengths

1. 6,800 retail locations.
2. Fully integrated producer.
3. Low-cost capabilities.

Weaknesses

1. Poor market research (totally misprojected VCR demand; company sells 10 percent of all audio equipment in United States but 1 percent of VCRs; phone sales 150 percent below projections).
2. Poor computer brand name (TRS-80 known as "Trash-80").
3. Computers not IBM compatible; lack software.
4. Store appearance more suited to hobbyist.
5. Prices above industry median.

Radio Shack used this assessment as input for decisions about a new strategy. Elements of Radio Shack's new strategy include:

1. Sell low-priced, IBM-compatible computers to individuals and very small businesses.
2. Use the Radio Shack and Tandy brand names and provide retail store-based training service to computer customers.
3. Revamp store appearance to attract women shoppers.

Continued on Page 220

> Strategy in Action 8–2 (*concluded*)
>
> 4. Focus on price-competitive versions of consumer electronic products in Radio Shack's traditional product areas.
> 5. Diversify into other discount electronics chains to take advantage of Tandy's highly integrated production capabilities.

true of the evaluation methods discussed above, the key determinants of success in an industry may be used to identify the internal strengths and weaknesses of a firm. By scrutinizing industry competitors, as well as customer needs, vertical industry structure, channels of distribution, costs, barriers to entry, availability of substitutes, and suppliers, a strategist seeks to determine whether a firm's current internal capabilities represent strengths or weaknesses in new competitive arenas. The previous discussion in Chapter 7 provides a useful framework—five industry forces—against which to examine potential strengths and weaknesses. General Cinema Corporation, the nation's largest movie theater operator, determined that its internal skills in marketing, site analysis, creative financing, and management of geographically dispersed operations provided key strengths relative to major success factors in the soft-drink bottling industry. This assessment proved accurate. Since entering the soft drink bottling industry in 1968, General Cinema has become the largest franchised bottler of soft drinks in the United States, handling Pepsi, 7UP, Dr Pepper, and Sunkist. Eastern Airlines, however, based its strategy on strengths and weaknesses derived from a historical comparison more so than an industry perspective. Strategy in Action 8–3 shows how this hurt Eastern in the long run.

Use of industry-level analysis to evaluate a firm's capacity for success and to help devise future strategy has become a popular technique.[8] Its relevance as an aid to comprehensive internal analysis is discussed more fully in a subsequent section of this chapter.

Quantitative versus Qualitative Approaches in Evaluating Internal Factors

Numerous quantitative tools are available for evaluating selected internal capabilities of a firm. These entail measurement of a firm's effectiveness vis-à-vis each relevant factor and comparative analysis of this measurement against both competitors (directly or through industry averages) and the historical experience of the firm. Ratio analysis is useful for evaluating selected financial, marketing, and operating factors. The firm's balance sheet and in-

---

[8] Michael E. Porter, *Competitive Strategy: Techniques for Analyzing Industries and Competitors* (New York: Free Press, 1980), offers broad, in-depth coverage of numerous techniques for evaluating the strengths and weaknesses of a firm and its competitors. Chapter 7 presents key aspects underlying Professor Porter's analytical approaches.

Strategy in Action 8–3
Eastern Airlines "Misses the Boat"

Eastern, seeking to calm nervous investors and employees, went to unusual lengths to communicate the basis for its 1984–85 corporate strategy. One key ingredient was its assessment of internal capabilities. Six key points were presented by Eastern management:

1. We will have the resources to substantially expand our operation.
   a. An average of 13 additional aircraft, primarily B-757s delivered in 1983, will be available for scheduled service.
   b. The pilot agreement permits additional hours to be flown with the existing work force. Similar productivity improvements are expected to limit the required increase in other personnel.
2. There are identified schedule opportunities at our established hubs for using the additional aircraft.
   a. Restoration of daytime service to the levels that preceded the air traffic controllers' (PATCO) strike at Atlanta and LaGuardia alone would effectively use the 13 aircraft.
3. Our position in the marketplace has been strong and improving.
   a. As measured by revenue per airplane seat-mile (ASM), we led all major airlines in 1982 and continued to outperform the industry in the first quarter of 1983.
4. Committed increases in employee compensation require increases in productivity that realistically can be achieved through both normal attrition and basic airline expansion.
   a. The pilot agreement includes improvements in productivity that are fundamental to our success. Similar improvements must be made elsewhere in the corporation.
5. In the aftermath of recent negotiations with the airline mechanics union, employee attitudes—morale and the willingness of different groups to work together—clearly are a major concern. Effectively addressing this issue is a major challenge for 1984.
6. Our balance sheet and cash situation require constant attention.

Eastern's management identified excess capacity as a key strength, ASM performance as an indicator of high customer demand (even though Eastern's high ASM is artificially high due to its New York-to-DC commuter service), financial position as a weakness, and morale/productivity as a pivotal question mark.

Continued on Page 222

Strategy in Action 8–3 (*concluded*)

But all of these were primarily based on Eastern's history rather than on comparison with competitors and changing requirements for success in the airline industry. The airline industry was rapidly changing, and competitive pressures were increasing. As a result, Eastern's strategy failed. Eastern subsequently avoided bankruptcy in late 1986 by selling out to Texas Air.

come statement are important sources from which to derive meaningful ratios. The appendix at the end of this chapter illustrates the use of these techniques for internal analysis.

Dun & Bradstreet and Robert Morris Associates regularly publish sets of ratios for a variety of industries.[9] Trade publications for specific types of firms are another source of comparative information. Information from these sources and from the firm's past performance are useful if ratio analysis is used to evaluate an internal factor. Examples of other quantitative or analytical tools include cash flow analysis, sensitivity analysis, and elasticity and variability analysis.[10]

Quantitative tools cannot be applied to all internal factors, and the normative judgments of key planning participants may be used in evaluation. Company or product image and prestige are examples of internal factors more amenable to qualitative evaluation. But, even though qualitative and judgmental criteria are used, identification and serious evaluation of this type of factor are necessary and important aspects of a thorough internal analysis. Research by Harold Stevenson found this to be particularly true in evaluating weaknesses.[11] Stevenson interviewed 50 executives in six medium to large firms and found the following criteria used to identify and evaluate strengths and weaknesses:

	Degree of use	
Type of criteria	*Strengths*	*Weaknesses*
Historical experience	90%	10%
Industry/competitor comparison	67	33
Normative judgment	21	79

---

[9] *Dun's Review,* published monthly by Dun & Bradstreet, N.Y.; RMA: *Annual Statement Studies* published annually by Robert Morris Associates, Philadelphia.

[10] O. M. Joy, *Introduction to Financial Management* (Homewood, Ill.: Richard D. Irwin, 1980), pp. 119–28, 207–9, provides a useful discussion of cash flow analysis and sensitivity analysis; C. W. Hofer and D. Schendel, *Strategy Formulation: Analytical Concepts* (St. Paul, Minn.: West Publishing, 1978), especially chap. 2, provides a discussion of sensitivity analysis, elasticity analysis, variability analysis, and the product life-cycle concept as tools for evaluating a business's strengths and weaknesses.

[11] Stevenson, "Defining Strengths," pp. 64–68.

While managers used past performance and competitive comparison in evaluating tentative strengths, they relied heavily on normative judgment (qualitative assessment and opinion) in evaluating probable weaknesses. Stevenson suggested that this was true because weaknesses often reflect competencies or areas in which the firm (and its managers) lack experience. And because they have no experience in these areas, managers must use qualitative assessment and opinion to evaluate the weakness. Stevenson's research probably does not reflect how all business firms evaluate strengths and weaknesses, but it provides a vivid illustration of how often typical managers employ normative judgments in internal analysis.

Summary: Viewing Internal Analysis as a Process

Figure 8–6 diagrams the development of a company profile as a four-step process you should find useful in guiding internal analysis. It also conveniently summarizes all that we have discussed in this chapter regarding internal analysis.

In step 1, managers audit and examine key aspects of the business's operation, seeking to target key areas for further assessment. Areas targeted are those deemed central to the firm's strategic direction. As such, they are called "strategic internal factors."

Step 2 has managers evaluating the firm's status on these factors by comparing their current condition with past abilities of the firm. This is where most managers start their planning efforts. How do we compare with last year? Have we improved over the last year? Are we better able to do key things than we were last year? Does each key factor represent a favorable or an unfavorable situation?

The third step is very critical. Managers seek some comparative basis—linked to key industry or product/market conditions—against which to more accurately determine whether the company's condition on a particular factor represents a potential strength or weakness. Managers use three perspectives to do this: (1) requirements for success across different product/market stages of evolution, (2) what competitors are capable of doing, and (3) perceived key requirements for success in the market/industry segments in which they compete.

The results of the third step should be a determination of whether key strategic internal factors are:

a. *Competitive advantages*—factors providing the company with an edge compared to its competitors, and therefore key factors around which to build the firm's strategy.

b. *Basic business requirements*—factors that are important capabilities for the firm to have but are also typical of every viable competitor; does not represent a potential source of any strategic advantage.

Figure 8–6
Steps in the development of a company profile*

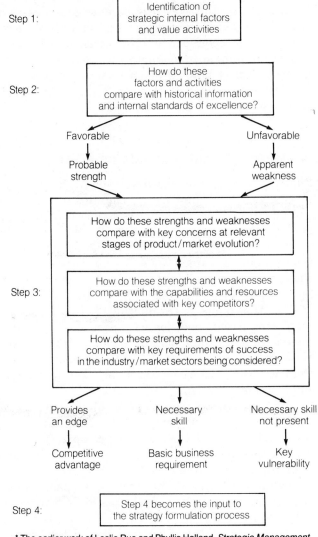

Step 1:   Identification of strategic internal factors and value activities

Step 2:   How do these factors and activities compare with historical information and internal standards of excellence?

Favorable — Probable strength

Unfavorable — Apparent weakness

Step 3:
How do these strengths and weaknesses compare with key concerns at relevant stages of product/market evolution?

How do these strengths and weaknesses compare with the capabilities and resources associated with key competitors?

How do these strengths and weaknesses compare with key requirements of success in the industry/market sectors being considered?

Provides an edge — Competitive advantage

Necessary skill — Basic business requirement

Necessary skill not present — Key vulnerability

Step 4:   Step 4 becomes the input to the strategy formulation process

* The earlier work of Leslie Rue and Phyllis Holland, *Strategic Management* (New York: McGraw-Hill, 1986), provided an important foundation from which to portray these steps.

c. *Key vulnerabilities*—factors on which the company currently lacks the necessary skill, knowledge, or resources to compete effectively. This assessment is also a key input into the strategic management process because managers will want to avoid choosing strategies that depend on factors in this category. And managers usually target key vulnerabilities as areas for special attention so as to remediate and change this situation.

The final step in internal analysis is to provide the results, or company profile, as input into the strategic management process. This input is vital during the early, strategy formulation phase in the strategic management process.

While this summary and Figure 8–6 explain internal analysis as a process, it is important to remember that each step in the process often overlaps another step. Thus separating each step helps explain the process of internal analysis; but, in practice, efforts to distinguish each step are seldom emphasized because the process is very interactive.

The process of internal analysis, when matched with the results of management's environmental analyses and mission priorities, provides the critical foundation for strategy formulation. When the internal analysis is accurate, thorough, and timely, managers are in a better position to formulate effective strategies. The next chapter describes basic strategy alternatives any company may consider.

Questions for Discussion

1. Describe the process used to identify key internal factors in a firm's strategic management process. Why does this appear to be an important part of the strategic management process?

2. Apply the two broad steps of internal analysis to yourself and your career aspirations. What are your major strengths and weaknesses? How might these be used to develop your future career plans?

3. Select one business in your area that appears to be doing well and another that appears to be doing poorly. Form two small teams with the help of your instructor. Have each team take one of the businesses and schedule a brief interview with a key manager. Obtain a *specific* assessment of each firm's internal strengths and weaknesses. Compare the results in a subsequent class. Are there substantial differences? Is one more comprehensive and specific than the other? Do strengths and weaknesses vary by type of business?

4. Explain why a firm might emphasize historical experience over competitor comparison in evaluating its strengths and weaknesses. When would the reverse emphasis be more relevant?

Bibliography

Barnard, Chester. *Functions of the Executive*. Cambridge, Mass.: Harvard University Press, 1939, chap. 14.

Buchele, Robert B. "How to Evaluate a Firm." *California Management Review,* Fall 1962, pp. 5–17.

Doyle, Peter. "The Realities of the Product Life Cycle." *Quarterly Review of Marketing,* Summer 1976, pp. 1–6.

Dun's Review. New York: Dun & Bradstreet, published monthly.

Fox, Harold. "A Framework for Functional Coordination." *Atlantic Economic Review,* November–December 1973, p. 18.

Gilmore, Frank. "Formulating Strategy in Smaller Companies." *Harvard Business Review,* May–June 1971, pp. 71–81.

Henry, Harold W. "Appraising a Company's Strengths and Weaknesses." *Managerial Planning,* July–August 1980, pp. 31–36.

Joy, O. M. *Introduction to Financial Management.* Homewood, Ill.: Richard D. Irwin, 1980, pp. 119–28 and 207–9.

Kotler, Philip. *Marketing Management.* 6th ed. Englewood Cliffs, N.J.: Prentice-Hall, 1988.

Mintzberg, Henry. "Strategy Making in Three Modes." *California Management Review* 16, no. 2 (1973), pp. 44–53.

Porter, Michael E. *Competitive Advantage.* New York: Free Press, 1985.

RMA: *Annual Statement Studies.* Philadelphia: Robert Morris Associates, published annually.

South, Stephen E. "Competitive Advantage: The Cornerstone to Strategic Thinking." *Journal of Business Strategy* 1, no. 4 (1981), pp. 15–25.

Stevenson, Howard H. "Defining Corporate Strengths and Weaknesses." *Sloan Management Review,* Spring 1976, pp. 51–68.

Appendix

Using Financial Analysis

One of the most important tools for assessing the strength of an organization within its industry is financial analysis. Managers, investors, and creditors all employ some form of this analysis as the beginning point for their financial decision making. Investors use financial analyses in making decisions about whether to buy or sell stock, and creditors use them in deciding whether or not to lend. They provide managers with a measurement of how the company is doing in comparison with its performance in past years and with the performance of competitors in the industry.

Although financial analysis is useful for decision making, there are some weaknesses that should be noted. Any picture that it provides of the company is based on past data. Although trends may be noteworthy, this picture should not automatically be assumed to be applicable to the future. In addition, the analysis is only as good as the accounting procedures that have provided the information. When making comparisons between companies, one should keep in mind the variability of accounting procedures from firm to firm.

There are four basic groups of financial ratios: liquidity, leverage, activity, and profitability.

Depicted in Exhibit 8–1 are the specific ratios calculated for each of the basic groups. Liquidity and leverage ratios represent an assessment of the risk of the firm. Activity and profitability ratios are measures of the return

Prepared by Elizabeth Gatewood, University of Georgia. © Elizabeth Gatewood, 1985. Reprinted by permission of Elizabeth Gatewood.

Exhibit 8–1
Financial ratios

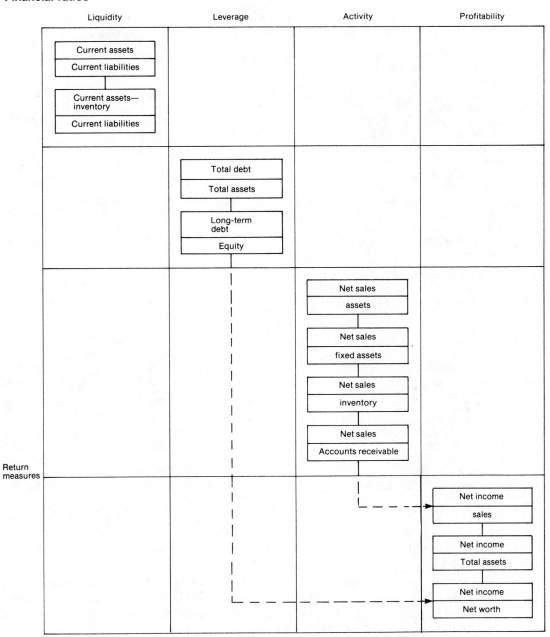

Exhibit 8–2

ABC COMPANY
Balance Sheet
As of December 31

	1989		1988	
Assets				
Current assets				
Cash		$ 140,000		$ 115,000
Accounts receivable		1,760,000		1,440,000
Inventory		2,175,000		2,000,000
Prepaid expenses		50,000		63,000
Total current assets		4,125,000		3,618,000
Fixed assets				
Long-term receivables		1,255,000		1,090,000
Property and plant	$2,037,000		$2,015,000	
Less: Accumulated depreciation	862,000		860,000	
Net property and plant		1,175,000		1,155,000
Other fixed assets		550,000		530,000
Total fixed assets		2,980,000		2,775,000
Total assets		$7,105,000		$6,393,000
Liabilities and Stockholders' Equity				
Current liabilities				
Accounts payable		$1,325,000		$1,225,000
Bank loans payable		475,000		550,000
Accrued federal taxes		675,000		425,000
Current maturities (long-term debt)		17,500		26,000
Dividends payable		20,000		16,250
Total current liabilities		2,512,500		2,242,250
Long-term liabilities		1,350,000		1,425,000
Total liabilities		3,862,500		3,667,250
Stockholders' equity				
Common stock (104,046 shares outstanding in 1985;				
101,204 shares outstanding in 1984)		44,500		43,300
Additional paid-in capital		568,000		372,450
Retained earnings		2,630,000		2,310,000
Total stockholders' equity		3,242,500		2,725,750
Total liabilities and stockholders' equity		$7,105,000		$6,393,000

generated by the assets of the firm. The interaction between certain groups of ratios is indicated by arrows.

Typically two common financial statements are used in financial analyses: the balance sheet and the income statement. Exhibit 8–2 is a balance sheet and Exhibit 8–3 an income statement for the ABC Company. These statements will be used to illustrate the financial analyses.

Exhibit 8–3

ABC COMPANY
Income Statement
For the Years Ending December 31

	1989	1988
Net sales	$8,250,000	$8,000,000
Less: Cost of goods sold $5,100,000		$5,000,000
Administrative expenses 1,750,000		1,680,000
Other expenses 420,000		390,000
Total	7,270,000	7,070,000
Earnings before interest and taxes	980,000	930,000
Less: Interest expense	210,000	210,000
Earnings before taxes	770,000	720,000
Less: Federal income taxes	360,000	325,000
Earnings after taxes (net income)	$ 410,000	$ 395,000
Common stock cash dividends	$ 90,000	$ 84,000
Addition to retained earnings	$ 320,000	$ 311,000
Earnings per common share	$ 3.940	$ 3.90
Dividends per common share	$ 0.865	$ 0.83

Liquidity Ratios

Liquidity ratios are used as indicators of a firm's ability to meet its short-term obligations. These obligations include any current liabilities, including currently maturing long-term debt. Current assets move through a normal cash cycle of inventories—sales—accounts receivable—cash. The firm then uses cash to pay off or reduce its current liabilities. The best-known liquidity ratio is the current ratio: current assets divided by current liabilities. For the ABC Company, the current ratio is calculated as follows:

$$\frac{\text{Current assets}}{\text{Current liabilities}} = \frac{\$4,125,000}{\$2,512,500} = 1.64 \, (1989)$$

$$= \frac{\$3,618,000}{\$2,242,250} = 1.61 \, (1988)$$

Most analysts suggest a current ratio of 2 to 3. A large current ratio is not necessarily a good sign; it may mean that an organization is not making the most efficient use of assets. The optimum current ratio will vary from industry to industry, with the more volatile industries requiring higher ratios.

Since slow-moving or obsolescent inventories could overstate a firm's ability to meet short-term demands, the quick ratio is sometimes preferred to assess a firm's liquidity. The quick ratio is current assets minus inventories, divided by current liabilities. The quick ratio for the ABC Company is calculated as follows:

$$\frac{\text{Current assets} - \text{Inventories}}{\text{Current liabilities}} = \frac{\$1,950,000}{\$2,512,500} = 0.78 \ (1989)$$

$$= \frac{\$1,618,000}{\$2,242,250} = 0.72 \ (1988)$$

A quick ratio of approximately 1 would be typical for American industries. Although there is less variability in the quick ratio than in the current ratio, stable industries would be able to safely operate with a lower ratio.

Leverage Ratios

Leverage ratios identify the source of a firm's capital—owners or outside creditors. The term *leverage* refers to the fact that using capital with a fixed interest charge will "amplify" either profits or losses in relation to the equity of holders of common stock. The most commonly used ratio is total debt divided by total assets. Total debt includes current liabilities and long-term liabilities. This ratio is a measure of the percentage of total funds provided by debt. A total debt/total assets ratio higher than 0.5 is usually considered safe only for firms in stable industries.

$$\frac{\text{Total debt}}{\text{Total assets}} = \frac{\$3,862,500}{\$7,105,000} = 0.54 \ (1989)$$

$$= \frac{\$3,667,250}{\$6,393,000} = 0.57 \ (1988)$$

The ratio of long-term debt to equity is a measure of the extent to which sources of long-term financing are provided by creditors. It is computed by dividing long-term debt by the stockholders' equity.

$$\frac{\text{Long-term debt}}{\text{Equity}} = \frac{\$1,350,000}{\$3,242,500} = 0.42 \ (1989)$$

$$= \frac{\$1,425,000}{\$2,725,750} = 0.52 \ (1988)$$

Activity Ratios

Activity ratios indicate how effectively a firm is using its resources. By comparing revenues with the resources used to generate them, it is possible to establish an efficiency of operation. The asset turnover ratio indicates how efficiently management is employing total assets. Asset turnover is calculated by dividing sales by total assets. For the ABC Company, asset turnover is calculated as follows:

$$\text{Asset turnover} = \frac{\text{Sales}}{\text{Total assets}} = \frac{\$8,250,000}{\$7,105,000} = 1.16 \text{ (1989)}$$

$$= \frac{\$8,000,000}{\$6,393,000} = 1.25 \text{ (1988)}$$

The ratio of sales to fixed assets is a measure of the turnover on plant and equipment. It is calculated by dividing sales by net fixed assets.

$$\text{Fixed asset turnover} = \frac{\text{Sales}}{\text{Net fixed assets}} = \frac{\$8,250,000}{\$2,980,000} = 2.77 \text{ (1989)}$$

$$= \frac{\$8,000,000}{\$2,775,000} = 2.88 \text{ (1988)}$$

Industry figures for asset turnover will vary with capital-intensive industries, and those requiring large inventories will have much smaller ratios.

Another activity ratio is inventory turnover, estimated by dividing sales by average inventory. The norm for American industries is 9, but whether the ratio for a particular firm is higher or lower normally depends upon the product sold. Small, inexpensive items usually turn over at a much higher rate than larger, expensive ones. Since inventories are normally carried at cost, it would be more accurate to use the cost of goods sold in place of sales in the numerator of this ratio. Established compilers of industry ratios such as Dun & Bradstreet, however, use the ratio of sales to inventory.

$$\text{Inventory turnover} = \frac{\text{Sales}}{\text{Inventory}} = \frac{\$8,250,000}{\$2,175,000} = 3.79 \text{ (1989)}$$

$$= \frac{\$8,000,000}{\$2,000,000} = 4 \text{ (1988)}$$

The accounts receivable turnover is a measure of the average collection period on sales. If the average number of days varies widely from the industry norm, it may be an indication of poor management. A too low ratio could indicate the loss of sales because of a too restrictive credit policy. If the ratio is too high, too much capital is being tied up in accounts receivable, and management may be increasing the chance of bad debts. Because of varying industry credit policies, a comparison for the firm over time or within an industry is the only useful analysis. Because information on credit sales for other firms is generally unavailable, total sales must be used. Since not all firms have the same percentage of credit sales, there is only approximate comparability among firms.

$$\frac{\text{Accounts}}{\text{receivable turnover}} = \frac{\text{Sales}}{\text{Accounts receivable}} = \frac{\$8,250,000}{\$1,760,000} = 4.69 \text{ (1989)}$$

$$= \frac{\$8,000,000}{\$1,440,000} = 5.56 \text{ (1988)}$$

$$\text{Average collection period} = \frac{360}{\text{Accounts receivable turnover}}$$

$$= \frac{360}{4.69} = 77 \text{ days (1989)}$$

$$= \frac{360}{5.56} = 65 \text{ days (1988)}$$

Profitability Ratios

Profitability is the net result of a large number of policies and decisions chosen by an organization's management. Profitability ratios indicate how effectively the total firm is being managed. The profit margin for a firm is calculated by dividing net earnings by sales. This ratio is often called return on sales (ROS). There is wide variation among industries, but the average for American firms is approximately 5 percent.

$$\frac{\text{Net earnings}}{\text{Sales}} = \frac{\$410,000}{\$8,250,000} = 0.0497 \text{ (1989)}$$

$$= \frac{\$395,000}{\$8,000,000} = 0.0494 \text{ (1988)}$$

A second useful ratio for evaluating profitability is the return on invest-ment—or ROI, as it is frequently called—found by dividing net earnings by total assets. The ABC Company's ROI is calculated as follows:

$$\frac{\text{Net earnings}}{\text{Total assets}} = \frac{\$410,000}{\$7,105,000} = 0.0577 \text{ (1989)}$$

$$= \frac{\$395,000}{\$6,393,000} = 0.0618 \text{ (1988)}$$

The ratio of net earnings to net worth is a measure of the rate of return or profitability of the stockholders' investment. It is calculated by dividing net earnings by net worth, the common stock equity and retained earnings account. ABC Company's return on net worth, also called ROE, is calculated as follows:

$$\frac{\text{Net earnings}}{\text{Net worth}} = \frac{\$410,000}{\$3,242,500} = 0.1264 \ (1989)$$

$$= \frac{\$395,000}{\$2,725,750} = 0.1449 \ (1988)$$

It is often difficult to determine causes for lack of profitability. The Du Pont system of financial analysis provides management with clues to the lack of success of a firm. This financial tool brings together activity, profitability, and leverage measures and shows how these ratios interact to determine the overall profitability of the firm. A depiction of the system is set forth in Exhibit 8–4.

The right side of the figure develops the turnover ratio. This section breaks down total assets into current assets (cash, marketable securities, accounts receivable, and inventories) and fixed assets. Sales divided by these total assets gives the turnover on assets.

The left side of the figure develops the profit margin on sales. The individual expense items plus income taxes are subtracted from sales to produce net profits after taxes. Net profits divided by sales gives the profit margin on sales. When the asset turnover ratio on the right side of Exhibit 8–4 is multiplied by the profit margin on sales developed on the left side of the figure, the product is the return on assets (ROI) for the firm. This can be shown by the following formula:

$$\frac{\text{Sales}}{\text{Total assets}} \times \frac{\text{Net earnings}}{\text{Sales}} = \frac{\text{Net earnings}}{\text{Total assets}} = \text{ROI}$$

The last step in the Du Pont analysis is to multiply the rate of return on assets (ROI) by the equity multiplier, which is the ratio of assets to common equity, to obtain the rate of return on equity (ROE). This percentage rate of return could, of course, be calculated directly by dividing net income by common equity. However, the Du Pont analysis demonstrates how the return on assets and the use of debt interact to determine the return on equity.

The Du Pont system can be used to analyze and improve the performance of a firm. On the left, or profit, side of the figure, attempts to increase profits and sales could be investigated. The possibilities of raising prices to improve profits (or lowering prices to improve volume) or seeking new products or markets, for example, could be studied. Cost accountants and production engineers could investigate ways to reduce costs. On the right, or turnover, side, financial officers could analyze the effect of reducing investment in various assets as well as the effect of alternative financial structures.

There are two basic approaches to using financial ratios. One approach is to evaluate the corporation's performance over several years. Financial ratios are computed for different years, and then an assessment is made as to whether there has been an improvement or deterioration over time. Financial ratios

Exhibit 8–4
Du Pont's financial analysis

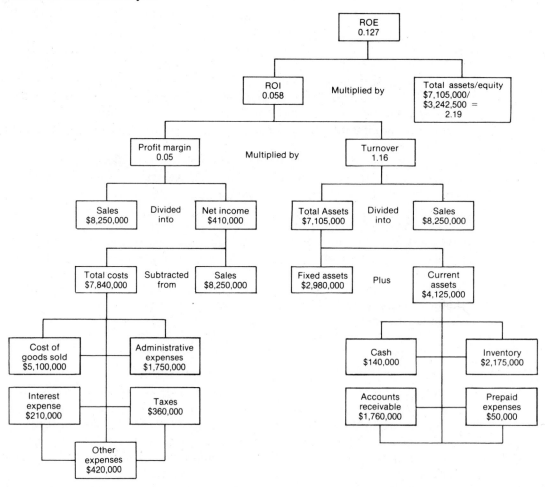

can also be computed for projected, or pro forma, statements and compared with present and past ratios.

The other approach is to evaluate a firm's financial condition and compare it with the financial conditions of similar firms or with industry averages in the same period. Such a comparison gives insight into the firm's relative financial condition and performance. Financial ratios for industries are provided by Robert Morris Associates, Dun & Bradstreet, and various trade association publications. (Associations and their addresses are listed in the *Encyclopedia of Associations* or the *Directory of National Trade Associations*.) Information about individual firms is available through *Moody's Manual,* Standard & Poor's manuals and surveys, annual reports to stockholders, and the major brokerage houses.

To the extent possible, accounting data from different companies must be standardized so that companies can be compared or so that a specific company can be compared with an industry average. It is important to read any footnotes of financial statements, since various accounting or management practices can have an effect on the financial picture of the company. For example, firms using sale-leaseback methods may have leverage pictures that are quite different from what is shown as debts or assets on the balance sheet.

Analysis of the Sources and Uses of Funds

The purpose of this analysis is to determine how the company is using its financial resources from year to year. By comparing balance sheets from one year to the next, one may determine how funds were obtained and the way in which these funds were employed during the year.

To prepare a statement of the sources and uses of funds it is necessary to (1) classify balance sheet changes that increase cash and changes that decrease cash, (2) classify from the income statement those factors that increase or decrease cash, and (3) consolidate this information on a sources and uses of funds statement form.

Sources of funds that increase cash are as follows:

1. A net decrease in any asset other than a depreciable fixed asset.
2. A gross decrease in a depreciable fixed asset.
3. A net increase in any liability.
4. Proceeds from the sale of stock.
5. The operation of the company (net income, and depreciation if the company is profitable).

Uses of funds include:

1. A net increase in any asset other than a depreciable fixed asset.
2. A gross increase in depreciable fixed assets.
3. A net decrease in any liability.
4. A retirement or purchase of stock.
5. Payment of cash dividends.

We compute gross changes to depreciable fixed assets by adding depreciation from the income statement for the period to net fixed assets at the end of the period and then subtracting from the total the net fixed assets at the beginning of the period. The residual represents the change in depreciable fixed assets for the period.

For the ABC Company, the following change would be calculated:

Net property and plant (1989)	$1,175,000
Depreciation for 1989	+ 80,000
	$1,255,000
Net property and plant (1988)	−1,155,000
	$ 100,000

To avoid double counting, the change in retained earnings is not shown directly in the funds statement. When the funds statement is prepared, this account is replaced by the earnings after taxes, or net income, as a source of funds and dividends paid during the year as a use of funds. The difference between net income and the change in the retained-earnings account will equal the amount of dividends paid during the year. The accompanying sources and uses of funds statement was prepared for the ABC Company.

A funds analysis is useful for determining trends in working-capital positions and for demonstrating how the firm has acquired and employed its funds during some period.

ABC COMPANY
Sources and Uses of Funds Statement
For 1989

Sources:		
Prepaid expenses	$	13,000
Accounts payable		100,000
Accrued federal taxes		250,000
Dividends payable		3,750
Common stock		1,200
Additional paid-in capital		195,500
Earnings after taxes (net income)		410,000
Depreciation		80,000
Total sources		1,053,500
Uses:		
Cash		25,000
Accounts receivable		320,000
Inventory		175,000
Long-term receivables		165,000
Property and plant		100,000
Other fixed assets		20,000
Bank loans payable		75,000
Current maturities of long-term debt		8,500
Long-term liabilities		75,000
Dividends paid		90,000
Total uses		1,053,500

Exhibit 8–5
A summary of the financial position of a firm

Ratios and working capital	1985	1986	1987	1988	1989	Trend	Industry average	Interpretation
Liquidity: Current								
Quick								
Leverage: Debt/assets								
Debt/equity								
Activity: Asset turnover								
Fixed asset ratio								
Inventory turnover								
Accounts receivable turnover								
Average collection period								
Profitability: ROS								
ROI								
ROE								
Working-capital position								

Conclusion

It is recommended that you prepare a chart such as Exhibit 8–5 so that you can develop a useful portrayal of these financial analyses. The chart allows a display of the ratios over time. The Trend column could be used to indicate your evaluation of the ratios over time (for example, "favorable," "neutral," or "unfavorable"). The Industry Average column could include recent industry averages on these ratios or those of key competitors. These would provide information to aid interpretation of the analyses. The Interpretation column can be used to describe your interpretation of the ratios for this firm. Overall, this chart gives a basic display of the ratios that provides a convenient format for examining the firm's financial condition.

Finally, Exhibit 8–6 is included to provide a quick reference summarizing the calculation and meaning of ratios discussed earlier.

Exhibit 8–6
A summary of key financial ratios

Ratio	*Calculation*	*Meaning*
Liquidity ratios		
Current ratio	$\dfrac{\text{Current assets}}{\text{Current liabilities}}$	The extent to which a firm can meet its short-term obligations.
Quick ratio	$\dfrac{\text{Current assets—Inventory}}{\text{Current liabilities}}$	The extent to which a firm can meet its short-term obligations without relying upon the sale of its inventories.
Leverage ratios		
Debt-to-total-assets ratio	$\dfrac{\text{Total debt}}{\text{Total assets}}$	The percentage of total funds that are provided by creditors.
Debt-to-equity ratio	$\dfrac{\text{Total debt}}{\text{Total stockholders' equity}}$	The percentage of total funds provided by creditors versus by owners.
Long-term-debt-to-equity ratio	$\dfrac{\text{Long-term debt}}{\text{Total stockholders' equity}}$	The balance between debt and equity in a firm's long-term capital structure.
Times-interest-earned ratio	$\dfrac{\text{Profits before interest and taxes}}{\text{Total interest charges}}$	The extent to which earnings can decline without the firm becoming unable to meet its annual interest costs.
Activity ratios		
Inventory turnover	$\dfrac{\text{Sales}}{\text{Inventory of finished goods}}$	Whether a firm holds excessive stocks of inventories and whether a firm is selling its inventories slowly compared to the industry average.
Fixed assets turnover	$\dfrac{\text{Sales}}{\text{Fixed assets}}$	Sales productivity and plant and equipment utilization.
Total assets turnover	$\dfrac{\text{Sales}}{\text{Total assets}}$	Whether a firm is generating a sufficient volume of business for the size of its asset investment.
Accounts receivable turnover	$\dfrac{\text{Annual credit sales}}{\text{Accounts receivable}}$	(In percentage terms) the average length of time it takes a firm to collect credit sales.
Average collection period	$\dfrac{\text{Accounts receivable}}{\text{Total sales/365 days}}$	(In days) the average length of time it takes a firm to collect on credit sales.

Exhibit 8–6 (concluded)

Ratio	Calculation	Meaning
Profitability ratios		
Gross profit margin	$\dfrac{\text{Sales} - \text{Cost of goods sold}}{\text{Sales}}$	The total margin available to cover operating expenses and yield a profit.
Operating profit margin	$\dfrac{\text{Earnings before interest and taxes (EBIT)}}{\text{Sales}}$	Profitability without concern for taxes and interest.
Net profit margin	$\dfrac{\text{Net income}}{\text{Sales}}$	After-tax profits per dollar of sales.
Return on total assets (ROA)	$\dfrac{\text{Net income}}{\text{Total assets}}$	After-tax profits per dollar of assets; this ratio is also called return on investment (ROI).
Return on stockholders' equity (ROE)	$\dfrac{\text{Net income}}{\text{Total stockholders' equity}}$	After-tax profits per dollar of stockholders' investment in the firm.
Earnings per share (EPS)	$\dfrac{\text{Net income}}{\text{Number of shares of common stock outstanding}}$	Earnings available to the owners of common stock.
Growth ratios		
Sales	Annual percentage growth in total sales	Firm's growth rate in sales.
Income	Annual percentage growth in profits	Firm's growth rate in profits.
Earnings per share	Annual percentage growth in EPS	Firm's growth rate in EPS.
Dividends per share	Annual percentage growth in dividends per share	Firm's growth rate in dividends per share.
Price–earnings ratio	$\dfrac{\text{Market price per share}}{\text{Earnings per share}}$	Faster-growing and less risky firms tend to have higher price–earnings ratios.

Chapter 8 Cohesion Case Illustration

Internal Analysis at Holiday Inns, Inc.

At Holiday Inns, internal analysis must be conducted at both the business and corporate levels. To do this, strengths and weaknesses within each business group should be examined first. After these analyses have been completed, they should be pulled together in an integrated overview of the strengths and weaknesses of Holiday Inns as a multibusiness firm.

Exhibit 1
Hotel group: Internal analysis*

Strengths	*Weaknesses*
HI dominates the industry in number of rooms available. It has the largest market share of lodging revenue dollars. *(21)*	Increasing average age of the typical property suggests increased maintenance and renovation expense. *(6, 7)*
Name, image, and customer awareness. *(17, 20)*	Dependent on the traveling public, which faces increased gasoline prices. *(21, 22)*
Extensive and steadily growing franchise network (80 percent of all units), with franchise revenues inflation-immune because they are based on a percentage of gross revenues. *(4)*	Hotels/motels are energy wasters that can disturb margins in an era of rapidly increasing energy costs. *(16)*
Massive real estate holdings rising steadily in value, providing an expanding asset base. Also, older mortgage rates provide a relative advantage against the cost newer competitors must encounter. *(69)*	HI has become the moderate- to high-priced accommodation relative to the rapidly expanding budget chains. *(23)*
Accumulated lodging experience both domestically and abroad. Extensive managerial talent and resources as evidenced by franchisee Winegardner's move to the top. *(20)*	A maturing domestic lodging industry with limited expansion opportunities, as evidenced by the net decline in the number of company-owned facilities over the last five years. *(6)*
Generally stable occupancy rate, revenues per room, gross revenue, and profit margin. *(66)*	Sensitivity to economic downturns as people curtail pleasure travel. *(21, 22)*
Well-balanced locations for interstate, airport, resort, and downtown traveler needs. *(6, 20, 21, 75)*	Rapidly escalating price competition on the one end (Days Inn, Best Western) and quality competition (Hilton, Marriott, Hyatt) on the other cuts at HI's large middle market. Also, relative to price competition, HI's built-in overhead—like 16-hour restaurants, big lobbies, room service—limits flexibility in lowering operating margins. *(21, 22)*
Quality control system. *(17)*	Cash drain on hotel group to support corporate-level overhead and ventures into new areas. Related attitude of franchisees regarding use of their fees to support this versus occupancy-enhancing activities. *(66)*
Food and lounge facilities at every location.	Challenges to the franchise agreement and relative dependence on franchisees. *(9)*

* Italicized numbers in parentheses refer to appropriate paragraphs of the Cohesion Case in Chapter 1. Exhibits in vicinity of appropriate paragraphs may also support this point.

Exhibit 2
Transportation group: Internal analysis

Strengths	Weaknesses
Increasing cost of auto travel should bolster ridership on Trailways. Some executives feel that Trailways' riders could complement hotel operations, especially tour and charter services. *(73, 76)*	Major competition from Greyhound, the number one bus line, as well as from air and train transportation. *(27, 28)*
Second-largest domestic bus service. *(26)*	Unsure whether the typical Trailways passenger is the typical HI motel/hotel customer. *(29, 32)*
Steady increase in transportation group revenues, particularly package express services. *(31)*	Rising maintenance and energy-related costs, while at the same time engaging in a price war with Greyhound. *(29, 30)*
Steady increase in net bus income, although no improvement in income as percent of revenues and a major drop within the steamship component.	Privately owned and maintained terminal facilities instead of the municipally owned terminals airlines enjoy. *(32)*
Growing revenue in package express services and the existence of Trailways' already-established intercity bus network to provide these services. *(31)*	Condition and rising maintenance/replacement costs of Trailways bus terminals. *(32)*
Delta Steamship (cargo) represents an operating base not directly tied to vacation and business travel. *(35)*	Growing popularity of airlines for both leisure and business travel based on a price/time in-transit comparison. *(27)*
Cargo business, with strong presence in South American and African routes, suggests a solid presence serving U.S. exports to Third World countries. *(35, 36)*	Growing number and variety of companies providing package express services. The questionable ability of Trailways to deliver *anywhere* within 24 hours. *(31)*
LASH technology is a distinct cargo cost advantage. *(37)*	Extent of managerial expertise in transportation—bus and marine cargo—is rather limited. *(26, 38)*
Cruise ship passenger service is a high-margin business. *(37)*	Heavy capital investment in marine cargo and ocean passenger business. *(66)*
	Small market share in marine transport and ocean passenger markets. *(39)*
	Lack of clear synergy between Delta operations and Trailways or both and the hotel group. *(32)*

Hotel Group. Clearly, this is the key business group for internal analysis. The hotel group is the core of Holiday Inns' diversified operations. It provides over 48 percent of total corporate revenues and over 59 percent of corporate income before taxes. Based on the Cohesion Case material, the strengths and weaknesses of the hotel group are shown in Exhibit 1.

Transportation Group. This is a growing segment of Holiday Inns, Inc.'s overall corporate endeavor. Two rather different businesses make up the transportation group—Continental Trailways bus system and Delta Steamship. Trailways seeks to provide moderate- to low-priced domestic intercity travel, while Delta provides marine cargo service and, increasingly, ocean pleasure cruises. Based on the case material, the strengths and weaknesses of this business group are outlined in Exhibit 2.

Exhibit 3
Restaurant group: Internal analysis

Strengths	Weaknesses
Perkins provides an immediate presence in the freestanding restaurant business via 360 company-owned and franchised operations in 30 states.	Must be integrated into a growingly complex and diversely focused corporate management.
HI is experienced in restaurant operation.	Faces stiff competition from similar firms like Sambo's, Shoney's, Denny's, and fast-food firms like McDonald's, Burger King, and Wendy's. *(48)*
Perkins is positioned as a family restaurant with a customer profile quite similar to that of the HI hotel guest. *(43)*	Limited geographic emphasis—northern United States. *(42)*
It is a franchise-based business, again deriving synergy from past experiences and hotel expertise at HI. *(42)*	
Provides economy-of-scale advantage in purchasing and advertising with restaurant business. *(45)*	

Exhibit 4
Gaming group: Internal analysis

Strengths	Weaknesses
Most casinos include hotels and sizable food and beverage operations, a natural synergy with HI's core expertise. *(54)*	Philosophical contradiction with founding principles at HI, such as family environment. *(52)*
Casino gaming revenue is fast growing, and profitability is quite high. *(56)*	While HI has hospitality experience, it has little gambling experience. *(57)*
The demographic profile of the typical casino customer is quite similar to that of the typical HI hotel guest. *(54)*	Gambling is only legal in a few areas. *(52)*
	Because of lack of experience, the cost of entry (real estate, etc.) is quite high. *(53)*
	Compatibility with corporate image and organized crime inference. *(52)*

Restaurant and Casino Groups.   In late 1979, Holiday Inns, Inc., moved into the freestanding restaurant market with its purchase of Perkins Cake and Steak, Inc., and its joint venture into casino operations in Atlantic City and Las Vegas. Because these are relatively new business groups, the case material is rather limited. You are encouraged to seek outside information from such sources as *Moody's* and *Standard & Poor's Industry Surveys* to round out the assessment of strengths and weaknesses provided here. Tentative strengths and weaknesses are listed in Exhibits 3 and 4.

Exhibit 5
Corporate-level internal analysis

Strengths	Weaknesses
The hotel business provides an excellent cash generator to support growth areas.	Management capability to absorb a rapidly increasing number of businesses may be severely challenged, especially in the short term.
Substantial and appreciating real estate holdings enhance corporatewide debt capacity.	Hotels and now restaurants represent a major dependence of outside franchisees—with several threatening legal challenges in progress.
Synergy between the hotel core and restaurant (Perkins) and casino operations should produce a distinct advantage.	Questionable whether some operations (especially Trailways buses, ocean cruises, and, to some extent, institutional products) clearly fit with other businesses in a related diversification strategy.
Casino gaming and increasing resort emphasis within company-owned expansion provide a logical synergy.	
Delta Steamship provides an avenue for lessening the travel-based, cyclical exposure of other HI businesses.	Severity of the budget chain threat and eventual price/cost squeeze on the essential cash generator—the hotel group—during a time of rapid cash outflows to gain positions in other business arenas.
Restaurants, casinos, and possibly marine transport provide reasonable growth avenues as the lodging industry matures.	Philosophical divisions among long-time managers over certain diversifications, especially casinos and restaurants, have corporatewide effect.
Franchising and marketing expertise across multiple businesses.	Revenues in the restaurant and gaming groups in 1980–81 indicate that these businesses may be more sensitive to recessionary business cycles than originally thought.
The 9⅝ percent convertible subordinate debentures represent $144 million of potential equity if they can be converted. Management estimates a stock price of over $22 (in 1982) would be necessary to issue a successful call.	The debt/total capitalization ratio, at a 10-year low in 1978 (34.6 percent), stood at a comparative high (over 42 percent) in 1981.

Having completed a basic internal analysis of each business group, Holiday Inns, Inc.'s strengths and weaknesses must be examined from an overall corporate standpoint. The focus in Exhibit 5 is on the overall business portfolio and the strengths and weaknesses it provides as corporate management views internal corporate capabilities.

These are some of the key strengths and weaknesses facing Holiday Inns, Inc., at the business and corporate levels. Compared with the environment analyses in Chapters 4 through 7, this internal analysis provides the basis for generating alternative strategies. The Chapter 10 Cohesion Case Illustration will look at this comparison. Before leaving internal analysis, however, do you agree with the strengths and weaknesses identified? Are any key factors missing? Are any factors identified as strengths that could be weaknesses or vice versa?

Formulating Long-Term Objectives and Grand Strategies

The company mission was described (in Chapter 3) as encompassing the broad aims of the organization. The most specific statement of wants appeared as the goals of the firm. However, these goals, which commonly dealt with profitability, growth, and survival, were stated without specific targets or time frames. They were always to be pursued but could never be fully attained. So, while they gave a general sense of direction, goals were not intended to provide specific benchmarks for evaluating the company's progress in achieving its aims. That is the function of objectives.[1]

In the first part of this chapter, the focus will be on long-term objectives. These are statements of the results a business seeks to achieve over a specified period of time, typically five years. In the second part of the chapter, focus will shift to formulation of grand strategies. These provide a comprehensive general approach guiding major actions designed to accomplish long-term business objectives.

The chapter has two major aims: (1) to discuss in detail the concept of long-term objectives, the topics they cover, and the qualities they should exhibit and (2) to discuss in detail the concept of grand strategies, the 12 principal options available, and two approaches to grand strategy selection.

---

[1] Throughout this text the terms *goals* and *objectives* are each used to convey a special meaning, with *goals* being the less specific and more encompassing concept. Most writers agree with this usage of the terms. However, some authors use the two words interchangeably, while others reverse the definitions.

Long-Term Objectives

Strategic managers recognize that short-run profit maximization is rarely the best approach to achieving sustained corporate growth and profitability. An often-repeated adage states that if impoverished people are given food they will enjoy eating it but will continue to be impoverished. However, if they are given seeds and tools and shown how to grow crops, they will be able to permanently improve their condition. A parallel situation confronts strategic decision makers:

1. Should they eat the seeds by planning for large dividend payments, by selling off inventories, and by cutting back on research and development to improve the near-term profit picture, or by laying off workers during periods of slack demand?

2. Or should they sow the seeds by reinvesting profits in growth opportunities, by committing existing resources to employee training in the hope of improving performance and reducing turnover, or by increasing advertising expenditures to further penetrate a market?

For most strategic managers the solution is clear—enjoy a small amount of profit now to maintain vitality, but sow the majority to increase the likelihood of a long-term supply. This is the most frequently used rationale in selecting objectives.

To achieve long-term prosperity, strategic planners commonly establish long-term objectives in seven areas:

Profitability.   The ability of any business to operate in the long run depends on attaining an acceptable level of profits. Strategically managed firms characteristically have a profit objective usually expressed in earnings per share or return on equity.

Productivity.   Strategic managers constantly try to improve the productivity of their systems. Companies that can improve the input–output relationship normally increase profitability. Thus, businesses almost always state an objective for productivity. Number of items produced or number of services rendered per unit of input are commonly used. However, productivity objectives are sometimes stated in terms of desired decreases in cost. This is an equally effective way to increase profitability if unit output is maintained. For example, objectives may be set for reducing defective items, customer complaints leading to litigation, or overtime.

Competitive Position.   One measure of corporate success is relative dominance in the marketplace. Larger firms often establish an objective in terms of competitive position to gauge their comparative ability for growth and profitability. Total sales or market share are often used; and an objective describing competitive position may indicate a corporation's priorities in the long term. For example, in 1975 Gulf Oil set an objective of moving by 1981 from third to second place as a producer of high-density polypropylene. Total sales were to be the measure.

Employee Development. Employees value growth and career opportunities in an organization. With such opportunities, productivity is often increased and expensive turnover decreased. Therefore, strategic decision makers frequently include an employee development objective in their long-range plans. For example, PPG has declared an objective of developing highly skilled and flexible employees, thereby providing steady employment for a reduced number of workers.

Employee Relations. Companies actively seek good employee relations, whether or not they are bound by union contracts. In fact, a characteristic concern of strategic managers is taking proactive steps in anticipation of employee needs and expectations. Strategic managers believe productivity is partially tied to employee loyalty and perceived management interest in worker welfare. Therefore, strategic managers set objectives to improve employee relations. For example, safety programs, worker representation on management committees, and employee stock option plans are all normal outgrowths of employee relations objectives.

Technological Leadership. Businesses must decide whether to lead or follow in the marketplace. While either can be a successful approach, each requires a different strategic posture. Therefore, many businesses state an objective in terms of technological leadership. For example, Caterpillar Tractor Company, which manufactures large earth movers, established its early reputation and dominant position in the industry on being a forerunner in technological innovation.

Public Responsibility. Businesses recognize their responsibilities to customers and society at large. In fact, many actively seek to exceed the minimum demands made by government. Not only do they work to develop reputations for fairly priced products and services, but they also attempt to establish themselves as responsible corporate citizens. For example, they may establish objectives for charitable and educational contributions, minority training, public or political activity, community welfare, and urban renewal.

Qualities of Long-Term Objectives

What distinguishes a good objective from a bad one? What qualities of an objective improve its chances of being attained?

Perhaps the best answer to these questions is found in relation to seven criteria that should be used in preparing long-term objectives: acceptable, flexible, measurable over time, motivating, suitable, understandable, and achievable.

Acceptable.   Managers are most likely to pursue objectives that are consistent with perceptions and preferences. If managers are offended by the objectives (e.g., promoting a nonnutritional food product) or believe them to be inappropriate or unfair (e.g., reducing spoilage to offset a disproportionate fixed overhead allocation), they may ignore or even obstruct achievement. In addition, certain long-term corporate objectives are frequently designed to be acceptable to major interest groups external to the firm. An example might involve air-pollution abatement efforts undertaken at the insistence of the Environmental Protection Agency.

Flexible.   Objectives should be modifiable in the event of unforeseen or extraordinary changes in the firm's competitive or environmental forecasts. At the same time, flexibility is usually increased at the expense of specificity. Likewise, employee confidence may be tempered because adjustment of a flexible objective may affect their job. One recommendation for providing flexibility while minimizing associated negative effects is to allow for adjustments in the level rather than the nature of an objective. For example, an objective for a personnel department "to provide managerial development training for 15 supervisors per year over the next five-year period" can easily be adjusted by changing the number of people to be trained. In contrast, changing the personnel department's objective after three months to "assisting production supervisors in reducing job-related injuries by 10 percent per year" would understandably create dissatisfaction.

Measurable.   Objectives must clearly and concretely state what will be achieved and within what time frame. Numerical specificity minimizes misunderstandings; thus, objectives should be measurable over time. For example, an objective to "substantially improve our return on investment" would be better stated as "increase the return on investment on our line of paper products by a minimum of 1 percent a year and a total of 5 percent over the next three years."

Motivating.   Studies have shown that people are most productive when objectives are set at a motivating level—one high enough to challenge but not so high as to frustrate or so low as to be easily attained. The problem is that individuals and groups differ in their perceptions of high enough. A broad objective that challenges one group frustrates another and minimally interests a third. One valuable recommendation is to develop multiple objectives, some aimed at specific groups. More sweeping statements are usually seen as lacking appreciation for individual and somewhat unique situations. Such tailor-made objectives require time and involvement from the decision maker, but they are more likely to serve as motivational forces.

Suitable.   Objectives must be suited to the broad aims of the organization, which are expressed in the statement of company mission. Each objective should be a step toward attainment of overall goals. In fact, objectives that do not coincide with company or corporate missions can subvert the aims of the firm. For example, if the mission is growth oriented, an objective of reducing the debt-to-equity ratio to 1.00 to improve stability would probably be unsuitable and counterproductive.

Understandable.   Strategic managers at all levels must have a clear understanding of what is to be achieved. They must also understand the major criteria by which their performance will be evaluated. Thus, objectives must be stated so that they are understandable to the recipient as they are to the giver. Consider the potential misunderstandings over an objective "to increase the productivity of the credit card department by 20 percent within five years." Does this mean: Increase the number of cards outstanding? Increase the use of outstanding cards? Increase the employee workload? Make productivity gains each year? Or hope that the new computer-assisted system, which should automatically improve productivity, is approved by year five? As this simple example illustrates, objectives must be prepared in clear, meaningful, and unambiguous fashion.

Achievable.   Finally, objectives must be possible to achieve. This is easier said than done. Turbulence in the remote and operating environments adds to the dynamic nature of a business's internal operations. This creates uncertainty, limiting strategic management's accuracy in setting feasible objectives. For example, the wildly fluctuating prime interest rates in 1980 made objective setting extremely difficult for 1981 to 1985, particularly in such areas as sales projections for consumer durable goods companies like General Motors and General Electric.

An especially fine example of long-term strategic objectives is provided in the 1981 to 1986 plan of Hawkeye Savings and Loan, a prominent financial organization in Iowa. Shown in Strategy in Action 9–1 are five of Hawkeye's major objectives for the period, specific performance targets for 1981 and 1982, and results from 1981. Hawkeye's approach is wholly consistent with the list of desired qualities for long-term objectives. In particular, Hawkeye's objectives are flexible, measurable over time, suitable, and understandable.

Grand Strategies[2]

Despite variations in implementing the strategic management approach, designers of planning systems generally agree about the critical role of *grand*

---

[2] Portions of this section are adapted from John A. Pearce II, "Selecting among Alternative Grand Strategies," *California Management Review,* Spring 1982, pp. 23–31.

Strategy in Action 9–1
Long-Range Objectives of Hawkeye Savings and Loan, 1981–1985

Objective 1.   Hawkeye should earn, after taxes, not less than 15 percent on average stockholder equity annually and, by December 31, 1985, be earning up to 20 percent on average stockholder equity. Per-share earnings should increase 10 percent annually.

	1981 objectives	1981 results	1982 objectives
Average stockholder equity	$84.5 million	$86.3 million	$110.0 million
Return on equity	16.3%	15.5%	14.6%
Earnings per share	2.75	2.50	2.56

Objective 2.   Hawkeye will grow from $1 billion in assets to $2 billion by December 31, 1985. This will be accomplished by: (*a*) acquiring $100 million in assets annually and (*b*) internal growth of 8 percent per annum.

	1981 objectives	1981 results	1982 objectives
Beginning assets	$1,100 million	$1,153 million	$1,408 million
Acquisitions	100	146	100
Internal growth	80	109	112
Ending assets	$1,280 million	$1,408 million	$1,620 million

Objective 3.   Hawkeye will maintain capital and reserves in subsidiary banks in an amount not less than 7 percent of assets, realizing regulatory authorities may require amounts in excess of that amount. The parent company will maintain a debt ratio under 35 percent of total capitalization and 40 percent of stockholders' equity.

	1981 objectives	1981 results	1982 objectives
Year-end stockholders' equity	$97.0 million	$105.2 million	$115.0 million
Parent company debt	39.0 million	39.6 million	46.0 million
Average subsidiary bank capital and reserves-to-asset ratio	8.0%	8.7%	8.0%

Continued on Page 250

Strategy in Action 9–1 (*concluded*)

Objective 4. Hawkeye's basic mission of "helping Iowans achieve their financial goals" requires that member banks be willing to loan funds. The willingness of Hawkeye's banks to loan funds also requires the bank to collect funds loaned.

	1981 objectives	1981 results	1982 objectives
Total loans	$650 million	$696 million	$708 million
Of the average total loans, total loan loss not to exceed	0.15%	0.242%	0.15%
Classified loans not to exceed	2.00%	1.750%	2.00%
Credit card delinquencies not to exceed	10.00%	6.790%	10.00%
Loan-to-deposit ratio not to exceed	73.50%	62.900%	73.50%

Objective 5. The Financial Services Group will expand the number and variety of financial services offered in keeping with Hawkeye Bancorporation's mission to build a regional financial corporation. These activities will account for an increasing share of Hawkeye profits.

	After-tax earnings objectives		
	1981 estimate	1981 actual	1982 estimate
Hawkeye Insurance Services, Inc.	$260,000	$169,000	$ 217,000
Central Hawkeye Life Insurance Company	137,000	171,000	480,000
Hawkeye Investment Management, Inc.	26,000	33,000	1,000
Hawkeye Farm Management	13,000	13,000	19,000
Iowa Higher Education Loan Program	80,000	145,000	196,000
Credit Card Center (service fees only)	34,000	47,000	187,000
Hawkeye Mortgage Company	16,000	(68,000)	87,000
STFIT	0	180,000	360,000
	$566,000	$690,000	$1,547,000

strategies.[3] Grand strategies, which are often called *master* or *business* strategies, are intended to provide basic direction for strategic actions. Thus, they are seen as the basis of coordinated and sustained efforts directed toward achieving long-term business objectives.

As theoretically and conceptually attractive as the idea of grand strategies has proved to be, two problems have limited use of this approach in practice. First, decision makers often do not recognize the range of alternative grand strategies available. Strategic managers tend to build incrementally from the status quo. This often unnecessarily limits their search for ways to improve corporate performance. Other executives have simply never considered the options available as attractive grand strategies.

Second, strategic decision makers may generate lists of promising grand strategies but lack a logical and systematic approach to selecting an alternative. Few planning experts have attempted to proffer viable evaluative criteria and selection tools.

The purpose of this section is therefore twofold: (1) to list, describe, and discuss 12 business-level grand strategies that should be considered by strategic planners and (2) to present approaches to the selection of an optimal grand strategy from available alternatives.

Grand strategies indicate how long-range objectives will be achieved. Thus, a grand strategy can be defined as a comprehensive general approach that guides major actions. As an example, Strategy in Action 9–2 presents a form of the grand strategy of Eastern Air Lines.

Any one of the 12 principal grand strategies could serve as the basis for achieving major long-term objectives of a single business: concentration, market development, product development, innovation, horizontal integration, vertical integration, joint venture, concentric diversification, conglomerate diversification, retrenchment/turnaround, divestiture, and liquidation. When a company is involved with multiple industries, businesses, product lines, or customer groups—as many firms are—several grand strategies are usually combined. However, for clarity, each of these grand strategies is described independently in this section with examples to indicate some of their relative strengths and weaknesses.

Concentration

The most common grand strategy is *concentration* on the current business. The firm directs its resources to the profitable growth of a single product, in a single market, and with a single technology. Some of America's largest

---

[3] Among recent such models or theories of strategic management are those of Pearce (1981), Steiner (1979), Higgins (1979), Ansoff (1979), King and Cleland (1978), and Steiner and Miner (1977), all listed in the bibliography to this chapter.

Strategy in Action 9–2
The 1984 Grand Strategy of Eastern Air Lines*

The past five years have been turbulent for the airline industry. Deregulation was quickly followed by a dramatic increase in oil prices; high inflation; skyrocketing interest rates; the most severe and prolonged recession since the Great Depression; the formation of new, low-cost airlines; and the PATCO strike, resulting in imposition of new government controls on operations. Under these circumstances, it should not be surprising that one trunk carrier has gone bankrupt and that others are in perilous financial condition.

During this period, Eastern's basic strategy has remained consistent:

A commitment to a modern, efficient fleet and support facilities, necessarily accompanied by some financial risk.

Growth through productivity.

Protection of job security to the maximum extent possible.

Protection of yields by selectively and carefully offering competitive prices in our markets.

Formation of a route structure which permits efficient development of our marketing strength at our primary traffic hubs.

Protection of our traditional major markets.

Development of new market opportunities.

A commitment to quality.

While Eastern's financial results have been unsatisfactory, the success of this strategy can be measured by Eastern's performance relative to that of other major carriers. In 1982, Eastern ranked first among the trunk carriers in operating margin; and, as measured by Merrill Lynch's "Passenger Profitability Index," Eastern ranks behind only Southwest and USAir.

Thus, our strategy will remain essentially intact. There will be changes in emphasis to reflect an improving external environment, our financial structure, and the employee productivity improvements we are anticipating. However, the basic direction remains unchanged.

* The details of a company's grand strategy are among its most closely guarded secrets. Since this statement of Eastern Air Line's grand strategy was *intended* for public consumption, it necessarily omitted the huge volumes of detailed analysis that preceded this extremely abbreviated and superficial overview.

and most successful companies have traditionally adopted the concentration approach. Examples include W. K. Kellogg and Gerber Foods, which are known for their product; Shaklee, which concentrates on geographic expansion; and Lincoln Electric, which bases its growth on technological advances.

The reasons for selecting a concentration grand strategy are easy to understand. Concentration is typically lowest in risk and in additional resources required. It is also based on the known competencies of the firm. On the negative side, for most companies concentration tends to result in steady but slow increases in growth and profitability and a narrow range of investment options. Further, because of their narrow base of competition, concentrated firms are especially susceptible to performance variations resulting from industry trends.

Concentration strategies succeed for so many businesses—including the vast majority of smaller firms—because of the advantages of business-level specialization. By concentrating on one product, in one market, and with one technology, a firm can gain competitive advantages over its more diversified competitors in production skill, marketing know-how, customer sensitivity, and reputation in the marketplace.

A grand strategy of concentration allows for a considerable range of action. Broadly speaking, the business can attempt to capture a larger market share by increasing present customers' rate of usage, by attracting competitors' customers, or by interesting nonusers in the product or service. In turn, each of these actions suggests a more specific set of alternatives. Some of these options are listed in the top section of Figure 9–1.

When strategic managers forecast that the combination of their current products and their markets will not provide the basis for achieving the company mission, they have two options that involve moderate cost and risk: market development and product development.

Market Development

Market development commonly ranks second only to concentration as the least costly and least risky of the 12 grand strategies. It consists of marketing present products, often with only cosmetic modifications, to customers in related market areas by adding different channels of distribution or by changing the content of advertising or the promotional media. Several specific approaches are listed under this heading in Figure 9–1. Thus, as suggested by the figure, businesses that open branch offices in new cities, states, or countries are practicing market development. Likewise, companies that switch from advertising in trade publications to newspapers or add jobbers to supplement their mail-order sales efforts are using a market development approach.

Figure 9–1
Specific options under the grand strategies of concentration, market development, and product development

Concentration (increasing use of present products in present markets):
1. Increasing present customers' rate of usage.
    a. Increasing the size of purchase.
    b. Increasing the rate of product obsolescence.
    c. Advertising other uses.
    d. Giving price incentives for increased use.
2. Attracting competitors' customers.
    a. Establishing sharper brand differentiation.
    b. Increasing promotional effort.
    c. Initiating price cuts.
3. Attracting nonusers to buy the product.
    a. Inducing trial use through sampling, price incentives, and so on.
    b. Pricing up or down.
    c. Advertising new uses.

Market development (selling present products in new markets):
1. Opening additional geographical markets.
    a. Regional expansion.
    b. National expansion.
    c. International expansion.
2. Attracting other market segments.
    a. Developing product versions to appeal to other segments.
    b. Entering other channels of distribution.
    c. Advertising in other media.

Product development (developing new products for present markets):
1. Developing new product features.
    a. Adapt (to other ideas, developments).
    b. Modify (change color, motion, sound, odor, form, shape).
    c. Magnify (stronger, longer, thicker, extra value).
    d. Minify (smaller, shorter, lighter).
    e. Substitute (other ingredients, process, power).
    f. Rearrange (other patterns, layout, sequence, components).
    g. Reverse (inside out).
    h. Combine (blend, alloy, assortment, ensemble; combine units, purposes, appeals, ideas).
2. Developing quality variations.
3. Developing additional models and sizes (product proliferation).

Source: Adapted from Philip Kotler, *Marketing Management: Analysis, Planning, and Control,* 5th ed., 1984, p. 58. Reprinted by permission of Prentice-Hall, Inc., Englewood Cliffs, N.J.

Product Development

Product development involves substantial modification of existing products or creation of new but related items that can be marketed to current customers through established channels. The product development strategy is often adopted either to prolong the life cycle of current products or to take advantage of favorable reputation and brand name. The idea is to attract satisfied customers to new products as a result of their positive experience with the company's initial offering. The bottom section of Figure 9–1 lists some of the many specific options available to businesses undertaking product development. Thus, a revised edition of a college textbook, a new car style, and a second formula of shampoo for oily hair each represents a product development strategy.

Strategy in Action 9–3 shows how Kohler Company was able to combine market and product development into an extremely effective grand strategy.

Innovation

In many industries it is increasingly risky not to innovate. Consumer as well as industrial markets have come to expect periodic changes and improvements in the products offered. As a result, some businesses find it profitable to base their grand strategy on *innovation*. They seek to reap the initially high profits associated with customer acceptance of a new or greatly improved product. Then, rather than face stiffening competition as the basis of profitability shifts from innovation to production or marketing competence, they move on to search for other original or novel ideas. The underlying philosophy of a grand strategy of innovation is creating a new product life cycle, thereby making any similar existing products obsolete. Thus, this approach differs from the

---

Strategy in Action 9–3
A Tub-and-Toilet Dynasty

In 1983, with the home-building industry in a long-running slump, profits in the plumbing fixtures business were swirling down the drain. For companies that made tubs, toilets, sinks, and showers, it seemed a time to retrench.

Not, however, for the privately held Kohler Company of Kohler, Wisconsin, creator of the Infinity Bath, the Super Spa, and other exotica for people who want their bathrooms to be fun as well as functional. Even though Kohler had to lay off 300 of its 6,000 workers because of slow sales of some products, the company was going ahead with its most ambitious capital spending program ever. In 1983 Kohler invested $50 million, more than 10 percent of its expected

Continued on Page 256

Strategy in Action 9–3 (*concluded*)

sales of $400 million. The plan included a big expansion of its factories in Brownwood, Texas.

Unlike most American executives, who were often criticized for trying to boost short-run profits at the expense of long-range investment, Chairman Herbert Kohler could afford to disregard the short-term bottom line. His family and relatives owned or controlled 90 percent of the Kohler stock. While the typical U.S. company reinvested 60 percent of its earnings, Chairman Kohler claimed to put 90 percent of his profits back into the firm.

Kohler viewed a recession as a grand opportunity to increase his share of the kitchen and bathroom business. Because of the slump, he pointed out, some building materials cost less than they did in 1980, and thus the construction of new factories was comparatively inexpensive. During the recession in 1973–75, Kohler expanded its facilities enough to overtake American Standard as the largest manufacturer of luxury plumbing fixtures in the United States.

When Herbert Kohler became chairman in 1972, he decided that plumbing had not reached its potential. Said he, "I felt we could innovate with shapes and colors to change the whole function of the bathroom and make it something stimulating, possibly even social."

The company has since introduced the Infinity Bath, a kidney-shaped tub for two (price: $2,000), and the Super Spa, a giant whirlpool ($4,000) that can come with a built-in table for those who, for example, want to play poker as they soak. Kohler's masterpiece is the $12,500 Environment, a pleasure chamber that pampers bathers with "tropic rain, jungle steam, chinook winds, and Baja sun," all accompanied by soothing stereo music.

Though plumbing fixtures are rarely mentioned in the same breath with computers or robots, Kohler was convinced that the bathroom business had considerable growth potential. He expected to see the day when whirlpools were virtually standard in middle-class homes.

Source: "Rub-a-Dub-Dub," *Time*, July 26, 1982, p. 37.

product development strategy of extending an existing product's life cycle. The automobile industry provides many excellent examples. Ford Motor Company's 1981 introduction of the sporty, economical, two-seater EXP was an effort to interest a segment of American drivers who traditionally bought foreign-made sports cars in trying a Ford product. This was an innovation strategy because a new life cycle had been started for Ford. At the same time, Ford modified the Fairmont to make it lighter and more fuel efficient. This was a product development strategy since the Fairmont life cycle was extended.

While most growth-oriented firms appreciate the need to be innovative occasionally, a few companies use it as their fundamental way of relating to their markets. An outstanding example is Polaroid, which heavily promotes each of its new cameras until competitors are able to match their technological innovation. By this time, Polaroid is normally prepared to introduce a dramatically new or improved product. For example, in short succession consumers were introduced to the Swinger, the SX-70, the One Step, and the Sun Camera 660.

Few innovative ideas prove profitable because research, development, and premarketing costs incurred in converting a promising idea into a profitable product are extremely high. A study by the management research department of Booz Allen & Hamilton Inc. provides some understanding of the risks. As shown in Figure 9–2, Booz Allen & Hamilton Inc. studied 51 companies and found that less than 2 percent of the innovative projects initially considered eventually reached the marketplace. Specifically, out of every 58 new product ideas, only 12 pass an initial screening test that finds them compatible with the company's mission and long-term objectives. Only seven of these remain after an evaluation of their product potential, and only three survive actual attempts to develop the product. Two of these still appear to have profit potential after test marketing; but, on the average, only one will be commercially successful. In fact, other studies show this success rate to be overly optimistic. For example, the results of one research project disclosed failure rates for commercial products to be as high as 89 percent.[4]

Horizontal Integration

When the long-term strategy of a firm is based on growth through the acquisition of one or more similar businesses operating at the same stage of the production-marketing chain, its grand strategy is called *horizontal integration*. Such acquisitions provide access to new markets for the acquiring firm and eliminate competitors. For example, Warner-Lambert Pharmaceutical Company's acquisition of Parke Davis reduced competition in the ethical drugs field for Chilcott Laboratories, a company Warner-Lambert had previously acquired. A second example is the long-range acquisition pattern of White Consolidated Industries, which expanded in the refrigerator and freezer market through a grand strategy of horizontal integration. In 1967 it acquired the Franklin Appliance Division of Studebaker, in 1978 it bought the Kelvinator Appliance Division of American Motors, in 1971 it acquired the Refrigerator Products Division of Bendix Westinghouse Automotive Air Brake, and finally in 1979 it bought Frigidaire Appliance from General Motors. For yet another example of a successful horizontal integration grand strategy, read the case of the

---

[4] Burt Schorr, "Many New Products Fizzle, Despite Careful Planning, Publicity," *The Wall Street Journal,* April 5, 1961.

Figure 9–2
Decay of new product ideas (51 companies)

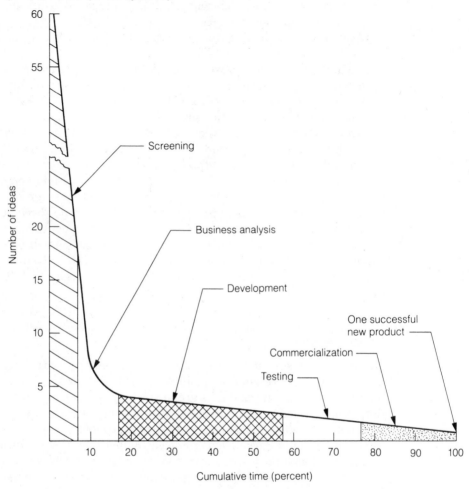

Santa Fe and Southern Pacific railroads in Strategy in Action 9–4. Thus, the combinations of two textile producers, two shirt manufacturers, or two clothing store chains would be classified as horizontal integrations.

Vertical Integration

When the grand strategy of a firm involves the acquisition of businesses that either supply the firm with inputs (such as raw materials) or serve as a customer for the firm's outputs (such as warehousers for finished products), *vertical integration* is involved. For example, if a shirt manufacturer acquires a textile producer—by purchasing its common stock, buying its assets, or through an exchange of ownership interests—the strategy is a vertical integration. In this case it is a *backward* vertical integration since the business acquired operates at an earlier stage of the production/marketing process. If the shirt manufacturer had merged with a clothing store, it would have been an example of *forward* vertical integration—the acquisition of a business nearer to the ultimate consumer.

Strategy in Action 9–4
Merging to Build a New Empire

In 1983 the Santa Fe and Southern Pacific railroads joined forces to form the third largest railroad in the United States, with 26,000 miles of track. Due to the $6.3 billion merger, only the Burlington Northern railroad (28,900 miles) and CSX (26,400) were bigger. The combined Santa Fe–Southern Pacific network stretched from Chicago in the North to New Orleans in the South to Portland in the West.

The new company was to be not just a railroad, but a business empire. Chicago-based Santa Fe Industries (1982 revenues: $3.16 billion) has gas wells, coal and uranium mines, and a forest-products division. The company was one of the largest U.S. producers of heavy crude oil. San Francisco–based Southern Pacific (1982 revenues: $3.1 billion) operated petroleum pipelines and leased executive aircraft, truck fleets, computers, mining machinery, and communications equipment. With huge holdings of farm land, timberland, and urban real estate, Southern Pacific was the largest private landlord in California.

[Southern Pacific] also owned the nation's only operational coal-slurry pipeline, which ran 273 miles between Arizona and Nevada. The pipeline allowed coal that has been mixed with water to be transported swiftly and cheaply.

Santa Fe and Southern Pacific saw their union as the best way to compete with two other big Western railroads that were built up through mergers: Burlington Northern and Union Pacific. Santa Fe and Southern Pacific intended to become more efficient by abandoning duplicate routes and pooling equipment. The combined 57,000-member work force of the two railroads would shrink but through attrition rather than layoffs.

Source: "Merging to Build New Empires," *Time,* October 10, 1983, p. 50.

Figure 9–3
Vertical and horizontal integrations

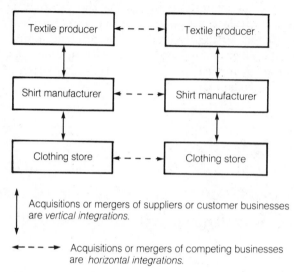

Acquisitions or mergers of suppliers or customer businesses are *vertical integrations.*

Acquisitions or mergers of competing businesses are *horizontal integrations.*

Figure 9–3 depicts both horizontal and vertical integration. The principal attractions of a horizontal integration grand strategy are readily apparent. The acquiring firm is able to greatly expand its operations, thereby achieving greater market share, improving economies of scale, and increasing efficiency of capital usage. Additionally, these benefits are achieved with only moderately increased risk, since the success of the expansion is principally dependent on proven abilities.

The reasons for choosing a vertical integration grand strategy are more varied and sometimes less obvious. The main reason for backward integration is the desire to increase the dependability of supply or quality of raw materials or production inputs. The concern is particularly great when the number of suppliers is small and the number of competitors is large. In this situation, the vertically integrating firm can better control its costs and thereby improve the profit margin of the expanded production/marketing system. Forward integration is a preferred grand strategy if the advantages of stable production are particularly high. A business can increase the predictability of demand for its output through forward integration, that is, through ownership of the next stage of its production/marketing chain.

Some increased risks are associated with both types of integration grand strategies. For horizontally integrated firms, the risks stem from the increased commitment to one type of business. For vertically integrated firms, the risks result from expansion of the company into areas requiring strategic managers

Figure 9–4
Typical joint ventures in the oil pipeline industry

Pipeline company (assets in $ millions)	Co-owners	Percent held by each
Colonial Pipeline Co. ($480.2)	Amoco	14.3
	Atlantic Richfield	1.6
	Cities Service	14.0
	Continental	7.5
	Phillips	7.1
	Texaco	14.3
	Gulf	16.8
	Sohio	9.0
	Mobil	11.5
	Union Oil	4.0
Olympic Pipeline Co. ($30.7)	Shell	43.5
	Mobil	29.5
	Texaco	27.0
West Texas Gulf Pipeline Co. ($19.8)	Gulf	57.7
	Cities Service	11.4
	Sun	12.6
	Union Oil	9.0
	Sohio	9.2
Texas–New Mexico Pipeline Co. ($30.5)	Texaco	45.0
	Atlantic Richfield	35.0
	Cities Service	10.0
	Getty	10.0

Source: Testimony of Walter Adams in *Horizontal Integration of the Energy Industry*, hearings before the Subcommittee on Energy of the Joint Economic Committee, 94th Congress, 1st sess. (1975), p. 112.

to broaden the base of their competencies and assume additional responsibilities.

Joint Venture

Occasionally two or more capable companies lack a necessary component for success in a particular competitive environment. For example, no single petroleum firm controlled sufficient resources to construct the Alaskan pipeline. Nor was any single firm capable of processing and marketing the volume of oil that would flow through the pipeline. The solution was a set of *joint ventures*. As shown in Figure 9–4, these cooperative arrangements could provide both the necessary funds to build the pipeline and the processing and marketing capacity to profitably handle the oil flow.

Strategy in Action 9–5
Moscow Woos Westerners for Joint Ventures

The Soviet government today set guidelines for joint business ventures between Soviet and Western firms, in an all-out bid to engage Western capital, technology, and management in the revision of the Soviet Union's socialist economy.

The rules leave no doubt that the partnerships will be dominated by Soviet firms, however. The partnerships should have "not less than" 51 percent Soviet ownership, a Soviet chairman of the board and general director, and "mainly" Soviet personnel, according to the Council of Ministers resolution released today by the official news agency, Tass.

The firms will be based in the Soviet Union, and Soviet and Western employees will be subject to Soviet employment regulations, with some exceptions possible for foreign workers.

The publication of the rules climaxes several months of Kremlin efforts to attract Western companies.

Since the concept of joint Soviet and Western enterprises first surfaced publicly here last spring, exploratory talks have been held with leading officials and business executives from at least a dozen Western countries, including the Netherlands, Britain, Finland, the United States, and Japan.

The aim of the efforts, today's announcement said, is to boost industrial output, "to attract into the national economy advanced foreign technology, managerial expertise, additional material and financial resources, [and] to develop the country's export base and reduce irrational imports."

Foreign shareholders are guaranteed the right to transfer hard currency earnings out of the Soviet Union.

Moscow has sweetened its courtship of Western companies with inducements. According to the new rules, the ventures will be tax free for the first two years and thereafter will be taxed at the after-deduction rate of 30 percent, considered modest by Western standards.

Despite the Soviet drive, Western diplomats and business executives based in Moscow who are skeptical about the chances for Soviet–Western joint ventures criticized today's release.

While the rules confirm Soviet interest in attracting Western business, Westerners in Moscow said they fail to demonstrate chances of reasonable profitability.

In addition, Western business executives balk at the stipulations placing employees under Soviet employment rules, many of which are unpublished. "It seems to take away the right of Western companies to hire and fire," one U.S.

Continued on Page 263

Strategy in Action 9–5 (*concluded*)

business executive in Moscow said. "That really undermines a Western business-man's means of exercising quality control."

The rules also prohibit joint ventures from direct marketing in the Soviet Union; instead, they must sell through a go-between—a Soviet foreign trade organization.

One big attraction is the vast warehouse of Soviet raw materials. The Soviet Union has several times the forest land of neighboring Finland, for example, but produces approximately the same amount of paper. In fact, paper pulp, along with machine building, chemical, light, and food production, are the key areas Moscow has pinpointed for joint ventures.

Source: Gary Lee, "Moscow Woos Westerners for Joint Ventures," *Washington Post,* January 27, 1987.

The particular form of joint venture discussed above is joint ownership.[5] In recent years it has become increasingly appealing for domestic firms to join foreign businesses through this form. For example, Bethlehem Steel acquired an interest in a Brazilian mining venture to secure a raw material source. The stimulus for this joint ownership venture was grand strategy, but such is not always the case. Certain countries virtually mandate that foreign companies entering their markets do so on a joint ownership basis. India and Mexico are good examples. The rationale of these countries is that joint ventures minimize the threat of foreign domination and enhance the skills, employment, growth, and profits of local businesses.

One final note: Strategic managers in the typical firm rarely seek joint ventures. This approach admittedly presents new opportunities with risks that can be shared. On the other hand, joint ventures often limit partner discretion, control, and profit potential while demanding managerial attention and other resources that might otherwise be directed toward the mainstream activities of the firm. Nevertheless, increasing nationalism in many foreign markets may require greater consideration of the joint venture approach if a firm intends to diversify internationally. These points are made vividly in Strategy in Action 9–5.

Concentric Diversification

Grand strategies involving diversification represent distinctive departures from a firm's existing base of operations, typically the acquisition or internal generation (spin-off) of a separate business with synergistic possibilities coun-

---

[5] Other forms of joint ventures (such as leasing, contract manufacturing, and management contracting) offer valuable support strategies. However, because they are seldom employed as grand strategies, they are not included in the categorization.

terbalancing the two businesses' strengths and weaknesses. For example, Head Ski initially sought to diversify into summer sporting goods and clothing to offset the seasonality of its snow business. However, diversifications are occasionally undertaken as unrelated investments because of their otherwise minimal resource demands and high profit potential.

Regardless of the approach taken, the motivations of the acquiring firms are the same:

Increase the firm's stock value. Often in the past, mergers have led to increases in the stock price and/or price-earnings ratio.

Increase the growth rate of the firm.

Make an investment that represents better use of funds than plowing them into internal growth.

Improve the stability of earnings and sales by acquiring firms whose earnings and sales complement the firm's peaks and valleys.

Balance or fill out the product line.

Diversify the product line when the life cycle of current products has peaked.

Acquire a needed resource quickly; for example, high-quality technology or highly innovative management.

Tax reasons, purchasing a firm with tax losses that will offset current or future earnings.

Increase efficiency and profitability, especially if there is synergy between the two companies.[6]

When diversification involves the addition of a business related to the firm in terms of technology, markets, or products, it is a *concentric diversification*. With this type of grand strategy, the new businesses selected possess a high degree of compatability with the current businesses. The ideal concentric diversification occurs when the combined company profits increase strengths and opportunities, as well as decrease weaknesses and exposure to risk. Thus, the acquiring company searches for new businesses with products, markets, distribution channels, technologies, and resource requirements that are familiar but not identical, synergistic but not wholly interdependent.

Conglomerate Diversification

Occasionally a firm, particularly a very large one, plans to acquire a business because it represents the most promising investment opportunity available. This type of grand strategy is commonly known as *conglomerate diversification*. The principal and often sole concern of the acquiring firm is the profit pattern

---

[6] William F. Glueck, *Business Policy and Strategic Management* (New York: McGraw-Hill, 1980), p. 213.

of the venture. There is little concern given to creating product/market synergy with existing businesses, unlike the approach taken in concentric diversification. Financial synergy is what is sought by conglomerate diversifiers such as ITT, Textron, American Brands, Litton, U.S. Industries, Fuqua, and I.C. Industries. For example, they may seek a balance in their portfolios between current businesses with cyclical sales and acquired businesses with counter-cyclical sales, between high-cash/low-opportunity and low-cash/high-opportunity businesses, or between debt-free and highly leveraged businesses.

The principal difference between the two types of diversification is that concentric acquisitions emphasize some commonality in markets, products, or technology, whereas conglomerate acquisitions are based principally on profit considerations.

Retrenchment/Turnaround

For any of a large number of reasons a business can find itself with declining profits. Economic recessions, production inefficiencies, and innovative break-throughs by competitors are only three causes. In many cases strategic managers believe the firm can survive and eventually recover if a concerted effort is made over a period of a few years to fortify basic distinctive competencies. This type of grand strategy is known as *retrenchment*. It is typically accomplished in one of two ways, employed singly or in combination:

1. *Cost reduction.* Examples include decreasing the work force through employee attrition, leasing rather than purchasing equipment, extending the life of machinery, and eliminating elaborate promotional activities.
2. *Asset reduction.* Examples include the sale of land, buildings, and equipment not essential to the basic activity of the business, and elimination of "perks" like the company airplane and executive cars.

If these initial approaches fail to achieve the required reductions, more drastic action may be necessary. It is sometimes essential to lay off employees, drop items from a production line, and even eliminate low-margin customers.

Since the underlying purpose of retrenchment is to reverse current negative trends, the method is often referred to as a *turnaround* strategy. Interestingly, the turnaround most commonly associated with this approach is in management positions. In a study of 58 large firms, researchers Schendel, Patton, and Riggs found that turnaround was almost always associated with changes in top management.[7] Bringing in new managers was believed to introduce needed new perspectives of the firm's situation, to raise employee morale,

---

[7] Dan G. Schendel, G. Richard Patton, and James Riggs, "Corporate Turnaround Strategies: A Study of Profit Decline and Recovery," *Journal of General Management* 3 (1976), pp. 3–11.

and to facilitate drastic actions, such as deep budgetary cuts in established programs.

Divestiture

A *divestiture strategy* involves the sale of a business or a major business component. When retrenchment fails to accomplish the desired turnaround, strategic managers often decide to sell the business. However, because the intent is to find a buyer willing to pay a premium above the value of fixed assets for a going concern, the term *marketing for sale* is more appropriate. Prospective buyers must be convinced that because of their skills and resources, or the synergy with their existing businesses, they will be able to profit from the acquisition.

The reasons for divestiture vary. Often they arise because of partial mismatches between the acquired business and the parent corporation. Some of the mismatched parts cannot be integrated into the corporation's mainstream and thus must be spun off. A second reason is corporation financial needs. Sometimes the cash flow or financial stability of the corporation as a whole can be greatly improved if businesses with high market value can be sacrificed. A third, less frequent reason for divestiture is government antitrust action when a corporation is believed to monopolize or unfairly dominate a particular market.

Although examples of grand strategies of divestiture are numerous, an outstanding example in the last decade is Chrysler Corporation, which in quick succession divested itself of several major businesses to protect its mission as a domestic automobile manufacturer. Among major Chrysler sales were its Airtempt air-conditioning business to Fedders and its automotive subsidiaries in France, Spain, and England to Peugeot–Citroen. These divestitures yielded Chrysler a total of almost $500 million in cash, notes, and stock and, thus, in the relatively short term, improved its financial stability. Other corporations that have recently pursued this type of grand strategy include Esmark, which divested Swift and Company, and White Motors, which divested White Farm.

An example of the value of divestiture is shown in Strategy in Action 9–6. As discussed, Gulf & Western used the proceeds of divestitures together with savings from selective retrenchments to create tax write-offs and reduce the firm's huge level of long-term debt.

Liquidation

When the grand strategy is that of *liquidation*, the business is typically sold in parts, only occasionally as a whole, but for its tangible asset value and not as a going concern. In selecting liquidation, owners and strategic managers

Strategy in Action 9–6
Gulf & Western Slims Down

Charles Bluhdorn was one of the earliest and flashiest conglomerateurs, a master of the unfriendly takeover. Starting with a small auto-parts company in 1958, he assembled an incredible array of disparate businesses into Gulf & Western Industries (1982 sales: $5.3 billion). Bluhdorn eventually bought some 100 companies large and small, ranging from Paramount Pictures to publisher Simon & Schuster to New York City's Madison Square Garden. In one six-year period, he brought 80 firms into what became jokingly known as "Engulf and Devour." Bluhdorn died in February 1983, at 56, after a heart attack, and his successors were in no mood to keep up that pace. They contracted Gulf & Western almost as fast as Bluhdorn had expanded it.

In 1983, a new management team headed by Vice Chairman and Chief Executive Martin Davis, 56, announced a major streamlining program to rid the company of low-profit operations. Among the cast-offs: Arlington Park race track near Chicago and Roosevelt Raceway in New York, manufacturer E. W. Bliss, and Sega's video-game unit. The moves saved the company about $470 million in tax write-offs, but produced a loss of $215 million in the first year.

The divestitures were just the latest ordered by Davis, who went to Gulf & Western from Paramount in 1969 and took over immediately after Bluhdorn's death. Davis had earlier moved to sell off $650 million of company-owned stock in 30 companies, leaving the conglomerate with some $150 million in such holdings. The money was used to bring down the company's mountain of debt to $1.2 billion. Davis then also sold Gulf & Western's 21.4 percent stake in Brunswick, the sports equipment manufacturer, for $97 million. Davis likewise chopped away at the company's work force, reducing it by about 10,000 to 47,000.

Pointless mixing of dissimilar firms seemed finished at Gulf & Western. Said Shearson/American Express analyst Scott Merlis: "Few of their businesses were related to their other businesses." Instead, the company now seemed determined to focus sharply on a few areas: consumer products (apparel, Kayser-Roth; home furnishings, Simmons), entertainment (Paramount), and financial services (Associates Corp.).

Gulf & Western was only one of several companies to follow the newly fashionable divestiture route. Such firms as Beatrice Foods, Quaker Oats, and General Electric all sold off major holdings during 1982–1983.

Source: "The Big Sell-Off," *Time,* August 29, 1983, p. 45.

of a business are admitting failure and recognize that this action is likely to result in great hardships to themselves and their employees. For these reasons liquidation is usually seen as the least attractive of all grand strategies. However, as a long-term strategy it minimizes the loss to all stakeholders of the firm. Usually faced with bankruptcy, the liquidating business tries to develop a planned and orderly system that will result in the greatest possible return and cash conversion as the business slowly relinquishes its market share.

Planned liquidation can be worthwhile. For example, the Columbia Corporation, a $130 million diversified firm, liquidated its assets for more cash per share than the market value of its stock.

Selection of Long-Term Objectives and Grand Strategy Sets

At first glance the strategic management model, which provides the framework for study throughout this book, seems to suggest that strategic choice decision making leads to the *sequential* selections of long-term objectives and grand strategy. In fact, however, strategic choice is the *simultaneous* selection of long-range objectives and grand strategy. Figure 9–5 depicts the actual process. When strategic planners study their opportunities, they try to determine which are most likely to result in achieving various long-range objectives. Almost simultaneously they try to forecast whether an available grand strategy can take advantage of preferred opportunities so that the tentative objectives can be met. In essence, then, three distinct but highly interdependent choices are being made at one time. Usually several triads or sets of possible decisions are considered.

A simplified example of this process is shown in Figure 9–6. In this example the business has determined that six strategic choice options are available. These options stem from three different interactive opportunities (e.g., West Coast markets) that present little competition. Because each of these interactive opportunities can be approached through different grand strategies—in options 1 and 2 they are horizontal integration and market development—each offers the potential for achieving long-range objectives to varying degrees. Thus, a business can rarely make a strategic choice only on the basis of its preferred opportunities, long-range objectives, or grand strategy. Instead, the three elements must be considered simultaneously because only in combination do they constitute a strategic choice.

In an actual decision situation the strategic choice would be complicated by a wider variety of interactive opportunities, feasible company objectives, promising grand strategy options, and evaluative criteria. Nevertheless, Figure 9–6 does partially reflect the nature and complexity of the process by which long-term objectives and grand strategy are selected.

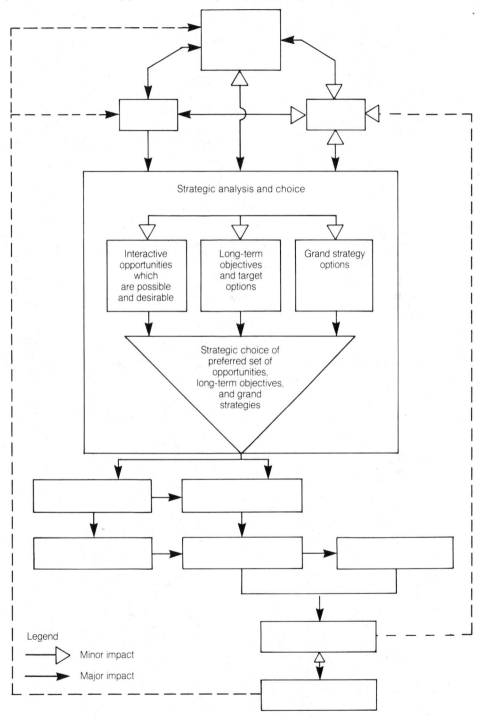

Strategic analysis and choice

Interactive opportunities which are possible and desirable

Long-term objectives and target options

Grand strategy options

Strategic choice of preferred set of opportunities, long-term objectives, and grand strategies

Legend

Minor impact

Major impact

Figure 9–6
A profile of strategic choice options

	Six strategic choice options					
	1	2	3	4	5	6
Interactive opportunities	West Coast markets present little competition		Current markets sensitive to price competition		Current industry product lines after too narrow a range of markets	
Appropriate long-range objectives (limited sample):						
Average 5-year ROI	15%	19%	13%	17%	23%	15%
Company sales by year 5	+50%	+40%	+20%	+0%	+35%	+25%
Risk of negative profit	.30	.25	.10	.15	.20	.05
Grand strategies	Horizontal integration	Market development	Concentration	Selective retrenchment	Product development	Concentration

In the next chapter, the strategic choice process will be fully explained. However, knowledge of long-term objectives and grand strategies is essential to understanding that process. Thus, the topics were presented here first, even though a company's specific selections of long-term objectives and grand strategies are actually outputs based on choice, as the strategic management process model shows.

Sequence of Objectives and Strategy Selection

The selection of long-term objectives and grand strategies involves simultaneous rather than sequential decisions. While it is true that objectives are needed so that the company's direction and progress are not determined by random forces, it is equally true that objectives are valuable only if strategies can be implemented, making achievement of objectives realistic. In fact, the selection of long-term objectives and grand strategies is so interdependent that until the 1970s most business consultants and academicians did not stress the need to distinguish between them. Most popular business literature and practicing executives still combine long-term objectives and grand strategies under the heading of company strategy.

However, the distinction has merit. Objectives indicate what strategic managers *want* but provide few insights as to *how* this will be achieved. Conversely, strategies indicate what type of *actions* will be taken but do not define what *ends* will be pursued or what criteria will serve as constraints in refining the strategic plan.

The latter view of objectives as constraints on strategy formulation rather than as ends toward which strategies are directed is stressed by several prominent management experts.[8] They argue that strategic decisions are designed (1) to satisfy the minimum requirements of different company groups, for example, the production department's need for more inventory capacity, or the marketing department's need to increase the sales force and (2) to create synergistic profit potential given these constraints.

Does it matter whether strategic decisions are made to achieve objectives or to satisfy constraints? No, because constraints are objectives themselves. The constraint of increased inventory capacity is a desire (an objective), not a certainty. Likewise, the constraint of a larger sales force does not assure that it will be achieved given such factors as other company priorities, labor market conditions, and the firm's profit performance.

---

[8] See, for example, P. F. Drucker, *The Practice of Management* (New York: Harper & Row, 1954); R. M. Cyert, and J. G. March, *A Behavioral Theory of the Firm* (Englewood Cliffs, N.J.: Prentice-Hall, 1963); H. A. Simon, "On the Concept of Organizational Goals," *Administrative Science Quarterly* 9 (1964), pp. 1–22; and M. D. Richards, *Organizational Goal Structures* (St. Paul, Minn.: West Publishing, 1978).

Summary

Before learning how strategic decisions are made, it was important to understand the two principal components of any strategic choice, namely, long-term objectives and grand strategy. Such understanding was the purpose of the chapter.

Long-term objectives were defined as the results a business seeks to achieve over a specified period of time, typically five years. Seven common long-term objectives were discussed: profitability, productivity, competitive position, employee development, employee relations, technological leadership, and public responsibility. These, or any other long-term objectives, should be acceptable, flexible, measurable over time, motivating, suitable, understandable, and achievable.

Grand strategies were defined as comprehensive approaches guiding major actions designed to achieve long-term business objectives. Twelve specific grand strategy options were discussed. They included concentration, market development, product development, innovation, horizontal integration, vertical integration, joint ventures, concentric diversification, conglomerate diversification, retrenchment/turnaround, divestiture, and liquidation.

Questions for Discussion

1. Think of the business community nearest to your college or university. Identify businesses you believe are using each of the 12 grand strategies.
2. Try to identify businesses in your community that appear to rely principally on 1 of the 12 grand strategies. What kind of information did you use to classify the firms?
3. Write a long-term objective for your school of business that exhibits the seven qualities of long-term objectives described in this chapter.
4. Distinguish between the following pairs of grand strategies:
    a. Horizontal and vertical integration.
    b. Conglomerate and concentric diversification.
    c. Product development and innovation.
5. Rank each of the 12 grand strategy options on the following three scales:

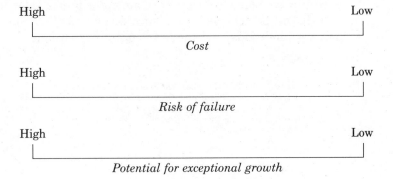

High   Low

Cost

High   Low

Risk of failure

High   Low

Potential for exceptional growth

6. Identify companies that use one of the eight specific options shown in Figure 9–1 under the grand strategies of concentration, market development, and product development.

Bibliography

Ansoff, H. I. "Strategies for Diversification." *Harvard Business Review,* September–October 1957, pp. 113–24.

————. *Corporate Strategy.* New York: McGraw-Hill, 1965.

————. *Strategic Management.* New York: John Wiley & Sons, 1979.

Cyert, R. M., and J. G. March. *A Behavioral Theory of the Firm.* Englewood Cliffs, N.J.: Prentice-Hall, 1963.

Drucker, P. F. *The Practice of Management.* New York: Harper & Row, 1954.

Glueck, W. F. *Business Policy and Strategic Management.* New York: McGraw-Hill, 1980.

Higgins, J. M. *Organizational Policy and Strategic Management.* Hinsdale, Ill.: Dryden Press, 1979.

King, R., and D. I. Cleland. *Strategic Planning and Policy.* New York: Van Nostrand Reinhold, 1978.

Kotler, P. *Marketing Management.* Englewood Cliffs, N.J.: Prentice-Hall, 1972.

Luck, D. J., and A. E. Prell. *Market Strategy.* New York: Appleton-Century-Crofts, 1968.

Osborn, A. F. *Applied Imagination.* 3rd rev. ed. New York: Charles Scribner's Sons, 1968.

Pearce, J. A., II. "An Executive-Level Perspective on the Strategic Management Process." *California Management Review,* Summer 1981, pp. 39–48.

————. "Selecting among Alternative Grand Strategies." *California Management Review,* Spring 1982.

Richards, M. D. *Organizational Goal Structures.* St. Paul, Minn.: West Publishing, 1978.

Schendel, Dan G.; G. R. Patton; and J. Riggs. "Corporate Turnaround Strategies: A Study of Profit Decline and Recovery." *Journal of General Management* 3 (1976), pp. 3–11.

Schorr, B. "Many New Products Fizzle, Despite Careful Planning, Publicity." *The Wall Street Journal,* April 5, 1961.

Simon, H. A. "On the Concept of Organizational Goals." *Administrative Science Quarterly,* 1964, pp. 1–22.

Steiner, G. A. *Strategic Planning.* New York: Free Press, 1979.

Steiner, G. A., and J. B. Miner. *Management Policy and Strategy.* New York: Macmillan, 1977.

Chapter 9 Cohesion Case Illustration

Long-Term Objectives and Grand Strategies at Holiday Inns, Inc.

Long-term objectives at Holiday Inns, Inc., exist at both the corporate and business levels. Selected examples of long-term objectives are provided below:

Corporate Long-Term Objectives:

Increase corporatewide return on equity to 17.5 percent by 1984.

Achieve and maintain a debt-to-invested-capital ratio that does not exceed a 40–50 percent range.

Improve the corporatewide after-tax margin to a minimum of 7 percent by 1984.

Ensure a corporationwide sales growth that will maintain hotel group contribution at less than 60 percent of sales by 1984.

Business Group Long-Term Objectives:

Increase the number of rooms in the HI system by 70,000 between 1982 and 1987. *(Hotel group)*

Improve hotel operating margins to 20 percent by 1984. *(Hotel group)*

Triple the number of company-owned properties in multiuser locations by 1987. *(Hotel group)*

Increase the cash flow generated by Delta for corporatewide use from $25 million in 1980 to $60 million in 1985. *(Transportation group)*

Increase the ROI from gaming operations to 15 percent by 1987. *(Casino group)*

Increase the average daily customer count at Perkins restaurants to 1,000 people per day by 1987. *(Restaurant group)*

These objectives provide examples of the strategic focus that long-term objectives can provide the firm. Strategic direction is further clarified through grand strategies.

Twelve fundamental grand strategies were discussed in Chapter 9. Each grand strategy is illustrated below as it might apply to a particular business group:

Concentration.   The *hotel group* might consider that continued emphasis on expansion of selected company-owned and franchised Holiday Inn properties has sufficient potential to achieve long-term objectives. This would call for a concentration on growth via the group's current approach with emphasis on maintaining and improving operating advantages and effectiveness.

Market Development.   The *hotel group* might determine that domestic growth potential is decreasing. If so, it might pursue a strategy that emphasizes major international expansion of the Holiday Inns network.

Product Development.   *Perkins* might determine that inadequate menu selection is one reason for its mediocre performance. A product development strategy would therefore pursue growth via systematic development and expansion of menu items.

Innovation.   The *transportation group* might consider pursuing growth via the systematic development of a revolutionary new ship design for shipping operations. This innovation-based strategy would be one option (probably a remote one) for the transportation group.

Horizontal Integration.   One way for the *gaming group* to grow rapidly would be to acquire casinos in key markets where the group currently competes or desires to compete.

Vertical Integration.   Vertical integration can be either *forward* or *backward*. For example, *Delta Steamships* might see growth via route expansion as fairly limited. As a result it might seek manufacturing capacity for LASH containers *(backward integration)* to serve its needs and those of other shippers. Another alternative is involvement in warehousing or brokering *(forward integration)* as a basis for shipping-related growth.

Joint Ventures.   The *hotel group* may project faster growth in the high-priced and budget-priced lodging segments than in the broad middle segment. It may seek joint ventures with chains in one or both of these segments to get a foothold and a possible expansion base.

Retrenchment.   Profits of the *transportation group* declined for several years in the late 1970s. A retrenchment strategy cutting out unprofitable routes, unnecessary overhead, and level of terminal services was a possible grand strategy for this group.

Divestiture. The *restaurant group* may determine that the best way to achieve long-term ROI objectives is to sell several subpar restaurant locations. Selling these as going concerns would represent a divestiture strategy if it represented the group's key orientation.

Liquidation. The *hotel group* acquired over 30 businesses supplying its institutional products needs in the 1960s. Most of these businesses solely supplied Holiday Inns' institutional and printing needs. The hotel group might choose to sell the equipment used by some of these businesses if sale of the business as a going concern is not realistic. This would be a liquidation strategy.

Concentric Diversification. The best way to view this grand strategy at Holiday Inns, Inc., is to look at selected decisions made at Holiday Inns when it was predominantly a hotel chain. Holiday Inns' expansion into the freestanding restaurant business and the casino-gaming business is a concentric diversification strategy in relation to Holiday Inns, Inc.'s dominant core business.

Conglomerate Diversification. From the same perspective, Holiday Inns, Inc.'s acquisition of Trailways and Delta Steamship represents a conglomerate diversification strategy in that these businesses were essentially unrelated to Holiday Inns' core businesses.

These examples illustrate each grand strategy concept. As you can see, each grand strategy is a possible alternative for at least one of Holiday Inns, Inc.'s businesses.

10

Strategic Analysis and Choice

The previous chapter described basic characteristics of major strategic alternatives that a firm might consider. Several questions remain. How does a company identify alternative strategies? What are some of the diagnostic tools used to identify and evaluate realistic alternative strategies in multibusiness companies? What factors influence the ultimate choice of strategy?

This chapter will examine possible answers to these questions. Techniques used to aid strategic choice at the corporate and business levels will be explored. Managerial, political, and behavioral factors affecting the choice of strategy will also be discussed.

The search for alternative strategies is both incremental and creative in that strategists begin by considering alternatives they are familiar with and think will work. These are usually incremental alterations of past strategies. Systematic comparison of external and internal factors is often used to search for alternative strategies. Creativity can be important in this internal/external comparison. The search for multiple alternatives depends on systematic comparison of the strengths, weaknesses, risks, and trade-offs of each alternative. Several alternatives are generated and systematically evaluated in a comparative framework. The quality of the ultimate choice is thereby logically enhanced. Evaluation of alternative strategies is much the same whether new alternatives or the old strategy is considered. The focus is the future. Both old and new strategies must be subjected to the same systematic evaluation if a logical choice is to be made.

Figure 10–1
The process of strategic analysis

	Corporate-level strategy	Business-level strategy
Time	Analysis of the overall company *portfolio* of businesses in terms of relative business unit strength *matched* with relative industry attractiveness and stage of development.	Analysis of the *match* between the business's current strategic position (company profile) and the major strategic opportunities and threats (environmental analysis) that exist or will exist in the planning time period.
	Identification of probable corporate performance if the current business unit portfolio is maintained with respective strategies.	Examining the probable results of pursuing the current strategy in light of the new business–environment match.
	Comparison of this projected corporate performance with tentative corporate objectives to identify major performance gaps.	Comparison of these results with tentative business objectives to identify major performance gaps and strategic concerns.
	Identification of alternative portfolios (including different strategy combinations at the business unit level) to close performance gaps.	Identification of alternative strategies to close performance gaps and confront (or avoid) strategic concerns.
	Evaluation of the alternatives and strategic choice.	Evaluation of the alternatives and strategic choice.

The process of strategic analysis and choice involves five incremental phases. Figure 10–1 identifies these phases at the business and corporate levels. Because strategic choice is a judgmental/analytical process meant to ascertain the future impact of one or more strategies on corporate (and/or business unit) performance, the answers to three basic questions are sought:

1. How effective has the existing strategy been?
2. How effective will that strategy be in the future?
3. What will be the effectiveness of selected alternative strategies (or changes in the existing strategy) in the future?

Strategic Analysis at the Corporate Level

A fundamental method of corporate strategic analysis in diversified, multi-industry companies is the business portfolio approach. General Electric, for example, has over 40 strategic business units (SBUs).[1] Thus, General Electric must decide how this portfolio of businesses should be managed to achieve corporate objectives. A corporate strategy is sought that sets the basic "strategic

---

[1] General Electric combined selected businesses or operations, regardless of organizational level, into SBUs for planning purposes.

An SBU is generally created when the following requirements are met by the component:

1. It has a unique business mission.
2. It has an identifiable set of competitors.
3. It is a viable competitor.
4. The SBU strategic manager can make or implement a strategic decision relatively independent of other SBUs.
5. Crucial operating decisions can be made within the SBU.

thrust" for each business unit in a manner consistent with the resource capabilities of the overall company.

The *portfolio approach,* with analysis of corporate-level strategy distinct from business-level strategy, is adaptable to multiproduct market firms in which each product/market is managed as a separate business or profit center and the firm is not dominated by one product/market. The approach involves examining each business as a separate entity and as a contributor to the corporation's total *portfolio* of businesses. In dominant product/market companies and single product/market firms, corporate strategy considerations are not separate and distinct from business-level considerations.

In a broad sense, corporate strategy is concerned with generation and allocation of corporate resources. The firm's portfolio of businesses are, to varying degrees, the generators and recipients of these resources. The portfolio approach provides a simple, visual way of identifying and evaluating alternative strategies for the generation and allocation of corporate resources.

The BCG Growth/Share Matrix

One of the most widely used portfolio approaches to corporate strategic analysis has been the growth/share matrix pioneered by the Boston Consulting Group (BCG) and illustrated in Figure 10–2. This matrix facilitates corporate strategic analysis of likely "generators" and optimum "users" of corporate resources. Strategy in Action 10–1 provides a description of the use of the BCG matrix at Mead Corporation.

To use the BCG matrix, each of the company's businesses is plotted according to market growth rate (percentage growth in sales) and relative competitive position (market share). Market growth rate is the projected rate of sales growth for the market to be served by a particular business. It is usually measured as the percentage increase in a market's sales or unit volume over the two most recent years. Market growth rate provides an indicator of the relative attractiveness of the markets served by each of the businesses in the corporation's portfolio of businesses. Relative competitive position is usually expressed as the ratio of a business's market share divided by the market share of the largest competitor in that market. Relative competitive position thus provides a basis for comparing the relative strengths of different businesses in the business portfolio in terms of the "strength" of their position in each business's respective market.

Businesses are plotted on the matrix once their market growth rate and relative competitive positions have been computed. Figure 10–2 represents the BCG matrix for a company with nine businesses. Each circle represents a business unit. The size of the circle represents the proportion of corporate revenue generated by that business unit. This provides visualization of the current importance of each business as a revenue generator.

Market growth rate is frequently separated into "high" and "low" areas by an arbitrary 10 percent growth line. Relative competitive position is usually

Figure 10–2
BCG's growth/share matrix

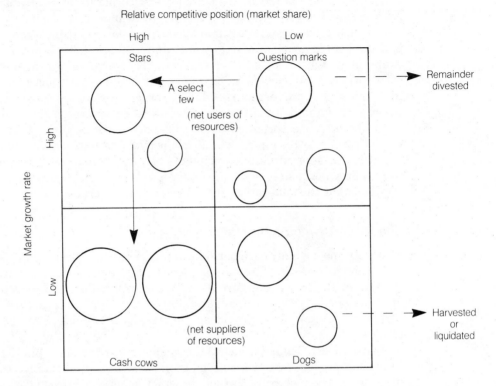

divided at a relative market share between 1.0 and 1.5, so that a "high" position signifies market leadership. Once plotted, businesses in the BCG matrix will be in one of four cells with differing implications for their role in an overall corporate-level strategy.

High-Growth/High Competitive Position. The *stars,* as the BCG matrix labeled them, are businesses in rapidly growing markets with large market shares. Stars represent the best long-run opportunities (growth and profitability) in the firm's portfolio. These businesses require substantial investment to maintain (and expand) their dominant position in a growing market. This investment requirement is often in excess of what can be generated internally. Therefore, these businesses are short-term, priority consumers of corporate resources within the overall business portfolio.

Low-Growth/High Competitive Position. *Cash cows* are high-market-share businesses in maturing, low-growth markets or industries. Because of their strong position and minimal reinvestment requirements for growth, these

Strategy in Action 10–1
Portfolio Management at Mead Corporation

Mead Corporation, under the direction of Chairman and CEO J. W. McSwiney, was one of the pioneers in the use of a portfolio approach in the strategic management of its numerous forest-products-related businesses. The following is excerpted from a presentation by J. W. McSwiney, President Warren L. Batts, and Vice Chairman William W. Wommack to Paper and Forest Products Analysts at the Princeton Club in New York about Mead's early experience using portfolio planning:

> As the first step toward achieving Mead's corporate goals, Mr. McSwiney assigned Bill Wommack full-time responsibility for developing a new strategic philosophy, a planning system, and then a strategy for each of Mead's businesses. The strategic concept he developed was straightforward and very effective:
>
> Obtain market leadership in markets we serve.
>
> If market leadership is not possible, redeploy our assets to markets where leadership potential exists.
>
> This concept can be translated into a matrix as follows:

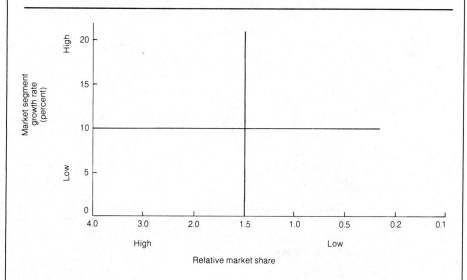

Continued on Page 282

Strategy in Action 10–1 (*continued*)

We consider a high-growth market to be one that is growing by at
least 10 percent in real terms. To us, relative market share is what counts.
We consider a leadership position exists when a business has a market
share that is at least 1.5 times the share of its next largest competitor, as
shown by the vertical line at 1.5 in the figure above.

Starting with the upper right-hand quadrant:

For a business in a high-growth market with a low market share, we assess
our chances for leadership, and either grow our share aggressively or
get out.

In a high-growth market with a high market share, we grow our share as
rapidly as we can and invest to become the most cost-effective producer.

In a low-growth market with a high market share, we maintain our market
share and cost effectiveness. We also generate cash for the balance of the
company.

In a low-growth market with low market share, we operate to generate cash—
we have generally found this means we get out.

When we classified our businesses on this matrix, we found many were
competing in low-growth segments with low market share. We decided
that within five years we should eliminate those low-growth and low-market-
share businesses and allocate capital to the remaining businesses so that
they could attain greater market share and grow larger.

Our first step was to dispose of 15 businesses where it was not
practical to become a leader. They were essentially the low-growth, low-
market-share businesses. This step generated $80 million in cash, plus it
saved $25 million we would have had to invest if we'd kept them. Especially
important, these actions immediately improved our mix of businesses and
the total return from our assets.

Second, we had to change the way our managers managed; plus we all
had to operate in a more highly focused manner. We started with formal
in-house training programs for some 300 Mead managers. [Our strategy]
would not be carried out unless key managers truly understood the new
. . . philosophy . . . and how to use the underlying analytical techniques.
But even when managers understood what we were trying to do, some
were unable to accept the discipline required. We had to reorganize several
businesses and change a number of managers. Five of our six operating
group vice presidents were changed, as well as 19 of our 24 division
presidents. Fortunately, the talent to effect these changes was largely in-
house.

Finally, we put increased emphasis on managing our assets. We consider
return on net assets the true measure of operating performance, so we
tied each general manager's compensation to a balance between his business
unit's earnings and its net assets.

Continued on Page 283

Strategy in Action 10–1 (*concluded*)

We categorized and managed our businesses from a strategic point of view as follows:

Poor businesses.

Those businesses which had good strategies in place.

Those businesses which needed a change in strategy.

Examining these categories demonstrates how we improved our results by:

Shifting assets.

Improving performance.

Carefully investing.

Category	Asset mix		Return on net assets	
	Year 1	Year 5	Year 1	Year 5
Poor businesses	13.2%	2.1%	2.4%	4.2%
No change	38.5	53.4	8.8	9.6
Change	48.3	44.5	2.8	11.8
Total corporate	100.0%	100.0%	4.7%	10.4%

In year 1 our sales totaled $1.1 billion. Four years later sales totaled $1.6 billion. This was a 9 percent compound growth rate, even though we had disposed of businesses having sales of $180 million. It is worth noting that sales of our Forest Products category increased at a 15 percent rate, so that percentage of the total rose to 56 percent.

Pretax earnings during this period increased from about $39 million to $167 million, or a 34 percent compound growth rate. Again, earnings in our Forest Products category increased sixfold.

We continually review our businesses, and we will reclassify a business and change its strategy when it's prudent to do so.

I believe we now have the fundamentals for long-term success firmly in place—both in the physical sense of good businesses serving growing markets, and in the management sense of realistic objectives, sound strategies—and the internal discipline to carry them out.

Source: Mead executive management presentation to Paper and Forest Product Analysts at the Princeton Club, New York, February 8, 1977. Reprinted with permission.

businesses often generate cash in excess of their needs. Therefore, these businesses are selectively "milked" as a source of corporate resources for deployment elsewhere (to stars and question marks). Cash cows are yesterday's stars and remain the current foundation of their corporate portfolios. They provide the cash to pay corporate overhead and dividends and also provide debt capacity. They are managed to maintain their strong market share while efficiently generating excess resources for corporatewide use.

Low-Growth/Low Competitive Position. The BCG matrix calls businesses with low market share and low market growth the *dogs* in the firm's portfolio. These businesses are in saturated, mature markets with intense competition and low profit margins. Because of their weak position, these businesses are managed for short-term cash flow (through ruthless cost cutting, for example) to supplement corporate-level resource needs. According to the original BCG prescription, they are eventually divested or liquidated once the short-term harvesting is maximized.

Recent research has questioned the notion that all *dogs* should be destined for divestiture/liquidation.[2] The thrust of this research suggests that *well-managed dogs* turn out to be positive, highly reliable resource generators (although still far less resource rich than cows). The well-managed dogs, according to these studies, combine a narrow business focus, emphasis on high product quality and moderate prices, strenuous cost cutting and cost control, and limited advertising. While suggesting that well-managed dogs can be a useful component of a business portfolio, these studies warn that ineffective dogs should still be considered prime candidates for harvesting, divestiture, or liquidation.

High-Growth/Low Competitive Position. *Question mark* businesses have considerable appeal because of their high growth rate yet present questionable profit potential because of low market share. Question mark businesses are known as cash guzzlers because their cash needs are high as a result of rapid growth, while their cash generation is low due to a small market share. Because market growth rate is high, a favorable market share (competitive position) should be easier to obtain than with the dogs in the portfolio. At the corporate level the concern is identifying the question marks that would most benefit from extra corporate resources resulting in increased market share and movement into the star group. When this long-run shift in a business's position from question mark to star is unlikely, the BCG matrix suggests divesting the business to reposition the resources more effectively in the remaining portfolio.

---

[2] Carlyn Y. Woo and Arnold C. Cooper, "Strategies of Effective Low-Market-Share Businesses," *Harvard Business Review,* November–December 1982, pp. 106–13; Donald Hambrick and Ian MacMillan, "Dogs," *Boardroom Reports,* October 15, 1981, pp. 5–6.

The BCG matrix was a valuable initial development in the portfolio approach to corporate-level strategy evaluation. The goal of the BCG approach is to determine the corporate strategy that best provides a balanced portfolio of business units. BCG's ideal, balanced portfolio would have the largest sales in cash cows and stars, with only a few question marks and very few dogs (the latter with favorable cash flow).

The BCG matrix makes two major contributions to corporate strategic choice: the assignment of a specific role or mission for each business unit and the integration of multiple business units into a total corporate strategy. By focusing simultaneously on comparative growth/share positions, the underlying premise of corporate strategy becomes exploitation of competitive advantage.

While the BCG matrix is an important visual tool with which to analyze corporate (business portfolio) strategy, strategists must recognize six limitations:

1. Clearly defining a *market* is often difficult. As a result, accurately measuring *share* and *growth rate* can be a problem. This, in turn, creates the potential for distortion or manipulation.

2. Dividing the matrix into four cells based on a *high/low* classification scheme is somewhat simplistic. It does not recognize the markets with *average* growth rates or the businesses with *average* market shares.

3. The relationship between market share and profitability underlying the BCG matrix—the *experience curve* effect—varies across industries and market segments. In some industries a large market share creates major advantages in unit costs; in others it does not. Furthermore, some companies with low market share can generate superior profitability and cash flow with careful strategies based on differentiation, innovation, or market segmentation. Mercedes-Benz and Polaroid are two examples.

4. The BCG matrix is not particularly helpful in comparing relative investment opportunities across different business units in the corporate portfolio. For example, is every star better than a cash cow? How should one question mark be compared to another in terms of whether it should be built into a star or divested?[3]

5. Strategic evaluation of a set of businesses requires examination of more than relative market shares and market growth. The attractiveness of an industry may increase based on technological, seasonal, competitive, or other considerations as much as on growth rate. Likewise, the value of a business within a corporate portfolio is often linked to considerations other than market share.[4]

---

[3] Derek F. Abell and John S. Hammond, *Strategic Market Planning* (Englewood Cliffs, N.J.: Prentice-Hall, 1979), p. 212.

[4] For an interesting elaboration of this point, see Walter E. Ketchell III, "Oh Where Oh Where Has My Little Dog Gone? Or My Cash Cow? Or My Star?" *Fortune*, November 2, 1981, pp. 148–52.

6. The four colorful classifications in the BCG matrix somewhat oversimplify the types of businesses in a corporate portfolio. Likewise, the simple strategic missions recommended by the BCG matrix often don't reflect the diversity of options available, as shown earlier in discussing dogs.

Before leaving the BCG matrix, the use of labels associated with this matrix deserves further comment. A recent survey of numerous executives in large firms using portfolio-planning techniques found widespread dislike of the *dog, question mark, cash cow,* and *star* terminology. Typical executive comments were as follows:

> To the extent that a division manager was to see a chart and see the word "dog" written next to his division, it's bound to create motivational problems. It's much easier to say that your mission is to reduce investment and you will be paid for achieving that objective and not for maximizing sales growth than to say you are a cash cow or a dog.
>
> We try to avoid the use of words such as cash cow or dog like the plague. If you call a business a dog, it'll respond like one. It's one thing to know that you are an ugly duckling—much worse to be told explicitly that you are.[5]

While criticism was widespread regarding BCG labels, there was strong support for use of more meaningful labels associated with positions in the BCG matrix or the GE planning grid (see Figure 10–3). Typical comments were as follows:

> In our company, the business unit labels are made explicit. In fact, the business unit managers are the ones who recommend what the strategy for their businesses should be. If we did not use explicit strategy labels, such as "build," "hold," and "harvest," the room for confusion over exactly what a business unit's strategy is would be very high. At the same time, it is important to remember that a business that's harvest today might need to have a build strategy tomorrow.
>
> Our business units know their strategies in terms such as "grow," "maintain," and "shrink." Only "withdraw" is not made explicit. Making strategy explicit helps in implementation; for example, it ensures that harvest managers won't ask for resources. . . . We don't label managers, but only their businesses; we keep moving people around since the idea is to develop well-rounded managers.[6]

This study suggests a preference for such strategy labels as *build, hold, harvest,* and *withdraw* rather than *star, cash cow, question mark,* and *dog* in the strategic planning activities of major multibusiness firms. The reasons are apparently threefold:

1. Some of the BCG terms are seen as negative and unnecessarily graphic.
2. The BCG terms are somewhat "static," while "build/hold/harvest" are more dynamic and action oriented.

---

[5] Anil K. Gupta and V. Govindarajan, "Build, Hold, Harvest: Converting Strategic Intentions into Reality," *Journal of Business Strategy,* March 1984, pp. 34–47.

[6] Ibid., p. 40.

Figure 10–3
General Electric's nine-cell planning grid

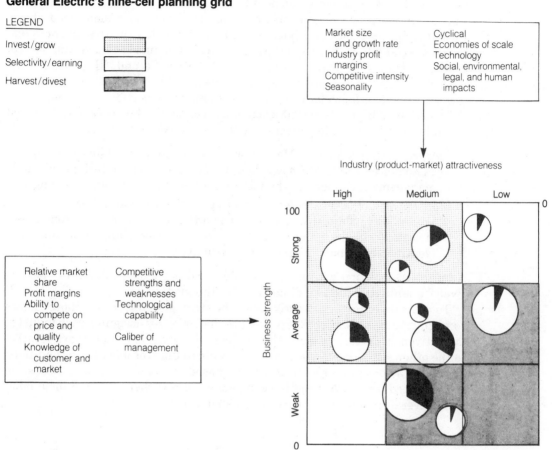

3. Terms like "dog/star/cash cow" have meaning only within a BCG context, while "build/hold/harvest" have universal validity and clarity of strategic intent even without a portfolio planning approach.

One executive's comment perhaps best illustrates the value of the preferred set of strategy labels:

> We have [generally] shied away from using any portfolio model. Yet we recognize that different businesses may need to have different strategic missions. In fact, our strategy documents require business unit managers to indicate explicitly the strategies for their units in terms such as "build," "hold," "harvest," "withdraw," and "explore."[7]

---

[7] Ibid., p. 35.

The GE Nine-Cell Planning Grid[8]

General Electric popularized an adaptation of the BCG approach (Figure 10–3) that attempts to overcome some of the matrix limitations mentioned above. First, the GE grid uses multiple factors to assess industry attractiveness and business strength, rather than the single measures (market share and market growth, respectively) employed in the BCG matrix. Second, GE expanded the matrix from four cells to nine—replacing the high/low axes with high/medium/low axes to make finer distinction between business portfolio positions.

To use the GE planning grid, each of the company's business units is rated on multiple sets of strategic factors within each axis of the grid:

Business strength factors: Market share, profit margin, ability to compete, customer and market knowledge, competitive position, technology, and management caliber are the factors contributing to business strength.

Industry attractiveness factors: Market growth, size and industry profitability, competition, seasonality and cyclical qualities, economies of scale, technology, and social/environmental/legal/human factors are identified as enhancing industry attractiveness.

A business's position within the planning grid is then calculated by "subjectively" quantifying the two dimensions of the grid.

To measure industry attractiveness, the strategist first selects those factors contributing to this aspect. The procedure then involves assigning each industry attractiveness factor a weight that reflects its perceived importance relative to the other attractiveness factors. Favorable to unfavorable future conditions for those factors are forecast and rated based on some scale (a 0- to-1 scale is illustrated below). A weighted composite score is then obtained for a business's overall industry attractiveness as show below.

Industry attractiveness factor	*Weight*	*Rating**	*Score*
Market size	20	0.5	10.0
Project market growth	35	1.0	35.0
Technological requirements	15	0.5	7.5
Concentration (a few large competitors)	30	0	0
Political and regulatory factors	Must be nonrestrictive	—	—
Total	100		52.5

* High = 1.0; Medium = 0.5; Low = 0.0.

---

[8] Label terminology in the GE planning grid is more consistent with executives' preferences. The discussion of the GE labels is cross-referenced to BCG terminology to show the overlap between the two sets of labels.

To assess business strength, a similar procedure is followed in selecting factors, assigning weights to them, and then rating the business on these dimensions, as illustrated below.

Business strength factor	Weight	Rating*	Score
Relative market share	20	0.5	10
Production			
Capacity	10	1.0	10
Efficiency	10	1.0	10
Location	20	0	—
Technological capability	20	0.5	10
Marketing			
Sales organization	15	1.0	15
Promotion advantage	5	0	—
	100		55

* High = 1.0; Medium = 0.5; Low = 0.0.

These examples illustrate how one business within a corporate portfolio might be assessed using the GE planning grid. It is important to remember that what should be included or excluded as a factor, as well as how it should be rated and weighted, is primarily a matter of managerial judgment; and usually several managers are involved during the planning process. The result of such ratings is a high, medium, or low classification in terms of both the projected strength of the business and the projected attractiveness of the industry, as shown in Figure 10–3.

Three basic strategic approaches are suggested for any business in the corporate portfolio depending on its location within the grid: (1) invest to grow, (2) invest selectively and manage for earnings, or (3) harvest or divest for resources. The resource allocation decisions remain quite similar to those in the BCG approach. Businesses classified as *invest to grow* would be treated like the *stars* in the BCG matrix. These businesses would be accorded resources to pursue growth-oriented strategies. Strategy in Action 10–2 describes Kodak's search for new "star" businesses and allocation of resources to them as a way to examine new strategic thrusts. Businesses classified in the *harvest/ divest* category would be managed like the *dogs* in the BCG matrix. They would follow strategies that provided net resources for use in other business units. Businesses classified in the *selectivity/earnings* category would either be managed as *cash cows* (providing maximum earnings for corporatewide use) or as *question marks* (selectivity chosen for investment or divestment).

While the strategic recommendations generated by the GE planning grid are similar to those from the BCG matrix, the GE nine-cell grid improves on the BCG matrix in three fundamental ways. First, as research discussed earlier pointed out, the terminology associated with the GE grid is preferable because it is less offensive and more universally understood. Second, the multiple measures associated with each dimension of the GE grid tap more factors relevant to business strength and market attractiveness than simply market share and market growth. This provides (or even forces) broader assessment during the planning process; considerations of strategic importance both in strategy formulation *and* in strategy implementation are brought to light.

Strategy in Action 10–2
Strategic Analysis at Kodak

By 1986, Kodak management decided to break its monolithic management into small groups that could help the company grow by entering new markets like electronics and biotechnology. For years, Kodak had relied on its high market share in its photographic equipment business. But with the "amateur film market," the main market served by Kodak, growing at only 6 percent versus a historical 10–15 percent and profits plunging by 51 percent to $565 million, Kodak had to look for new business to compliment its "cash cow."

Thanks largely to its overreliance on the photographic equipment business, Kodak had neglected to enter such markets as instant photography, 35-mm cameras, and VCRs even though they were natural extensions of Kodak's basic photography business. By 1986, 85 percent of Kodak's sales were related to its photographic equipment business.

The company has divided management in order to explore new ventures that range from cattle feed nutrients to medical equipment to electronic publishing, all of which relate to Kodak's expertise in pictures, graphics, or chemicals. Kodak is counting on its reputation for quality and its distribution strength to help propel the company into some of these new markets.

One of the key markets Kodak plans to enter is electronic imaging—systems that manipulate graphics and photographs the way computers manipulate text. The company has unveiled a $500,000 system that locates stored microfilm and scans it so that a computer can read it. Similar initiatives are under way to enter the medical markets with diagnostic equipment linked to Kodak's basic scientific skills.

All of Kodak's initiatives are part of an ongoing process of strategic analysis whereby company managers are trying to experimentally find Kodak's niches for the 1990s in ways that take advantage of its fundamental strengths of the past.

Source: Based on "Kodak Is Trying to Break Out of Its Shell," *Business Week,* June 10, 1985.

Finally, the nine-cell format obviously allows finer distinction between portfolio positions (most notably for "average" businesses) than does the four-cell BCG format.

The portfolio approach is useful for examining alternative corporate-level strategies in multi-industry companies. Portfolio planning offers three potential benefits. First, it aids in generating good strategies by promoting competitive analysis at the business level and substantive, comparative discussion across the company's business units, resulting in a strategy that capitalizes on the benefits of corporate diversity. Second, it promotes selective resource allocation trade-offs by providing a visualization of the corporatewide strategic issues and a standardized, "neutral" basis for resource negotiation. Thus, power struggles within the company can be more objectively focused and channeled. Third, some users feel portfolio approaches help in implementation of corporate strategy because increased focus and objectivity enhance commitment.[9]

Its visual appeal notwithstanding, the portfolio approach is useful in evaluation because it allows a thorough and comparative analysis of market share, market growth, industry attractiveness, competitive position, and/or product/market evolution of each business unit. This portfolio evaluation must be conducted routinely and repeatedly. In this way, the effectiveness of resource generation and allocation decisions in achieving corporate objectives can be monitored, updated, and altered.

Once portfolio strategies have been identified, business strategies must be determined. Portfolio approaches help clarify and determine broad strategic intent. But this is not enough. Basic decisions involving allocation of corporate resources and the general manner in which a business unit will be managed (invest to grow, for example) do not complete the process of strategic analysis and choice. Each business unit must examine and select a specific grand strategy to guide its pursuit of long-term objectives.

Grand Strategy Selection at the Business Level

Once business units in a multi-industry firm have been identified in terms of invest, hold, or harvest, each business unit must identify and evaluate its grand strategy options. If a unit has been identified as a resource generator within the corporate portfolio strategy, for example, several alternative grand strategies are available for fulfilling this role.

What factors should a single business consider in selecting its grand strategy? What is the relative attractiveness of each of the 12 grand strategy options discussed in Chapter 9 for a single business? Three approaches to answering these questions are the focus of this section.

---

[9] A discussion of the uses and limits of portfolio planning, including coverage of companies and industries in terms of portfolio usage, is found in P. Haspelslagh's "Portfolio Planning: Uses and Limits," *Harvard Business Review* 60, no. 2 (1982), pp. 58–73.

SWOT Analysis

SWOT is an acronym for the internal *S*trengths and *W*eaknesses of a business and environmental *O*pportunities and *T*hreats facing that business. SWOT analysis is a systematic identification of these factors and the strategy that reflects the best match between them. It is based on the logic that an effective strategy maximizes a business's strengths and opportunities but at the same time minimizes its weaknesses and threats. This simple assumption, if accurately applied, has powerful implications for successfully choosing and designing an effective strategy.

Environmental/industry analysis (Chapters 4 through 7) provides the information to identify key opportunities and threats in the firm's environment. These can be defined as follows:

Opportunities.   An *opportunity* is *a major favorable situation in the firm's environment.* Key trends represent one source of opportunity. Identification of a previously overlooked market segment, changes in competitive or regulatory circumstances, technological changes, and improved buyer or supplier relationships could represent opportunities for the firm.

Threats.   A *threat* is *a major unfavorable situation in the firm's environment.* It is a key impediment to the firm's current and/or desired future position. The entrance of a new competitor, slow market growth, increased bargaining power of key buyers or suppliers, major technological change, and changing regulations could represent major threats to a firm's future success.

Consumer acceptance of home computers was a major opportunity for IBM. Deregulation of the airline industry was a major opportunity for regional carriers (such as USAir) to serve routes that were previously closed to additional service. Some traditional carriers (such as Eastern) saw deregulation as a major threat and credit deregulation with a rapid decline in profitability in high-traffic routes. So opportunity for one firm can be a strategic threat to another. And the same factor can be seen as both a potential opportunity and a potential threat. For example, as the baby boom generation moves into the prime earning years, a major opportunity is arising for financial service firms, such as Merrill Lynch.[10] However, this group wants convenient financial services, which is a major threat to Merrill Lynch's established broker network.

Understanding the key opportunities and threats facing a firm helps managers identify realistic options from which to choose an appropriate strategy. Such understanding clarifies the most effective niche for the firm.

The second fundamental focus in SWOT analysis is identifying key *strengths*

---

[10] "Merrill Lynch's Dilemma," *Business Week,* January 6, 1984, p. 60.

and *weaknesses* based on examination of the company profile (Chapter 8). Strengths and weaknesses can be defined as follows:

Strengths.   A *strength* is *a resource, skill, or other advantage* relative to competitors and the needs of markets a firm serves or anticipates serving. A strength is *a distinctive competence* that gives the firm a comparative advantage in the marketplace. Financial resources, image, market leadership, and buyer/supplier relations are examples.

Weaknesses.   A *weakness* is *a limitation or deficiency in resources, skills, and capabilities* that seriously impedes effective performance. Facilities, financial resources, management capabilities, marketing skills, and brand image could be sources of weaknesses.

Sheer size and level of customer acceptance proved to be key strengths around which IBM built its successful strategy in the personal computer market. Braniff's limited financial capacity was a weakness that management did not sufficiently acknowledge, leading to an unsuccessful route expansion strategy and eventual bankruptcy after deregulation. Relative financial capacity was a weakness recognized by Piedmont Airlines, which charted a selective route expansion strategy that has been quite successful in a deregulated airline industry.

Understanding the key strengths and weaknesses of the firm further aids in narrowing the choice of alternatives and selecting a strategy. Distinct competence and critical weakness are identified in relation to key determinants of success for different market segments; this provides a useful framework for making the best strategic choice.

SWOT analysis can be used in at least three ways in strategic choice decisions. The most common application provides a logical framework guiding systematic discussions of the business's situation, alternative strategies, and, ultimately, the choice of strategy. What one manager sees as an opportunity, another may see as a potential threat. Likewise, a strength to one manager may be a weakness from another perspective. Different assessments may reflect underlying power considerations within the organization, as well as differing factual perspectives. The key point is that systematic SWOT analysis ranges across all aspects of a firm's situation. As a result, it provides a dynamic and useful framework for choosing a strategy.

A second application of SWOT analysis is illustrated in Figure 10–4. Key external opportunities and threats are systematically compared to internal strengths and weaknesses in a structured approach. The objective is identification of one of four distinct patterns in the match between the firm's internal and external situations. These patterns are represented by the four cells in Figure 10–4. Cell 1 is the most favorable situation; the firm faces several environmental opportunities and has numerous strengths that encourage pursuit of such opportunities. This condition suggests growth-oriented strategies

Figure 10–4
SWOT analysis diagram

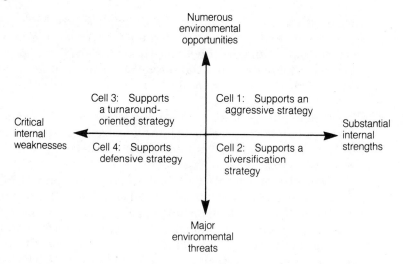

to exploit the favorable match. IBM's intensive market development strategy in the personal computer market was the result of a favorable match between strengths in reputation and resources and the opportunity for impressive market growth. Cell 4 is the least favorable situation, with the firm facing major environmental threats from a position of relative weakness. This condition clearly calls for strategies that reduce or redirect involvement in the products/ markets examined using SWOT analysis. Chrysler Corporation's successful turnaround from the verge of bankruptcy in the early 1980s is an example of such a successful strategy developed from a SWOT analysis that revealed mainly environmental threats and internal weaknesses.

In Cell 2, a firm with key strengths faces an unfavorable environment. In this situation, strategies would use current strengths to build long-term opportunities in other products/markets. Greyhound, possessing many strengths in intercity bus transportation, still faces an environment predominated by fundamental, long-term threats, such as airline competition and labor costs. The result was product development into nonpassenger (freight) services, followed by diversification into other businesses (e.g., financial services). A business in Cell 3 faces impressive market opportunity but is constrained by several internal weaknesses. Businesses in this predicament are like the question marks in the BCG matrix. The focus of strategy for such firms is eliminating internal weaknesses to more effectively pursue market opportunity. Apple's redirection of its "Lisa" technology to multiple products was an attempt to reformulate the company's technology-based strategy across several new product offerings in the microcomputer industry.

A major challenge in using SWOT analysis lies in identifying the position the business is actually in. A business that faces major opportunities may likewise face some key threats in its environment. It may have numerous internal weaknesses but also have one or two major strengths relative to key competitors. Fortunately, the value of SWOT analysis does not rest solely on careful placement of a firm in one particular cell. Rather, it lets the strategist visualize the overall position of the firm in terms of the product/market conditions for which a strategy is being considered. Does the SWOT analysis suggest that the firm is dealing from a position of major strength? Or must the firm overcome numerous weaknesses in the match of external and internal conditions? In answering these questions, SWOT analysis helps resolve one fundamental concern in selecting a strategy: *What will be the principal purpose of the grand strategy?* Is it to take advantage of a strong position or to overcome a weak one?[11] SWOT analysis provides a means of answering this fundamental question. And this answer is input to one dimension in a second, more specific tool for selecting grand strategies: the *grand strategy selection matrix.*

Grand Strategy Selection Matrix

A second valuable guide to the selection of a promising grand strategy is the matrix shown in Figure 10–5.[12] The basic idea underlying the matrix is that two variables are of central concern in the selection process: (1) the principal purpose of the grand strategy and (2) the choice of an internal or external emphasis for growth and/or profitability.

In the 1950s and 1960s, planners were advised to follow certain rules or prescriptions in their choice of strategies. Most experts now agree that strategy selection is better guided by the unique set of conditions that exist for the planning period and by company strengths and weaknesses. It is valuable to note, however, that even early approaches to strategy selection were based on matching a concern for internal versus external growth with a principal desire to either overcome weakness or maximize strength.

The same concerns led to the development of the grand strategy selection matrix. A firm in Quadrant I often views itself as overly committed to a particular business with limited growth opportunities or involving high risks because the company has "all its eggs in one basket." One reasonable solution

---

[11] A recent broad-based empirical study [L. G. Hrebiniak and C. Snow, "Top-Management Agreement and Organizational Performance," *Human Relations* 35, no. 12 (1982), pp. 1139–58], offers strong support that using SWOT analysis in this manner contributes to effective strategic choice. Examining 247 top-level managers in 88 organizations *and* eliminating the effects of other variables (types of planning, prior performance, industry), this study found strong, positive relationships between top management's agreement on the firm's strengths and weaknesses in relation to its environmental context and the measure of organizational performance—return on assets—used in the study. In other words, a comprehensive SWOT analysis, agreed upon by top management, provided one key input in the selection of an appropriate, effective strategy for the firm.

[12] John A. Pearce II, "Selecting among Alternative Grand Strategies," *California Management Review* 30, no. 2 (Spring 1982), pp. 23–31.

Figure 10–5
Grand strategy selection matrix

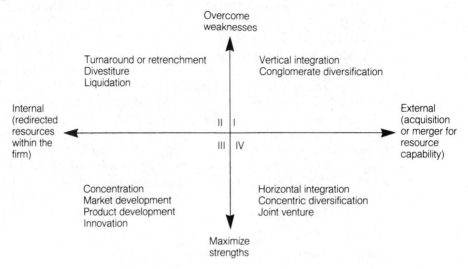

Overcome
weaknesses

Turnaround or retrenchment
Divestiture
Liquidation

Vertical integration
Conglomerate diversification

Internal
(redirected
resources
within the
firm)

II | I

III | IV

External
(acquisition
or merger for
resource
capability)

Concentration
Market development
Product development
Innovation

Horizontal integration
Concentric diversification
Joint venture

Maximize
strengths

Source: John A. Pearce II, "Selecting among Alternative Grand Strategies," *California Management Review* 30, no. 2 (Spring 1982), p. 29.

is *vertical integration,* which enables the firm to reduce risk by reducing uncertainty either about inputs or about access to customers. Alternatively, a firm may choose *conglomerate diversification,* which provides a profitable alternative for investment without diverting management attention from the original business. However, the external orientation to overcoming weaknesses usually results in the most costly grand strategies. The decision to acquire a second business demands both large initial time investments and sizable financial resources. Thus, strategic managers considering these approaches must guard against exchanging one set of weaknesses for another.

A more conservative approach to overcoming weakness is found in Quadrant II. Firms often choose to redirect resources from one business activity to another within the company. While this approach does not reduce the company's commitment to its basic mission, it does reward success and enables further development of proven competitive advantages. The least disruptive of the Quadrant II strategies is *retrenchment,* the pruning of a current business's activities. If weaknesses arose from inefficiencies, retrenchment can actually serve as a *turnaround* strategy, meaning the business gains new strength by streamlining its operations and eliminating waste. However, when the weaknesses are a major obstruction to success in the industry, and when the costs of overcoming the weaknesses are unaffordable or are not justified by a cost-benefit analysis, then eliminating the business must be considered. Strategy in Action 10–3 illustrates a systematic divestiture and refocus strategy at Honeywell. *Divestiture* offers the best possibility for recouping the company's investment, but even *liquidation* can be an attractive option when the alternatives are an unwarranted drain on organizational resources or bankruptcy.

A common business adage states that a company should build from strength. The premise is that growth and survival depend on an ability to capture a market share that is large enough for essential economies of scale. If a firm believes profitability will derive from this approach and prefers an internal emphasis for maximizing strengths, four alternative grand strategies hold considerable promise. As shown in Quadrant III, the most common approach is *concentration* on the business, that is, market penetration. The business that selects this strategy is strongly committed to its current products and markets. It will strive to solidify its position by reinvesting resources to fortify its strength.

Two alternative approaches are *market* and *product development*. With either of these strategies the business attempts to broaden its operations. Market development is chosen if strategic managers feel that existing products would be well received by new customer groups. Product development is preferred when existing customers are believed to have an interest in products related to the firm's current lines. This approach may also be based on special technological or other competitive advantages. A final alternative for Quadrant III firms is *innovation*. When the business's strengths are in creative product design or unique production technologies, sales can be stimulated by accelerating perceived obsolescence. This is the principle underlying an innovative grand strategy.

Maximizing a business's strength by aggressively expanding its basis of operations usually requires an external emphasis in selecting a grand strategy. Preferred options here are shown in Quadrant IV. *Horizontal integration* is attractive because it enables a firm to quickly increase output capability. The skills of the original business's managers are often critical in converting new facilities into profitable contributors to the parent company; this expands a fundamental competitive advantage of the firm—management.

Concentric diversification is a good second choice for similar reasons. Because the original and newly acquired businesses are related, the distinctive competencies of the diversifying firm are likely to facilitate a smooth, synergistic, and profitable expansion.

The final option for increasing resource capability through external emphasis is a *joint venture*. This alternative allows a business to extend its strengths into competitive arenas that it would be hesitant to enter alone. A partner's production, technological, financial, or marketing capabilities can significantly reduce financial investment and increase the probability of success to the point that formidable ventures become attractive growth alternatives.

Strategy in Action 10–3
Honeywell Creates a New Strategy

One of the "BUNCH" is leaving the mainframe computer business. After a phased withdrawal that started three years ago, Honeywell, one of the makers in the group of mainframe manufacturers commonly known as the BUNCH (Burroughs, Univac, NCR, Control Data, Honeywell), is leaving to concentrate on factory automation, where its century-old expertise gives the company a chance for leadership.

Honeywell started in the computer business in 1955, through a joint venture with Raytheon, and decided to compete directly with IBM. Believing size to be critical, it bought GE's computer operation in 1970 and Xerox's computer business in 1976 when both decided to get out of the business. But by 1986, IBM controlled 71 percent of the mainframe computer business versus 3 percent for Honeywell.

Honeywell will concentrate on its strengths. The company has a growing $1.9-billion-a-year aerospace and defense business making torpedoes and navigational equipment. It has a $2.8 billion controls business where the company is the leader in both heat and air-conditioning controls for buildings and process controls for industry.

The company wants to concentrate on factory automation as its next growth vector. The company is pursuing the opportunity through logical development of its core control business, not through merger. Honeywell is focusing on the "brain" end of automation, as opposed to the "muscle" end (robots and machine tools). The brain end involves sensors, programmable controllers, software, and minicomputers—all conveniently similar to its control business competencies. The brain segment is worth $10 billion in sales annually and is growing at 15 percent annually.

Source: Based on "Strategic Withdrawal," *Forbes*, February 10, 1986.

Model of Grand Strategy Clusters

A third guide to selecting a promising grand strategy involves Thompson and Strickland's modifications of the BCG growth share portfolio matrix.[13] As shown in Figure 10–6, a business's situation is defined in terms of the growth rate of the general market and the company's competitive position in that market. When these factors are considered simultaneously, a business

---

[13] Arthur A. Thompson, Jr., and A. J. Strickland III, *Strategic Management: Concepts and Cases,* 3rd ed. (Plano, Tex.: Business Publications, 1984), p. 99. The BCG matrix was discussed earlier in this chapter.

Figure 10–6
Model of grand strategy clusters

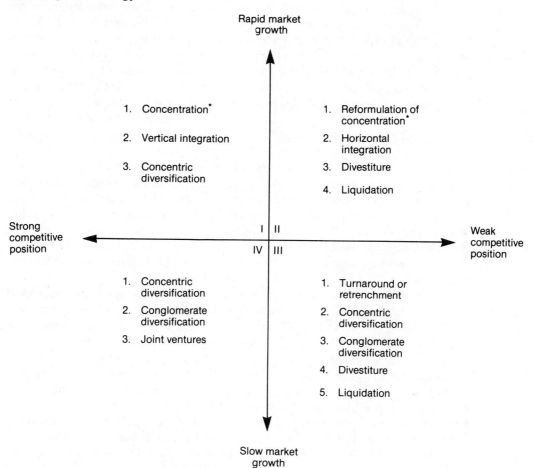

The grand strategy of innovation was omitted from this model. Apparently the authors felt that the notion of market growth was incompatible with the assumptions underlying the innovation approach.

Grand strategies are listed in probable order of attractiveness.

* In this model the grand strategy of concentration was meant to encompass market development and product development.

Source: Adapted from Arthur A. Thompson, Jr., and A. J. Strickland III, *Strategic Management: Concepts and Cases,* 4th ed. (Plano, Tex.: Business Publications, 1987).

can be broadly categorized in one of four quadrants: (I) strong competitive position in a rapidly growing market, (II) weak position in a rapidly growing market, (III) weak position in a slow-growth market, or (IV) strong position in a slow-growth market. Each of these quadrants suggests a set of promising possibilities for selection of a grand strategy.

Firms in Quadrant I are in an excellent strategic position. One obvious grand strategy for such firms is continued concentration on their current business as it is presently defined. Because consumers seem satisfied with the firm's current strategy, it would be dangerous to shift notably from the established competitive advantages. However, if the business has resources that exceed the demands of a concentration strategy, it should consider vertical integration. Either forward or backward integration helps a business protect its profit margins and market share by ensuring better access to either consumers or material inputs. Finally, a Quadrant I firm might be wise to consider concentric diversification to diminish the risks associated with a narrow product or service line; with this strategy, heavy investment in the company's basic area of proven ability continues.

Firms in Quadrant II must seriously evaluate maintaining their present approach to the marketplace. If a firm has competed long enough to accurately assess the merits of its current grand strategy, it must determine (1) the reasons its approach is ineffectual and (2) whether the company has the capability to compete effectively. Depending on the answers to these questions, the firm should choose one of four grand strategy options: formulation or reformulation of a concentration strategy, horizontal integration, divestiture, or liquidation.

In a rapidly growing market, even a small or relatively weak business is often able to find a profitable niche. Thus, formulation or reformulation of a concentration strategy is usually the first option to consider. However, if the firm lacks either a critical competitive element or sufficient economies of scale to achieve competitive cost efficiencies, then a grand strategy that directs company efforts toward horizontal integration is often a desirable alternative. A final pair of options involve deciding to stop competing in the market or product area. A multiproduct firm may conclude that the goals of its mission are most likely to be achieved if this one business is dropped through divestiture. Not only does this grand strategy eliminate a drain on resources, it may also provide additional funds to promote other business activities. As an option of last resort, a firm may decide to liquidate the business. In practical terms this means that the business cannot be sold as a going concern and is at best worth only the value of its tangible assets. The decision to liquidate is an undeniable admission of failure by a firm's strategic management and is thus often delayed—to the further detriment of the company.

Strategic managers tend to resist divestiture because it is likely to jeopardize their control of the firm and perhaps even their jobs. By the time the desirability of divestiture is acknowledged, the business has often deteriorated to the point of failing to attract potential buyers as a business. The consequences of such delays are financially disastrous for the owners of the firm, because the value of a going concern is many times greater than simple asset value.

Strategic managers who have a business in the position of Quadrant III and feel that continued slow market growth and a relatively weak competitive position are going to continue will usually attempt to decrease their resource commitment to that business. Minimal withdrawal is accomplished through retrenchment; this strategy has the side benefits of making resources available for other investments and of motivating employees to increase their operating efficiency. An alternative strategy is to divert resources for expansion through investment in other businesses. This approach typically involves either concentric or conglomerate diversification, because the firm usually wants to enter more promising arenas of competition than forms of integration or development would allow. The final options for Quadrant III businesses are divestiture, if an optimistic buyer can be found, and liquidation.

Quadrant IV businesses (strong competitive position in a slow-growth market) have a basis of strength from which to diversify into more promising growth areas. These businesses have characteristically high cash flow levels and limited internal growth needs. Thus, they are in an excellent position for concentric diversification into ventures that utilize their proven business acumen. A second choice is conglomerate diversification, which spreads investment risk and does not divert managerial attention from the present business. The final option is joint ventures, which are especially attractive to multinational firms. Through joint ventures a domestic business can gain competitive advantages in promising new fields while exposing itself to limited risks. Strategy in Action 10–4 describes Anheuser-Busch's approach to strategy analysis and choice under Quadrant IV circumstances.

Behavioral Considerations Affecting Strategic Choice

Strategic choice is a decision. At both the corporate and the business levels, this decision determines the future strategy of the firm.

After alternative strategies are examined, strategic choice is made. This is a decision to adopt one of the alternatives scrutinized. If the examination identified a clearly superior strategy, or if the current strategy will clearly meet future company objectives, then the decision is relatively simple. Such clarity is the exception, however, making the decision judgmental and difficult. Strategic decision makers, after comprehensive strategy examination, are often confronted with several viable alternatives rather than the luxury of a clear-cut, obvious choice. Under these circumstances, several factors influence the strategic choice decision. Some of the more important are:

1. Role of past strategy.
2. Degree of the firm's external dependence.
3. Attitudes toward risk.
4. Internal political considerations and the CEO.
5. Timing.
6. Competitive reaction.

Strategy in Action 10–4
Anheuser-Busch's Choice of Strategy for the 1980s

In 1985 Anheuser-Busch completed a $2 billion, five-year expansion program that will increase its capacity 40 percent and add significantly to its 29 percent share of the beer market.

The St. Louis brewer is evaluating three options for its growth in the 1990s:

1. Diversification.
2. Overseas expansion.
3. A combination of both.

To evaluate and ultimately choose its strategy, Anheuser-Busch is using what its managers call learning probes—miniventures or experiments relative to each alternative strategy.

Anheuser-Busch's first learning probe was into the soft drink business. From the start, the test was the subject of considerable second-guessing. "Would Coke and Pepsi enter the beer industry from scratch and go up against Anheuser-Busch and Miller?" asks a skeptical rival brewer. "I think the answer would be no."

Anheuser-Busch's answer, after two years of testing, was no. "We learned it's a competitive jungle out there," says August Busch III, chairman, "Just like us and Miller in the brewing industry."

Root 66 beer and its sugar-free version—sold in five cities since 1980—have a respectable market share, but competitors contend it was achieved mostly through cents-off discounts offered to consumers. Chelsea, a citrus beverage that could have had the snob appeal and profit margin of Perrier, was hooted off the market by nurses and others who objected to the alcoholic content (0.4 percent) and beer-like appearance of the "not-so-soft drink."

Beer distributors were used for the soft drink test and also for a look at the snack business, where Anheuser-Busch is selling its new Eagle line in bars. One sign of success: distribution is being widened to 54 cities from a handful.

The third learning probe, less prominent than snacks or soda but more encouraging to several followers of Anheuser-Busch, is the company's development of Sesame Place educational parks in conjunction with Children's Television Workshop, producers of "Sesame Street."

The other alternative strategy, which requires even less capital and could pay off sooner than the others, is overseas expansion of the brewing business.

Continued on Page 303

Strategy in Action 10–4 (*concluded*)

International sales account for less than 1 percent of Anheuser-Busch's beer volume.

Company officials, reluctant to disclose much about the prospects for their learning probes, acknowledged that "beer earnings and share growth may slow as we approach our long-term 40 percent market share goal." The brewer is planning for that day by "getting our feet wet in new business areas, not massive diversification efforts."

Source: "If Anheuser-Busch Gets Its Way, Saying 'Bud' Won't Say It All." Reprinted by permission of *The Wall Street Journal,* © Dow Jones & Company, Inc., January 15, 1981, p. 25. All rights reserved.

Role of Past Strategy

A review of past strategy is the point at which the process of strategic choice begins. As such, past strategy exerts considerable influence on the final strategic choice.

Current strategists are often the architects of past strategies. Because they have invested substantial time, resources, and interest in these strategies, the strategists would logically be more comfortable with a choice that closely parallels past strategy or represents only incremental alterations.

This familiarity and commitment to past strategy permeate the organization. Thus, lower-level management reinforces the top manager's inclination toward continuity with past strategy during the choice process. In one study, during the planning process, lower-level managers suggested strategic choices that were consistent with current strategy and likely to be accepted while withholding suggestions with less probability of approval.[14]

Research by Henry Mintzberg suggests that the past strategy strongly influences current strategic choice.[15] The older and more successful a strategy has been, the harder it is to replace. Similarly, a strategy, once initiated, is very difficult to change because organizational momentum keeps it going.

Mintzberg's work and research by Barry Staw found that even as the strategy begins to fail due to changing conditions, strategists often increase their commitment to the past strategy.[16] Firms may thus replace key executives when performance has been inadequate for an extended period because replacing

---

[14] Eugene Carter, "The Behavioral Theory of the Firm and Top-Level Corporate Decisions," *Administrative Science Quarterly* 16, no. 4 (1971), pp. 413–28.

[15] Henry Mintzberg, "Research on Strategy Making," *Proceedings of the Academy of Management,* Minneapolis, 1972.

[16] Barry M. Staw, "Knee-Deep in the Big Muddy: A Study of Escalating Commitment to a Chosen Course of Action," *Organizational Behavior and Human Performance,* June 1976, pp. 27–44; Mintzberg, "Research on Strategy."

top executives lessens the influence of unsuccessful past strategy on future strategic choice.

Degree of the Firm's External Dependence

A comprehensive strategy is meant to effectively guide a firm's performance in the larger external environment. Owners, suppliers, customers, government, competitors, and unions are a few of the elements in a firm's external environment, as elaborated on in Chapters 4 through 7. A major constraint on strategic choice is the power of environmental elements in supporting this decision. If a firm is highly dependent on one or more environmental factors, its strategic alternatives and ultimate choice must accommodate this dependence. The greater a firm's external dependence, the lower its range and flexibility in strategic choice.

Two examples highlight the influence of external dependence on strategic choice. For many years Whirlpool sold most of its major appliance output to one customer, Sears. With its massive retail coverage and access to alternate suppliers, Sears was a major external dependence for Whirlpool. Whirlpool's strategic alternatives and ultimate choice of strategy were limited and strongly influenced by Sears' demands. Whirlpool's grand strategy and important related decisions in areas such as research and development, pricing, distribution, and product design were carefully narrowed and chosen with the firm's critical dependence on Sears in mind. Chrysler Corporation's dependence on federal loan guarantees and financial concessions by labor considerably limited the strategic choices available in the early 1980s. The decision of Chrysler's Lee Iaccoca to pay off several federal obligations before they were due was partially meant to increase Chrysler's flexibility by reducing one restrictive external dependence.

These examples show that a firm's flexibility in strategic choice is lessened when environmental dependence increases. If external dependence is critical, firms may include representatives of the external factor (government, union, supplier, bank) in the strategic choice process. In 1980, Chrysler, for example, took the unprecedented action of including Leonard Woodcock, president of the United Auto Workers, on its board of directors.

Attitudes toward Risk

Attitudes toward risk exert considerable influence on strategic choice. These attitudes may vary from eager risk taking to strong aversion to risk, and they influence the range of available strategic choices. Where attitudes favor risk, the range and diversity of strategic choices expand. High-risk strategies are acceptable and desirable. Where management is risk averse, the diversity of choices is limited, and risky alternatives are eliminated before strategic choices are made. Risk-oriented managers prefer offensive, opportunistic strategies. Risk-averse managers prefer defensive, safe strategies. Past strategy

Figure 10–7
Managerial risk propensity and strategic choices

Risk averse		*Risk prone*
Decrease choices	————————————————	Expand choices
Defensive strategies	————————————————	Offensive strategies
Stability	←————————————→	Growth
Incremental	←————————————→	Innovation
Minimize company weaknesses	←————————————→	Maximize company strengths
Strong ties to past strategy	←————————————→	Fewer ties to past strategy
Stable industry	————————————————	Volatile industry
Maturing product/market evolution	←————————————→	Early product/market evolution

is quite influential in the strategic choices made by risk-averse managers, but it is less of a factor for risk-oriented managers. Figure 10–7 illustrates the relationship between attitudes toward risk and strategic choice.

Industry volatility influences managerial propensity toward risk. In highly volatile industries, top managers must absorb and operate with greater amounts of risk than their counterparts in stable industries. Therefore, managers in volatile industries consider a broader, more diverse range of strategies in the strategic choice process.

Product/market evolution is another determinant of managerial risk propensity. If a firm is in the early stages of product/market evolution, it must operate with considerably greater risk than a firm later in the product/market evolution cycle.

In making a strategic choice, risk-oriented managers lean toward opportunistic strategies with higher payoffs. They are drawn to offensive strategies based on innovation, company strengths, and operating potential. Risk-averse managers lean toward safe, conservative strategies with reasonable, highly probable returns. The latter are drawn to defensive strategies to minimize a firm's weaknesses and external threats, as well as the uncertainty associated with innovation-based strategies.

A recent study examined the relationship between the willingness of strategic business unit (SBU) managers to take risks and SBU performance. The study found a link between risk taking and strategic choice. Looking first at SBUs assigned build or star strategic missions within a corporate portfolio, researchers found that the general managers of higher-performing SBUs had *greater willingness to take risks* than did their counterparts in lower-performing build or star SBUs. Looking next at SBUs assigned harvest strategies, successful units had general managers *less willing to take risks* than general managers in lower-performing harvest SBUs.[17]

This study supports the idea that managers make different decisions depending on their willingness to take risks. Perhaps most important, the study suggests that being either risk prone or risk averse is not inherently good or bad. Rather, SBU performance is more effective when the risk orientation of the general manager is consistent with the SBU's strategic mission (build or harvest). While this is only one study and not a final determination of the influence of risk orientation on strategic choice, it helps illustrate the importance of risk orientation on the process of making and implementing strategic decisions.

Internal Political Considerations

Power/political factors influence strategic choice. The existence and use of power to further individual or group interests is common in organizational life. An early study by Ross Stagner found that strategic decisions in business organizations were frequently settled by power rather than by analytical maximization procedures.[18]

A major source of power in most organizations is the chief executive officer (CEO). In smaller enterprises, the CEO is consistently the dominant force in strategic choice, and this is also often true in large firms, particularly those with a strong or dominant CEO. When the CEO begins to favor a particular choice, it is often unanimously selected.

Cyert and March identified another power source that influences strategic choice, particularly in larger firms.[19] They called this the *coalition* phenomenon. In large organizations, subunits and individuals (particularly key managers) have reason to support some alternatives and oppose others. Mutual interest often draws certain groups together in coalitions to enhance their position on major strategic issues. These coalitions, particularly the more powerful ones (often called *dominant coalitions*), exert considerable influence in the strategic choice process. Numerous studies confirm the use of power and coalitions on a frequent basis in strategic decision making. Interestingly, one study found that managers occasionally try to hide the fact that they prefer judgmental/political bargaining over systematic analysis and that when politics was a factor, it slowed decision-making.[20]

---

[17] Gupta and Govindarajan, "Build, Hold, Harvest."

[18] Ross Stagner, "Corporate Decision Making," *Journal of Applied Psychology* 53, no. 1 (1969), pp. 1–13.

[19] Richard M. Cyert and James G. March, *A Behavorial Theory of the Firm* (Englewood Cliffs, N.J.: Prentice-Hall, 1963).

[20] See, for example, H. Mintzberg, D. Raisinghani, and Andre Theoret, "The Structure of Unstructured Decision Process," *Administrative Science Quarterly,* June 1976, pp. 246–75; and William Guth, "Toward a Social System Theory of Corporate Strategy," *Journal of Business,* July 1976, pp. 374–88.

Figure 10-8
Political activities in phases of strategic decision making

Phases of strategic decision making	Focus of political action	Examples of political activity
Identification and diagnosis of strategic issues	Control of: Issues to be discussed Cause-and-effect relationships to be examined	Control of agenda Interpretation of past events and future trends
Narrowing the alternative strategies for serious consideration	Control of alternatives	Mobilization Coalition formation Resource commitment for information search
Examining and choosing the strategy	Control of choice	Selective advocacy of criteria Search and representation of information to justify choice
Initiating implementation of the strategy	Interaction between winners and losers	Winners attempt to "sell" or co-opt losers Losers attempt to thwart decisions and trigger fresh strategic issues
Designing procedures for evaluation of results	Representing oneself as successful	Selective advocacy of criteria

Source: Adapted from Liam Fahey and V. K. Naroyanan, "The Politics of Strategic Decision Making," in *The Strategic Management Handbook,* ed. Kenneth J. Albert (New York: McGraw-Hill, 1983), p. 21-20.

Figure 10–8 illustrates the focus of political activity across phases of strategic decision making. It illustrates how the *content* of strategic decisions and the *processes* of arriving at such decisions are politically intertwined. Each phase in the process of strategic choice presents a real opportunity for political action intended to influence the outcome. The challenge to strategists is in recognizing and managing this political influence. If such processes are not carefully overseen, various managers can bias the content of strategic decisions in the direction of their own interests.[21] For example, selecting the criteria used to compare alternative strategies or collecting and appraising information regarding these criteria may be particularly susceptible to political influence. This must be recognized and, where critical, "managed" to avoid dysfunctional political bias. Reliance on different sources for obtaining *and* appraising information might be effective in this context.

Rather than simply being denoted as "bad" or inefficient, organizational politics must be viewed as an inevitable dimension of organizational decision making that must be accommodated in strategic management. Some authors argue that politics are a key ingredient in the "glue" that holds an organization together. Formal and informal negotiating and bargaining between individuals, subunits, and coalitions are indispensable mechanisms for organizational

---

[21] Liam Fahey and V. K. Naroyanan, "The Politics of Strategic Decision Making," in *The Strategic Management Handbook,* ed. Kenneth J. Albert (New York: McGraw-Hill, 1983), p. 21-18.

coordination.[22] Recognizing and accommodating this in choosing future strategy will result in greater commitment and more realistic strategy. The costs are likely to be increased time spent on decision making and incremental (as opposed to drastic) change.

Timing Considerations

The time element can have considerable influence on strategic choice. Consider the case of Mech-Tran, a small manufacturer of fiberglass piping that found itself in financial difficulty. At the same time it was seeking a loan guarantee through the Small Business Administration (SBA), it was approached by KOCH Industries (a Kansas City–based supplier of oil field supplies) with a merger offer. The offer involved 100 percent sale of Mech-Tran stock and a two-week response deadline, while the SBA loan procedure could take three months. Obviously, management's strategic decision was heavily influenced by external time constraints, which limited analysis and evaluation. Research by Peter Wright indicates that under such a time constraint, managers put greater weight on negative than on positive information and prefer defensive strategies.[23] The Mech-Tran owners decided to accept the KOCH offer rather than risk losing the opportunity and subsequently being turned down by the SBA. Thus, faced with time constraints, management opted for a defensive strategy consistent with Wright's findings.

There is another side to the time issue—the timing of a strategic decision. A good strategy may be disastrous if it is undertaken at the wrong time. Winnebago was the darling of Wall Street in 1970, with its stock rising from $3 to $44 per share in one year. Winnebago's 1972 strategic choice, focusing on increasing its large, centralized production facility, was a continuation of the strategy that had successfully differentiated Winnebago in the recreational vehicle industry. The 1973 Arab oil embargo with subsequent rises in gasoline prices and overall transportation costs had dismal effects on Winnebago. The strategy was good, but the timing proved disastrous. On the other hand, IBM's decision to hold off entering the rapidly growing personal computer market until 1982 appeared to be perfectly timed. Welcomed by Apple with a full-page advertisement in *The Wall Street Journal*, IBM assumed the market share lead by early 1983.

A final aspect of the time dimension involves the lead time required for alternative choices and the time horizon management is contemplating. Management's primary attention may be on the short or long run, depending on current circumstances. Logically, strategic choice will be strongly influenced by the match between management's current time horizon and the lead time

---

[22] Ibid.

[23] Peter Wright, "The Harrassed Decision Maker," *Journal of Applied Psychology* 59, no. 5 (1974), pp. 555–61.

(or payoff time) associated with different choices. As a move toward vertical integration, Du Pont went heavily into debt to acquire Conoco in a 1982 bidding war. By 1983, the worldwide oil glut meant that Du Pont could have bought raw materials on more favorable terms in the open market. This short-term perspective was not of great concern to Du Pont management, however, because the acquisition was part of a strategy to stabilize Du Pont's long-term position as a producer of numerous petroleum-based products.

Competitive Reaction

In weighing strategic choices, top management frequently incorporates perceptions of likely competitor reactions to different options. For example, if management chooses an aggressive strategy that directly challenges a key competitor, that competitor can be expected to mount an aggressive counterstrategy. Management of the initiating firm must consider such reactions, the capacity of the competitor to react, and the probable impact on the chosen strategy's success.

The beer industry provides a good illustration. In the early 1970s, Anheuser-Busch dominated the industry. Miller Brewing Company, recently acquired by Philip Morris, was a weak and declining competitor. Miller's management, contemplating alternative strategies, made the decision to adopt an expensive, advertising-oriented strategy. While this strategy challenged the big three (Anheuser-Busch, Pabst, and Schlitz) head-on, Miller anticipated that the reaction of the other brewers would be delayed due to Miller's current declining status in the industry. Miller proved correct and was able to reverse its trend in market share before Anheuser-Busch countered with an equally intense advertising strategy.

Miller's management took another approach in their next major strategic decision. In the mid-1970s they introduced (and heavily advertised) a low-calorie beer—Miller Lite. Other industry members had introduced such products without much success. Miller chose a strategy that did not directly challenge key competitors and, Miller anticipated, would not elicit immediate and strong counterattacks. This choice proved highly successful, because Miller was able to establish a dominant share of the low-calorie market before major competitors decided to react. In both cases, Miller's expectation of competitor reaction was a key determinant of strategic choice.

Contingency Approach to Strategic Choice

Ultimate strategic choices often depend on various assumptions about future conditions. The success of the strategy chosen is contingent, to varying degrees, on future conditions. And changes in the industry and environment may differ from forecasts and assumptions.

For example, Winnebago's strategy of centralized, economy-of-scale production and extensive inventories of large recreational vehicles (RVs) was contingent on a continued supply of plentiful, inexpensive gasoline for future customer use. With the Arab oil embargo, this contingency changed dramatically. Winnebago was left with extensive inventories of large RVs and high-break-even–oriented production facilities for large RVs. As a result, Winnebago was still trying to recover a decade later.

To improve their ability to cope in similar circumstances, an increasing number of firms have adopted a contingency approach to strategic choice. The critical assumptions on which success of the chosen strategy depends are identified. Conditions that may turn out to be different from the basic forecast or assumptions for these critical contingencies are identified, particularly negative ones.[24] A downturn in the economy, a labor strike, an increase in the prime rate, a technological breakthrough, or a shortage of critical material are examples of such contingencies. Once these scenarios are identified, managers develop alternative, contingency strategies for the firm. Such contingency strategies can be short and/or long term and are appropriate at the corporate-, business-, and/or functional levels. Firms using this contingency approach often identify trigger points to alert management that a contingency strategy should be considered. The trigger points are specific deviations in key forecasts of industry or environmental conditions (like the supply and price of gasoline) and are set to alert management to the need to consider the alternative strategy and allow sufficient lead time for implementation of the contingency response.

Summary

This chapter has presented and examined several considerations in strategic analysis and choice. The form of strategic analysis and choice varies considerably according to the stage of development of the firm, and the focus differs at the corporate and business levels.

For multi-industry and multiproduct/market firms, strategic analysis begins at the corporate level. Different strategies are examined in terms of generating and allocating corporate resources. The portfolio approach is one method of strategy examination at the corporate level. Portfolio matrixes and stage of product/market evolution are conceptual tools guiding the portfolio approach.

Strategic analysis and choice do not end with corporate-level strategy. Alternative business-level strategies must be examined within the context of each business unit in multi-industry firms, much as strategy is evaluated in single-product/service firms. Three approaches that facilitate grand strategy selection at the business level were discussed.

---

[24] Positive as well as negative alternatives should be considered. If circumstances are unusually positive, the firm may not be in a position to exploit the favorable circumstances. However, most firms are primarily concerned with negative deviation in key contingencies.

Strategic analysis often limits alternatives to several viable choices. Strategic choice seldom involves the luxury of making an obvious choice. Nonetheless, a choice must be made. Several factors influence strategic choice, such as propensity for risk, past strategy, and coalitions, which are outside the realm of purely analytical consideration. Some firms attempt a contingency approach to strategic choice by incorporating the flexibility to alter a chosen strategy if underlying assumptions change.

Choosing corporate- and business-level strategies is not the end of the strategic management process. Functional strategies must be identified and implemented to initiate and control daily business activities in a manner consistent with business strategy, as must organizational systems and processes to implement and control the strategy. The next section of this book examines the implementation phase of the strategic management process.

Questions for Discussion

1. How does strategic analysis at the corporate level differ from strategic analysis at the business level? How are they related?
2. Why would multi-industry companies find the portfolio approach to strategy evaluation useful?
3. Explain the role of SWOT analysis as a tool facilitating strategic choice at the business level. How is it similar/dissimilar to the grand strategy selection matrix and the model of grand strategy clusters?
4. What role does politics play in the development and evaluation of alternative strategies? Please explain.
5. Explain and illustrate the role of three behavioral considerations in strategy examination and choice.

Bibliography

Abell, Derek F. "Strategic Windows." *Journal of Marketing,* July 1978, pp. 21–26.

Buzzell, Robert D.; T. G. Bradley; and Ralph Sultan. "Market Share: A Key to Profitability." *Harvard Business Review,* January–February 1975, pp. 97–106.

Christensen, H. K.; A. C. Cooper; and C. A. DeKluyver. "The 'Dog' Business: A Reexamination." *Proceedings of the Academy of Management,* 1981 pp. 26–30.

Gupta, Anil K., and V. Govindarajan. "Build, Hold, Harvest: Converting Strategic Intentions into Reality." *Journal of Business Strategy,* March 1984, pp. 34–47.

_____. "Business Unit Strategy, Managerial Characteristics, and Business Unit Effectiveness at Strategy Implementation." *Academy of Management Journal* 27, no. 1 (1984), pp. 27–36.

Guth, William. "Toward a Social System Theory of Corporate Strategy." *Journal of Business,* July 1976, pp. 374–88.

Hambrick, D. C.; I. C. MacMillan; and D. L. Day. "Strategic Attributes and Performance in the MCG Matrix—A PIMS–Based Analysis of Industrial-Product Businesses." *Academy of Management Journal* 25, no. 3 (1982), pp. 510–31.

Haspeslagh, P. "Portfolio Planning: Uses and Limits." *Harvard Business Review,* January–February 1982, p. 58.

Hax, Arnoldo C., and Nicolas S. Majluf. "The Use of the Growth-Share Matrix in Strategic Planning." *Interfaces* 13, no. 1 (1983), pp. 8–21.

————. "The Use of the Industry Attractiveness–Business Strength Matrix in Strategic Planning." *Interfaces* 13, no. 2 (1983), pp. 54–71.

Hedley, Barry. "Strategy and the Business Portfolio." *Long-Range Planning,* February 1977, pp. 8–15.

Hofer, Charles W. "Toward a Contingency Theory of Business Strategy." *Academy of Management Journal,* December 1975, pp. 784–810.

Hofer, Charles, and Dan Schendel. *Strategy Formulation: Analytical Concepts.* St. Paul, Minn.: West Publishing, 1978.

Macmillan, I. *Strategy Formulation: Political Concepts.* St. Paul, Minn.: West Publishing, 1978.

Mintzberg, Henry. "Research on Strategy Making." *Proceedings of the Academy of Management,* 1972, pp. 218–22.

————. "Strategy Making in Three Modes." *California Management Review,* Winter 1973, pp. 44–53.

Mintzberg, Henry; D. Raisinghani; and Andre Theoret. "The Structure of Unstructured Decision Process." *Administrative Science Quarterly,* June 1976, pp. 246–75.

Murray, E., Jr. "Strategic Choice as a Negotiated Outcome." *Management Science* 24, no. 9 (1978), pp. 960–72.

Pearce, John A., II. "Selecting among Alternative Grand Strategies." *California Management Review* 30, no. 2 (1982), pp. 23–31.

Schoeffler, Sidney; Robert Buzzell; and Donald Heany. "Impact of Strategic Planning on Profit Performance." *Harvard Business Review,* March–April 1974, pp. 137–45.

Stagner, Ross. "Corporate Decision Making." *Journal of Applied Psychology,* February 1969, pp. 1–13.

Staw, Barry M. "Knee-Deep in the Big Muddy: A Study of Escalating Commitment to a Chosen Course of Action." *Organizational Behavior and Human Performance,* June 1976, pp. 27–44.

"Wanted: A Manager to Fit Each Strategy." *Business Week,* February 25, 1980, p. 166.

Chapter 10 Cohesion Case Illustration

Strategic Analysis and Choice at Holiday Inns, Inc.

Before evaluating alternatives and choosing a strategy for the 1990s at Holiday Inns, Inc., take a few minutes to review what has been done in the cohesion case sections up to this point. First, the company mission was examined. An essential issue that surfaced was whether Holiday Inns is in the travel business, hospitality business, or some broader combination of the two. Holiday Inns' executives have traditionally used the travel definition, although the mission must be readdressed as you evaluate and choose a strategy. Second, consecutive sections have examined the present and projected environment of Holiday Inns and analyzed the internal strengths and weaknesses of Holiday Inns at the corporate and business-group levels. Comparing these external and internal analyses is a key basis for generating, evaluating, and choosing corporate- and business-level strategies. Finally, different possible grand strategies for each business group were examined. Now, realistic alternative strategies for Holiday Inns must be identified, evaluated, and the strategies chosen that will guide Holiday Inns through the 1990s.

How is strategy analyzed and chosen at Holiday Inns? To begin, the distinction between corporate- and business-level strategy must be recognized. With both levels applicable at Holiday Inns, this illustration will concentrate initial identification at the business level. In other words, alternative grand strategies for each of Holiday Inns' business units will be identified. Subsequent evaluation and choice of business-level strategies will follow evaluation and choice of corporate-level strategy.

For each business group at Holiday Inns, what are the most appropriate grand strategy options? Exhibit 1 provides an answer. It places each business in its appropriate cell on the grand strategy selection matrix, which was discussed in this chapter (Figure 10–5). This helps identify the more appropriate grand strategies for each Holiday Inns business. At Trailways, for example, the key grand strategies to be evaluated are turnaround/retrenchment or divestiture (Quadrant II). In the restaurant group, Quadrants III and IV must be evaluated because there are attractive possibilities in both areas. Thus, it is important to look at market development or joint venture and concentration or horizontal integration.

How is the business placed in an appropriate quadrant? This cohesion case section will illustrate the placement of two of Holiday Inns' businesses and leave to you the assignment of fitting the other businesses in the two matrix dimensions.

Exhibit 1
Grand strategy selection matrix for Holiday Inns, Inc.

Purpose of the grand strategy	Areas of emphasis	
	Internal: Redirect resources within the firm	External: Acquisition of the resource capacity
Overcome weakness and threats	Quadrant II • Turnaround or retrenchment • Divestiture • Liquidation Trailways Restaurant	Quadrant I • Vertical integration • Conglomerate diversification
Maximize strengths and opportunities	Quadrant III • Concentration • Market development • Product development • Innovation Hotels Delta	Quadrant IV • Horizontal integration • Concentric diversification • Joint venture Casinos

Trailways.   Trailways faced numerous environmental threats—heavy competition, rising energy costs, lack of subsidies for terminals, and significant internal weaknesses (price/cost squeeze, aging terminals, inferior image). The primary focus of its ultimate strategy will necessarily have to overcome these weaknesses and threats. To pursue its ultimate strategy, Trailways will depend on and emphasize internal operating capabilities—it already has buses, terminals, and so on—rather than develop operating capacity through external acquisitions. Combining these two assessments, Trailways logically fits in Quadrant II of the grand strategy selection matrix.

Exhibit 2
Grand strategy options at each of Holiday Inns' businesses

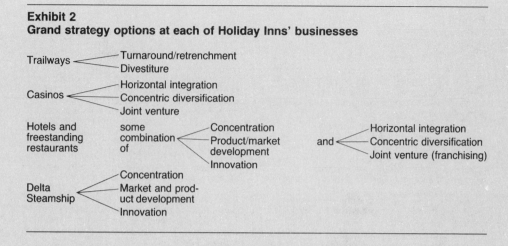

Trailways — Turnaround/retrenchment / Divestiture

Casinos — Horizontal integration / Concentric diversification / Joint venture

Hotels and freestanding restaurants — some combination of — Concentration / Product/market development / Innovation   and — Horizontal integration / Concentric diversification / Joint venture (franchising)

Delta Steamship — Concentration / Market and product development / Innovation

Restaurant Group.   The restaurant group faces key environmental opportunities (eating-out, age, and single-household trends) yet a mixture of threats (growing competition and industry leaders—Shoneys, etc.). Perkins has some internal strengths (franchising expertise, synergy with the core hotel business, Perkins' northern U.S. position) yet a conspicuous weakness—its poor track record. Group executives would surely argue that the purpose of its grand strategy is to maximize strengths and opportunities. The area of emphasis for anticipated growth is both internal and external. They would argue that the company is positioned to carry out company-owned growth (internal emphasis) and external operating capacity through franchising and possible acquisition of additional chains. CEO Mike Rose's comments suggest great concern about lack of success and inability to confront powerful competitors successfully. This suggests the Perkins operation may well be a Quadrant II candidate.

Other Groups.   It should now be possible to surmise why the other Holiday Inns businesses were placed as shown in Exhibit 1. These decisions can be briefly summarized. The hotel group has attractive strengths and environmental opportunities, while it (like restaurants) must emphasize both company-owned (internal) and franchise (external) growth. Delta Steamship has limited but important opportunities (growing Third World markets) and strengths (major U.S.–flag carrier) while depending primarily on internal resource capability. The casinos group, while facing impressive opportunities, must look outside for operational capabilities in the near future, thus its placement in Quadrant IV.

This analysis suggests that the key grand strategy options for each of Holiday Inns' businesses are as shown in Exhibit 2.

**Exhibit 3
Hotel group**

Strategy alternatives	*Strategy analysis*
Pursue rapid growth through domestic and international expansion while seeking to become increasingly price competitive with quality budget chains. (Market development and joint venture franchising)	Hotels are HI's core business, the major profit contributor, and its greatest distinctive competencies. Rapid growth can only be achieved by taking on the lower-priced competitors because available locations are limited. But with markets maturing, and either increased financing or dependence on franchisees required, this alternative is risky.
Selective growth with company-owned movement into multiuser properties (resorts, airports, downtown) and gradual franchise expansion while maintaining the traditional upper-medium focus in price with high-quality service. (Concentration and joint venture franchising)	Consistent with changing travel patterns and shorter vacations for business and family travelers. Allows company-owned positioning in the more lucrative markets. Maintains favorable profit margins and positive cash generator role for corporate activity. Risks continual threat from quality budget chains, especially for the broad franchise base.

**Exhibit 4
Transportation group**

Strategy alternatives	*Strategy analysis*
Trailways: Stabilize market share and profitability through a combination of price competition, improved image, elimination of inefficient routes and equipment, more efficient terminals, and linking with motel network. (Retrenchment/turnaround) Divestiture of the Trailways bus operation. (Divestiture)	Transportation market is quite competitive, with Greyhound as well as the deregulated airline industry. Could increase ridership, but lowering prices in face of rising energy costs would threaten profit margins. Questionable whether Trailways' ridership is compatible with HI guest profile. Possibly extreme and even detrimental because the bus operation has contributed at a steadily growing rate of approximately 23 percent of corporate revenue since 1974. However, profitability has steadily declined, and the bus operation is not compatible with all other groups in terms of customer profile. Managerial and financial resources might be better used elsewhere.
Delta Steamship: Steady growth in new LASH cargo services seeking to exploit and expand market share in South American routes. (Concentration/market development) Divestiture of Delta Steamship. (Typical strategy consideration that would be introduced at the corporate level)	Delta has competitive start with LASH technology and a strong South American/West African route structure. Ships provide useful tax shelter and government subsidies against foreign competition. Cargo emphasis, however, is getting way outside. Drastic improvement in sales and profits in 1978 makes Delta quite marketable. Steamship cargo and passenger services are increasingly removed from HI's core competencies, suggesting divestiture. But, as of now, an increasingly profitable unit to harvest until the right buyer appears.

Exhibit 5
Restaurant group

Strategy alternatives	Strategy analysis
Rapid expansion into freestanding restaurant business through additional acquisition as well as geographic expansion with Perkins franchises. (Market development, joint venture franchising, and horizontal integration) Concentration and steady growth via the Perkins chain above. (Concentration and joint venture franchising)	A growing primary market, but strong competition nationwide. Organizational capacity of HI to absorb and manage rapid acquisition of additional regional chains is doubtful. Risk of a market shakeout with heavy level of competition is a real possibility. Perkins provides an established, competitive base and competent management to guide its stable growth, backed as necessary by corporate resources. Allows HI to evaluate this new operating area before making additional acquisition or resource commitments.

Exhibit 6
Casino group

Strategy alternatives	Strategy analysis
Casinos: Rapid expansion into the four major U.S. areas for legalized gambling via direct investment and particularly joint ventures or acquisition. (Horizontal integration, joint ventures)	A rapidly expanding market that offers exceptional profit potential. A logical extension of HI's lodging and restaurant expertise, particularly when matched with another firm's gaming expertise. Limited U.S. areas having legalized gambling, so should move rapidly to secure a foothold in each area. Offers a natural international spin-off and ultimate lessening of corporate dependence on roadside travel accommodations and franchisees.
Stabilize with current endeavors into gaming and only gradually commit further resources. (Joint venture holding pattern)	Lets HI make sure gaming is an area it should be in before committing sizable resources. However, with limited areas available, could fall behind competition or newcomers (like Ramada Inns) in establishing a foothold.

Several specific grand strategy alternatives could be generated for subsequent analysis. To illustrate the discussion in Chapter 10, a limited range of strategy alternatives for subsequent analysis and choice will be presented.

Exhibits 3 through 6 show a limited range of alternative strategies within each of Holiday Inns' business groups. This set of alternative business strategies will then be used to generate a limited range of alternative corporate-level strategies. Each alternative will provide a brief analysis, which both illustrates the analysis of strategy and gives a basis for strategic choice.

When the analysis of each business group's alternative strategies is complete,

Exhibit 7
Business portfolio matrix for Holiday Inns

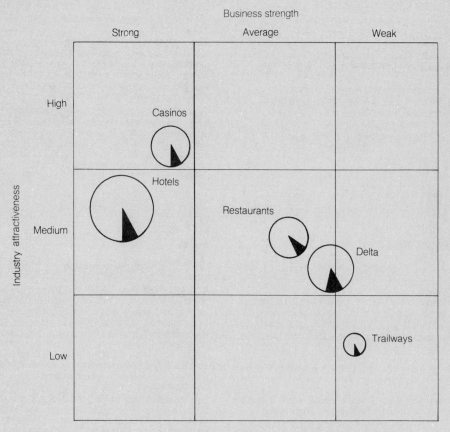

a choice must be made. To ensure consistent business-level choices, this choice must be made at the corporate level and finalized at each business level.

The critical issue at the corporate level for Holiday Inns, Inc., returns to its overall mission. Which of the following does it see as its mission?

1. Diversified firm in travel- and transportation-related industries.
2. Diversified firm in the travel-related industry.
3. Diversified firm in the hospitality industry.

Clearly, Holiday Inns' current business portfolio would align itself with the first mission statement. However, Holiday Inns has traditionally perceived itself within mission statement 2. Its corporatewide expertise and distinctive competence are strongest relative to statement 3. So, to choose a strategy, Holiday Inns, Inc., must also clarify its overall mission.

To illustrate corporate-level strategic choice, we have placed HI businesses in a business portfolio matrix in Exhibit 7. This matrix gives several insights into corporate-level strategy evaluation and choice.

> HI's strongest position is in the hospitality-related area, with hotels providing stable growth and strong cash flow, while casinos also represent key areas for corporate growth.
>
> Perkins restaurants are questionable, with a moderately attractive industry but continued weakness in historical performance.
>
> Bus operation is the weakest portfolio member, with Trailways of questionable long-term value to the firm.
>
> Delta provides a steadily profitable business, though without the potential of the hospitality group and clearly unrelated to that group.

The portfolio matrix suggests two basic corporate strategy choices for Holiday Inns, Inc.:

1. Stabilize and improve the current business portfolio.
2. Extend the success of the hotel business (concentration, product and market development), with major growth emphasis (particularly) in casinos.

The choice is related to the need for clarification of the company mission mentioned earlier, so that two points must be dealt with: the mission must be clarified and the corporate strategy chosen. This will set the parameters for business-level strategic choices. Holiday Inns' decision for the 1990s can be summarized as follows:

> Company mission and corporate strategy: "Our strategy for the coming decade will be to grow consistently from our leadership base in *the hospitality industry,* seeking major positions in the closely related fields of hotels and casino gaming."

Business group strategies (refer to the earlier discussion):

Hotel group—option 2, product development with aggressive franchise growth and entry into new lodging segments.

Trailways—option 2, divestiture with a $15 million loss.

Delta—combination of options 1 and 2, continued cargo service expansion until profitable divestiture can be made.

Restaurants—option 2, turnaround or possible divestiture of Perkins.

Casinos—option 1, rapid growth into four major regions.

And the long-term objectives associated with the corporate strategy might be as follows:

"The primary goal of HI management is to maximize the value of HI stock to its shareholders."

Dividend payout of 25 to 30 percent of normalized earnings.

Maintain a debt/capital ratio under 50 percent.

Return on equity to exceed 17 percent annually.

Develop a favorable climate for the company in the communities in which it conducts its business through corporate philanthrophy, with an annual goal of $1.5 million in donations.

STRATEGIC MANAGEMENT MODEL

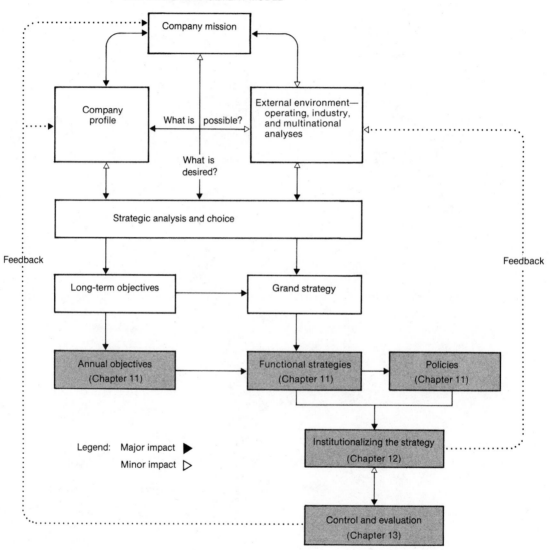

PART THREE

Strategy Implementation

The last part of this book examines what is often called the action phase of the strategic management process: implementation of the chosen strategy. Up to this point, three major phases have been covered: strategy formulation, analysis of alternative strategies, and strategic choice. While these phases are important, they alone cannot ensure success. The strategy must be translated into concrete action, and that action must be carefully implemented. Otherwise, accomplishment is left to chance. The three chapters in this section discuss key aspects of the implementation phase of strategic management.

Implementation is successfully initiated in three interrelated stages:

1. Identification of measurable, mutually determined *annual objectives*.
2. Development of specific *functional strategies*.
3. Development and communication of concise *policies* to guide decisions.

Annual objectives guide implementation by converting long-term objectives into specific, short-term ends. Functional strategies translate grand strategy at the business level into current action plans for subunits of the company. Policies provide specific guidelines for operating managers and their subordinates in executing strategies. Chapter 11 examines how to maximize the use of annual objectives, operating strategies, and policies to operationalize a strategy.

A new strategy must be institutionalized—must permeate the very day-to-day life of the company—to be effectively implemented. In Chapter 12, three organizational elements providing fundamental, long-term means of institutionalizing the company's strategy are discussed:

1. *Structure* of the organization.
2. *Leadership* of the CEO and key managers.
3. The fit between the strategy and the company's *culture*.

Strategy is implemented in a changing environment. Thus, execution must be controlled and evaluated if the strategy is to be successfully implemented and adjusted to changing conditions. The control and evaluation process must include at least three fundamental dimensions:

1. *Establish strategic controls* that "steer" strategy execution.
2. *Operations control systems* that monitor performance, evaluate deviations, and initiate corrective action.
3. *Reward systems* that motivate control and evaluation.

Chapter 13 examines each dimension of the control and evaluation process.

11

Operationalizing the Strategy: Annual Objectives, Functional Strategies, and Business Policies

Even after the grand strategies are determined and long-term objectives tentatively set, the strategic management process is far from complete. The tasks of operationalizing, institutionalizing, and controlling the strategy still remain. These tasks signal a critical new phase in the strategic management process: translating strategic thought into strategic action. Shifting from formulation to implementation gives rise to three interrelated concerns:

1. Identification of measurable, mutually determined annual objectives.
2. Development of specific functional strategies.
3. Communication of concise policies to guide decisions.

Annual objectives translate long-range aspirations into this year's budget. If annual objectives are well developed, they provide clarity, which is a powerful, motivating facilitator of effective strategy implementation. This chapter looks at how to develop annual objectives that maximize implementation-related payoffs.

Functional strategies translate grand strategy at the business level into action plans for subunits of the company. Operating managers assist in developing these strategies, which, in turn, helps clarify what the managers' units are expected to do in implementing the grand strategy. This chapter examines the value and characteristics of functional strategies and the key areas in an organization for which operating strategies enhance implementation of the grand strategy.

Policies are specific guides for operating managers and their subordinates. Policies, often misunderstood and misused, can provide a powerful tool for strategy implementation if they are clearly linked to operating strategies and long-term objectives. This chapter explains how to use policies in the implementation and control of a company's strategies.

Annual Objectives

Chapter 9 dealt with the importance of long-term objectives as benchmarks for corporate and business strategies. Such measures as market share, ROI, return on equity (ROE), stock price, and new market penetration provide guidance in assessing the ultimate effectiveness of a chosen strategy. While such objectives clarify the long-range purpose of a grand strategy and the basis for judging its success, they are less useful in guiding the operating strategies and immediate actions necessary to implement a grand strategy.

A critical step in successful implementation of grand strategy is the identification and communication of annual operating objectives that relate logically to the strategy's long-term objectives.[1] Accomplishment of these annual objectives adds up to successful execution of the business's overall long-term plan. A comprehensive set of annual objectives also provides a specific basis for monitoring and controlling organizational performance. Such objectives can aid in the development of "trigger points" that alert top management to variations in key performance areas that might have serious ramifications for the ultimate success of a strategy.

Qualities of Effective Annual Objectives

Annual objectives are specific, measurable statements of what an organization subunit is expected to achieve in contributing to the accomplishment of the business's grand strategy. Although this seems rather obvious, problems in strategy implementation often stem from poorly conceived or stated annual objectives. To maximize these objectives' contribution, certain basic qualities must be incorporated in developing and communicating them.

Linkage to Long-Term Objectives.   An annual objective must be clearly linked to one or more long-term objectives of the business's grand strategy. However, to accomplish this, it is essential to understand how the two types of objectives differ. Four basic dimensions distinguish annual and long-term objectives:

---

[1] An *annual* time frame is the most popular short-term planning horizon in most firms. Short-term objectives, particularly for a key project, program, or activity, may involve a shorter time horizon (e.g., a three- or six-month horizon). The discussion in this section accommodates such shorter horizons.

1. *Time frame.* Long-term objectives are focused usually five years or more into the future. Annual objectives are more immediate, usually involving one year.
2. *Focus.* Long-term objectives focus on the future position of the firm in its competitive environment. Annual objectives identify specific accomplishments for the company, functional areas, or other subunits over the next year.
3. *Specificity.* Long-term objectives are broadly stated. Annual objectives are very specific and directly linked to the company, a functional area, or other subunit.
4. *Measurement.* While both long-term and annual objectives are quantifiable, long-term objectives are measured in broad, relative terms; for example, 20 percent market share. Annual objectives are stated in absolute terms, such as a 15 percent increase in sales in the next year.

Annual objectives add breadth and specificity in identifying *what* must be accomplished in order to achieve the long-term objective. For example, the long-term objective "to obtain 20 percent market share in five years" clarifies where the business wants to be. But achieving that objective can be greatly enhanced if a series of specific annual objectives identify what must be accomplished each year to achieve that objective. If market share is now 10 percent, then one likely annual objective would be "to achieve a minimum 2 percent increase in relative market share in the next year."

Specific annual objectives should provide targets for performance of operating areas if the long-term objective is to be achieved. "Open two regional distribution centers in the Southeast in 1990" might be one annual objective that marketing and production managers agree is essential in achieving a 20 percent market share in five years. "Conclude arrangements for a $10 million line of credit at 1 percent above prime in 1989" might be the annual objective of financial managers to support the operation of new distribution centers and the additional purchases necessary to increase output in reaching the long-term objective.

The link between short-term and long-term objectives should resemble cascades through the business from basic long-term objectives to numerous specific annual objectives in key operating areas. Thus, long-term objectives are segmented and reduced to short-term (annual) objectives. The cascading effect has the added advantage of providing a clear reference for vertical communication and negotiation, which may be necessary to ensure integrated objectives and plans at the operating level.[2]

---

[2] Lawrence G. Hrebiniak and William F. Joyce, *Implementing Strategy* (New York: Macmillan, 1984), p. 110.

Figure 11–1
Logistic priorities in a manufacturing firm

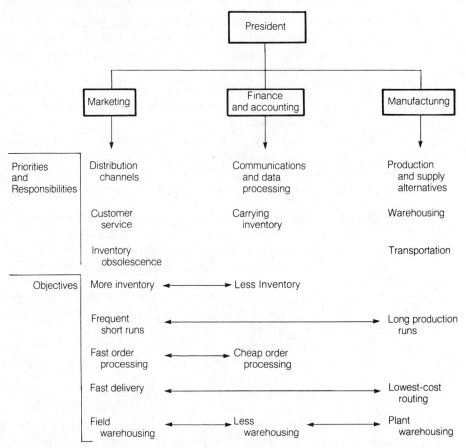

Source: Adapted from John F. Stolle, "How to Manage Physical Distribution," *Harvard Business Review*, July–August 1967, p. 95.

Integrated and Coordinated Objectives.   Implementation of grand strategies requires objectives that are *integrated and coordinated*. However, subunit managers (e.g., vice president of finance, vice president of marketing, vice president of production) may not consider such a "superordinate" purpose in setting annual objectives. Consider the example in Figure 11–1. As can be seen, priorities of the marketing function can easily conflict with those of manufacturing or finance/accounting. For example, manufacturing might logically prefer long production runs and plant warehousing to maximize efficiency. On the other hand, marketing might be better served by frequent, short production runs and field warehousing to maximize customer convenience. Other functional conflicts are evident in Figure 11–1. Without concerted effort to integrate and coordinate annual objectives, these natural conflicts can contribute to the failure of long-term objectives (and the grand strategy), even though the separate annual objectives are well designed.

Successful implementation of strategy depends on coordination and integration of operating units. This is encouraged through the development of short-term (annual) objectives. Expressed another way, annual objectives provide a focal point for raising and resolving conflicts between organizational subunits that might otherwise impede strategic performance.

Managers should be involved at key points in the planning process so that annual objectives are integrated and coordinated. These managers are brought together to discuss important data, assumptions, and performance requirements. This promotes discussion of key interdependencies and a clearer, possibly negotiated determination of annual objectives in key performance areas. Particularly if major strategic change is involved, participation is essential both to establish the relationship of short-term operating activities and long-term strategy *and* to integrate and coordinate operating plans and programs.

Consistency in Annual Objectives

Experience indicates that managers in the same organization will have different ways of developing objectives. For example, managers in different functions, departments, or other subunits will often emphasize different criteria. Due to this lack of consistency, units may not be comparable, commitment to objectives may differ, and the interdependence of units may be dysfunctional. For example, if the marketing area of the firm in Figure 11–1 had very clear, specific objectives regarding delivery time to customers while the manufacturing area's objectives in this regard were ill defined, conflict might be frequent and counterproductive to the strategic success of the firm.

Annual objectives are more consistent when each objective clearly states *what* is to be accomplished, *when* it will be done, and *how* accomplishment will be *measured*. Objectives can then be used to monitor both the effectiveness of an operating unit and, collectively, progress toward the business's long-term objectives. Figure 11–2 illustrates several effective and ineffective annual objectives. If objectives are measurable and state what is to be done and when it will be achieved in a clear, understandable manner, misunderstanding is less likely to occur among the interdependent operating managers who must implement the grand strategy.

Measurable. *Measurability* cannot be overemphasized as a key quality of annual objectives. Unfortunately, some key results are easier to measure than others. *Line* units (e.g., production) may easily be assessed by clear, quantifiable measures, while criteria for certain *staff* areas (e.g., personnel) are more difficult to measure. However, successful implementation requires setting measurable

Figure 11–2
Operationalizing measurable annual objectives

Examples of deficient annual objectives	*Examples of annual objectives with measurable criteria for performance*
To improve morale in the divisions (plant, department, etc.).	To reduce turnover (absenteeism, number of rejects, etc.) among sales managers by 10 percent by January 1, 1989.
	Assumption: Morale is related to measurable outcomes (i.e., high and low morale are associated with different results).
To improve support of the sales effort.	To reduce the time lapse between order date and delivery by 8 percent (two days) by June 1, 1989.
	To reduce the cost of goods produced by 6 percent to support a product price decrease of 2 percent by December 1, 1989.
	To increase the rate of before- or on-schedule delivery by 5 percent by June 1, 1989.
To develop a terminal version of the SAP computer program.	To develop a terminal version of SAP capable of processing X bits of information in time Y at cost not to exceed Z per 1,000 bits by December 1, 1989.
	Assumption: There is virtually an infinite number of "terminal" or operational versions. Greater detail or specificity defines the objective more precisely.
To enhance or improve the training effort.	To increase the number of individuals capable of performing X operation in manufacturing by 20 percent by April 15, 1989.
	To increase the number of functional heads capable of assuming general management responsibility at the division level by 10 percent by July 15, 1989.
	To provide sales training to X number of individuals, resulting in an average increase in sales of 4 percent within six months after the training session.
To improve the business's image.	To conduct a public opinion poll using random samples in the five largest U.S. metropolitan markets and determine average scores on 10 dimensions of corporate responsibility by May 15, 1989.
	To increase our score on those 10 items by an average of 7.5 percent by May 1, 1990.

Source: Adapted from Laurence G. Hrebiniak and William F. Joyce, *Implementing Strategy* (New York: Macmillan, 1984), p. 116.

annual objectives in these difficult areas, as well. This is usually accomplished by initially focusing on *measurable activity,* followed by the identification of acceptable, measurable *outcomes.*

Other qualities of good objectives discussed in Chapter 9—acceptable, flexible, suitable, motivating, understandable, and achievable—also apply to annual objectives. While these will not be discussed here, the reader should review the earlier discussion to appreciate the qualities common to all objectives.

Figure 11–3
A case of misplaced priorities

CITIBANK

Citibank (New York State), N.A.
P.O. Box 227
Cheektowaga, New York 14225

January 18, 1988

Dear Silver Card Customer:

Several months ago we at Citibank began issuing The Silver Card to Goodyear customers.

The Silver Card revolving loan plan was established and offered by Citibank to provide a more effective nationwide tire and auto service credit card for customers of Goodyear's retail outlets.

As a national credit card, The Silver Card will offer you far more convenience than previously available. Our objective is to make The Silver Card the best credit card available anywhere.

Providing The Silver Card to over a million customers was an ambitious and complex effort and it resulted in account processing problems for some account holders. We understand how frustrating these types of problems can be for you. We are working around the clock to assure that any problems will be corrected promptly.

In the meantime, we trust that you will continue to patronize your Goodyear retail outlet as they will render you the finest products and service available anywhere.

We apologize for any inconvenience we may have caused you and we thank you for your patience and understanding.

Sincerely,

CITIBANK

Source: Mailed to the author, a Goodyear credit customer.

Priorities.   Another critical quality of annual objectives involves the need to prioritize short-term objectives. Due to timing considerations and relative impact on strategic success, annual objectives often have *relative* priorities.

Timing considerations often necessitate initiating or completing one activity before another is started. Figure 11–3 shows how this became a problem for Citibank in implementing a program designed to expand its credit card base as part of an ambitious market development strategy in the financial services industry. Citibank's objective for establishing the accounting procedures needed to support the marketing program was not given sufficient priority.

While all annual objectives are important, some deserve additional attention because of their particular impact on the success of a strategy. If such priorities are not discussed and indicated, conflicting assumptions about the relative importance of annual objectives might inhibit progress toward strategic effectiveness.[3] Facing the real possibility of bankruptcy in 1983, Eastern Air Lines formulated a retrenchment strategy with several important annual objectives in labor relations, routes, fleet, and financial condition. But its highest priority involved maintaining the integrity of selected debt-related measures that would satisfy key creditors who could otherwise move to force bankruptcy.

Priorities are usually established in one of several ways. A simple *ranking* may be based on discussion and negotiation during the planning process. However, this does not necessarily communicate the *real* difference in the importance of objectives, so terms such as *primary, top, or secondary* may be used to indicate priority. Some businesses assign weights (for example, 0–100 percent) to establish and communicate the relative priority of each objective. Whatever the method, recognizing the priorities of annual objectives is an important dimension in implementing the strategy.

Benefits of Annual Objectives

Systematic development of annual objectives provides a tangible, meaningful focus through which managers can translate long-term objectives and grand strategies into specific action. Annual objectives give operating managers and personnel a better understanding of their role in the business's mission. This *clarity of purpose* can be a major force in effectively mobilizing the "people assets" of a business.[4] Strategy in Action 11–1 illustrates how specific annual objectives help focus a declining NBA.

A second benefit involves the process required to derive annual objectives. If these objectives have been developed through the participation of managers responsible for their accomplishment, they provide an "objective" basis for addressing and accommodating conflicting political concerns that might interfere with strategic effectiveness. Effective annual objectives become the essential link between strategic intentions and operating reality.

Well-developed annual objectives provide another major benefit: *a basis for strategic control.* The question of controlling strategy will be examined in greater detail in Chapter 13; but it is important to recognize here the simple yet powerful benefit of annual objectives in developing budgets, schedules, trigger points, and other mechanisms for controlling strategy implementation.

Annual objectives can provide motivational payoffs in strategy implementa-

---

[3] Ibid., p. 119.

[4] One recent book that supports this point is Thomas J. Peters and R. H. Waterman, Jr., *In Search of Excellence* (New York: Harper & Row, 1982). Extensive literature on one of the best-known management techniques, management by objectives (MBO), supports the value of objective setting in achieving desired performance. For a useful discussion of MBO, see Karl Albrecht, *Successful Management by Objectives* (Englewood Cliffs, N.J.: Prentice-Hall, 1978).

Strategy in Action 11–1

Annual Objectives and Functional Strategies at the National Basketball Association

By the mid-1980s, a safe bet around sport circles was that the NBA would not survive to the 1990s. Sixteen of 23 teams were losing money, TV ratings were dropping, and buyers for "for sale" franchises were nowhere to be found. In 1987, Commissioner David J. Stern identified three annual objectives and five functional strategies to turn the situation around.

Annual Objective for the NBA. Commissioner Stern set three objectives for 1988:

1. Gross league revenues will be $325 million.
2. All 23 teams will generate a profit.
3. The NBA's TV ratings will increase by 10 percent.

Functional Strategies for the NBA. Stern used five functional strategies designed to accomplish these objectives:

1. *Stop overspending for players.* Selected NBA teams had courted bankruptcy by overspending for players. The new salary strategy sets a salary pool beyond which a team cannot (normally) spend. The figure is arrived at by totaling NBA revenues, multiplying by 53 percent, and apportioning that amount equally among the 23 teams.
2. *Recruit businesspersons to buy sagging franchises.* Commissioner Stern personally took charge of targeting and recruiting successful businesspeople to acquire sagging NBA franchises. He felt such owners would understand, appreciate, and restore financial sanity to these problem franchises.
3. *Reduce overexposure on TV.* In 1984, over 200 NBA games were televised nationally on cable and network TV. This avalanche of available games depressed NBA ratings, which reduced advertising rates and league revenue. Commissioner Stern reduced the number of televised games to 55 regular season games and 20 playoff games. This strategy improved audience size and raised ratings, which, in turn, increased TV revenues.
4. *Institute a league MIS system.* The NBA developed an MIS system that offers each team an item-by-item revenue-and-expense comparison with other teams and NBA averages.
5. *Institute an antidrug program.* The NBA took the forefront among professional sports in fighting the drug problem. It developed a comprehensive drug program for its athletes, which allowed the NBA to generate sizable goodwill toward the league.

Source: Based on "Basketball: Business Is Booming," *Business Week*, October 28, 1986.

tion. If objectives clarify personal and group roles in a business's strategies and are also measurable, realistic, and challenging, they can be powerful motivators of managerial performance—particularly when they are linked to the business's reward structure.

While annual objectives provide a powerful tool in operationalizing business strategy, they aren't sufficient in themselves. Functional strategies, the *means* to accomplish these objectives, must be clearly identified to encourage successful implementation.

Developing Functional Strategies

A *functional strategy* is the short-term game plan for a key functional area *within* a company. Such strategies clarify grand strategy by providing more specific details about how key functional areas are to be managed in the near future.

Functional strategies must be developed in the key areas of marketing, finance, production/operations, R&D, and personnel. They must be consistent with long-term objectives and grand strategy. Functional strategies help in implementation of grand strategy by organizing and activating specific subunits of the company (marketing, finance, production, etc.) to pursue the business strategy in daily activities. In a sense, functional strategies translate thought (grand strategy) into action designed to accomplish specific annual objectives. For every major subunit of a company, functional strategies identify and coordinate actions that support the grand strategy and improve the likelihood of accomplishing annual objectives. Strategy in Action 11–1 illustrates key functional strategies used to implement the NBA's turnaround in the late 1980s.

Figure 11–4 illustrates the important role of functional strategies in implementing corporate and business strategy. The corporate strategy defined General Cinema Corporation's general posture in the broad economy. The business strategy outlined the competitive posture of its operations within the domestic movie exhibition industry. But to increase the likelihood that these strategies will be successful, more specific guidelines are needed for the business's operating components. Thus, functional strategies clarify the business strategy, giving specific, short-term guidance to operating managers. The example in Figure 11–4 shows possible functional strategies in the functional areas of operations, marketing, and finance. Additional functional strategies are necessary, most notably in the personnel area.

Differences between Business and Functional Strategies

To better understand the role of functional strategies within the strategic management process, they must be differentiated from grand strategies. Three basic characteristics differentiate functional and grand strategies:

Figure 11–4
Role of functional strategies at General Cinema Corporation

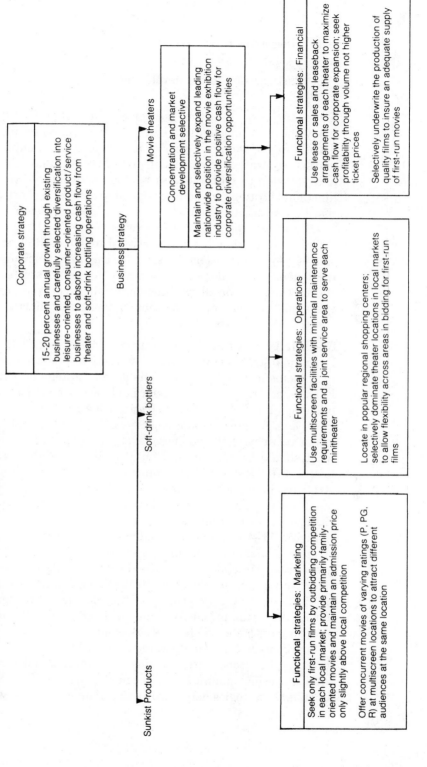

1. Time horizon covered.
2. Specificity.
3. Participation in the development.

Time Horizon.   The time horizon of a functional strategy is usually comparatively short. Functional strategies identify and coordinate short-term actions, usually undertaken in a year or less. Sears, for example, might implement a marketing strategy of increasing price discounts and sales bonuses in its appliance division to reduce excess appliance inventory over the next year. This functional strategy would be designed to achieve a short-range (annual) objective that ultimately contributes to the goal of Sears' grand strategy in its retail division over the next five years.

This shorter time horizon is critical to successfully implementing a grand strategy for two reasons. First, it focuses functional managers' attention on what needs to be done *now* to make the grand strategy work. Second, the shorter time horizon allows functional managers to recognize current conditions and adjust to changing conditions in developing functional strategies.

Specificity.   A functional strategy is more specific than a grand strategy. Functional strategies guide functional actions taken in key parts of the company to implement grand strategy. The grand strategy provides general direction. Functional strategies give specific guidance to managers responsible for accomplishing annual objectives. Such strategies are meant to ensure that managers know *how* to meet annual objectives. It is not enough to identify a general grand strategy at the business level. There must also be strategies outlining what should be done in each functional area if the annual (and ultimately long-term) objectives of the company are to be achieved. Specific functional strategies improve the willingness (and ability) of operating managers to implement strategic decisions, particularly when those decisions represent major changes in the current strategy of the firm.

Figure 11–4 illustrates the difference in specificity of grand and operating strategies. General Cinema's grand strategy for its movie theater division gives broad direction on how the division should pursue a concentration and selective market development strategy. Two functional strategies illustrated in the marketing area give specific direction to managers on what types of movies (first-run, primarily family-oriented, P, PG, R) and what pricing strategy (competitive in the local area) should be followed.

Specificity in functional strategies contributes to successful implementation for several reasons. First, it adds substance, completeness, and meaning to what a specific subunit of the business must do. The existence of numerous functional strategies helps ensure that managers know what needs to be done and can focus on accomplishing results.[5] Second, specific functional strategies clarify for top management how functional managers intend to accomplish the grand strategy. This increases top management's confidence in and sense of control over the grand strategy. Third, specific functional strategies facilitate coordination between operating units *within* the company by clarifying areas of interdependence and potential conflict.

Participants.   Different people participate in strategy development at the functional and business levels. Business strategy is the responsibility of the general manager of a business unit. Development of functional strategy is typically delegated by the business-level manager to principal subordinates charged with running the operating areas of the business. The business manager must establish long-term objectives and a strategy that corporate management feels contributes to corporate-level goals. Key operating managers similarly establish annual objectives and operating strategies that help accomplish business objectives and strategies. Just as business strategies and objectives are approved through negotiation between corporate managers and business managers, the business manager typically ratifies the annual objectives and functional strategies developed by operating managers.[6]

The involvement of operating managers in developing functional strategies contributes to successful implementation because understanding of what needs to be done to achieve annual objectives is thereby improved. And perhaps most critical, active involvement increases commitment to the strategies developed.

It is difficult to generalize about the development of strategies across functional areas. For example, key variables in marketing, finance, and production are different. Furthermore, within each functional area, the importance of key variables varies across business situations. Thus, in the next several sections, we will not exhaustively treat each functional area but will attempt to indicate the key decision variables that should receive attention in the functional strategies of typical areas.

Functional Strategies in the Marketing Area

The role of the marketing function is to profitably bring about the sale of products/services in target markets for the purpose of achieving the business's

---

[5] While a company typically has one grand strategy, it should have a functional strategy for each major subunit and several operating strategies within the subunit. For example, a business may specify distinct pricing, promotion, and distribution strategies as well as an overall strategy to guide marketing operations.

[6] A. A. Thompson, Jr., and A. J. Strickland III, *Strategy Formulation and Implementation,* 2nd ed. (Plano, Tex.: Business Publications, 1983), p. 77.

Figure 11–5
Functional strategies in marketing

Key functional strategies	Typical questions that should be answered by the functional strategy
Product (or service)	Which products do we emphasize?
	Which products/services contribute most to profitability?
	What is the product/service image we seek to project?
	What consumer needs does the product/service seek to meet?
	What changes should be influencing our customer orientation?
Price	Are we primarily competing on price?
	Can we offer discounts or other pricing modifications?
	Are pricing policies standard nationally or is there regional control?
	What price segments are we targeting (high, medium, low, etc.)?
	What is the gross profit margin?
	Do we emphasize cost/demand or competition-oriented pricing?
Place	What level of market coverage is necessary?
	Are there priority geographic areas?
	What channels of distribution are key?
	What are the channel objectives, structure, and management?
	Should the marketing managers change their degree of reliance on distributors, sales reps, and direct selling?
	What sales organization do we want?
	Is the sales force organized around territory, market, or product?
Promotion	What are key promotion priorities and approaches?
	Which advertising/communication priorities and approaches are linked to different products, markets, and territories?
	Which media would be most consistent with the total marketing strategy?

goals. Functional strategies in the marketing area should guide this endeavor in a manner consistent with the grand strategy and other functional strategies. Effective marketing strategies guide marketing managers in determining who will sell what, where, when, to whom, in what quantity, and how. Marketing strategies must therefore entail four components: product, price, place, and promotion. Figure 11–5 illustrates the types of questions that operating strategies must address in terms of these four components. Strategy in Action 11–2 shows how marketing strategies were used to implement a new business strategy at K mart.

Strategy in Action 11–2
K mart Operationalizes a New Business Strategy

Not long ago, employees in K mart discount department stores began shuffling shelves, replacing racks, moving whole departments, and blazing new aisles. When they finished, the stores had a new look, and K mart Corp., the world's second-largest retailer, had started on a new merchandising tack.

The trouble is that K mart can no longer rely entirely on its old strategy of growth through building new stores. Since the first K mart opened in 1962, offering everything from baby oil to motor oil at cut-rate prices, the stores have proliferated, turning the former S. S. Kresge Company from a so-so five-and-dime chain into the biggest retailer next to Sears Roebuck & Co.

Now, with stores in nearly all the 300 top metropolitan areas in the country, some of which are saturated, K mart's growth through expansion is increasingly limited. The answer is to try for more volume, and more profitable volume per store, from the cost-conscious consumers attracted by K mart's low prices. K mart can't risk losing its discount appeal, but at the same time it must move more and higher-quality goods. To achieve this new business strategy, K mart is relying heavily on a sophisticated operating strategy in merchandising. The standard K mart—a cavernous building of plain design filled with racks, bins, and metal shelves—has been changed here to emphasize the merchandise at least as much as the price tags and signs. Displays of clothing and other goods are being altered to stimulate impulse buying. In addition, higher-quality goods are being offered.

K mart's heavy advertising consistently has attracted customers, especially cost-conscious middle- and upper-income customers. "But too often we fail to merchandise all of the items that customers would buy from us after we get them into the store," said K mart's CEO. "We simply aren't getting enough of their spendable dollars."

Although the changes in K marts seem subtle, they're designed to create an atmosphere conducive to free spending. In women's apparel, rows and rows of long piperacks have been replaced by multilevel, circular, and honeycomb racks that allow customers to see whole garments. Higher-quality, more fashionable soft goods hang on the new racks. Delicatessen and snack counters have moved to a wall from their front-and-center position. Now, jewelry greets shoppers inside the entrances. "We wanted to get the popcorn out from in front of the door," said a K mart vice president. The jewelry includes higher-quality pieces and more brand-name items. Sales of women's wear and jewelry have increased in the redesigned stores, K mart managers say.

Source: "Mass Appeal," *Forbes*, May 5, 1986.

A functional strategy for the *product component* of the marketing function should clearly identify the customer needs the firm seeks to meet with its product and/or service. An effective functional strategy for this component should guide marketing managers in decisions regarding features, product lines, packaging, accessories, warranty, quality, and new product development. This strategy should provide a comprehensive statement of the product/service concept and the target market(s) the firm is seeking to serve. This, in turn, fosters consistency and continuity in the daily activity of the marketing area.

A product or service is not much good to a customer if it is not available when and where it is wanted. So, the functional strategy for the *place component* identifies where, when, and by whom the product/services are to be offered for sale. The primary concern here is the channel(s) of distribution—the combination of marketing institutions through which the products/services flow to the final user. This component of marketing strategy guides decisions regarding channels (for example, single versus multiple channels) to ensure consistency with the total marketing effort.

The *promotion component* of marketing strategy defines how the firm will communicate with the target market. Functional strategy for the promotion component should provide marketing managers with basic guides for the use and mix of advertising, personal selling, sales promotion, and media selection. It must be consistent with other marketing strategy components and, due to cost requirements, closely integrated with financial strategy.

Functional strategy regarding the *price component* is perhaps the single most important consideration in marketing. It directly influences demand and supply, profitability, consumer perception, and regulatory response. The approach to pricing strategy may be cost oriented, market oriented, or competition (industry) oriented. With a cost-oriented approach, pricing decisions center on total cost and usually involve an acceptable markup or target price ranges. Pricing is based on consumer demand (e.g., gasoline pricing in a deregulated oil industry) when the approach is market oriented. With the third approach, pricing decisions center around those of the firm's competitors. The discount pricing that occurred in the U.S. automobile industry in the 1980s, with several domestic and foreign producers usually following Chrysler's discount pricing initiatives, is an example of competitor-based pricing. While one approach (e.g., market demand) may predominate in a firm's pricing strategy, the strategy is always influenced to some degree by the other orientations.

Functional Strategies in Finance/Accounting

While most operating strategies guide implementation in the immediate future, the time frame for financial functional strategies varies because strategies in this area direct the use of financial resources in support of the business strategy, long-term goals, and annual objectives. Financial operating strategies with longer time perspectives guide financial managers in long-term capital

Figure 11–6
Functional strategies in finance

Key functional strategies	Typical questions that should be answered by the functional strategy
Capital acquisition	What is an acceptable cost of capital?
	What is the desired proportion of short- and long-term debt; preferred and common equity?
	What balance is between internal and external funding?
	What risk and ownership restrictions are appropriate?
	What level and forms of leasing should be used in providing assets?
Capital allocation	What are the priorities for capital allocation projects?
	On what basis is final selection of projects to be made?
	What level of capital allocation can be made by operating managers without higher approval?
Dividend and working capital management	What portion of earnings should be paid out as dividends?
	How important is dividend stability?
	Are things other than cash appropriate as dividends?
	What are the cash flow requirements; minimum and maximum cash balances?
	How liberal/conservative should credit policies be?
	What limits, payment terms, and collection procedures are necessary?
	What payment timing and procedure should be followed?

investment, use of debt financing, dividend allocation, and the firm's leveraging posture. Operating strategies designed to manage working capital and short-term assets have a more immediate focus. Figure 11–6 highlights some key questions financial strategies must answer for successful implementation.

Long-term financial strategies usually guide capital acquisition in the sense that priorities change infrequently over time. The desired level of debt versus equity versus internal long-term financing of business activities is a common issue in capital acquisition strategy. For example, Delta Airlines has a long-standing operating strategy that seeks to minimize the level of debt in proportion to equity and internal funding of capital needs. General Cinema Corporation has a long-standing strategy of long-term leasing to expand its theater and soft-drink bottling facilities. The debt-to-equity ratios for these two firms are approximately 0.50 to 2.0, respectively. Both have similar records of steady profitable growth over the last 20 years and represent two different yet equally effective operating strategies for capital acquisition.

Another financial strategy of major importance is capital allocation. Growth-oriented grand strategies generally require numerous major investments in facilities, projects, acquisitions, and/or people. These investments cannot generally be made immediately, nor are they desired to be. Rather, a capital allocation strategy sets priorities and timing for these investments. This also helps manage conflicting priorities among operating managers competing for capital resources.

Retrenchment or stability often require a financial strategy that focuses on the reallocation of existing capital resources. This could necessitate pruning product lines, production facilities, or personnel to be reallocated elsewhere in the firm. The overlapping careers and aspirations of key operating managers clearly create an emotional setting. Even with retrenchment (perhaps even more so!), a clear operating strategy that delineates capital allocation priorities is important for effective implementation in a politically charged organizational setting.

Capital allocation strategy frequently includes one additional dimension—level of capital expenditure delegated to operating managers. If a business is pursuing rapid growth, flexibility in making capital expenditures at the operating level may enable timely responses to an evolving market. On the other hand, capital expenditures may be carefully controlled if retrenchment is the strategy.

Dividend management is an integral part of a firm's internal financing. Because dividends are paid on earnings, lower dividends increase the internal funds available for growth, and internal financing reduces the need for external, often debt, financing. However, stability of earnings and dividends often makes a positive contribution to the market price of a firm's stock. Therefore, a strategy guiding dividend management must support the business's posture toward equity markets.

Working capital is critical to the daily operation of the firm, and capital requirements are directly influenced by seasonal and cyclical fluctuations, firm size, and the pattern of receipts and disbursements. The working capital component of financial strategy is built on an accurate projection of cash flow and must provide cash management guidelines for conserving and rebuilding the cash balances required for daily operation.

Functional Strategies in Research and Development

With the increasing rate of technological change in most competitive industries, research and development (R&D) has assumed a key functional role in many organizations. In the technology-intense computer and pharmaceutical industries, for example, firms typically spend between 4 and 6 percent of their sales dollars on R&D. In other industries, such as the hotel/motel and construction industries, R&D spending is less than 1 percent of sales. Thus, R&D may be a vital function—a key instrument of business strategy—although in stable, less innovative industries, R&D is less critical as a functional strategy than is marketing or finance.

Figure 11–7 illustrates the types of questions addressed by an R&D operating

Figure 11–7
Functional strategies in R&D

R&D decision area	Typical questions that should be answered by the functional strategy
Basic research versus commercial development	To what extent should innovation and break-through research be emphasized? In relation to the emphasis on product development, refinement, and modification?
	What new projects are necessary to support growth?
Time horizon	Is the emphasis short term or long term?
	Which orientation best supports the business strategy? marketing and production strategy?
Organizational fit	Should R&D be done in-house or contracted out?
	Should it be centralized or decentralized?
	What should be the relationship between the R&D unit(s) and product managers? marketing managers? production managers?
Basic R&D posture	Should the firm maintain an offensive posture, seeking to lead innovation and development in the industry?
	Should the firm adapt a defensive posture, responding quickly to competitors' developments?

strategy. First, R&D strategy should clarify whether basic research or product development research will be emphasized. Several major oil companies now have solar energy subsidiaries with R&D strategy emphasis on basic research, while smaller competitors emphasize product development research.

Directly related to the choice of emphasis between basic research and product development is the time orientation for these efforts mandated by R&D strategy. Should efforts be focused on the near or the long term? The solar subsidiaries of the major oil companies have long-term perspectives, while their smaller competitors appear to be focusing on the immediate future. These orientations are consistent with each business's strategy if the major oil companies want to ensure their long-term position in the energy field, while the smaller companies want to establish a competitive niche in the growing solar industry.

R&D strategy should also guide organization of the R&D function. For example, should R&D efforts be conducted solely within the firm or should portions of the work be contracted outside? A closely related issue is whether R&D should be a centralized or decentralized function.

The basic R&D posture of the firm influences each of these decisions because strategy in this area can be offensive, defensive, or a combination of these. If the R&D strategy is offensive, technological innovation and new product development are emphasized as the basis for the firm's future success, as is true for small, high-technology firms. However, this orientation entails high risk (and high payoff) and demands considerable technological skill, forecasting expertise, and the ability to quickly transform basic innovations into commercial products.

A defensive R&D strategy emphasizes product modification and the ability to copy or acquire new technology to maintain a firm's position in the industry. American Motors (AMC) is a good example. Faced with the massive R&D budgets of General Motors, Ford, and foreign competitors, AMC has placed R&D emphasis on bolstering the product life cycle of its prime products (particularly Jeeps) and acquiring small-car technology through a partnership arrangement with Renault of France.

A combination of offensive and defensive R&D strategy is often used by large companies with some degree of technological leadership. GE in the electrical industry, IBM in the computer industry, and Du Pont in the chemical industry all have defensive R&D strategies for currently available products *and* emphasis on an offensive R&D posture in basic, long-term research.

Functional Strategies in Production/Operations

Production/operations management (POM) is the core function in the business firm. POM is the process of converting inputs (raw material, supplies, people, and machines) into value-enhanced output. This function is most easily associated with manufacturing firms. However, it applies equally to all other types of businesses (including service and retail firms, for example).

Functional strategies in POM must guide decisions regarding: (1) the basic nature of the firm's POM system, seeking an optimum balance between investment input and production/operations output and (2) location, facilities design, and process planning on a short-term basis. Figure 11–8 illustrates these concerns by highlighting key decision areas in which the POM strategies should provide guidance.

The facilities and equipment component of POM strategy involves decisions regarding plant location, size, equipment replacement, and facilities utilization that should be consistent with grand strategy and other operating strategies. In the mobile home industry, for example, Winnebago's plant and equipment strategy entailed one large, centralized production center (in Iowa) located near its raw materials with modernized equipment and a highly integrated production process. Fleetwood, Inc., a California-based competitor, opted for dispersed, decentralized production facilities located near markets. Fleetwood emphasizes maximum equipment life and less integrated, labor-intensive production processes. Both are leaders in the mobile home industry.

The purchasing function is another area that should be addressed in the POM strategy. From a cost perspective, are a few suppliers an advantage or risky because of overdependence? What criteria (for example, payment requirements) should be used in selecting vendors? How should purchases be made in terms of volume and delivery requirements to support operations? If such questions are critical to the success of a grand strategy, functional strategy guidelines improve implementation.

Functional strategies for the planning and control component of POM provide guidelines for ongoing production operations. They are meant to encourage

Figure 11–8
Functional strategies in POM

Key operating strategies	Typical questions that should be answered by the functional strategy
Facilities and equipment	How centralized should the facilities be? (One big facility or several small facilities?)
	How integrated should the separate processes be?
	To what extent will further mechanization or automation be pursued?
	Should size and capacity be oriented toward peak or normal operating levels?
Purchasing	How many sources are needed?
	How do we select suppliers and manage relationships over time?
	What level of forward buying (hedging) is appropriate?
Operations planning and control	Should work be scheduled to order or to stock?
	What level of inventory is appropriate?
	How should inventory be used (FIFO/LIFO), controlled, and replenished?
	What are the key foci for control efforts (quality, labor cost, downtime, product usage, other)?
	Should maintenance efforts be preventive or breakdown oriented?
	What emphasis should be placed on job specialization? plant safety? use of standards?

efficient organization of production/operations resources to match long-range, overall demand. Often this component dictates whether production/operations will be demand oriented, inventory oriented, or subcontracting oriented. If demand is cyclical or seasonal, then POM strategy must ensure that production/operations processes are efficiently geared to this pattern. A bathing suit manufacturer would prefer inventories to be at their highest in the early spring, for example, not the early fall. If demand is less cyclical, a firm might emphasize producing to inventory, wanting a steady level of production and inventories. When demand fluctuations are less predictable, many firms subcontract to handle sudden increases in demand while avoiding idle capacity and excess capital investment. Thus, a POM strategy should aid in such decisions as:

What is the appropriate inventory level? Purchasing procedure? Level of quality control?

What is the trade-off in emphasizing cost versus quality in production/operations? What level of productivity is critical?

How far ahead should we schedule production? Guarantee delivery? Hire personnel?

What criteria should be followed in adding or deleting equipment, facilities, shifts, and people?

Figure 11–9
Operations management concerns associated with different elements of a strategy

Possible elements of strategy	Concomitant conditions that may affect or place demands on the operations function
1. Compete as low-cost provider of goods or services	Broadens market. Requires longer production runs and fewer product changes. Requires special-purpose equipment and facilities.
2. Compete as high-quality provider	Often possible to obtain more profit per unit, and perhaps more total profit from a smaller volume of sales. Requires more quality-assurance effort and higher operating cost. Requires more precise equipment, which is more expensive. Requires highly skilled workers, necessitating higher wages and greater training efforts.
3. Stress customer service	Requires broader development of servicepeople and service parts and equipment. Requires rapid response to customer needs or changes in customer tastes, rapid and accurate information system, careful coordination. Requires a higher inventory investment.
4. Provide rapid and frequent introduction of new products	Requires versatile equipment and people. Has higher research and development costs. Has high retraining costs and high tooling and changeover in manufacturing. Provides lower volumes for each product and fewer opportunities for improvements due to the learning curve.
5. Strive for absolute growth	Requires accepting some projects or products with lower marginal value, which reduces ROI. Diverts talents to areas of weakness instead of concentrating on strengths.
6. Seek vertical integration	Enables company to control more of the process. May not have economies of scale at some stages of process. May require high capital investment as well as technology and skills beyond those currently available within the organization.
7. Maintain reserve capacity for flexibility	Provides ability to meet peak demands and quickly implement some contingency plans if forecasts are too low. Requires capital investment in idle capacity. Provides capability to grow during the lead time normally required for expansion.
8. Consolidate processing (centralize)	Can result in economies of scale. Can locate near one major customer or supplier. Vulnerability: one strike, fire, or flood can halt the entire operation.
9. Disperse processing of service (decentralize)	Can be near several market territories. Requires more complex coordination network: perhaps expensive data transmission and duplication of some personnel and equipment at each location. If each location produces one product in the line, then other products still must be transported to be available at all locations. If each location specializes in a type of component for all products, the company is vulnerable to strike, fire, flood, etc. If each location provides total product line, then economies of scale may not be realized.
10. Stress the use of mechanization, automation, robots	Requires high capital investment. Reduces flexibility. May affect labor relations. Makes maintenance more crucial.

Figure 11–9 (*concluded*)
Operations management concerns associated with different elements in a strategy

Possible elements of strategy	Concomitant conditions that may affect or place demands on the operations function
11. Stress stability of employment	Serves the security needs of employees and may develop employee loyalty.
	Helps to attract and retain highly skilled employees.
	May require revisions of make-or-buy decisions, use of idle time, inventory, and subcontractors as demand fluctuates.

Source: From *Production and Operations Management: Manufacturing and Nonmanufacturing*, 2nd ed., by J. Dilworth. Copyright © 1983 by Random House, Inc. Reprinted by permission of the publisher.

POM operating strategies must be coordinated with marketing strategy if the firm is to succeed. Careful integration with financial strategy components (such as capital budgeting and investment decisions) and the personnel function are also necessary. Figure 11–9 helps illustrate the importance of such coordination by showing the different POM concerns that arise when different marketing/financial/personnel strategies are required as elements of the grand strategy.

Functional Strategies in Personnel

The strategic importance of functional strategies in the personnel area has become more widely accepted in recent years. Personnel management aids in accomplishing grand strategy by ensuring the development of managerial talent, the presence of systems to manage compensation and regulatory concerns, and the development of competent, well-motivated employees. Functional strategies in personnel should guide the effective utilization of human resources to achieve both the annual objectives of the firm and the satisfaction and development of employees. These strategies involve the following areas:

Employee recruitment, selection, and orientation.
Career development and counseling, performance evaluation, and training and development.
Compensation.
Labor/union relations and Equal Employment Opportunity Commission (EEOC) requirements.
Discipline, control, and evaluation.

Operating strategy for recruitment, selection, and orientation guides personnel management decisions for attracting and retaining motivated, productive employees. This involves such questions as: What are the key human resource needs to support a chosen strategy? How do we recruit for these needs? How sophisticated should the selection process be? How should new employees be introduced to the organization? The recruitment, selection, and orientation component of personnel strategy should provide basic parameters for answering these questions.

The development and training component should guide personnel actions taken to meet future human resource needs of the grand strategy. Merrill Lynch, a major brokerage firm, has a long-term corporate strategy of becoming a diversified financial service institution. In addition to handling stock transactions, Merrill Lynch is actively moving into such areas as investment banking, consumer credit, and venture capital. In support of these far-reaching, long-term objectives, Merrill Lynch has incorporated extensive early-career training and ongoing career development programs to meet its expanding need for personnel with multiple competencies.

Functional strategies in the personnel area are needed to guide decisions regarding compensation, labor relations, EEOC requirements, discipline, and control to enhance the productivity and motivation of the work force. Involved are such concerns as: What are the standards for promotion? How should payment, incentive plans, benefits, and seniority policies be interpreted? Should there be hiring preference? What are appropriate disciplinary steps? These are specific personnel decisions that operating managers frequently encounter. Functional strategies in the personnel area should guide such decisions in a way that is compatible with business strategy, strategies for other functional areas, and the achievement of annual objectives.

To summarize, functional strategies are important because they provide specifics on *how* each major subactivity contributes to the implementation of the grand strategy. This specificity, and the involvement of operating managers in its development, help ensure understanding of and commitment to the chosen strategy. Annual objectives, linked to both long-term objectives and functional strategies, reinforce this understanding and commitment by providing measurable targets that operating managers have agreed on. The next step in implementing a strategy involves the identification of *policies* that guide and control decisions by operating managers and their subordinates.

Developing and Communicating Concise Policies

Policies are directives designed to guide the thinking, decisions, and actions of managers and their subordinates in implementing an organization's strategy. Policies provide guidelines for establishing and controlling ongoing operations in a manner consistent with the firm's strategic objectives. Often referred to as "standard operating procedures," policies serve to increase managerial effectiveness by standardizing many routine decisions and controlling the discretion of managers and subordinates in implementing operational strategies. Logically, policies should be derived from functional strategies (and, in some instances, from corporate or business strategies) with the key purpose of aiding in strategy execution.[7] Strategy in Action 11–3 illustrates selected policies from several well-known companies.

The Purpose of Policies

Policies communicate specific guides to decisions. They are designed to control and reinforce the implementation of functional strategies and the grand strategy, and they fulfill this role in several ways:

1. *Policies establish indirect control over independent action* by making a clear statement about how things are *now* to be done. By limiting discretion, policies in effect control decisions and the conduct of activities without direct intervention by top management.

2. *Policies promote uniform handling of similar activities.* This facilitates coordination of work tasks and helps reduce friction arising from favoritism, discrimination, and disparate handling of common functions.

3. *Policies ensure quicker decisions* by standardizing answers to previously answered questions that would otherwise recur and be pushed up the management hierarchy again and again.

4. *Policies help institutionalize basic aspects of organization behavior.* This minimizes conflicting practices and establishes consistent patterns of action in terms of how organizational members attempt to make the strategy work.

5. *Policies reduce uncertainty in repetitive and day-to-day decision making,* thereby providing a necessary foundation for coordinated, efficient efforts.

6. *Policies can counteract resistance to or rejection of chosen strategies by organization members.* When major strategic change is undertaken, unambiguous operating policies help clarify what is expected and facilitate acceptance, particularly when operating managers participate in policy development.

7. *Policies offer a predetermined answer to routine problems,* giving managers more time to cope with nonroutine matters; dealing with ordinary and extraordinary problems is greatly expedited—the former by referring to established policy and the latter by drawing on a portion of the manager's time.

---

[7] The term *policy* has various definitions in management literature. Some authors and practitioners equate policy with strategy. Others do this inadvertently by using "policy" as a synonym for company mission, purpose, or culture. Still other authors and practitioners differentiate policy in terms of "levels" associated respectively with purpose, mission, and strategy. "Our policy is to make a positive contribution to the communities and societies we live in" and "our policy is not to diversify out of the hamburger business" are two examples of the breadth of what some call policies. This book defines *policy* much more narrowly as specific guides to managerial action and decisions in the implementation of strategy. This definition permits a sharper distinction between the formulation and implementation of functional strategies. And, of even greater importance, it focuses the tangible value of the policy concept where it can be most useful—as a key administrative tool to enhance effective implementation and execution of strategy.

Strategy in Action 11–3
Selected Policies that Aid Strategy Implementation

Wendy's has a *purchasing policy* to give local store managers the authority to buy fresh meat and produce locally rather than from regionally designated or company-owned sources.

(This policy supports Wendy's functional strategy of having fresh, unfrozen hamburgers daily.)

General Cinema has a *financial policy* that requires annual capital investment in movie theaters not to exceed annual depreciation.

(By keeping capital investment no greater than depreciation, this policy supports General Cinema's financial strategy of maximizing cash flow—in this case, all profit—to growth areas of the company. It also reinforces General Cinema's financial strategy of leasing as much as possible.)

Holiday Inns has a *personnel policy* that every new innkeeper attend Holiday Inns University's three-week innkeeper program within one year of being hired.

(This policy supports Holiday Inns' functional (POM) strategy of strict compliance with specific standards at every HI location by ensuring standardized training of every new innkeeper at every Holiday Inn whether company owned or franchised.)

IBM originally had a *marketing policy* not to give free IBM personal computers (PCs) to any person or organization.

(This policy attempted to support IBM's image strategy as a professional, high-value, service business and its effort to retain that image as it seeks to dominate the PC market.)

Crown, Cork and Seal Company has an *R&D policy* not to invest any financial or people resources in basic research.

(This policy supports Crown, Cork and Seal's functional strategy, which emphasizes customer service, not technical leadership.)

First National Bank of South Carolina has an *operating policy* that requires annual renewal of the financial statement of all personal borrowers.

(This policy supports First National's financial strategy, which seeks to maintain a loan/loss ratio below the industry norm.)

8. *Policies afford managers a mechanism for avoiding hasty and ill-conceived decisions in changing operations.* Prevailing policy can always be used as a reason for not yielding to emotion-based, expedient, or temporarily valid arguments for altering procedures and practices.[8]

Policies may be written and formal or unwritten and informal. The positive reasons for informal, unwritten policies are usually associated with some strategic need for competitive secrecy. Some unwritten policies, such as "promotion from within," are widely known (or expected) by employees and implicitly sanctioned by management. However, unwritten, informal policies may be contrary to the long-term success of a strategy. Still, managers and employees often like the latitude "granted" when policies are unwritten and informal. There are at least seven advantages to formal written policies:

1. Managers are required to think through the policy's meaning, content, and intended use.
2. The policy is explicit so misunderstandings are reduced.
3. Equitable and consistent treatment of problems is more likely.
4. Unalterable transmission of policies is ensured.
5. Authorization or sanction of the policy is more clearly communicated, which can be helpful in many cases.
6. A convenient and authoritative reference can be supplied to all concerned with the policy.
7. Indirect control and organizationwide coordination, key purposes of policies, are systematically enhanced.[9]

Policies can vary in their level of strategic significance. Some, such as travel reimbursement procedures, are really work rules that are not necessarily linked to the implementation of a specific strategy. At the other extreme, such organizationwide policies as Wendy's requirement that every location invest 1 percent of gross revenue in local advertising are virtually functional strategies.

Policies can be externally imposed or internally derived. Policies regarding EEOC practices are often developed in compliance with external (government) requirements. Likewise, policies regarding leasing or depreciation may be strongly influenced by current tax regulations.

Regardless of the origin, formality, and nature of the policy, the key point to bear in mind is the valuable role policies can play in strategy implementation.

---

[8] These eight points are adapted from related discussions by Richard H. Buskirk, *Business and Administrative Policy* (New York: John Wiley & Sons, 1971), pp. 145–55; Thompson and Strickland, *Strategy Formulation,* pp. 377–79; Milton J. Alexander, *Business Strategy and Policy* (Atlanta: University Publications, 1983), chap. 3.

[9] Adapted from Robert G. Murdick, R. Carl Moor, Richard H. Eckhouse, and Thomas W. Zimmerer, *Business Policy: A Framework for Analysis* (Columbus, Ohio: Grid, 1984), p. 65.

Carefully constructed policies enhance strategy implementation in several ways. Obviously, it is imperative to examine existing policies and ensure the existence of policies necessary to guide and control operating activities consistent with current business and functional strategies. Ensuring communication of specific policies will help overcome resistance to strategic change and foster greater organizational commitment for successful strategy implementation.

Summary

The first concern in the implementation of a grand strategy is to operationalize that strategy throughout the organization. This chapter discussed three important tools to accomplish this: annual objectives, functional strategies, and policies.

Annual objectives guide implementation by translating long-term objectives into current targets. Annual objectives are derived from long-term objectives, but they differ in time frame, focus, specificity, and measurement. For annual objectives to be effective in strategy implementation, they must be integrated and coordinated. They must also be consistent, measurable, and prioritized.

Functional strategies are a second important tool for effective implementation of a grand strategy. Functional strategies are derived from business strategy and provide specific, immediate direction to key functional areas within the business in terms of what must be done to implement the grand strategy.

Policies provide another means of directing and controlling decisions and actions at operating levels of the firm in a manner consistent with business and functional strategies. Effective policies channel actions, behavior, decisions, and practices to promote strategic accomplishment.

While annual objectives, functional strategies, and policies represent the start of implementation, much more remains. The strategy must be institutionalized—must permeate the basic foundation of the company. The next chapter examines the institutionalization phase of strategy implementation.

Questions for Discussion

1. Explain the phrase "translate thought into action." How does this relate to the relationship between grand strategy and operating strategy? between long-term and short-term objectives?
2. How do functional strategies differ from corporate and business strategies?
3. What key concerns must be addressed by functional strategies in marketing? finance? POM? personnel?
4. How do policies aid strategy implementation? Illustrate your answer.
5. Illustrate a policy, an objective, and an operating strategy in your personal career strategy.
6. Why are annual objectives needed when long-term objectives are already available? What function do they serve?

Bibliography

Albrecht, Karl. *Successful Management by Objectives*. Englewood Cliffs, N.J.: Prentice-Hall, 1978.

Alexander, Milton J. *Business Strategy and Policy*. Atlanta: University Publications, 1983, chap. 3.

Fox, Harold. "A Framework for Functional Coordination." *Atlanta Economic Review,* November–December 1973, pp. 10–11.

Friend, J. K. "The Dynamics of Policy Changes." *Long-Range Planning,* February 1977, pp. 40–47.

Helfert, E. A. *Techniques of Financial Analysis,* 4th ed. Homewood, Ill.: Richard D. Irwin, 1978.

Heskett, James L. "Logistics—Essential to Strategy." *Harvard Business Review,* November–December 1977, pp. 85–96.

Hobbs, John, and Donald Heany. "Coupling Strategy to Operating Plans." *Harvard Business Review,* May–June 1977, pp. 119–26.

Hofer, Charles. "Conceptual Scheme for the Implementation of Organizational Strategy." Boston: Intercollegiate Case Clearing House 9–378–737, 1977.

Hrebiniak, Lawrence G., and William F. Joyce. *Implementing Strategy.* New York: Macmillan, 1984.

Ingrasia, Paul. "McDonald's Seeks to Boost Dinner Sales to Offset Surge in Costs and Competition." *The Wall Street Journal,* October 16, 1978.

Kotler, Phillip. *Marketing Management: Analysis, Planning, and Control,* 3rd ed. Englewood Cliffs, N.J.: Prentice-Hall, 1976.

MacMillan, Ian C. "Strategy and Flexibility in the Smaller Business." *Long-Range Planning,* June 1975, pp. 62–63.

McCarthy, E. J., and William D. Perreault, Jr. *Basic Marketing,* 8th ed. Homewood, Ill.: Richard D. Irwin, 1984.

Murdick, Robert G.; R. Carl Moor; Richard H. Eckhouse; and Thomas W. Zimmerer. *Business Policy: A Framework for Analysis.* Columbus, Ohio: Grid, 1984.

Peters, Thomas J., and R. H. Waterman, Jr. *In Search of Excellence.* New York: Harper & Row, 1982.

Shapiro, Benson P. "Can Marketing and Manufacturing Coexist?" *Harvard Business Review,* September–October 1977, pp. 105–14.

Shirley, R. C.; M. H. Peters; and A. I. El-Ansary. *Strategy and Policy Formation: A Multifunctional Orientation,* 2nd ed. New York: John Wiley & Sons, 1981.

Stolle, John F. "How to Manage Physical Distribution." *Harvard Business Review,* July–August 1967, p. 95.

Tellier, Richard. *Operations Management: Fundamental Concepts and Methods.* New York: Harper & Row, 1978.

Vancil, Richard. "Strategy Formulation in Complex Organizations." *Sloan Management Review,* Winter 1976, pp. 2–5.

Weston, J. F., and E. F. Brigham. *Essentials of Managerial Finance,* 7th ed. Hinsdale, Ill.: Dryden Press, 1985.

Chapter 11 Cohesion Case Illustration

Functional Strategies at Holiday Inns, Inc.

The cohesion case in Chapter 10 dealt with strategy analysis and choice. It concluded with the identification of Holiday Inns' choice of corporate-level and business-level strategies. But choice of strategies is not the end of the strategic management process. The strategies must be implemented–translated into appropriate organizational action. The first step in implementation is making the strategy operational. This requires identification of annual objectives, functional strategies, and key policies.

Illustrating the process for each business group at Holiday Inns, Inc., would require extensive text. Instead, this section will isolate one business group—hotels—to identify annual objectives, operating strategies, and policies as discussed in this chapter. It should be kept in mind, however, that a similar effort would be required for each business group at Holiday Inns to effectively implement corporatewide and business-level strategies.

Exhibit 1 highlights key long-term objectives and the business-level strategy (concentration and market development) the hotel group seeks to pursue in its five-year plan.

Annual objectives, functional strategies, and policies must be linked to the grand strategy and long-term objectives in Exhibit 1 if the strategy is to be effectively implemented. Exhibit 2 briefly summarizes key annual objectives and the functional strategies used to implement the hotel group's strategy.

Exhibit 1
Long-term objectives and business-level strategy in the hotel group

Long-term objectives (five years)	Business-level strategy
Net addition of 70,000 new rooms by 1988	Maintain and expand HI's leadership position in the lodging industry by providing the largest number of high-quality, moderately priced, full-service lodging facilities worldwide with emphasis on selective, company-owned expansion into multiuser-oriented properties and steady expansion through franchising with continuous updating or elimination of older properties.
217,000 new and extensively renovated rooms in HI system by 1988	
95 percent of all HI-owned properties in multiuser areas	
50 new franchised properties per year	
17 percent return on investment	
40 percent debt-to-capitalization ratio	Maintain the leadership position as the number one brand preference among lodging customers.
Best price/value ratio in industry	

Exhibit 2
Operationalizing the hotel business strategy: Annual objectives and functional strategies

Annual objectives	*Functional strategies*

Maintain a 70 percent systemwide occupancy rate annually.

Clear identification of customer profile and changes in same on an annual basis.

Maintain 33 percent or greater customer preference for Holiday Inns next year.

Lead the industry in the number of reservations each year.

Prebook over one third of systemwide room-nights each year.

Average 50 new franchised properties per year for the next three years.

Have 50 percent or higher of new franchised units built by existing franchises in 1988.

Have every managerial or supervisory employee at both company-owned and franchised properties trained at HI University by 1988.

35 percent debt-to-capitalization ratio next year.

17 percent operating margin (before taxes) each year.

17 percent average return on equity each year.

Ensure that every property failing two consecutive inspections is out of the HI system within one year.

Marketing. Clearly identify the typical HI guest, provide superior price/value lodging services desired, and ensure customer awareness that these services exist.

Marketing research. Make sure HI knows clearly who its customers are, what they want, and when and where to provide it via a continuous $1.2 million annually budgeted consumer research program.

Advertising. Extensive magazine and TV advertising with largest industry budget and most recognized campaign—No Excuses—in the industry.

Sales. Offer the most advanced reservation system in the industry.

Franchising. Maintain high level of franchise satisfaction and gradual expansion of franchise units systemwide.

Personnel. Ensure highly skilled operating personnel for all hotel properties. To accomplish this, HI University offers one- to three-week courses for all new hotel managers, assistant managers, food and beverage managers, front office, sales, maintenance, and housekeeping supervisors, with mandatory attendance.

Financial. Maintain a financially sound capital structure relative to industry averages by using 50 percent internal and/or equity financing of company-owned expansion. Maintain profitability and stable growth by improving operating margins and a steady return on equity. Call the 9⅝ percent convertible subordinate debentures as soon as the stock price exceeds $22 per share.

Operations. Ensure high-quality, standardized, superior-service lodging facilities throughout the HI network. Emphasize quality control, particularly at existing facilities, and update services offered systemwide to match changing customer profile and needs.

Quality control. At least one unannounced quality control inspection at every property annually. Also, achieve 50 percent of all systemwide rooms being either new or substantially renovated every five years.

Up-to-date services. Continuous improvement of services/facilities offered to match customer preferences. For example: HI-NET satellite communications network for multicity meetings and more king-sized beds for increasing number of single and business guests.

Annual objectives help clarify long-term objectives. For example, Holiday Inns' annual objective of at least 50 new franchised properties feeds directly into the five-year objective of 70,000 rooms in the system. With the average property consisting of approximately 225 rooms, 50 properties would add 11,250 rooms per year. The balance needed would be just under 14,000 (or 2,750 per year), well within the stated preferences for 80 percent franchisee and 20 percent company-owned hotels in the system. Five years at this rate would mean 56,250 franchised rooms.

Functional strategies guide managers while attempting to ensure synergy with the grand strategy. For example, Holiday Inns' quality control strategy of two unannounced visits annually with expulsion from the system if both are failed clarifies for quality control managers, property managers, and franchisees the implicit priorities of the grand strategy.

Finally, organizational policies help guide strategy implementation at Holiday Inns. For example, Holiday Inns has a systemwide policy that every new managerial or supervisory employee at a hotel property—innkeeper, restaurant manager, etc.—must attend Holiday Inns University's course (usually two or three weeks) for that position. This policy helps instill the "Holiday Inns way" and ensures that service standards related to the firm's leadership strategy are consistently implemented at the day-to-day operating level.

This section has highlighted annual objectives, functional strategies, and policies in the hotel group. Are other necessary areas that were not mentioned here useful in implementing the hotel group's strategy? Apply the vehicles for operationalizing grand strategies to each of Holiday Inns' other business units.

12

Institutionalizing the Strategy: Structure, Leadership, and Culture

Annual objectives, functional strategies, and specific policies provide important means of communicating what must be done to implement the overall strategy. By translating long-term intentions into short-term guides to action, they make the strategy operational. But the strategy must also be *institutionalized*— permeate the very day-to-day life of the company—if it is to be effectively implemented. Three organizational elements provide the fundamental, long-term means for institutionalizing the firm's strategy: (1) structure, (2) leadership, and (3) culture.

In the first part of this chapter, the focus will be on organizational structure, the formal reporting relationships and responsibilities within a company. In the second part, focus will shift to the leadership of top management in the accomplishment of strategic objectives. The final part of this chapter will focus on organizational culture—the shared values and beliefs of organization members.

The chapter has three major aims: (1) to present structural alternatives, their advantages and disadvantages, and their role in strategy implementation; (2) to discuss the key dimensions of leadership that are important in strategy implementation; and (3) to discuss the concept of organizational culture, explain how it influences organizational life, and examine ways to manage the strategy–culture relationship.

Structural Considerations

An organization is necessary if strategic purpose is to be accomplished. Thus, organizational structure is a major priority in implementing a carefully formulated strategy. If activities, responsibilities, and interrelationships are not organized in a manner that is consistent with the strategy chosen, the structure is left to evolve on its own. If structure and strategy are not coordinated, the result will probably be inefficiencies, misdirection, and fragmented efforts.

The need for structure becomes apparent as a business evolves. In a small firm where one person manages current operations and plans for the future, organizational structure is relatively simple. Owner-managers have no organizational problem until their hurried trips to the plant, late-night sessions assimilating financial information for their CPA, and pressed calls on potential customers are inadequate to meet the demands of a business's increasing volume. As the magnitude of business activity increases, the need to subdivide activities, assign responsibilities, and provide for the integration and coordination of the new organizational parts becomes imperative. Thus, how to structure the organization to effectively execute the business's strategy has become a major concern.

What is structure? A basically simple concept: the division of tasks for efficiency and clarity of purpose, and coordination between the interdependent parts of the organization to ensure organizational effectiveness. Structure balances the need for specialization with the need for integration. It provides a formal means of decentralizing *and* centralizing consistent with the organizational and control needs of the strategy.

Structure is not the only means for getting "organized" to implement the strategy. Reward systems, planning procedures, and information and budgetary systems are other examples that should be employed. In the day-to-day implementation of strategy, these elements operate *inter*dependently with the formal organizational structure to shape how things are done. These other means may also be important, but it is through structure that strategists attempt to balance internal efficiency and overall effectiveness within a broader environment.

What are the structural choices? Five basic types are currently used by most business firms:

1. Simple.
2. Functional.
3. Divisional.
4. Strategic business unit.
5. Matrix.

Diversity and size create unique structural needs for each firm, but these five structural choices involve basic underlying features common to most business organizations.

Strategy in Action 12–1
Ford Motor Company Organizes the Taurus Success

In the early 1980s, amidst a recession in the automobile business, Ford executives finally realized that fuel economy was not the only reason why consumers were buying import cars. They realized that Ford car quality was not comparable to Japanese products, and they set out to correct the problem. Company managers decided to take radical steps in planning, production, and labor relations in order to build a new, higher-quality car. Ford executives backed up this commitment by investing $3 billion on the development of the new cars and decided that the new models would replace the company's most stable line—Ford LTD and Mercury Marquis—which sold 273,000 units in 1985.

The first thing Ford did was change its traditional structure for building new cars. Instead of the sequential five-year process (in which each component works in isolation without communication between each component), Ford adopted a "Program Management" approach whereby representatives from each unit— planning, design, engineering, and manufacturing—worked together as a group and took final responsibility for the car.

The group first set out to determine which were the world's best-designed and -engineered automotive features. The group determined the 400 "best in class features," and then it determined how they were designed, assembled, and manufactured. And 80 percent of those features were incorporated in the Taurus.

In order to determine consumer preferences, Ford launched its largest series of market studies ever. Interviews at grocery stores, schools, car washes, self-service filling stations, focus groups, and other settings led to the identification of 1,401 suggested features. Ford incorporated over 700 of these "wants" in the Taurus and Sable cars.

Finally, Ford did something no one had done in the U.S. auto industry. It asked assembly line workers for their advice before the car was designed. Numerous suggestions were incorporated in the design. The Taurus team also signed long-term contracts with suppliers and invited them to participate in planning sessions as well.

The approach paid off. By 1987, Taurus had become the top U.S. automobile. Ford has 100,000-plus backlogs in orders. Elated dealers say that customers— some of whom haven't set foot in a domestic producer's showroom for years— are content to wait patiently for two months or more for a Taurus or Sable.

Source: Based on "Ford's Idea Machine," *Newsweek,* November 24, 1986; and "How Ford Hit the Bull's-Eye with Taurus," *Business Week,* June 30, 1986.

Figure 12–1
Simple and functional organizational structures

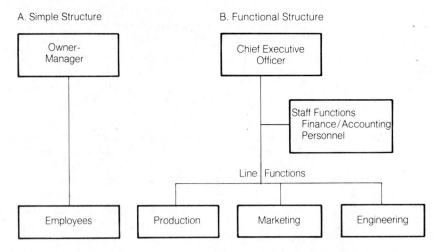

A. Simple Structure

B. Functional Structure

Advantages

1. Facilitates control of all the business's activities.
2. Rapid decision making and ability to change with market signals.
3. Simple and informal motivation/reward/control systems.

Disadvantages

1. Very demanding on the owner-manager.
2. Increasingly inadequate as volume expands.
3. Does not facilitate development of future managers.
4. Tends to focus owner-manager on day-to-day matters and not on future strategy.

Advantages

1. Efficiency through specialization.
2. Improved development of functional expertise.
3. Differentiates and delegates day-to-day operating decisions.
4. Retains centralized control of strategic decisions.

Disadvantages

1. Promotes narrow specialization and potential functional rivalry or conflict.
2. Difficulty in functional coordination and interfunctional decision making.
3. Staff-line conflict.
4. Limits internal development of general managers.

Structure is not an end in itself but rather a means to an end. It is a tool for managing the size and diversity of a business to enhance the success of its strategy. This section identifies structural options and examines the role of structure in strategy implementation.

Simple and Functional Organizational Structures

Figure 12–1 is a model of simple and functional organizational structures. In the smallest business enterprise, the simple structure prevails. All strategic and operating decisions are centralized in the owner-manager's domain. With the strategic concern primarily survival, and the likelihood that one bad decision could seriously threaten continued existence, this structure maximizes the owner's control. It also allows rapid response to product/market shifts and the ability to accommodate unique customer demands without coordination difficulties. Simple structures encourage employee involvement in more than one activity and are efficacious in businesses that serve a localized, simple product/market. This structure can be very demanding on the owner-manager and, as volume increases, can pressure the owner-manager to give increased attention to day-to-day concerns at the expense of time invested in strategic management activities.

Functional structure predominates in firms that concentrate on one or a few related products/markets. Functional structures group similar tasks and activities (usually production/operations, marketing, finance/accounting, research and development, personnel) as separate functional units within the organization. This specialization encourages greater efficiency and refinement of particular expertise and allows the firm to seek and foster distinct competencies in one or more functional areas. Expertise is critical to single-product/market companies and to firms that are vertically integrated. Strategy in Action 12–2 illustrates Crown, Cork and Seal's shift from a divisional structure to the centralized functional structure that was more consistent with its strategy. The functional structure allowed Crown, Cork and Seal to fine-tune its competitive advantage in understanding and responding to the technical needs of customers for hard-to-hold beverage containers. Strategy in Action 12–3 illustrates a similar move by Apple Computer Company.

The strategic challenge in the functional structure is effective coordination of the separate functional units. The narrow technical expertise sought through specialization can lead to limited perspectives and different priorities across different functional units. Specialists may not understand problems in other functional areas and may begin to see the firm's strategic issues primarily as "marketing" problems or "production" problems. This potential conflict makes the coordinating role of the chief executive critical if a strategy is to be effectively implemented using the functional structure. Integrating devices (such as project teams or planning committees) are frequently used in functionally organized businesses to enhance coordination and to facilitate understanding across functional areas.

Divisional Organizational Structure

When a firm diversifies its product/service lines, covers broad geographic areas, utilizes unrelated market channels, or begins to serve distinctly different customer groups, a functional structure rapidly becomes inadequate. For example, functional managers may wind up overseeing the production or marketing of numerous and different products or services. And coordination demands on top management are beyond the capacity of a functional structure. Some form of divisional structure is necessary to meet the coordination and decision-

Strategy in Action 12–2
From Divisional to Functional Structure at Crown, Cork and Seal

John Connelly became chief executive officer at Crown, Cork and Seal (CCS), a major company in the metal container industry, when CCS had fallen on hard times. In trying to compete on all fronts with much larger competitors like American Can and Continental Can, CCS had become overextended and was on the verge of bankruptcy. It had a product-oriented, divisional structure, similar to that of its larger competitors, which had been adopted to facilitate decentralized competition.

Connelly formulated a desperate retrenchment strategy to turn CCS around. The strategy focused CCS on the production of cans for hard-to-hold products, aerosol cans, and evolving international markets. The emphasis was to sell to large purchasers and provide extensive service in purchasers' canning operations. Thus, Connelly's strategy was to narrow CCS's scope to the most profitable product/market segments, build a service-related competitive advantage, and maintain tight fiscal control to overcome the imminent threat of bankruptcy.

Connelly quickly realized that the existing divisional structure was not consistent with the needs of the new strategy. Corporate-level overhead was both costly and unnecessary given the narrowed scope of CCS operations under the new strategy. To accommodate its narrow product/market scope and the need for tight fiscal control, Connelly reorganized CCS along functional lines, with three vice presidents—manufacturing, sales, and finance—reporting directly to him. This provided the centralized control needed for the retrenchment strategy and cut the managerial labor force by 24 percent. By making plant managers responsible for the profitability of their operations, he accommodated the strategy's need for tight control of geographically dispersed units within an efficient, streamlined functional structure.

CCS's strategy has been quite effective, with the company consistently leading the industry in return on equity, profitability, and return on investment. And the success of this strategy was clearly linked to an appropriate organizational structure and the strong, forceful leadership of John Connelly.

making requirements resulting from increased diversity and size. Such a structure is illustrated in Figure 12–2.

Days Inn's strategy to expand via new geographic markets in the 1970s required it to move from a functional structure to a divisional structure with three geographic divisions. Each division manager had major operating responsibility for company-owned properties in a particular geographic region of the United States. IBM has adopted a divisional organization based on different customer groups. For many years, Ford and General Motors adopted classic divisional structures organized by product groups.

A divisional structure allows corporate management to delegate authority for the strategic management of a distinct business entity. This can expedite critical decision making within each division in response to varied competitive environments, and it forces corporate management to concentrate on corporate-level strategic decisions. The semiautonomous divisions are usually given profit responsibility. The divisional structure thus seeks to facilitate accurate assessment of profit and loss.

Strategic Business Units

Some firms encounter difficulty in controlling their divisional operations as the diversity, size, and number of these units continues to increase. And corporate management may encounter difficulty in evaluating and controlling its numerous, often multi-industry divisions. Under these conditions, it may become necessary to add another layer of management to improve strategy implementation, promote synergy, and gain greater control over the diverse business interests. This can be accomplished by grouping various divisions (or parts of some divisions) in terms of common strategic elements. These groups,

Strategy in Action 12–3
Restructuring Apple Computer for the 1990s

Apple Computer, the pioneer of the personal computer industry, faced major challenges to its market position by the late 1980s from IBM and a host of others. Chairman John Sculley and the Apple management team adopted an aggressive strategy aimed at the business markets and centered on its MacIntosh line of computers.

To implement this strategy, Sculley and key Apple executives spent six weeks redesigning Apple's organizational structure. Below is the final memo from Sculley to all Apple employees and stockholders.

Continued on Page 364

Strategy in Action 12–3 (*continued*)

APPLE COMPUTER INTEROFFICE MEMO

Date: June 14, 1985
To: Board of directors
From: John Sculley
Subject: Company reorganization

The executive staff, key managers, and I have met almost daily over the past several weeks to develop a new organization. As you know, Apple has been a divisionalized company with several highly autonomous profit centers, which have acted almost like stand-alone companies:

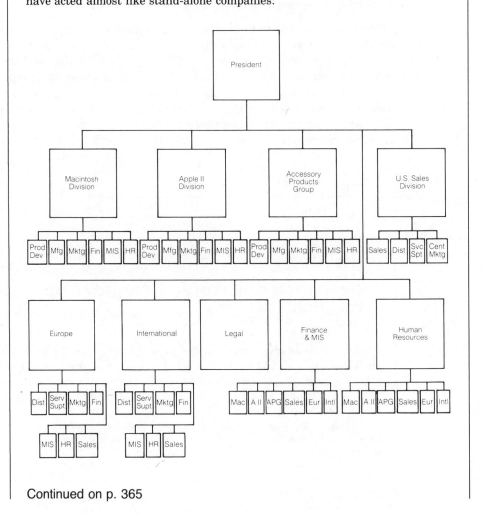

Continued on p. 365

Strategy in Action 12–3 (*concluded*)

I am pleased to announce a new structure, which is vastly simplified and organized around functions:

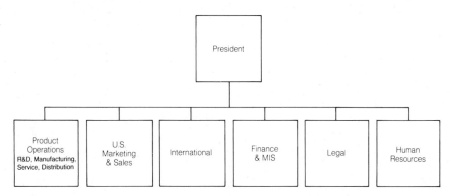

The new organization will reduce our break-even point. It should also simplify internal communication of company objectives and allow for greater consistency in their implementation.

We have selected leaders of each functional area who have had considerable experience in their specialty and in managing people.

In the process of moving to this new organization, we will reduce the number of jobs at Apple by 1,200. This is a painful and difficult decision. However, this streamlining will allow us to eliminate unnecessary job duplication in the divisional structure. (As shown in the organization chart, each division has had its own product development, manufacturing, finance, management information systems, and human resources staffs.)

The new organization should be more effective at providing products the marketplace wants and at providing them in a more timely manner. In addition to the greater effectiveness of the organization, it should also be more efficient— making us more profitable on lower sales than would have been the case with the former organization.

The reorganization will be costly in the short run. We take such a strong step only because it is clear that the new organization and management team will vastly improve Apple's probability for success as an industry leader.

Source: Apple Computer, Annual Report, 1985, p. 5.

commonly called strategic business units (SBUs), are usually structured based on the independent product/market segments served by the firm.

Figure 12–3 illustrates an SBU organizational structure. General Electric, faced with massive sales growth but little profit growth in the 1960s, was a pioneer in the SBU organization. GE restructured over 48 divisions into six

Figure 12–2
Divisional organization structure

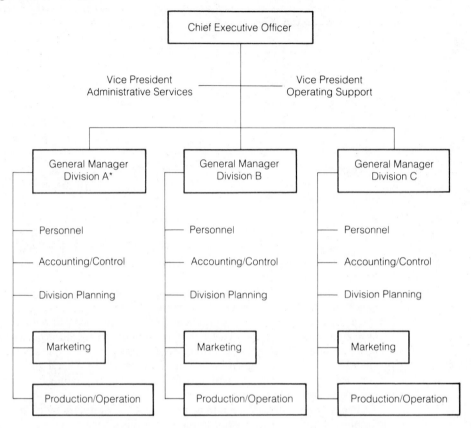

Advantages

1. Forces coordination and necessary authority down to the appropriate level for rapid response.
2. Places strategy development and implementation in closer proximity to the divisions' unique environment.
3. Frees chief executive officer for broader strategic decision making.
4. Sharply focuses accountability for performance.
5. Retains functional specialization within each division.
6. Good training ground for strategic managers.

Disadvantages

1. Fosters potentially dysfunctional competition for corporate-level resources.
2. Problem with the extent of authority given to division managers.
3. Potential for policy inconsistencies between divisions.
4. Problem of arriving at a method to distribute corporate overhead costs that is acceptable to different division managers with profit responsibility.

Figure 12–3
Strategic business unit organizational structure

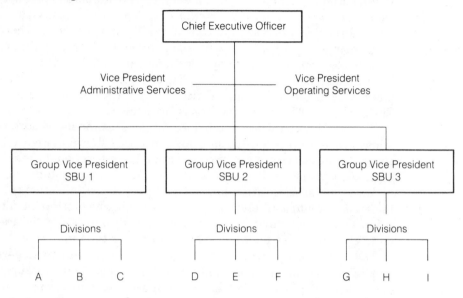

Advantages	Disadvantages
1. Improves coordination between divisions with similar strategic concerns and product/market environments.	1. Places another layer of management between the divisions and corporate management.
2. Tightens the strategic management and control of large, diverse business enterprises.	2. Dysfunctional competition for corporate resources may increase.
3. Facilitates distinct and in-depth business planning at the corporate and business levels.	3. The role of the group vice president can be difficult to define.
4. Channels accountability to distinct business units.	4. Difficulty in defining the degree of autonomy for the group vice presidents and division managers.

(sector) SBUs. For example, three separate divisions making food preparation appliances were merged into a single SBU serving the housewares market.[1] General Foods, after originally defining SBUs along product lines (which served overlapping markets), restructured along menu lines. SBUs for breakfast foods, beverages, main meals, desserts, and pet foods allowed General Foods to target specific markets.[2]

---

[1] William K. Hall, "SBUs: Hot, New Topic in the Management of Diversification," *Business Horizons,* February 1978, p. 19.

[2] Ibid.

Matrix Organization

In large companies, increased diversity leads to numerous product and project efforts, *all with major strategic significance.* The result is a need for an organizational form that provides and controls skills and resources where and when they are most useful. The *matrix organization,* pioneered by firms like defense contractors, construction companies, and large CPA firms, has increasingly been used to meet this need. The list of companies now using some form of matrix organization includes Citicorp, Digital Equipment, General Electric, Shell Oil, Dow Chemical, and Texas Instruments.

The matrix organization provides for dual channels of authority, performance responsibility, evaluation, and control, as shown in Figure 12–4. Essentially, subordinates are assigned to both a basic functional area and a project or product manager. The matrix form is included to combine the advantages of functional specialization and product/project specialization. In theory, the matrix is a conflict resolution system through which strategic and operating priorities are negotiated, power is shared, and resources are allocated internally on a "strongest case for what is best overall for the unit" basis.[3]

The matrix structure increases the number of middle managers exercising general management responsibilities and broadens their exposure to organizationwide strategic concerns. Thus, it can accommodate a varied and changing project, product/market, or technology focus and can increase the efficient use of functional specialists who otherwise might be idle.

Citicorp used the matrix organization to implement an international expansion strategy focusing on both geographically different financial service requirements and at the same time targeting the multinational corporation market segment. The change was designed to increase the priority given to large, international organizations. The strategy ultimately gave Citicorp a better understanding of the worldwide financial needs and activities of multinational corporations than even the chief financial officers of these corporations had. Matrix structure was a strategic tool that allowed Citicorp to gain a competitive advantage with this important segment.[4]

While the matrix structure is easy to design, it is difficult to implement. Dual chains of command challenge fundamental organizational orientations. Negotiating shared responsibilities, use of resources, and priorities can create misunderstanding or confusion among subordinates. Strategy in Action 12–4 illustrates the varied reactions in Shell Oil's move to a matrix structure.

To overcome the deficiencies that might be associated with a permanent matrix structure, some firms are using a "temporary" or "flexible" *overlay structure* to accomplish a particular strategic task. This approach, used recently

---

[3] Arthur A. Thompson, Jr., and A. J. Strickland III, *Strategy Formulation and Implementation* (Plano, Tex.: Business Publications, 1983), p. 335.

[4] Paul J. Stonich, *Implementing Strategy* (Cambridge, Mass.: Ballinger, 1982), p. 60.

Figure 12–4
Matrix organizational structure

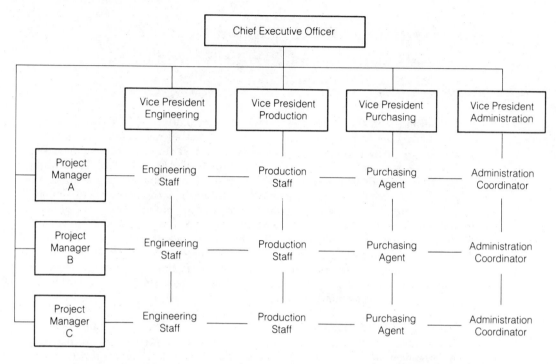

Advantages

1. Accommodates a wide variety of project-oriented business activity.
2. Good training ground for strategic managers.
3. Maximizes efficient use of functional managers.
4. Fosters creativity and multiple sources of diversity.
5. Broader middle-management exposure to strategic issues for the business.

Disadvantages

1. Dual accountability can create confusion and contradictory policies.
2. Necessitates tremendous horizontal and vertical coordination.

by firms like General Motors, IBM, and Texas Instruments, is meant to take *temporary* advantage of a matrix-type team while preserving the shape and spirit of the underlying divisional structure.[5] Thus, the basic idea of the matrix structure, to *simplify and amplify the focus of resources on a narrow but strategically important product, project, or market,* appears to be an important structural alternative within large, diverse organizations.

---

[5] Robert H. Waterman, Jr., T. J. Peters, and J. R. Phillips, "Structure Is Not Organization," *Business Horizons,* June 1980, p. 20.

Strategy in Action 12–4
Shell Oil: Matrix Structure to Implement Strategy

Fifteen miles off the coast of Louisiana, a giant platform called Cognac rattles and shakes under the ceaseless activity. Hard-hatted roughnecks are spudding a new well, sending drilling bits twisting 1,200 feet through the choppy waters to reach rich reservoirs of crude oil beneath the Gulf of Mexico's floor. Meanwhile, 60 other wells drilled from the massive midsea factory shoot crude through a ganglion of pipe to onshore refineries. Everything about the Cognac field is imposing. It represents a capital investment of about $800 million, and every 24 hours it gushes out an awesome return: 16,000 barrels of oil worth $576,000 at current prices. Cognac, a mere blip on the Shell balance sheets, is a microcosmic example of the stupefying risks and rewards of the modern oil business. Shell, which analysts consider one of the best-run companies in the industry, employs a strategy different from that of competitors. Shell's corporate strategy focuses almost exclusively on the development of energy resources and petrochemicals.

Managing by Matrix. To make and implement the far-reaching decisions this strategy requires, Shell management relies on a matrix system to structure its organization. Like most large corporations, Shell has managers who report to general managers who report to vice presidents. But it also has a network of interlevel, interdivisional teams that try to coordinate the activities of everyone from petroleum engineers to public relations specialists. As a result, more employees participate in decision making and understand the reasons for policies before they are dictated. And in theory, at least, the system helps guard against redundant activities. Instead of maintaining separate research projects for exploration and production, oil products, and chemicals, Shell has a single research division that serves the entire company.

The matrix can be exasperating at times. "We meet ourselves to death," complains Ken Spauling, manager of chemical-products plans. But it reinforces Shell's policy of delegating responsibility to "the level of maximum knowledge." J. B. Henderson, the president of Shell Chemical Co., for instance, doesn't decide whether or not to buy a certain cargo of crude oil for his facilities. "I can't make the decision intelligently," he says. "Someone in the buying department can."

The Role of Structure: Linking Structure to Strategy

Which structure is best? Considerable research has been done on this question, and the collective answer is that it depends on the strategy of the firm. The structural design ties together key activities and resources of the firm. Therefore, it must be closely aligned with the needs/demands of the firm's strategy.

Alfred Chandler provided a landmark study in understanding the choice of structure as a function of strategy.[6] Chandler studied 70 large corporations over an extended time period and found a common strategy–structure sequence:

1. Choice of a new strategy.
2. Emergence of administrative problems; decline in performance.
3. A shift to an organizational structure more in line with the strategy's needs.
4. Improved profitability and strategy execution.

General Electric's recent history supports Chandler's thesis. Operating with a simple divisional structure in the late 1950s, GE embarked on a broad diversification strategy. In the 1960s, GE experienced impressive sales growth. However, GE also experienced administrative difficulties in trying to control and improve the corresponding lack of increase in profitability. In the early 1970s, GE executives redesigned its organizational structure to accommodate the administrative needs of strategy (ultimately choosing the strategic business unit structure), subsequently improving profitability of and control over the diversification strategy.

Chandler's research and the GE example allow us to make four important observations. First, all forms of organizational structure are not equally effective in implementing a strategy. Second, structures seem to have a life of their own, particularly in larger organizations. As a result, the need for immediate and radical changes in structure is not immediately perceived. Once the need is perceived, lagging performance may be necessary before politically sensitive structure is changed or organizational power redistributed. Third, sheer growth can make restructuring necessary. Finally, as firms diversify into numerous related or unrelated products and markets, structural change appears to be essential if the firm is to perform effectively.

Research on corporate stages of development provides further understanding of the structure–strategy relationship.[7] After studying numerous business firms, these researchers concluded that companies move through several stages

---

[6] Alfred D. Chandler, *Strategy and Structure* (Cambridge, Mass.: MIT Press, 1962).

[7] Several authors have dealt with stages of development. Some of the more frequently cited include J. T. Cannon, *Business Strategy and Policy* (New York: Harcourt Brace Jovanovich, 1968), pp. 525–28; Malcomb Salter, "Stages of Corporate Development," *Journal of Business Policy* 1, no. 1 (1970), pp. 23–37; Bruce Scott, "Stages of Corporate Development—Parts I and II," mimeographed (Boston: Harvard Business School, 1970); and Donald H. Thain, "Stages of Corporate Development," *Business Quarterly*, Winter 1969, pp. 33–45.

Figure 12–5
Corporate stages of development

Stage	Characteristics of the firm	Typical structure
I	Simple, small business. Offering one product/service or one line of products/services to a small, distinct local or regionalized market.	Simple to functional
II	Singular or closely related line of products/services but to a larger and sometimes more diverse market (geography, channels, or customers).	Functional to divisional
III	Expanded but related lines of products/services to diverse, large markets.	Divisional to matrix
IV	Diverse, unrelated lines of products/services to large, diverse markets.	Divisional to SBUs

as size and diversity increase. Figure 12–5 is a synthesis of these stage-of-development theories. The figure shows that a firm moves through each stage, size, diversity, and competitive environment change.

To compete effectively at different stages requires, among other things, different structures. Again, the choice of structure appears contingent on the strategy of the firm in terms of size, diversity of the products/services offered, and markets served. Two firms in the metal container industry help illustrate this point. Continental Can, the industry leader, employs a divisional structure. This is used to implement a diversification strategy intended to serve virtually every user of metal containers, as well as to compete in unrelated markets like forest products. Crown, Cork and Seal, the industry's fourth largest company, employs a modified functional structure to serve a limited domestic and international market of users with specialized container needs. Both firms are successful. Both derive their greatest revenues from the same industry. But each employs a different organizational structure because their strategies (narrow versus broad product/market scope) are different.

The choice of structure must be determined by the firm's strategy. And the structure must segment key activities and/or strategic operating units to improve efficiency through specialization, response to a competitive environment, and freedom to act. At the same time, the structure must effectively integrate and coordinate these activities and units to accommodate interdependence of activities and overall control. The choice of structure reflects strategy in terms of the firm's (1) size, (2) product/service diversity, (3) competitive environment and volatility, (4) internal political considerations, and (5) information/coordination needs for each component.

Even a change in strategy, with its accompanying alteration of administrative needs, does not lead to an immediate change in structure. The research of Chandler and others suggests that commitment to a structure lingers even when it's become inappropriate for a current strategy.[8] Whether this is due

---

[8] Chandler, *Strategy and Structure;* and J. R. Galbraith and D. A. Nathanson, *Strategy Implementation: The Role of Structure and Process* (St. Paul, Minn.: West Publishing, 1978).

Strategy in Action 12–5
Leadership Practices at Intel Corporation

Andrew Grove, founder and president of Intel Corporation, has made a conscious effort to foster informality in the management and decision-making practices of the highly successful microelectronics company he started in 1968. Visible examples of informality are many: no reserved parking, no executive dining rooms, no corporate jets (*everyone* flies coach), and rather than offices every manager from the chairman of the board and president on down operates out of a maze of cubicles separated by 5-foot-high sound-proofed partitions. A journalist, puzzled by this, once asked Andrew Grove if his company's emphasis on visible signs of egalitarianism was just so much affectation. Grove replied that it was not affectation but a matter of survival and offered the following explanation:

> In traditional industries where the chain of command is precisely defined, a person making a certain kind of decision is a person occupying a particular position on an organization chart. As the saying goes, authority (to make decisions) goes with responsibility (position in the management hierarchy). In businesses that deal mostly with information and know-how, however, a manager has to cope with a new phenomenon. Here a rapid divergence develops between power based on position and power based on knowledge. The divergence occurs because the base of knowledge that constitutes the foundation of the business changes rapidly.
>
> What do I mean? When someone graduates from college with a technical education, at that time and for the next several years that person will be very up-to-date in the technology of the time. Hence, he possesses a good deal of knowledge-based power in the organization that hires him. If he does well, he will be promoted, and as the years pass his position power will grow. At the same time, his intimate familiarity with current technology will fade. Put another way, even if today's veteran manager was once an outstanding engineer, he is not now the technical expert he once was. At high-technology firms, we managers get a little more obsolete every day.
>
> So a business like ours has to employ a management process unlike that used in more conventional industries. If we had people at the top making all the decisions, then these decisions would be made by those unfamiliar with the technology of the day. In general, the faster the change in the know-how on which a business depends, the greater the divergence between knowledge and position power is likely to be.
>
> Since our business depends on what it knows to survive, we mix "knowledge-power people" with "position-power people" daily, so that together they make the decisions that will affect us for years to come. We

Continued on Page 374

Strategy in Action 12–5 (*concluded*)

at Intel frequently ask junior members of the organization to participate jointly in a decision-making meeting with senior managers. This only works if everybody at the meeting voices opinions and beliefs as equals, forgetting or ignoring status differentials. And it is much easier to achieve this if the organization doesn't separate its senior and junior people with limousines, plush offices, and private dining rooms. Status symbols do not promote the flow of ideas, facts, and points of view. So while our egalitarian environment may appear to be a matter of style, it is really a matter of necessity, a matter of long-term survival.

This idea of mixing knowledge-based and position-based power underlines the quality circle movement and the participative management concept. The real benefit of the quality circle movement, the participative management concept, and our informality at work is not cosmetic, nor is it really to make people feel better (although that is not a bad consequence, either). It is to team up people with hands-on knowledge with those in positions of power to create the best solutions in the interest of both.

Source: "Breaking the Chains of Command," *Newsweek,* October 3, 1983, p. 23. Condensed from *Newsweek.* Copyright 1983, by Newsweek, Inc. All rights reserved. Reprinted by permission.

to inertia, organizational politics, or a realistic assessment of the relative costs of immediate structural change, historical evidence suggests that the existing structure will be maintained and not radically redesigned until a strategy's profitability is increasingly disproportionate with increasing sales.[9]

Organizational Leadership

While organizational structure provides the overall framework for strategy implementation, it is not in itself sufficient to ensure successful execution. Within the organizational structure, individuals, groups, and units are the mechanisms of organizational action. And the effectiveness of their actions is a major determinant of successful implementation. In this context, two basic factors encourage or discourage effective action—leadership and culture.[10] This section examines the leadership dimension as a key element in strategy implementation. In the next section, the importance of organizational culture in effectively executing strategy will be illustrated and discussed.

---

[9] C. W. Hofer, E. A. Murray, Jr., R. Charan, and R. A. Pitts, *Strategic Management* (St. Paul, Minn.: West Publishing, 1984), p. 20.

[10] Leadership and organizational culture are interdependent phenomena. Each aspect of leadership ultimately helps shape organizational culture. Conversely, the prevailing organizational culture can profoundly influence a leader's effectiveness. The richness of this interdependence will become apparent. The topics are addressed in separate sections because it is important to develop an appreciation of the role of each in strategy implementation. Strategy in Action 12–5 gives a vivid illustration of the interdependence of leadership, cultural, and structural considerations in strategy implementation.

Leadership, while seemingly vague and esoteric, is an essential element in effective strategy implementation. And two leadership issues are of fundamental importance here: (1) the role of the chief executive officer (CEO) and (2) the assignment of key managers.

Role of the CEO

The chief executive officer is the catalyst in strategic management. This individual is most closely identified with and ultimately accountable for a strategy's success. In most firms, particularly larger ones, CEOs spend up to 80 percent of their time developing and guiding strategy.

The nature of the CEO's role is both *symbolic* and *substantive* in strategy implementation. First, the CEO is a symbol of the new strategy. This individual's actions and the perceived seriousness of his or her commitment to a chosen strategy, particularly if the strategy represents a major change, exert a significant influence on the intensity of subordinate managers' commitment to implementation. Lee Iaccoca's highly visible role in the early 1980s as spokesperson for the "New Chrysler Corporation" on television, in Chrysler factories and offices, and before securities analysts was intended to provide a strong symbol that Chrysler's desperate turnaround strategy could work.

Second, the firm's mission, strategy, and key long-term objectives are strongly influenced by the personal goals and values of its CEO. To the extent that the CEO invests time and personal values in the chosen strategy, he or she represents an important source for clarification, guidance, and adjustment during implementation.

Major changes in strategy are often preceded or quickly followed by a change in CEO. The timing suggests that different strategies require different CEOs if they are to succeed. The resignation of L. M. Clymer as CEO at Holiday Inns clearly illustrates this point. Holiday Inns' executive group was convinced that casinos provide a key growth area for the company. Clymer chose to resign because his personal values and perception of what Holiday Inns should be were not consistent with this change. Research has concluded that a successful turnaround strategy "will require almost without exception either a change in top management or a substantial change in the behavior of the existing management team."[11] Clearly, successful strategy implementation is directly linked to the unique characteristics, orientation, and actions of the CEO.

Assignment of Key Managers

A major concern of top management in implementing a strategy, particularly if it involves a major change, is that the right managers are in the right

---

[11] Charles W. Hofer, "Turnaround Strategies," *Journal of Business Strategy* 1, no. 1 (1980), p. 25.

positions for the new strategy. Of all the tools for ensuring successful implementation, this is the one CEOs mention first. Confidence in the individuals occupying pivotal managerial positions is directly and positively correlated with top-management expectations that a strategy can be successfully executed.

This confidence is based on the answers to two fundamental questions:

1. Who holds the current leadership positions that are especially critical to strategy execution?
2. Do they have the right characteristics to ensure that the strategy will be effectively implemented?[12]

What characteristics are most important in this context? It would be impossible to specify this precisely, but probable characteristics include: (1) ability and education, (2) previous track record and experience, and (3) personality and temperament.[13] These, combined with gut feeling and top managers' confidence in the individual, provide the basis for this key decision.

Recently, numerous attempts have been made to match "preferred" managerial characteristics with different grand strategies.[14] These efforts are meant to capsulize, for example, the behavioral characteristics appropriate for a manager responsible for implementing an "invest to grow" strategy in contrast to those for a manager implementing a "harvest" strategy. Despite widespread theoretical discussion of this idea, two recent studies covering a broad sample of companies did not find a single firm that matched managerial characteristics to strategic mission in a formal manner. However, they did find several firms addressing such considerations in an informal, intuitive manner.[15] The following comment summarizes these findings:

> Despite the near unanimity of belief that, for effective implementation, different strategies require different skills . . . many corporate executives avoid too rigid an approach to matching managerial characteristics and strategy [for three reasons]: (1) exposure to and experience at managing different kinds of strategies and businesses is viewed as an essential component of managerial development; (2) too rigid a differentiation is viewed as much more likely to result in some managers being typecast as "good builders" and some others as "good harvesters," thereby creating motivational problems for the latter; and (3) a "perfect match" between managerial characteristics and strategy is viewed as more likely to

---

[12] William F. Glueck, *Business Policy and Strategic Management* (New York: McGraw-Hill, 1980), pp. 306–7.

[13] Ibid., p. 307.

[14] See, for example, J. G. Wisseman, H. W. Van der Pol, and H. M. Messer, "Strategic Management Archetypes," *Strategic Management Journal* 1, no. 1 (1980), pp. 37–45; William F. Glueck and Lawrence R. Jauch, *Strategic Management and Business Policy* (New York: McGraw-Hill, 1984), p. 365; Boris Yavitz and William H. Newman, *Strategy in Action* (New York: Free Press, 1982), p. 167; and "Wanted, a Manager to Fit Each Strategy," *Business Week*, February 25, 1980, p. 166.

[15] Anil K. Gupta and V. Govindarajan, "Build, Hold, Harvest: Converting Strategic Intentions into Reality," *Journal of Business Strategy*, Winter 1984, p. 41; Peter Lorange, "The Human Resource Dimension in the Strategic Planning Process," mimeographed (Cambridge, Mass.: Sloan School, MIT, 1983), p. 13.

result in overcommitment [or] self-fulfilling prophecies (a harvester becoming *only* a harvester) as compared with a situation where there was some mismatch.[16]

One practical consideration in making key managerial assignments when implementing strategy is whether to emphasize current (or promotable) executives or bring in new personnel. This is obviously a difficult, sensitive, and strategic issue. Figure 12–6 highlights major advantages and disadvantages associated with either alternative.

While key advantages and disadvantages can be clearly outlined, actual assignment varies with the situation and the decision maker. Two fundamental aspects of the strategic situation strongly influence the managerial assignment decision: (1) the changes required to implement the new strategy and (2) the effectiveness of past organizational performance. Figure 12–7 and the following discussion illustrate how these aspects might affect managerial assignments.

Turnover Situation.   A company's performance has been ineffective for several years. The new strategy and the organizational requirements necessary to implement it represent major changes from the "way things have been done in the past." In this situation, the advantages of bringing in outside managers can be maximized. Because the experience necessary to implement the new strategy is unavailable or ineffective internally, outsiders are sought. Current executives may react defensively when faced with major changes, while outsiders generally undertake a new assignment with a positive commitment to the new direction and are not encumbered by internal commitments to people. Widespread changes will also be taken more seriously by employees if outsiders are brought in who possess skills that match the changes and supplement well-known inadequacies in current management.

Chrysler Corporation's situation in the early 1980s is a case in point. Following several years of ineffective, declining performance, Chrysler's board went outside the organization to recruit a new CEO (Lee Iaccoca) who was capable of redirecting Chrysler into a small-car-oriented strategy. Iacocca eventually brought in outsiders to fill over 80 percent of Chrysler's top-management positions because they had the new skills and commitment necessary to quickly and decisively implement Chrysler's new strategy.

Selective Blend.   A different emphasis in key managerial assignments is needed when a company's new strategy requires major changes but the need for change is not based on poor performance. The company has been an effective performer with its previous strategy, yet changing market, competitive, technological, or other environmental factors necessitate a change in the company's strategic posture. IBM's move into the personal computer industry is a good illustration.

---

[16] Gupta and Govindarajan, "Build, Hold, Harvest," p. 41.

Figure 12–6
Key considerations in managerial assignments to implement strategy

	Advantages	Disadvantages
Using existing executives to implement a new strategy	Already know key people, practices, and conditions	Less adaptable to major strategic changes because of knowledge, attitudes, and values
	Personal qualities better known and understood by associates	Past commitments may hamper hard decisions required in executing a new strategy
	Have established relationships with peers, subordinates, suppliers, buyers, etc.	Less ability to become inspired and credibly convey the need for change
	Symbolizes organizational commitment to individual careers	
Bringing in outsiders to implement a new strategy	Outsider may already believe in and have "lived" the new strategy.	Often costly, both in terms of compensation and "learning-to-work-together" time
	Outsider is unemcumbered by internal commitments to people.	Candidates suitable in all respects (i.e., exact experience) may not be available, leading to compromise choices
	Outsider comes to the new assignment with heightened commitment and enthusiasm.	Uncertainty in selecting the right person
	Bringing in an outsider can send powerful signals throughout the organization that change is expected.	The "morale" costs when an outsider takes a job several insiders wanted
		"What to do with poor ol' Fred" problem

Source: Adapted from Boris Yavitz and William H. Newman, *Strategy in Action* (New York: Free Press, 1982), chap. 10; and Paul J. Stonich, *Implementing Strategy* (Cambridge, Mass.: Ballinger, 1982), chap. 4.

The advantages and disadvantages associated with either source of managerial talent are applicable in this situation. Using existing executives rewards past effectiveness and takes advantage of the knowledge of "people practices" and relationships necessary to integrate changes into a previously successful system. It also reinforces the company's commitment to individual careers

Figure 12–7
Four managerial assignment situations

	Selective blend	Turnover
Many	Current executives via promotion and transfer where skills match new roles; otherwise, seek skills and experience via outsiders	Outsiders should be a high priority to provide new skills, motivation, and enthusiasm.
	Stability	**Reorientation**
Few	Current executives and internal promotions should be a major emphasis in order to reward, retain, and develop managerial talent.	Outsiders are important to replace weaknesses and "communication seriousness." Current executives should be a priority where possible via promotion, transfer, or role clarification.
	Effective	Ineffective

Changes required to implement the new strategy

Assessment of past organizational performance

and facilitates executive development. On the other hand, the outsider brings all the advantages described in Figure 12–6, especially skill and experience in one or more of the key change areas. But there is a critical difference—the past performance of this company. Thus, the advantage of the outsider as a "change agent" is much less important than his or her value as a provider of the key skills needed to *supplement* current management talent. Emphasis in this situation is a selective blend using current or promotable executives while objectively incorporating outsiders to provide needed knowledge and skill that is not available internally. Strategy in Action 12–6 illustrates the planned change of managers at successful McGraw-Hill to successfully institutionalize a very different strategic direction.

IBM's move into personal computers required major changes in the firm's past, highly successful market development strategy. IBM needed to sell and service a small computer primarily for numerous individual and small-business users. This was quite different than what was needed to lease or sell expensive computer systems and office equipment to large public and private organizations. IBM used existing talent to implement this small-computer strategy. Use of outsiders was primarily related to the development of direct retail outlets, a sales approach not used with past IBM products but critical to ensure IBM's long-term, profitable access to a broad, fragmented, and individualized market. So, IBM sought to selectively blend its "inside/outside" emphasis

Strategy in Action 12–6
Changing Management and Approach at McGraw-Hill

It seems like McGraw-Hill set out to prove that even in healthy organizations, change is often necessary. Even though the company had grown by a compounded rate of 17 percent, CEO Joseph Dionne set out to reorganize and refocus the company for the 1990s with the help of Harvard Business School professor Micheal Porter.

A central concern was to shift the assessment of management from quarterly results to a long-term vision. Dionne felt that with the company's old organization and style, the company was stifling the development of new products and that it would soon slow the company's growth. So, Dionne and Porter conceived of McGraw-Hill as a confederation of 19 market focus groups instead of a company organized around separate book, magazine, and statistical services divisions.

Each of the 19 market groups follows a specific industry like construction, transportation, and health care. Instead of gathering information for a single publication, the data goes into a giant database, which in turn can be drawn on by all to produce new products like specialty print publications or on-line services for personal computers.

While the virtual reconfiguration of McGraw-Hill's organization and the way it does business is exciting, it has thrown the company into turmoil. A host of managers have left the company, particularly managers from the publications divisions bitter at what they believe is mismanagement of the publications sector in order to make room for the payoff of electronics. Also hit with desertions is the econometrics forecasting group, Data Resources, which the company bought in 1979. Twenty percent of DR's executives have left since the reorganization was announced.

While the turnover and turmoil is difficult, top management at McGraw-Hill feels that most of these executives had grown with one media and that they were neither prepared nor receptive to the new technologies in information. They perceive the act of precipitating this turmoil as a proactive, astute decision that lets the company shape its destiny rather than waiting for the sales and earning declines that would have caused the same result—but with McGraw-Hill on the reacting, catch-up end of the equation.

The 19 market focus groups will have independence to chart their own course and make their own deals. The company is expecting revenues to exceed $1.5 billion in 1990 and reach $2.5 billion by 1995. Many remaining executives are unsure how much electronics can do for McGraw-Hill's big profit centers—magazines and books. Only time will tell whether these radical changes in the status quo will be effective.

Source: Adapted from "Marketing Is the Message at McGraw-Hill," *Fortune*, February 17, 1986, p. 27.

in new managerial assignments consistent with the key advantages of each approach.

Stability.   A stability situation is generally attractive in managing executive assignments. The company's past performance has been effective, and implementation requires only minor deviation from "the ways things were done in the past." The advantages associated with using current and promotable existing executives are maximized. These executives are familiar with people, practices, and the ways to get things done. They have established relationships with suppliers, buyers, peers, and subordinates. Past performance indicates that the managers have achieved assigned results. This is recognized through assignment to new responsibilities associated with the new strategy. In this situation, junior-level managers can be developed because an effective performance environment exists within which they will observe and acquire managerial and technical skills. The risk in this situation is that there are fewer opportunities to advance talented personnel who contributed to past effectiveness because change was minor and retaining the current executive teams was emphasized.

Wendy's hamburger chain was a firm facing this situation in the early 1980s. The firm had quite effectively carved a profitable niche in the fast-food industry. Its new strategy for the 1980s sought to emphasize three things: market penetration, product development, and diversification via Sister's Chicken 'n Biscuits. While this was an aggressive new strategy, the changes required were relatively minor: market penetration necessitated a slight shift in Wendy's franchising approach; product development efforts were well underway; and the Sister's chicken implementation plan would be modeled exactly after the Wendy's approach in the hamburger segment. Wendy's assignment of managerial positions emphasized the use of current management. The Sister's venture was seen as an ideal way to open up career opportunities for talented operating personnel. By 1984, 30 of the 37 members of Wendy's executive committee (its "top-management team") were new, but only 2 of the 30 new members came from outside the Wendy's organization.

Reorientation.   Some companies face a situation in which the fundamental changes required to implement a new strategy are minor—the basic strategy appears appropriate—yet past performance has been ineffective. With IBM at the top of the personal computer market in early 1984, the former leader, Apple, was in just such a situation. Its new strategy was an attempt to refocus on its formerly successful product development strategy by making key (yet relative few) organizational changes. For example, Steven Jobs (Apple's co-founder) sought to reinvigorate R&D efforts by personal involvement. Key managerial assignments in marketing and finance were filled from outside the company to systematically reorient Apple's competitive posture against IBM. Apple added a new CEO from outside the organization to oversee this effort. At the same time, Apple sought to transfer and clarify the roles of several current managers, particularly younger managers with product development skills, to aid in reinvigorating Apple's technological reputation.

Apple is an example of a company with a sound strategy but ineffective implementation. A key issue in this context is whether the ineffectiveness can be linked to inadequate skills or capabilities of the management team. If such inadequacies are found, outsiders could play a key role in reorienting or refocusing organizational efforts toward an otherwise sound strategy.

Organizational Culture[17]

Organizational culture is the set of important assumptions (often unstated) that members of an organization share in common. Every organization has its own culture. Organizational culture is similar to an individual's personality—an intangible yet ever-present theme that provides meaning, direction, and the basis for action. Much as personality influences the behavior of an individual, shared assumptions (beliefs and values) among members of an organization set a pattern for activities, opinions, and actions within that firm. The purpose of the next several sections is to help you first gain an understanding of the concept of culture, then ways to identify a company's culture, and finally an analytical framework for managing the strategy–culture relationship.

Important Assumptions.   We have just defined culture as that set of important assumptions that organization members share. The *important* assumptions are sufficiently central to the life of the organization so as to have a major impact on it. Members of an organization hold two principal types of assumptions in common: beliefs and values.

Beliefs include basic assumptions about the world and how it actually works. They derive from personal experience and are reinforced by it. Individuals also rely to some degree on the judgment and expertise of others they trust or can identify with to help them decide what to believe or not to believe. Examples of beliefs include "Money is the most powerful motivator" or "Most people follow the leader."

Values are basic assumptions about which ideals are desirable or worth striving for. They derive from personal experience and identification with those who have had an important influence on one's personal development since early childhood. Values represent preferences for ultimate end-states, such as striving for success or avoiding debt at all costs.

It is important to note that these definitions do not refer to what people *say* are their beliefs and values but rather to the beliefs and values they *actually hold, whether consciously or otherwise.* To illustrate, an important

---

[17] This section draws heavily on the outstanding work by Vijay Sathe of the Harvard Business School. The primary reference in compiling this work is Vijay Sathe, *Culture and Related Corporate Realities* (Homewood, Ill.: Richard D. Irwin, 1985).

professional assumption for a lawyer is client confidentiality. This value is taken for granted, and a lawyer may become conscious of it only if it is challenged or violated. For example, a client might question the lawyer about it, or a fellow lawyer might violate it, either of which would draw attention to this important value. Even after drawing attention to it, this value remains present and potent. It is usually hard to change, as are other beliefs and values that the individual actually holds, consciously (openly) or otherwise.

With this clarification of culture as assumptions involving personal beliefs and values, the meaning of *shared* in the definition of culture can be made more explicit.

Shared Assumptions: Internalized Beliefs and Values that Organizational Members Hold in Common. A member of an organization can simply be aware of the organization's beliefs and values without sharing them in a personally significant way. Values and beliefs have more personal meaning if an individual complies with the set of values as a guide to appropriate behavior in the organization. The individual becomes fundamentally committed to the organization's beliefs and values when he or she internalizes them, that is, when the person comes to hold them as personal beliefs and values. In this case, the corresponding behavior is *intrinsically rewarding* for the individual—the person derives personal satisfaction from what he or she does in the organization because it is congruent with corresponding personal beliefs and values. *The assumptions become shared assumptions through the process of internalization by individual members of an organization.* And these shared, internalized beliefs and values shape the content and strength of an organization's culture.

Content of Culture. The content of an organization's culture ultimately derives from three sources. First, the influence of the business environment in general, and the industry in particular, is an important determinant of shared assumptions. For example, companies in industries characterized by rapid technological change, such as computers and electronics companies, normally have cultures that strongly value innovation. Second, founders, leaders, and organizational employees bring a pattern of assumptions with them when they join the organization. These assumptions often depend on these individuals' own experiences in the culture of the national, regional, ethnic, religious, occupational, and professional communities from which they came. Third, the actual experience people in the organization have had in working out solutions for coping with the basic problems the organization encounters molds shared assumptions. For example, two companies may each value cooperation and internal competition, but one company may emphasize cooperation more in decision making and resource allocation, while internal competition may predominate in the other. J. C. Penney is a good example of the former, while PepsiCo is a good example of the latter. The cultures of these two companies consequently have quite different content, even though some of their basic assumptions about cooperation and internal competition are the same.

Taken together, these three principle sources suggest that the content of culture derives from a combination of prior assumptions and new learning experiences. Several important implications follow from this understanding of culture's content. First, culture is subject to development and change due to the learning going on in the organization as it copes with its problems of external adaptation and internal integration. Second, because existing basic assumptions do not change readily, changing culture is normally incremental and evolutionary rather than radical and revolutionary. In other words, culture is fairly resistant to major change, especially in the short run. Third, because its roots are in the cultures of the wider communities from which the people in the organization come, the content of an organization's culture is apt to be a variation on the beliefs and values associated with these "associated" cultures.

Not all cultures produce equally powerful effects. Some cultures are stronger than others.

Strength of Culture.   The strength of a culture influences the intensity by which organizational members comply with it as they go about their day-to-day activities. The three specific features of culture that determine its strength are *thickness, extent of sharing,* and *clarity of ordering.*

The number of important shared assumptions varies from one organization to another. *Thick* cultures have many; *thin* cultures have few. Cultures with many layers of important shared beliefs and values generally have a stronger influence on behavior. IBM, for example, has a thick culture made up of numerous shared beliefs and values, including respect for the individual, encouragement of constructive rebellion, and doing what is right. Thinner cultures have fewer shared assumptions and thus have a weaker influence on organizational life.

Second, some important assumptions are more widely shared than others. Few are completely shared in the sense that every member of the organization has internalized them. Cultures with more widely shared beliefs and values have a more pervasive impact because more people are guided by them. At IBM, most of the cultural assumptions are very widely shared.

Finally, in some organizational cultures the shared beliefs and values are clearly ordered. Their relative importance and their relation to each other are fairly unambiguous. In less ordered cultures, relative priorities and interrelationships are not so clear. Cultures whose shared assumptions are clearly ordered have a more pronounced effect on behavior because members of the organization are sure of which values should prevail in cases of conflicting interests.

Whereas its content determines in *what direction* a culture will influence organizational behavior, the *intensity* of its effect on behavior depends on a culture's strength. The stronger cultures are thicker, more widely shared, and more clearly ordered; consequently, they have a more profound influence on organizational behavior. Strong cultures are also more resistant to change, which can represent a major asset or liability depending on the culture's compatibility with the needs of the organization's chosen strategy. We will examine this issue in greater detail after first describing how to "decipher" or read a culture.

Deciphering a Culture.   Reading a culture is an interpretive, subjective activity. One cannot decipher a culture simply by relying on what people say about it. Other evidence, both historical and current, must be taken into account to infer what the culture is. There are no exact answers, and two observers may come up with somewhat different descriptions of the same culture. The validity of deciphering a culture must be judged by the utility of the insights the diagnosis provides.

The framework presented in Figure 12–8 provides a systematic method to help decipher or infer an organization's culture. Each important shared assumption creating an organization's culture may be inferred from one or more shared things, shared sayings, shared doings, and shared feelings. People examining a culture may come up with a somewhat different list of "shared" things, doings, sayings, and feelings. The important point is to distill from these various cultural manifestations a much more concise set of important shared beliefs and values.

Figure 12–9 provides a useful illustration of this approach to deciphering or reading the culture at Cummins Engine Company. Sixteen "manifestations" of culture are distilled into five important, shared assumptions that help Cummins managers understand and read their culture. The most subjective and tricky part in the process of deciphering a culture is in distilling the content of culture from its many manifestations. To do it well, those attempting to read a culture must empathize with the people in question and try to understand them in their own terms, rather than in the observer's terms.

How Culture Influences Organizational Life

Culture is a strength that can also be a weakness. It is a strength because culture eases and economizes communications, facilitates organizational decision making and control, and may generate higher levels of cooperation and commitment in the organization. The result is efficiency in that these activities are accomplished with a lower expenditure of resources (such as time and money) than would otherwise be possible. The stronger the culture, the greater its efficiency.

Culture becomes a weakness when important shared beliefs and values interfere with the needs of the business, its strategy, and the people working on the company's behalf. To the extent that the content of a company's culture

Figure 12–8
Framework for deciphering culture

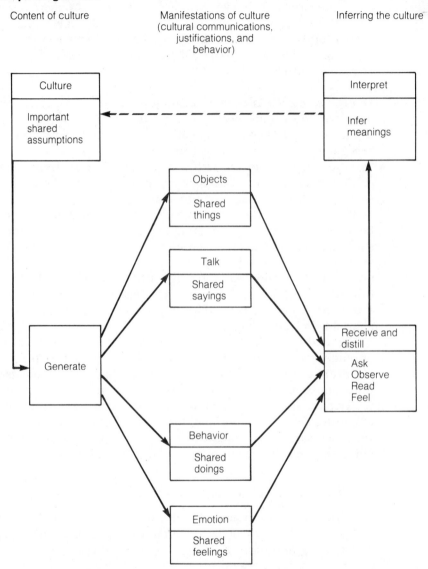

Content of culture   Manifestations of culture   Inferring the culture
(cultural communications,
justifications, and
behavior)

Culture

Important
shared
assumptions

Interpret

Infer
meanings

Objects

Shared
things

Talk

Shared
sayings

Generate

Behavior

Shared
doings

Emotion

Shared
feelings

Receive and
distill

Ask
Observe
Read
Feel

Source: Vijay Sathe, *Culture and Related Corporate Realities* (Homewood, Ill.: Richard D. Irwin, 1985), p. 17.

Figure 12–9
Inferring important shared assumptions from shared things, shared sayings, shared doings, and shared feelings for managers at Cummins Engine Company

Manifestations of the culture at Cummins	*Inferred culture at Cummins*

Shared things
  ST1. Shirt sleeves.
  ST2. One-company town.
  ST3. Open offices.
  ST4. No parking privileges.
Shared sayings
  SS1. Belief in travel, "get out there" to understand the customer.
  SS2. "Systems won't work" to meet customer needs.
  SS3. "Top management will tell us" what to do.
Shared doings
  SD1. Lots of meetings.
  SD2. Close direction from the top.
  SD3. Personal relationships and communications.
  SD4. Rallying to a crisis to meet the needs of the customer.
  SD5. Expediting behavior to achieve highly responsive service.
  SD6. Close relationships with union.
Shared feelings
  SF1. The company is good to me.
  SF2. We don't need to worry about what to do in a crisis.
  SF3. We take pride in shipping faster to the customer than our competition does.

Important shared assumptions
  1. Provide highly responsive, high-quality customer service (SS1, SS2, SD4, SD5, SF3).
  2. Get things done well and quickly ("expediting") (SD1, SD4, SD5, SF3).
  3. Operate informally without systems (ST1, ST3, SS2, SD3, SD6).
  4. Top management will tell us what to do if there is a problem (SS3, SD2, SF2).
  5. See the company as part of the family (ST2, ST4, SD6, SF1).

Source: Adapted from Vijay Sathe, *Culture and Related Corporate Realities* (Homewood, Ill.: Richard D. Irwin, 1985), p. 18.

leads its people to think and act in inappropriate ways, culture's efficiency will not help achieve effective results. This condition is usually a significant weakness because it is hard to change a culture's content.

To take a closer look at how culture influences organizational life, we need to examine five basic processes that lie at the heart of any organization— cooperation, decision making, control, communication, and commitment.

Cooperation.   True cooperation cannot ultimately be legislated. Management can resort to carefully worded employment contracts, spell out detailed expectations, and devise clever incentive schemes to reward just the right behavior. However, even well-thought-out formal procedures can never anticipate all contingencies. When something unforeseen occurs, the organization is at the mercy of the employee's willingness to act in the spirit of cooperation, which involves intent, goodwill, and mutual trust. The degree of true cooperation is influenced by the shared assumptions in this area. The example in Figure 12–9 suggests that shared beliefs and values of informality and family spirit generated high levels of true cooperation at Cummins Engine Company.

Decision Making.   Culture affects the decision-making process because shared beliefs and values give organizational members a consistent set of basic assumptions and preferences. This leads to a more efficient decision-making process because fewer disagreements arise over which premises should prevail.

As pointed out earlier, however, efficiency does not imply effectiveness. If the shared beliefs and values are not in keeping with the needs of the business, its strategy, and its members, dysfunctional consequences will result. In Figure 12–9's Cummins example, the reliance on the people at the top in crisis situations ("Top management will tell us what to do if there is a problem") was efficient but no longer effective in the complex, multiplant environment that Cummins' top management faced. This assumption had to be changed, and Cummins' CEO eventually succeeded in changing it.

Control.   The essence of control is the ability to take action to achieve planned results. The basis for action is provided by two different control mechanisms: formal procedures and clans.

Formal procedures rely on adjusting rules, procedures, guidelines, budgets, and directives. The *clan mechanism* relies on shared beliefs and values. In effect, shared beliefs and values constitute an organizational "compass" that members rely on to choose appropriate courses of action. Clan control derives from culture.

A strong culture facilitates the control process by enhancing clan control. Clan control is highly efficient; but again, efficiency and effectiveness should not be confused. Apple Computer, for instance, heavily used clan control in the 1970s. People responded to the rapid growth of the 1970s and the unexpected downturn in the early 1980s with "automatic pilot" responses. There was no reliance on special incentives to motivate and very little use of new systems, procedures, or directives. However, the clan method of control had become inefficient because of growth and expansion. Apple's CEO John Sculley attempted to change the Apple culture to place more value on using systems to do the routine work without giving up Apple's valued "go for growth" beliefs.

Communication.   The major reasons people miscommunicate daily in organizational and everyday life include the technical problem of distortion between the point where a communication starts out and the point where it is received. A good example is the familiar parlor game in which a sentence that one person speaks at the start of a human chain comes out distorted at the other end. A second and more important hurdle in communication concerns difficulties in interpretation. Even two-person, face-to-face communication, where the technical problem is minimal, is fraught with the danger of each person misunderstanding the other's meaning. More complex are the communication problems of one organization member trying to communicate with someone located in a different unit or of the corporate senior executive trying to communicate with the entire work force.

Culture reduces these dangers of miscommunication in two ways. First, there is no need to communicate in matters for which shared assumptions already exist; certain things go without saying. Second, shared assumptions provide guidelines and cues to help interpret messages that are received. Thus a strong culture encourages efficient and effective communication. And the advantage of this efficiency and effectiveness should not be underestimated; communications are the lifeblood of organizations.

Culture's content affects the content of communication. Some organizations' cultures value open communication: "Bad news is bad, but withholding it is worse." Other cultures do not value open communication. In these cultures, withholding relevant information that has not been specifically requested, secrecy, and outright distortion may prevail.

Commitment.   A person feels committed to an organization when he or she identifies with it and experiences some emotional attachment to it. A variety of incentives—salary, prestige, and personal sense of worth—tie the individual to the organization. Strong cultures foster strong identification and feelings through multiple beliefs and values that the individual can share with others.

In making decisions and taking actions, committed employees automatically evaluate the impact of alternatives on the organization. Committed people will put out the extra effort needed to get the organization out of a bind. For instance, at Cummins Engine Company the shared value of highly responsive customer service (see Figure 12–9) led the people to "move mountains" to meet intermittent and unexpected surges in product demand, without being given special incentives to do so. People had so thoroughly bought into the values of high-quality customer service and expediting behavior that these had become more than strategic objectives or operational directives. They were taken-for-granted assumptions for the people at Cummins.

Summary.   Culture has a pervasive influence on organizational life, but people working in an organization do not ordinarily recognize this because the basic assumptions and preferences guiding thought and action tend to operate at a preconscious level and remain outside their realm of awareness. Some of culture's manifestations—the shared words, actions, doings, and feelings indicated in Figures 12–8 and 12–9—may be apparent, but the underlying beliefs and values are frequently unstated and not always obvious. Their subtle quality is easily taken for granted. Like the fish who do not realize how much they depend on water, those who are most affected by culture often overlook its basic impact on cooperation, decision making, control, communication, and commitment.

The strength of culture determines its efficiency. However, the content of culture determines its effectiveness because content determines the direction in which culture influences organizational behavior. If the content of the culture guides organizational thinking and action in ways that are out of keeping with the needs of the business and its strategy, culture becomes ineffective, regardless of its efficiency. So, a key challenge facing strategic managers is to carefully manage the strategy–culture relationship to effectively implement the business's strategy.

The Strategy–Culture Connection

Culture gives employees a sense of how to behave, what they should do, and where to place priorities in getting the job done. Culture helps employees *fill in the gaps* between what is formally decreed and what actually takes place. As such, culture is of critical importance in the implementation of strategy.

A company's culture can be a major strength when it is consistent with strategy and thus can be a powerful driving force in implementation. The following examples at IBM and Delta Airlines illustrate how a supportive culture enhances employee efforts in implementing strategy:

> Delta Airlines has emphasized a market development strategy with a focus on customer service that requires a high degree of teamwork. Employees have become very receptive to substituting in other jobs to keep planes flying, baggage moving, and reservations confirmed. A simple story told in a recent book illustrates the degree to which these values are [inculcated] at Delta: A woman inadvertently missed out on a "Super Saver" ticket because the family had moved and, owing to a technicality, the ticket price was no longer valid. She called to complain. Delta's president intervened personally and, being there at the time, met her at the gate to give her the new ticket.[18]
>
> IBM's strategy in business machines has had as its basic premise offering unparalleled service to customers. A customer's explanation of his decision to choose IBM in a major computer system purchase for a hospital illustrates how values reinforcing this strategy permeate IBM employees: "Many of the others were ahead of IBM in technological wizardry. And heaven knows their software is easier to use. But IBM alone took the trouble to get to know us. They interviewed extensively up and down the line. They talked our language, no mumbo jumbo on computer innards. Their price was fully 25 percent higher. But they provided unparalleled guarantees of reliability and service. They even went so far as to arrange a backup connection with a local steel company in case our system

---

[18] Thomas J. Peters and Robert H. Waterman, Jr., *In Search of Excellence* (New York: Harper & Row, 1982), p. xxi.

crashed. Their presentations were to the point. Everything about them smacked of assurance and success. Our decision, even with severe budget pressure, was really easy.[19]

At both IBM and Delta Airlines, the beliefs and values (*culture*) that drive employee behavior are fully consistent with the "service-driven" strategies of the companies.

The opposite can occur. A culture can prevent a company from meeting competitive threats or adapting to changing economic or social environments that a new strategy is designed to overcome. One widely cited example is AT&T. AT&T adopted a marketing-oriented strategy for the 1980s to replace its service- and public-utility-oriented strategy. This new strategy was chosen in response to antitrust pressures, the Federal Communications Commission's decision to allow other companies to sell products in AT&T's once-captive markets, and the unregulated competition in the emerging telecommunications industry. AT&T has now labored for several years to behave like a marketing company, but with marginal success. Efforts to serve different market segments in different ways have run afoul of the strong values, beliefs, and norms managers have imbibed since the turn of the century—that it is important to furnish telephone service to everybody, and that you do so by not discriminating too much among different kinds of customers.[20] The solution seems obvious: change the culture. Changing the orientation of approximately 1 million employees is not easy.

A similar experience in the oil industry was reported in *Business Week:*

Five years ago the chief executives of two major oil companies determined that they would have to diversify out of oil because their current business could not support long-term growth and faced serious political threats. Not only did they announce their new long-range strategies to employees and the public, but they established elaborate plans to implement them. Each of the CEOs was unable to implement his strategy, not because it was theoretically wrong or bad, but because neither had understood that his company's culture was so entrenched in the traditions and values of doing business as oilmen that employees resisted (and sabotaged) the radical changes that the CEOs tried to impose. Oil operations require long-term investments for long-term rewards; but the new businesses needed short-term views and an emphasis on current returns. Successes had come from hitting it big in wildcatting, but the new success was to be based on such abstractions as market share or numbers growth—all seemingly nebulous concepts to them.[21]

After several years of pursuing diversification strategies, both companies are firmly back in the oil business, and the two CEOs have been replaced. *Business Week* analysts attributed each strategy's failure to the idea that

---

[19] Ibid., p. xx.

[20] "The Corporate Culture Vultures," *Fortune*, October 17, 1983, p. 66.

[21] "Corporate Culture," *Business Week*, October 27, 1980, p. 148.

"implementing them violated employees' basic beliefs about their roles in the company and the traditions that underlie the companies' cultures."[22]

These examples help demonstrate the important role of culture in institutionalizing a company's strategy. As a consequence, managing culture to successfully implement a strategy is critical. The issue is simple to state yet exceedingly difficult to effect. The critical issue that must be managed is whether the "fit" between the shared assumptions comprising an organization's culture is consistent with the implementation requirements of the chosen strategy.

Managing the Strategy–Culture Relationship

Managers have a difficult time thinking through the relationship between culture and the critical factors on which strategy depends. They quickly recognize, however, that key components of the company—structure, staff, systems, people, style—influence the way key managerial tasks are executed and critical management relationships are formed. And strategy implementation is largely concerned with adjustments in these components to accommodate the perceived needs of the new strategy. So, managing the strategy–culture relationship requires sensitivity to the interaction between the changes necessary to implement strategy and the compatibility or "fit" between those changes and the organization's culture. Figure 12–10 provides a simple but useful framework for managing the strategy–culture relationship by identifying four basic situations a company might face.

Link to Mission.   A company in cell 1 faces implementing a new strategy that requires several changes in structure, systems, managerial assignments, operating procedures, or other fundamental aspects of the organization. At the same time, most of the changes are potentially compatible with the existing organizational culture. Companies in this situation are usually those with a tradition of effective performance that are either seeking to take advantage of a major opportunity or attempting to redirect major product/market operations consistent with core, proven capabilities. Such companies are in a very promising position: they can pursue a strategy requiring major changes but still benefit from the power of cultural reinforcement.

Companies seeking to manage a strategy–culture relationship in this context need to emphasize four basic considerations. First, *key changes must be visibly linked to the basic company mission.* The mission provides a broad official foundation for the organizational culture. Therefore, top executives should use every internal and external forum available to reinforce the message that the changes are inextricably linked to the fundamental company mission. Second, *emphasis should be placed on using existing personnel* where possible to fill positions created in implementing the strategy. Existing personnel carry

---

[22] Ibid., p. 148.

Figure 12–10
Managing the strategy–culture relationship

		High	Low
	Many	Link changes to basic mission and fundamental organizational norms 1	Reformulate strategy or prepare carefully for long-term, difficult change 4
Changes in key organizational factors that are necessary to implement the new strategy	Few	2 Synergistic— Focus on reinforcing culture	3 Manage around the culture

Potential
compatibility of changes
with existing culture

with them the shared values and norms that help ensure cultural compatibility as major changes are implemented. Third, *care must be taken if adjustments are needed in the reward system.* These should be consistent with currently rewarded behavior. If, for example, a new product/market thrust requires significant changes in the way sales are made and therefore in incentive compensation, common themes (e.g., incentive-oriented) must be emphasized. In this way, current and future approaches are related and the changes are justified (encourage development of less familiar markets). Fourth, *key attention should be paid to changes that are least compatible with current culture* so that current norms are not disrupted. For example, a company may choose to subcontract an important step in a production process because the process would be incompatible with current culture.

IBM's strategy in entering the personal computer market is an illustration. The strategy required numerous organizational changes to serve a radically different market. To maintain maximum compatibility with its existing culture, IBM went to considerable public and internal effort to link its new PCs with the corporation's long-standing mission. The message relating the PC to IBM's tradition of top-quality service appeared almost daily on television and in magazines. Internally, every IBM manager was given a PC. The corporation also emphasized the use of IBM personnel where feasible to fill new positions. But because production requirements were not compatible with current operations, IBM subcontracted virtually all manufacturing for the PC.

Maximize Synergy. A company in cell 2 is in the enviable position of needing only a few organizational changes to implement a new strategy; and those changes are potentially quite compatible with the current culture. A company in this position should emphasize two broad themes: (1) *take advantage of this situation to reinforce and solidify the company's culture* and (2) *use this time of relative stability to remove organizational roadblocks to the desired culture.* Holiday Inns' move into casino gambling required few major organizational changes for the parent company. Casinos were seen as resort locations requiring lodging, dining, and gambling/entertainment services. Holiday Inns had only to incorporate gambling/entertainment expertise into its management team, which otherwise had the complete capability to manage the lodging and dining requirements of casino (or any other) resort locations. This single, major change was successfully inculcated in part by selling it internally as completely compatible with Holiday Inns' mission to provide high-quality accommodations for business and leisure travelers. The resignation of then CEO Roy Clymer removed one final organization roadblock, legitimizing a culture that prided itself on quality service to the middle- to upper-income business traveler rather than one that placed its highest priority on family-oriented service. The latter value was fast disappearing from the Holiday Inns' culture, with the encouragement of most of Holiday Inns' top management, but was not yet fully sanctioned because of personal beliefs shared by Clymer. His voluntary departure helped solidify the new values top management wanted.

Manage around the Culture.   A company in cell 3 must make a few major organizational changes to implement its new strategy. At the same time, these changes are potentially inconsistent with current organizational culture. The critical question for this firm is whether these changes can be made with a reasonable chance for success.

Consider, for example, a multibillion-dollar industry leader facing several major threats to its record of outstanding growth and profitability. To meet these threats, considerable effort is made to design a new organizational structure around major markets. After formally assessing the "cultural risks" of such a change, the proposal is rejected as too radical and too inconsistent with the company's functional culture. A positive alternative is available. Planning and coordination personnel can be increased to *manage around the culture* in implementing the strategy.[23] This can be an important means of implementation if a company faces changing a factor (like structure) that is inextricably linked to the organization's culture.

Several alternatives can facilitate managing around culture: create a separate company or division; use task forces, teams, or program coordinators; subcontract; bring in an outsider; or sell out. These are a few of the alternatives available, but the key idea is to create an alternative method of achieving the change desired without directly confronting the incompatible cultural

---

[23] Howard Schwartz and Stanley M. Davis, "Matching Corporate Culture and Business Strategy," *Organizational Dynamics,* Summer 1981, p. 43.

norms. As cultural resistance diminishes, the change may be absorbed into the organization.

Rich's is a highly successful, quality-oriented department store serving higher-income customers in several southeastern locations. With Sears and K mart experiencing rapid growth in mid- to lower-priced merchandise in the 1970s, Rich's decided to serve this market as well. Finding such merchandise inconsistent with the successful values and norms (a quality-merchandise, customer-service-oriented culture) of its traditional business, Rich's created a separate business called Richway to tap this growth area in retailing. Rich's found it necessary and appropriate to create an entire new store network to *manage around its culture*. Both businesses have since flourished, based in part on radically different cultures.

Reformulate.   A company in cell 4 faces the most difficult challenge in managing the strategy–culture relationship. The company must make numerous organizational changes to implement its new strategy. But the number and nature of the changes are incompatible with the current, usually entrenched, values and norms. AT&T, discussed earlier in this chapter, illustrates the substantial dilemma faced by a firm in this situation. Like AT&T, the company in this situation faces the awesome challenge of changing its culture—a complex, expensive, often long-term proposition. It is a challenge numerous organizational culture consultants say borders on an impossibility.[24] Strategy in Action 12–7 describes the decade-long experience at PepsiCo that was necessary to change its culture.

When faced with massive change and cultural resistance, a company should first examine whether strategy reformulation is appropriate. Is it really necessary to change many of the fundamental organizational factors? Can the changes be made with any real expectation that they will be acceptable and successful? If the answer to these questions is no, the business should seriously reconsider and reformulate its strategic plan. In other words, the strategy that the firm can realistically implement must be more consistent with established organizational norms and practices. Merrill Lynch & Co. provides a recent example of a firm that faced this dilemma. Seeking to remain number one in the newly deregulated financial services industry, Merrill Lynch chose to pursue a new, product development strategy in its brokerage business. The success of this strategy depends on Merrill Lynch's traditional, service-oriented brokerage network becoming sales and marketing oriented in order to sell a broader range of investment products to a more diverse customer base. Initial efforts to implement this strategy generated substantial resistance from Merrill Lynch's highly successful brokerage network. The strategy is fundamentally inconsistent with long-standing cultural norms at Merrill Lynch that emphasize personalized service and very close broker–client relationships.

---

[24] "Corporate Culture Vultures," p. 72.

Strategy in Action 12–7
The Pepsi Challenge: Creating an Aggressive Culture to Match an Aggressive Strategy

For decades, Coke's unchallenged position in the cola market was so complete that the brand name Coke became synonymous with cola drinks. It attained this distinction under Robert W. Woodruff, who served as chief executive for 32 years and was still chairman of the company's finance committee at age 90. Woodruff had an "almost messianic drive to get Coca-Cola [distributed] all over the world," according to Harvey Z. Yazijian, coauthor of *The Cola Wars*. So successful was Coke in accomplishing this under Woodruff and later J. Paul Austin that Coca-Cola became known as "America's second State Department." Its trademark became a symbol of American life itself.

"A real problem in the past," said Yazijian, "was that they had a lot of deadwood" among employees. Nevertheless, Coke's marketing and advertising were extremely effective in expanding consumption of the product. But the lack of serious competition and the company's relative isolation in its hometown of Atlanta allowed it to become "fat, dumb, and happy," according to one consultant. Coke executives are known to be extremely loyal to the company and circumspect to the point of secrecy in their dealings with the outside world.

In the mid-1950s, Pepsi, once a sleepy, New York–based bottler with a lame slogan, "Twice as much for a nickel too," began to develop into a serious threat under the leadership of Chairman Alfred N. Steele. The movement gathered momentum, and by the early 1970s, the company had become a ferocious competitor under chairman Donald M. Kendall and President Andrall E. Pearson, a former director of [the consulting firm] McKinsey & Co. The culture that these two executives were determined to create was based on the goal of becoming the number one marketer of soft drinks.

Severe pressure was put on managers to show continual improvement in market share, product volume, and profits. "Careers ride on 10ths of a market share point," offered John Sculley, a Pepsi vice president. This atmosphere pervades the company's nonbeverage units as well. "Everyone knows that if the results aren't there, you had better have your resume up-to-date," says a former snack-food manager.

To keep everyone on their toes, a "creative tension" is continually nurtured among departments at Pepsi, says another former executive. The staff is kept lean, and managers are moved to new jobs constantly, which results in people

Continued on Page 397

Strategy in Action 12–7 (*concluded*)

working long hours and engaging in political maneuvering "just to keep their jobs from being reorganized out from under them," says a headhunter.

Kendall himself sets a constant example. He once resorted to using a snowmobile to get to work in a blizzard, demonstrating the ingenuity and dedication to work he expects from his staff. This type of pressure has pushed many managers out. But a recent company survey shows that others thrive under such conditions. "Most of our guys are having fun," Pearson insists. They are the kind of people, elaborates Sculley, who "would rather be in the marines than in the army."

Like marines, Pepsi executives are expected to be physically fit as well as mentally alert: Pepsi employs four physical fitness instructors at its headquarters, and a former executive says it is an unwritten rule that to get ahead in the company, a manager must stay in shape. The company encourages one-on-one sports as well as interdepartmental competition in such games as soccer and basketball. In company team contests or business dealings, says Sculley, "the more competitive it becomes, the more we enjoy it." In such a culture, less competitive managers are deliberately weeded out. Even suppliers notice a difference today. "They are smart, sharp negotiators who take advantage of all opportunities," says one.

While Pepsi steadily gained market share in the 1970s, Coke was reluctant to admit that a threat existed, Yazijian says. Pepsi now has bested Coke in the domestic take-home market, and it is mounting a challenge overseas. At the moment, the odds are in favor of Coke, which sells one third of the world's soft drinks and has had Western Europe locked up for years. But Pepsi has been making inroads: Besides monopolizing the Soviet market, it has dominated the Arab Middle East ever since Coke was ousted in 1967, when it granted a bottling franchise in Israel. Still, Coke showed that it was not giving up. It cornered a potentially vast new market—China.

With Pepsi gaining domestic market share faster than Coke—in the last five years it has gained 7.5 percent to Coke's 5 percent—observers believe that Coke will turn more to foreign sales or food sales for growth. Roberto C. Goizueta, Coke's chairman, will not reveal Coke's strategy. But one tactic the company has already used is hiring away some of Pepsi's "tigers." Coke has lured Donald Breen, Jr., who played a major role in developing the "Pepsi Challenge"—the consumer taste test—as well as five other marketing and sales executives associated with Pepsi. Pepsi won its court battle to prevent Breen from revealing confidential information over the next 12 months.

The company's current culture may be unlikely to build loyalty. Pepsi may well have to examine the dangers of cultivating ruthlessness in its managers, say former executives.

Only time can tell if these comments are accurate or simply "sour grapes." Regardless, Pepsi has clearly sought to ensure consistency in every aspect of changing its culture from a passive to an aggressive one over the last 20 years.

Source: Based on the article "Corporate Culture: The Hard-to-Change Values that Spell Success or Failure," *Business Week*, October 27, 1980, p. 54.

Following the 1984 resignation of Merrill Lynch's CEO, numerous analysts reported serious reconsideration of this product development strategy toward one more consistent with traditional values and norms inculcated in the brokerage network.

For many businesses facing this dilemma, reformulation is not in the long-term interests of the firm. Oftentimes, as illustrated earlier in Strategy in Action 12–6 about McGraw-Hill, major external changes necessitate a new strategy that requires difficult changes in the fundamental culture of the organization. In the situation where the culture must be changed, several basic managerial actions—both symbolic and substantive—should be considered as the bases for cultural change. Five types of basic managerial actions that will aid in the difficult process of changing organizational culture are discussed below.

Chief Executive's Role. The CEO has to visibly lead the organization in *each* fundamental change. This is a symbolic role in communicating the need for change and recognizing initial successes; and it is a substantive role in making hard decisions. The top-management team must create the pressure for change and set an example that unequivocally demonstrates the seriousness of the new direction.

Who Is Hired and Promoted. One key way to begin the process of changing values and norms is to bring in new people who share the desired values. Likewise, indoctrination of new personnel into the company is a key time for clarifying and inculcating desired values. Companies can also remove employees who strongly resist or blunt efforts to revamp the old culture. In extreme cases, this can mean changing top management.

Change the Reward Structure. A powerful way of changing values and behavior is to link the reward structure and the desired change. This can be done individually and with subunits of the organization. Compensation is the most obvious reward, but resource allocation, perks, and other visible "rewards" help positively reinforce desired change.

Clarify Desired Behavior. Unless managers are fully aware of the behavior required to get things done in the new culture, they will not change how they approach tasks and relationships. So, planning teams and other educational vehicles must clarify what the "new rules" are and how the new behavior will enhance development and advancement in the company.[25]

Foster Consistency between Desired Changes and Rewards. One element appears certain in changing culture: employees cannot be fooled. They

---

[25] Schwartz and Davis, "Matching Corporate Culture," p. 44.

understand the "real" priorities in the company. At the first inconsistency they will become confused, then reluctant to change, and eventually intransigent. So, consistency between what is said to be important and what is rewarded as such is critical in cultural change. Indeed, consistency in every aspect of a culture is essential to its success, as PepsiCo's transformation into an archrival of Coke shows in Strategy in Action 12–7.

Changing an organizational culture takes time. Strategy in Action 12–6 describes efforts at McGraw-Hill that have been under way since 1985. Executives who have succeeded in fundamentally transforming a culture estimate that the process requires from 6 to 15 years.[26] So, in trying to change underlying organizational factors, strategists must recognize that reshaping "the way things are done" in a company is often an incremental process. Small opportunities should be sought for making a change or initiating an action that visibly reinforces the spirit and direction of the new culture. Top management should continually try (and urge their subordinates to try, as well) to gradually build and nurture the company's shared psychological and attitudinal commitment to the new strategy so that the fit between shared employee values and the new strategic mission continually improves.

Summary

This chapter examined the idea that a key aspect of implementing strategy is the need to *institutionalize* that strategy so that it permeates daily decisions and actions in a manner consistent with long-term strategic success. Three fundamental elements must be managed to "fit" the strategy if that strategy is to be effectively institutionalized: organizational *structure, leadership,* and *culture.*

Five fundamental organizational structures were examined, and the advantages and disadvantages of each were identified. Institutionalizing the strategy requires a good strategy–structure fit. This chapter dealt with how this need is often overlooked until performance becomes inadequate and examined conditions under which alternative structures would be more appropriate.

Organizational leadership is essential to effective strategy implementation. The CEO plays a critical role in this regard. Assignment of key managers, particularly within the top-management team, is an important aspect of organizational leadership. The question of promoting insiders versus hiring outsiders is often a central leadership issue in strategy implementation. This chapter provided a situational approach to making this decision in a manner that best institutionalizes the new strategy.

In recent years, organizational culture has been recognized as a pervasive force influencing organizational life. Culture is described as the shared beliefs and values of organizational members, and it may be a major asset or liability

---

[26] "Corporate Culture Vultures," p. 70.

when implementing strategy. An approach to managing the strategy–culture fit was discussed in this chapter. We identified four fundamentally different strategy–culture situations based on the changes necessary to implement the strategy and the "fit" of these changes with the company's culture. Recommendations for managing the strategy–culture fit vary across the four situations.

Questions for Discussion

1. What key structural considerations must be incorporated into strategy implementation? Why does structural change often lag a change in strategy?

2. Which structure is most appropriate for successful strategy implementation? Explain how stage of development affects your answer.

3. Why is leadership an important element in strategy implementation? Find an example in a major business periodical of the CEO's key role in strategy implementation.

4. Under what conditions would it be more appropriate to fill a key management position with someone from outside the company when a qualified insider is available?

5. What is organizational culture? Why is it important? Explain two different situations a firm might face in managing the strategy–culture relationship.

Bibliography

"Corporate Culture." *Business Week*, October 27, 1980, pp. 148–60.

"Corporate Culture Vultures." *Fortune*, October 17, 1983, pp. 66–73.

Deal, Terrence E., and Allan A. Kennedy. *Corporate Cultures*. Reading, Mass.: Addison-Wesley Publishing, 1982.

Fenton, Noel J. "Managing the Adolescent Company." *Management Review*, December 1976, pp. 12–19.

Galbraith, Jay R., and Daniel A. Nathanson. *Strategy Implementation: The Role of Structure and Process*. 2nd ed. St. Paul, Minn.: West Publishing, 1978.

Hrebiniak, Lawrence G., and William F. Joyce. *Implementing Strategy*. New York: Macmillan, 1984.

Leontiades, Milton. *Strategies for Diversification and Change*. Boston: Little, Brown, 1980, chaps. 2, 3, 6.

————. "Choosing the Right Manager to Fit the Strategy." *Journal of Business Strategy*, Fall 1982, pp. 58–69.

Miles, R. E., and C. C. Snow. *Organizational Strategy, Structure, and Process*. New York: McGraw-Hill, 1978.

Peters, Thomas J. "Beyond the Matrix Organization." *Business Horizons*, October 1979, pp. 15–27.

Peters, Thomas J., and Robert Waterman. *In Search of Excellence*. New York: Harper & Row, 1982.

Sathe, Vijay. *Culture and Related Corporate Realities*. Homewood, Ill.: Richard D. Irwin, 1985.

Stonich, Paul J. *Implementing Strategy*. Cambridge, Mass.: Ballinger, 1982.

Tichy, N. M.; C. J. Fombrun; and M. A. Devanna. "Strategic Human Resource Management." *Sloan Management Review*, Winter 1982, p. 47.

"Wanted: A Manager to Fit Each Strategy." *Business Week*, Febuary 25, 1980, p. 166.

Yavitz, Boris, and William H. Newman. *Strategy in Action*. New York: Free Press, 1982.

Chapter 12 Cohesion Case Illustration

Institutionalizing the Strategy at Holiday Inns, Inc.

Holidays Inns has emphasized three key elements to institutionalize its strategy for the 1990s: organizational structure, selection and assignment of key managers, and organizational culture.

Organizational Structure.   Exhibit 1 provides an abbreviated look at the organizational structure of Holiday Inns, Inc. As you can see, Holiday Inns has a divisional structure with four rather autonomous business groups. This clearly reflects the needs of its corporate diversification strategy by providing each business group with its own functional support and broad decision-making capability. Second, the formerly separate products group has been reorganized within the hotel group. This clearly reflects the strategy of retrenchment and divestiture within the products group limiting it primarily to a service role for the hotel group's furnishing and equipment needs. Finally, Delta Steamship and Perkins restaurants have been organized as fully independent and autonomous units. This distinguishes Delta and Perkins from the hospitality businesses and facilitates rapid divestiture should Holiday Inns find the right opportunity to do so (which it did with Delta in 1983 and with Perkins in 1986).

Assignment of Key Managers.   Several key managerial assignments reflect a deliberate choice at the corporate level to effectively implement Holiday Inns' diversification strategy. Holiday Inns' three nonhotel divisions have as their presidents the former CEOs at Harrah's, Perkins, and Delta, respectively. Instead of putting a Holiday Inns-trained executive in charge, corporate management deliberately chose to maintain autonomy and leadership to meet the unique needs of these new groups. Finally, reflecting a corporate portfolio strategy that emphasizes casinos as a key growth area, gaming is the only business group other than hotels to have representation on the board of directors and of the corporate management level.

Mike Rose (CEO) and Roy Winegardner (chairman of the board) were initially successful franchisees before becoming involved with Holiday Inns' top-management team. Thus, they understand franchisees—an attribute critical to the franchise-dominated hotel and restaurant businesses. They also (particularly Rose) had less of a tie to Holiday Inns' previous family-oriented hotel philosophy and widespread, transportation-related diversification. This made

Exhibit 1
Organizational structure at Holiday Corporation

Board of Directors

Chairman of the Board (Roy Winegardner)

President and Chief Executive Officer (Mike Rose)

- Vice President Administration
- Vice President Strategic Planning
- Vice President Communications
- Vice President Human Resources
- Senior Vice President Finance
- Vice President Government and Industrial Relations
- Vice President Management Information Systems
- Vice President Organizational Development

President Hotel Group
- Vice President Franchising
- Vice President Personnel
  - Vice President Marketing
  - Vice President International Operations
  - Vice President Domestic Operations
  - Vice President Finance, Development, Planning
  - Vice President Product Services

Chairman Gaming Group
- President
  - Vice President Operations
  - Vice President Marketing
  - Vice President Finance and Planning
  - Vice President Government Relations
  - Vice President Entertainment

President Perkins Restaurants
- Vice President Operations
- Vice President Marketing
- Vice President Finance
- Vice President Personnel

President Delta Steamship
- Vice President Finance and Planning
- Vice President Atlantic Division
- Vice President Gulf Division
- Vice President Pacific Division

them more objective and effective in addressing and implementing the casino decision and several major divestitures (product group and transportation businesses).

Two additions to the board reflect Holiday Inns' institutionalization of its hospitality strategy. Donald Smith, senior vice president with PepsiCo and president of its Food Service Division, brings well-respected food-service experience to Holiday Inns' top-management team. Smith was credited with turning Burger King into a viable competitor with McDonald's in fast foods. James Farley, chairman and CEO of Booz Allen & Hamilton (a worldwide consulting firm), reflects a serious commitment to systematic strategic planning for Holiday Inns' future.

Organizational Culture.   The structural and key managerial changes reflect a steady shift from an entrepreneurial to a professionally managed company. Refocusing on being a *hospitality* company in two industries—hotels and gaming—has been presented as the "new Holiday Corporation." The common threat for each operation is a strong service orientation that encourages and rewards superior individual performance. The "new" Holiday Inns sees its people assets as key to its service success, as reflected by its corporate philosophy and statements by Roy Winegardner, shown below:

Corporate Philosophy Statement:
   We are a forward-looking innovative industry leader with clearly defined goals, producing superior products/services and consistently high return for our shareholders.
   We will maintain integrity in both our internal and external relationsips, fostering respect for the individual and open two-way communications.
   We will promote a climate of enthusiasm, teamwork, and challenge, which attracts, motivates, and retains superior personnel and rewards superior performance.
   Our employees give us our greatest competitive advantage. We employ and develop high-quality people because they are the key to our continued leadership and growth.

13

Strategic Control: Guiding and Evaluating the Strategy

A strategy is selected and implemented over time so as to effectively position and guide a firm within an often rapidly changing environment. Strategies are forward looking, designed to be accomplished several years into the future, and based on management assumptions about numerous events that have not yet occurred.

How should managers undertake controlling a strategy? Traditional approaches to control seek to compare actual results against a standard. The work is done, the manager evaluates the work, and uses the evaluation as input to control future efforts. While this approach has its place, it is inappropriate as a means to control a strategy. Waiting until a strategy has been fully executed often involves five or more years, during which many changes occur that have major ramifications for the ultimate success of the strategy. Consequently, customary control concepts and approaches must be adjusted or replaced in favor of strategic controls that recognize the unique control needs of long-term strategies.

Strategic control is concerned with tracking the strategy as it is being implemented, detecting problems or changes in underlying premises, and making necessary adjustments. In contrast to post-action control, strategic control is concerned with controlling and guiding efforts on behalf of the strategy as action is taking place and while the end result is still several years into the future. Managers responsible for a strategy and its success are typically concerned with two sets of questions:

1. Are we moving in the proper direction? Are key things falling into place? Are our assumptions about major trends and changes correct? Are the critical things we need to do being done? Do we need to adjust or abort this strategy?

2. How are we performing? Are we meeting objectives and schedules? How are costs, revenues, and cash flows matching projections? Do we need to make operational changes?

Strategic controls, augmented by certain operational controls, are designed to answer these questions.

This chapter describes strategic controls and explains how to set them up. It then explains key operational control systems necessary to support strategic control. Reward systems are also explained in this chapter because they play a key role in directing strategy implementation and motivating strategic control. Finally, this chapter explains fundamental considerations in the evaluation of strategy once its implementation is complete.

Establishing Strategic Controls

Control of strategy can be characterized as a form of "steering control."[1] Ordinarily, a significant time span occurs between initial implementation of a strategy and achievement of its intended results. During that time, numerous projects are undertaken, investments are made, and actions are undertaken to implement the new strategy. Also during that time, both the environmental situation and the firm's internal situation are developing and evolving. Strategic controls are necessary to steer the firm through these events. They must provide the basis for correcting the actions and directions of the firm in implementing its strategy as developments and changes in its environmental and internal situations take place.

Prudential Insurance Company provides a useful example of the proactive, steering nature of strategic control. Several years ago, Prudential committed to a long-term market development strategy wherein it would seek to attain the top position in the life insurance industry by differentiating its level of service from other competitors in the industry. Prudential decided to establish regional home offices, thus achieving a differential service advantage. Exercising strategic control, Prudential managers used the experience at the first regional offices to reproject overall expenses and income associated with this strategy. In fact, the predicted expenses were so high that the location and original schedule for converting other regions had to be modified. Conversion of corporate headquarters was sharply revised on the basis of other early feedback. Thus the steering control (or strategic control) exercised by Prudential managers significantly altered the strategy long before the total plan

---

[1] B. Yavitz and W. H. Newman, *Strategy in Action* (New York: Free Press, 1982), p. 207.

was in place. In this case, major objectives remained in place while changes were made in the strategy; in other cases, strategic controls may initiate changes in objectives as well.

The four basic types of strategic control are:

1. Premise control.
2. Implementation control
3. Strategic survelliance.
4. Special alert control.

The nature of these four strategic controls is summarized in Figure 13–1.

Premise Control

Every strategy is based on assumed or predicted conditions. These assumptions or predictions are planning premises; a firm's strategy is designed around these predicted conditions. *Premise control is designed to check systematically and continuously whether or not the premises set during the planning and implementation process are still valid.* If a vital premise is no longer valid, then the strategy may have to be changed. The sooner an invalid premise can be recognized and revised, the better the chances that an acceptable shift in the strategy can be devised.

What Premises Should Be Monitored?   Premises are primarily concerned with two types of factors: environmental and industry. They are described below.

Environmental Factors.   A company has little or no control over environmental factors, but these factors exercise considerable influence over the success of the strategy. Inflation, technology, interest rates, regulation, and demographic/social changes are examples of such factors. Strategies are usually based on key premises about these factors.

Industry Factors.   These factors affect the performance of companies in a given industry. They differ among industries, and a company should be aware of the factors that influence success in its particular industry. Competitors, suppliers, substitutes, and barriers to entry are a few such factors about which strategic assumptions are made.

Premises, some major and some minor, are often made about numerous environmental and industry variables. To attempt to track every premise may be unnecessarily expensive and time-consuming. Therefore, managers must select those premises and variables that (*a*) are likely to change and (*b*) would have a major impact on the company and its strategy if they did.

Figure 13–1
Four types of strategic control

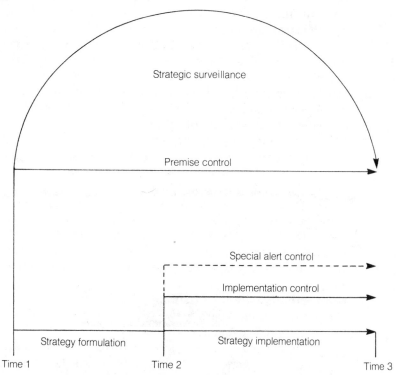

Source: Adapted from G. Schreyogg and H. Steinmann, "Strategic Control: A New Perspective," *Academy of Management Review* 12, no. 1 (1987), p. 96.

How Are Premise Controls Enacted?   The key premises should be identified during the planning process. The premises should be recorded, and responsibility for monitoring them should be assigned to the persons or departments who are qualified sources of information. For example, the sales force may be a valuable source for monitoring the expected price policy of major competitors, while the finance department might monitor interest rate trends. All premises should not require the same amount of effort; and, again, emphasis should be placed on key success premises so as to avoid information overload. Premises should be updated (new predictions) based on updated information. Finally, key areas within the company or key aspects of the strategy that the predicted changes may significantly impact should be preidentified so that adjustments necessitated by a revised premise can be determined and initiated. For example, senior marketing executives should be alerted about changes in competitors' pricing policies in order to determine if revised pricing, product repositioning, or other strategy adjustments are necessary.

Implementation Control

The action phase of strategic management is located in the series of steps, programs, investments, and moves undertaken over a period of time to implement the strategy. Special programs are undertaken. Functional areas initiate several strategy-related activities. Key people are added or reassigned. Resources are mobilized. In other words, managers convert broad strategic plans into concrete actions and results for specific units and individuals as they go about implementing strategy. And these actions take place incrementally over an extended period of time designed ultimately to enact the planned strategy and achieve long-term objectives.

Strategic control can be undertaken within this context. We refer to this type of strategic control as implementation control. *Implementation control is designed to assess whether the overall strategy should be changed in light of unfolding events and results associated with incremental steps and actions that implement the overall strategy.* The earlier example of Prudential Insurance Company updating cost and revenue projections based on early experiences with regional home offices is an illustration of an implementation control. The two basic types of implementation control are: (1) monitoring strategic thrusts (new or key strategic programs) and (2) milestone reviews.

Monitoring Strategic Thrusts. Implementing broad strategies often involves undertaking several new strategic projects—specific narrow undertakings that represent part of what needs to be done if the overall strategy is to be accomplished. These projects or thrusts provide a source of information from which managers can obtain feedback that helps determine whether the overall strategy is progressing as planned and whether it needs to be adjusted or changed.

While strategic thrusts seem a readily apparent type of control, using them as control sources is not always easy to do. Early experience may be difficult to interpret. Clearly identifying and measuring early steps and promptly evaluating the overall strategy in light of this early, isolated experience can be difficult.

Two approaches are useful in enacting implementation controls focused on monitoring strategic thrusts. One way is to agree early in the planning process on which thrusts, or phases of those thrusts, are *critical factors in the success of the strategy or of that thrust*. Managers responsible for these implementation controls single these out from other activities and observe them frequently.

The second approach for monitoring strategic thrusts is to use stop/go assessments linked to a series of meaningful thresholds (time, costs, research and development, success, etc.) associated with particular thrusts. Days Inns' nationwide market development strategy in the early 1980s included a strategic thrust of regional development via company-owned inns in the Rocky Mountain area. Time problems in meeting development targets led company executives to reconsider the overall strategy, ultimately deciding to totally change it and sell the company.

Milestone Reviews.   Managers often attempt to identify critical milestones that will occur over the time period the strategy is being implemented. These milestones may be critical events, major resource allocations, or simply the passage of a certain amount of time. In each case, *a milestone review usually involves a full-scale reassessment of the strategy and the advisability of continuing or refocusing the direction of the company.*

A useful example of strategic implementation control based on milestone review can be found in Boeing's product development strategy to enter the supersonic transport (SST) airplane market. Competition from the joint British/French Concord effort was intense. Boeing had invested millions of dollars and years of scarce engineering talent through phase I of its SST venture. The market was believed large, but the next phase represented a billion-dollar decision for Boeing. This phase was established as a milestone review by Boeing management. Cost estimates were greatly increased; relatively few passengers and predictions of rising fuel costs raised estimated operating costs; the Concord had massive government subsidy, while Boeing did not. All factors led Boeing management to withdraw, in spite of high sunk costs, pride, and patriotism. Only an objective, full-scale strategy reassessment could have led to such a decision.[2]

In this example, a major resource allocation decision point provided the appropriate point for a milestone review. Milestone reviews might also occur concurrent with the timing of a new major step in the strategy's implementation or when a key uncertainty is resolved. Sometimes managers may even set an arbitrary time period, say, two years, as a milestone review point. Whatever the basis for selecting the milestone point, the critical purpose of a milestone review is to undertake a thorough review of the firm's strategy so as to control the company's future.

Strategic Surveillance

By their nature, premise control and implementation control are focused control. The third type of strategic control, *strategic surveillance, is designed to monitor a broad range of events inside and outside the company that are likely to threaten the course of the firm's strategy.*[3] The basic idea behind strategic surveillance is that some form of general monitoring of multiple

---

[2] Ibid.

[3] G. Scheyogg and H. Steinmann, "Strategie Control: A New Perspective," *Academy of Management Review* 12, no. 1 (1987), p. 101.

information sources should be encouraged, with the specific intent being the opportunity to uncover important yet unanticipated information.

Strategic surveillance must be kept unfocused as much as possible and should be designed as a loose "environmental-scanning" activity. Trade magazines, *The Wall Street Journal,* trade conferences, conversations, and intended and unintended observations are all sources of strategic surveillance. While strategic surveillance is loose, its important purpose is to provide an ongoing, broad-based vigilance in all daily operations so as to uncover information that may prove relevant to the firm's strategy.

Special Alert Control

Another type of strategic control, really a subset of the other three, is special alert control. *A special alert control is the need to thoroughly, and often rapidly, reconsider the firm's basic strategy based on a sudden, unexpected event.* A political coup in the Middle East, an outside firm suddenly acquiring a leading competitor, an unexpected product difficulty like Tylenol's experience with poisoned capsules—all of these represent sudden changes that can drastically alter the company's strategy.

Such an occurrence should trigger an immediate and intense reassessment of the company's strategy and its current strategic situation. Many firms have developed crisis teams to handle initial response and coordination when faced with unforeseen occurrences that may have an immediate effect on the firm's strategy. Increasingly, companies are developing contingency plans along with crisis teams to respond to such circumstances as are illustrated in Strategy in Action 13–1.

Table 13–1 summarizes the major characteristics of the four types of strategic control. While each type of strategic control is different, they share a common purpose: to assess whether the strategic direction should be altered in light of unfolding events. Unlike operational controls, strategic controls are designed to continuously and proactively question the basic direction of the strategy.

Operations controls are concerned with providing action control. Strategic controls are concerned with "steering" the company's future direction. Both are needed to manage the strategic process effectively. The next section examines key types of operations control systems used to aid the strategic management process.

Operational Control Systems

Strategic controls are useful to top management in monitoring and steering the basic strategic direction of the company. But operating managers also need control methods appropriate to their level of strategy implementation. The primary concern at the operating level is allocation and use of the company's resources.

Strategy in Action 13–1
Examples of Strategic Controls

Premise Control at Citicorp

Citicorp has been pursuing an aggressive product development strategy intended to achieve earnings growth of 15 percent annually while becoming an institution capable of supplying clients with any kind of financial service anywhere in the world. A major problem Citicorp faces in achieving this earnings growth is its exposure because of earlier, extensive loans to troubled Third World countries. Citicorp remains sensitive to the wide variety of predictions about impending Third World defaults.

Citicorp established a basic planning *premise* that 10 percent of its Third World loans will default annually over the next five years. Yet it maintains active *premise control* by having each of its international branches monitor daily announcements from key governments and from inside contacts. When the premise is challenged, management attempts to adjust Citicorp's posture. For example, when Peru's president, Alan Garcia, stated that his country would not pay interest on its debt as scheduled, Citicorp raised its default charge to 20 percent of its $100 million Peruvian exposure.

Implementation Control at Days Inns

Pioneering the budget segment of the lodging industry, Days Inns' strategy placed primary emphasis on company-owned facilities as it insisted on maintaining roughly a 3-to-1 company-owned/franchise ratio. This ratio ensured total control over standards, rates, and so forth by the parent company.

As other firms moved into the budget segment, Days Inns saw the need to expand rapidly throughout the United States, and it decided to reverse its conservative franchise posture. This reversal would rapidly accelerate its ability to open new locations. Longtime executives, concerned about potential loss of control over local standards, instituted *implementation controls* requiring both regular franchise evaluation and annual milestone reviews. Two years into the program, executives were convinced a high franchise/company ratio was manageable, and they accelerated the growth of franchising by doubling the franchise sales department.

Continued on Page 412

Strategy in Action 13–1 (*concluded*)

Strategic Surveillance at IBM

In the early years of its attempt to make and sell computers (versus its staple typewriters and adding machines), IBM's strategy was targeted toward the scientific and research markets in government, universities, and industry. Its early experience was poor as these organizations appeared to have little money buying IBM's large, expensive mainframe computer. Yet no other organization or setting had a need for the volume computing capacity—at least that was IBM management's assumption.

Fortunately for IBM, one sales executive's reading included the *Librarian,* a trade magazine among librarians at the time. He noticed one article about the number of transactions handled in large libraries and the need for automated solutions.

This led to a suggestion to investigate libraries as a market for IBM's early mainframes. Executives also found libraries to be relatively flush with funds because of recent, generous funding from the New Carnegie Foundation. This market proved to be the basis for IBM's early success (some say its real survival) in the mainframe computer business. And the discovery of this early, important niche has been attributed to an IBM manager's regular readings—a form of strategic surveillance—which was the only source for information critical to IBM's ability to steer its mainframe computer strategy in a successful direction.

Special Alert Control at United Airlines

The sudden impact of an airplane crash could be devastating to a major airline. Few companies have made more elaborate preparations than United Airlines. Its executive vice president, James M. Guyette, heads a crisis team permanently prepared to respond. Members carry beepers and are always on call. If United's Chicago headquarters receives word that a plane has crashed, for example, they can be in a "war room" within an hour to direct the response.

Beds are set up nearby so participants can catch a few winks; while they sleep, alternates take their places. Members of this squad have been carefully screened through simulated crisis drills. "The point is to weed out those who don't hold up well under stress," says Guyette. Although the team was established to handle flight disasters, it has since assumed an expanded role. Earlier this year, the process was activated when American Airlines, Inc., launched a fare war. And, according to Gulette, "We're brainstorming about how we would be affected by everything from a competitor who had a serious problem to a crisis involving a hijacking or taking a United employee hostage."

Sources: Adapted from "Citicorp: What the New Boss Is up To," *Fortune,* February 17, 1986, p. 40; conversations with selected Days Inns executives; Peter Drucker, *Innovation and Entrepreneurship* (New York: Harper & Row, 1986); and "How Companies Prepare for the Worst," *Business Week,* December 23, 1985, p. 74.

Table 13–1
Summary characteristics of the four types of strategic control

Basic characteristics	Types of strategic control			
	Premise control	*Implementation control*	*Strategic surveillance*	*Special alerts*
Objects of control	Planning premises and projections	Key strategic thrusts and milestones	Potential threats and opportunities related to the strategy	Occurrence of recognizable but unlikely events
Degree of focusing	High	High	Low	High
Data acquisition				
Formalization	Medium	High	Low	High
Centralization	Low	Medium	Low	High
Use with:				
Environmental factors	Yes	Seldom	Yes	Yes
Industry factors	Yes	Seldom	Yes	Yes
Strategy-specific factors	No	Yes	Seldom	Yes
Company-specific factors	No	Yes	Seldom	Seldom

Source: Adapted from G. Scheyogg and H. Steinmann, "Strategic Control: A New Perspective," *Academy of Management Review* 12, no. 1 (1987), pp. 91–103.

Operational control systems guide, monitor, and evaluate progress in meeting annual objectives. While strategic controls attempt to steer the company over an extended time period (usually five years or more), operational controls provide post-action evaluation and control over short time periods—usually from one month to one year. To be effective, operational control systems must take four steps common to all post-action controls:

1. Set standards of performance.
2. Measure actual performance.
3. Identify deviations from standards.
4. Initiate corrective action or adjustment.

Three types of operational control systems are *budgets, schedules,* and *key success factors*. The nature and use of these three operational control systems are described in the next several sections.

Budgeting Systems

The budgetary process was the forerunner of strategic planning. Capital budgeting in particular provided the means for strategic resource allocations. With the growing use of strategic management, such allocations are now based on strategic assessment and priorities, not solely on capital budgeting.[4] Yet capital and expenditure budgeting, as well as sales budgeting, remain important control mechanisms in strategy implementation.

A budget is simply a resource allocation plan that helps managers coordinate operations and facilitates managerial control of performance. Budgets themselves do not control anything. Rather, they set standards against which action can be measured. They also provide a basis for negotiating short-term resource requirements to implement strategy at the operating level.

Most firms employ a budgeting system, not a singular budget, in controlling strategy implementation. Figure 13–2 represents a typical budgeting system for a manufacturing business. A budgeting system incorporates a series of different budgets fitting the organization's unique characteristics. Because organizations differ, so do their budgets. Yet most firms include three general types of budgets—revenue, capital, and expenditure—in their budgetary control system.

Revenue Budgets. Most firms employ some form of revenue budget to monitor their sales projections (or expectations), because this reflects a key objective of the chosen strategy. The revenue budget provides important information for the daily management of financial resources and key feedback as to whether the strategy is working. For evaluative purposes, the revenue budget may be derived from revenue forecasts arrived at in the planning process, or it may be linked to past revenue patterns. For example, most hotel/motel operators emphasize daily revenue compared to revenue for the same day in the previous year as a monitor of sales effectiveness.

A revenue budget is particularly important as a tool for control of strategy implementation. Revenue budgets provide an early warning system about the effectiveness of the firm's strategy. And if the deviation is considerably below or above expectations, this budgetary tool should initiate managerial action to reevaluate and possibly adjust the firm's operational or strategic posture.

Capital Budgets. Capital budgets outline specific expenditures for plant, equipment, machinery, inventories, and other capital items needed during the budget period.

To support their strategies, many firms require capital investment or divestiture. A firm committed to a strong growth strategy may need additional capacity or facilities to support increased sales. On the other hand, a firm intent on retrenchment may have to divest major parts of its current operations to generate additional resources. In both cases, the firm is concerned with management of significant financial resources, probably over an extended time period.

---

[4] Peter Lorange, *Corporate Planning* (Englewood Cliffs, N.J.: Prentice-Hall, 1980), p. 155.

Figure 13–2
A typical budgeting system for controlling strategy implementation

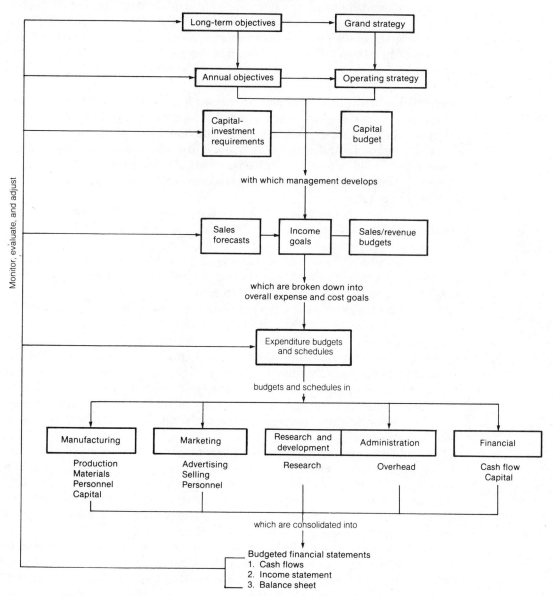

For effective control, a capital budget that carefully plans the acquisition and expenditure of funds, as well as the timing, is essential.

Two additional budgets are often developed to control the use of capital resources. A *cash budget* forecasts receipts and disbursements of cash—cash flow—during the budget period. And a *balance sheet budget* is usually developed to forecast the status of assets, liabilities, and net worth at the end of the budget period.

Expenditure Budgets.   Numerous expense/cost budgets will be necessary for budgetary control in implementation of strategy in various operating units of the firm. An expenditure budget for each functional unit and for subfunctional activities can guide and control unit/individual execution of strategy, thus increasing the likelihood of profitable performance. For example, a firm might have an expenditure budget for the marketing department and another for advertising activities.

In such budgets, dollar variables will be the predominant measure, although nondollar measures of physical activity levels may occasionally be used as a supplement.[5] For example, a production budget might include standards for expenditures as well as standards for output level or productivity. These nondollar variables might also include targets or milestones that provide evidence of necessary progress in particular strategic programs.

An expenditure or operating budget is meant to provide concrete standards against which operational costs and activities can be measured and, if necessary, adjusted to maintain effective strategy execution. The expenditure budget is perhaps the most common budgetary tool in strategy implementation. If its standards are soundly linked to strategic objectives, then it can provide an effective communication link between top management and operating managers about what is necessary for a strategy to succeed. It provides another warning system alerting management to problems in the implementation of the firm's strategy.

The budgeting system (see Figure 13–2) provides an integrated picture of the firm's operation as a whole. The effect on overall performance of a production decision to alter the level of work-in-process inventories or of a marketing decision to change sales organization procedures can be traced through the entire budget system. Thus, coordinating these decisions becomes an important consideration for the control of strategy implementation.

Figure 13–2 provides an illustration of how budgets can be coordinated to aid in coordinating operations. In this chart, production, raw material purchases, and direct labor requirements are coordinated with anticipated sales. In more comprehensive systems, other budgets may be included: manufacturing expense, inventories, building services, advertising, maintenance, cash flow, administrative overhead, and so on, as suggested earlier in this section.

---

[5] Ibid., p. 158.

Scheduling

Timing is often a key factor in the success of a strategy. Scheduling is simply a planning tool for allocating the use of a time-constrained resource or arranging the sequence of interdependent activities. The success of strategy implementation is quite dependent on both. So scheduling offers a mechanism with which to plan for, monitor, and control these dependencies. For example, a firm committed to a vertical integration strategy must carefully absorb expanded operations into its existing core. Such expansion, whether involving forward or backward integration, will require numerous changes in the operational practices of some of the firm's organizational units. A good illustration of this is Coors Brewery, which recently made the decision to integrate backward by producing its own beer cans. A comprehensive, two-year schedule of actions and targets for incorporating manufacture of beer cans and bottles into the product chain contributed to the success of this strategy. Major changes in purchasing, production scheduling, machinery, and production systems were but a few of the critical operating areas that Coors' scheduling efforts were meant to accommodate and control.

Key Success Factors

One useful way to effect operational control is to focus on "key success factors." Key success factors identify performance areas that must receive continuous management attention. These are the factors that are of greatest importance in implementing the company's strategies. Examples of key success factors focused on internal performance include: (1) improved productivity, (2) high employee morale, (3) improved product/service quality, (4) increased earnings per share, (5) growth in market share, and (6) completion of new facilities. Strategy in Action 13–2 illustrates the key success factors monitored by Chrysler management to control its turnaround strategy in the 1980s.

Each key success factor must have measurable performance indicators. Management of 1-2-3 from Lotus, for example, identified product quality, customer service, employee morale, and competition as the four key determinants of the success of their strategy to rapidly expend Lotus's software offerings. They identified three measures to monitor and control each key success factor as follows:

For product quality:
    Performance data versus specifications.
    Percentage of product returns.
    Number of customer complaints.

For customer service:
    Delivery cycle in days.
    Percentage of orders shipped complete.
    Field service delays.

Strategy in Action 13–2
Strategic Success Factors in Chrysler's Turnaround Strategy

When Lee Iacocca came to Chrysler in 1979, the Michigan State Fairgrounds were jammed with thousands of unsold, unwanted, rusting Chryslers, Dodges, and Plymouths. Foreign operations were leeching the lifeblood out of the company. And worst of all, cars were coming off the assembly line with loose doors, chipped paint, and crooked moldings.

According to Iacocca, the Chrysler experience highlighted four painful realities:

The quality of our products had declined.

Work practices had shortchanged productivity.

The government had become an enemy instead of an ally.

Foreign countries that the United States had defeated in war and rebuilt in peace were beating this country in its own markets.

Chrysler was faced with a choice. The company could go under—the suggestion of not a few—or efforts could be made to save the company, and with it, according to Iacocca, "the American way of doing business—with honesty, pride, ingenuity, and good old-fashioned hard work."

In charting Chrysler's turnaround strategy, Iacocca identified six key success factors essential to a successful turnaround. Chrysler executives used these six factors as the basis for their operational control of the turnaround strategy. Careful, systematic attention was given to monitoring progress on each factor as a key indicator of desired execution of the turnaround strategy.

1. Reduce *wage and salary expenses* by half the 1980 level. (Chrysler ultimately reduced its work force from 160,000 to 80,000 and received over $1.2 billion in wage and benefit sacrifices.)

2. Reduce *fixed cost* by over $4 billion. (Chrysler closed 20 plants and modernized the remaining 40 with state-of-the-art robot and computer technology.)

3. Reduce the *number of different parts* by one third. (Chrylser reduced the number of parts from 75,000 to 40,000, shaking $1 billion out of inventory in the process.)

4. Improve its *weak balance sheet*. (Chrysler retired its U.S. bank debt by converting $1.3 billion into preferred stock, and some preferred into common stock.)

Continued on Page 419

Strategy in Action 13–2 (*concluded*)

5. Improve the *quality of its components* and finished products. (Chrysler reduced warranty costs by 25 percent in 1982; it reduced scheduled maintenance costs to a level $20 to $200 below that of the competition.)
6. Implement a $6 billion *product improvement program.* (Chrysler has a lead in front-wheel-drive technology; it has the best fuel economy in the industry; it offers the industry's most extensive 50,000-mile warranty.)

Source: Based on Lee A. Iacocca, "The Rescue and Resuscitation of Chrysler," *Journal of Business Strategy* 4, no. 3 (1983), pp. 67–69.

For employee morale:
  Trends in employee attitude survey.
  Absenteeism versus plan.
  Employee turnover trends.
For competition:
  Number of firms competing directly.
  Number of new products introduced.
  Percentage of bids awarded versus standard.

Key success factors succinctly communicate the critical elements for which operational managers must be responsible in making the strategy successful. Because their achievement requires the successful performance of several key individuals, these factors can be a foundation for teamwork among managers in meeting the company's strategic objectives.

Budgeting, scheduling, and monitoring *key success factors* are important means to control the implementation of strategy at the operational level of the company. Common to each operational control system is the need to establish measurable standards and to monitor performance against these standards. The next section examines how to accomplish this important role.

Using Operational Control Systems: Monitoring Performance and Evaluating Deviations

Operating control systems require the establishment of performance standards. In addition, progress must be monitored and deviations from standards evaluated as the strategy is implemented. Timely information must be obtained so that deviations can be identified, the underlying cause determined, and actions taken to correct *or* exploit them.

Figure 13–3 illustrates a simplified report on the current status of key performance indicators linked to the firm's strategy. These performance indicators represent progress after two years of a five-year plan intended to differentiate the firm as a customer-service-oriented provider of high-quality products.

Figure 13–3
Monitoring and evaluating performance deviations

Key success factors	Objective, assumption or budget	Forecast performance at this time	Current performance	Current deviation	Analysis
Cost control: Ratio of indirect overhead to direct field and labor costs	10%	15%	12%	+3 (ahead)	Are we moving too fast or is there more unnecessary overhead than originally thought?
Gross profit	39%	40%	40%	0%	
Customer service:					
Installation cycle in days	2.5 days	3.2 days	2.7 days	+0.5 (ahead)	Can this progress be maintained?
Ratio of service to sales personnel	3.2	2.7	2.1	−0.6 (behind)	Why are we behind here? How can we maintain the installation cycle progress?
Product quality:					
Percentage of products returned	1.0%	2.0%	2.1%	−0.1% (behind)	Why are we behind here? Ramifications for other operations?
Product performance versus specification	100%	92%	80%	−12% (behind)	
Marketing:					
Sales per employee monthly	$12,500	$11,500	$12,100	+$600 (ahead)	Good progress. Is it creating any problems to support?
Expansion of product line	6	3	5	+2 products (ahead)	Are the products ready? Are the perfect standards met?
Employee morale in service area:					
Absenteeism rate	2.5%	3.0%	3.0%	(on target)	
Turnover rate	5%	10%	15%	−8% (behind)	Looks like a problem! Why are we so far behind?
Competition:					
New product introductions (average number)	6	3	6	−3 (behind)	Did we underestimate timing? Implications for our basic assumptions?

Management's concern is comparing *progress to date* with *expected progress* at this point in the plan. Of particular interest is the *current deviation* because it provides a basis for examining *suggested actions* (usually from subordinate managers) and for finalizing decisions on any necessary changes or adjustments in the company's operations.

In Figure 13–3, the company appears to be maintaining control of its cost structure. Indeed, it is ahead of schedule on reducing overhead. The company is well ahead of its delivery cycle target, while slightly below its service/sales personnel ratio objective. Product returns look OK, although product performance against specification is below standard. Sales per employee and expansion of the product line are ahead of schedule. Absenteeism in the service area is meeting projections, but turnover is higher than planned. Competitors appear to be introducing products more rapidly than expected.

After deviations and the underlying reasons for them are identified, the implications of these deviations for the ultimate success of the strategy must be seriously considered. For example, the rapid product line expansion indicated in Figure 13–3 may be in response to competitors' increased rate of product expansion. At the same time, product performance is still low and, while the installation cycle is slightly above standard (improving customer service), the ratio of service to sales personnel is below its target. Contributing to this substandard ratio (and perhaps reflecting a lack of organizational commitment to customer service) is the exceptionally high turnover in customer service personnel. The rapid reduction in indirect overhead costs might mean that administrative integration of customer service and product development requirements has been reduced too quickly.

As a result of this information, operations managers face several options. The deviations observed may be attributed primarily to internal factors or discrepancies. In this case, priorities can be scaled up or down. For example, greater emphasis might be placed on retaining customer service personnel while de-emphasizing overhead reduction and new product development. On the other hand, the management team could decide to continue as planned in the face of increasing competition and decide to accept or gradually improve the customer service situation. Another possibility is reformulating the strategy or a component of the strategy in the face of rapidly increasing competition. For example, the firm might decide to shift emphasis toward more standardized or lower-priced products to overcome customer service problems and take advantage of an apparently ambitious sales force.

This interpretation of Figure 13–3 is but one of many possible explanations. The important point is the critical need to monitor progress against standards and give serious, in-depth attention to both the reasons underlying observed deviations and the most appropriate responses to them.

Evaluations such as this are appropriate for organizational subunits, product groups, and operating units in a firm. Budgets, schedules, and other operating control systems with performance targets and standards linked to the strategic plan deserve this type of attention in detecting and evaluating deviations. The time frame is more compressed—usually quarterly or even monthly during the budgeted year. The operating manager typically reviews year-to-date progress against budgeted figures. After deviations are evaluated, slight adjustments may be necessary to keep progress, expenditures, or other factors in line with programmed needs of the strategy. In the unusual event that deviations are extreme—usually because of unforeseen changes—management is alerted to the possible need for revising the budget, reconsidering certain functional plans related to budgeted expenditures, or examining the units and effectiveness of the managers responsible.

An acceptable level of deviation should be allowed before action is taken; if not, the control process will become an administrative overload. Standards should not be regarded as absolute because the estimates used to formulate them are typically based on historical data, which, by definition, are "after the fact." Furthermore, absolute standards (keep equipment busy 100 percent of the time, or meet 100 percent of quota) are often used with no provision for variability. Standards are also often derived from averages, which, by definition, ignore variability. These difficulties suggest the need for defining acceptable *ranges* of deviation in budgetary figures or key indicators of strategic success. This approach helps in avoiding administrative difficulties, recognizing measurement variability, delegating more realistic authority to operating managers in making short-term decisions, and hopefully improves motivation.

Some companies use trigger points for clarification of standards, particularly in monitoring key success factors. A *trigger point* is a level of deviation of a key indicator or figure (such as a competitor's actions or a critical cost category) that management identifies in the planning process as representing either a major threat or an unusual opportunity. When that point is "hit," management is immediately alerted ("triggered") to consider necessary adjustments in the firm's strategy. Some companies take this idea a major step forward and develop one or more *contingency plans* to be implemented once predetermined trigger points are reached. These contingency plans redirect priorities and actions rapidly so that valuable reaction time is not "wasted" on administrative assessment and deliberation of the extreme deviation.

Correcting deviations in performance brings the entire management task into focus. Managers can correct performance by changing measures. Perhaps deviations can be resolved by changing plans. Management can eliminate poor performance by changing how things are done, by hiring new people, by retraining present workers, by changing job assignments, and so on. Correcting deviations from plans, therefore, can involve all of the functions, tasks, and responsibilities of operations managers. Operational control systems are intended to provide essential feedback so that company managers can make the necessary decisions and adjustments to implement the current strategy.

Reward Systems: Motivating Execution and Control

Execution and control of strategy ultimately depend on individual organizational members, particularly key managers. And motivating and rewarding good performance by individuals and organizational units are key ingredients in effective strategy implementation. While positive reinforcements are given primary emphasis, sanctions or negative reinforcements are important tools for controlling and adjusting poor performance. Motivating and controlling individual efforts, particularly those of managerial personnel, in execution of strategy is accomplished through a firm's reward–sanction mechanisms—compensation, raises, bonuses, stock options, incentives, benefits, promotions, demotions, recognition, praise, criticism, more (or less) responsibility, group norms, performance appraisal, tension, and fear. These mechanisms are positive and negative, short run and long run.

Control mechanisms align personal and subunit actions and objectives with the objectives and needs of the firm's strategy. This is not easy, and reward–sanction structures controlling strategy execution vary greatly across different firms. For example, Harold Geneen, former CEO of ITT, purportedly used an interesting combination of money (compensation and incentives), tension (strict accountability for results), and fear to control individual managers' efforts toward strategy implementation. According to one author:

> Geneen provides his managers with enough incentives to make them tolerate the system. Salaries all the way through ITT are higher than average—Geneen reckons 10 percent higher—so that few people can leave without taking a drop. As one employee put it: "We're all paid just a bit more than we think we're worth." At the very top, where the demands are greatest, the salaries and stock options are sufficient to compensate for the rigors. As someone said, "He's got them by their limousines."
>
> Having bound his men to him with chains of gold, Geneen can induce the tension that drives the machine. "The key to the system," one of his men explained, "is the profit forecast. Once the forecast has been gone over, revised, and agreed on, the managing director has a personal commitment to Geneen to carry it out. That's how he produces the tension on which the success depends." The tension goes through the company, inducing ambition, perhaps exhilaration, but always with some sense of fear: what happens if the target is missed?[6]

BIC Pen Company takes a different approach. Its reward structure involves incentive systems, wide latitude for operating managers, and clearly specified objectives to motivate and control individual initiative. All employees are invited to participate in a stock purchase plan whereby up to 10 percent of their salary can be used to purchase stock at a 10 percent discount from the market price. Functional managers are given wide rein in operational decisions

---

[6] Anthony Sampson, *The Sovereign State of ITT* (New York: Steig & Day, 1973), p. 132.

while being held strictly accountable for results. The director of manufacturing, for example, is free to spend up to $500,000 for a cost-saving machine, as long as profit margin objectives are maintained. Commenting on his approach to rewarding executives, BIC's president, Robert Adler, said:

> We have a unique bonus system, which I'm sure the Harvard Business School would think is crazy. Each year I take a percentage of profits before tax and give 40 percent to sales, 40 percent to manufacturing, and 20 percent to the treasurer to be divided up among executives in each area. Each department head keeps some for himself and gives the rest away. We never want bonuses to be thought of as salaries because they would lose their effect. So we change the bonus day each year so that it always comes as a pleasant surprise, something to look forward to.[7]

These two examples highlight several generalizations about the use of rewards and sanctions to control individuals, particularly managers, in strategy execution. Financial incentives are important reward mechanisms. They are particularly useful in controlling performance when they are directly linked to specific activities and results. Intrinsic, nonfinancial rewards, such as flexibility and autonomy in the job and visible control over performance, are important managerial motivators. And negative sanctions, such as withholding financial and intrinsic rewards or the tensions emanating from possible consequences of substandard performance, are necessary ingredients in directing and controlling managers' efforts.

The time horizon on which rewards are based is a major consideration in linking rewards and sanctions to strategically important activities and results. Numerous authors and business leaders have expressed concern with incentive systems based on short-term (typically annual) performance. They fear short-term reward structures can result in actions and decisions that undermine the long-term position of a firm. A marketing director who is rewarded based on the cost effectiveness and sales generated by the marketing staff might place significantly greater emphasis on established distribution channels than on "inefficient" nurturing and development of channels that the firm has not previously used. A reward system based on maximizing current profitability can potentially shortchange the future in terms of current investments (time, people, and money) from which the primary return will be in the future.[8] If the firm's grand strategy is growth through, among other means, horizontal integration of current products into new channels and markets, the reward structure could be directing the manager's efforts in a way that penalizes the ultimate success of the strategy. And the marketing director, having per-

---

[7] C. R. Christensen, K. R. Andrews, and J. L. Bower, *Business Policy: Text and Cases* (Homewood, Ill.: Richard D. Irwin, 1978), p. 318.

[8] W. R. King and D. I. Cleland, *Strategic Planning and Policy* (New York: Van Nostrand Reinhold, 1978), p. 364.

formed notably within the current reward structure, may have moved on to other responsibilities before the shortcomings emerge.

Short-term executive incentive schemes typically focus on last year's (or last quarter's) profits. This exclusive concentration on the bottom line has four weaknesses in terms of promoting a new strategy:[9]

1. It is backward looking. Reported results reflect past events and, to some extent, past strategy.

2. The focus is short term, even though many of the recorded transactions have effects over longer periods.

3. Strategic gains or losses are not considered due to, among other things, basic accounting methods.

4. Investment of time and money in future strategy can have a negative impact. Since such outlays and efforts are usually intermingled with other expenses, a manager can improve his or her bonus by *not* preparing for the future.

While there are clear dangers in incentive systems that encourage decidedly short-run thinking and neglect the longer term, there is real danger in hastily condemning short-term measures. Arguing that managers must be concerned with long-run performance is easy; it also may be too easy to make the mistake of concluding that short-term concerns are not important or that they are necessarily counterproductive to the strategic needs of the organization. Such a simplistic and quick conclusion can be dangerous. In an effectively implemented strategy, short-term objectives or aims support, and are critical to, the achievement of long-term strategic goals. The real problem is not the short- versus long-term concerns of management; it is the lack of integration of and consistency between long- and short-term plans and objectives in the control system that is vital to the successful implementation of strategy.[10] The critical ingredients for the achievement of this consistency are appropriate rewards and incentives.

To integrate long- and short-term concerns, reward systems must be based on the assessment and control of both the short-run and long-run (strategic) contributions of key managers. An effective reward system should provide payoffs that control and evaluate the creation of *potential* future performances as well as last year's results. Figure 13–4 illustrates a management reward system tied to a five-year cycle of strategy implementation. Review and evaluation in a specific year include *both* an assessment of performance during that year *and* an evaluation of progress toward the five-year strategic objectives. The annual objectives and incentives in each year can reflect adjustments

---

[9] Yavitz and Newman, *Strategy in Action,* pp. 204–9.

[10] Lawrence G. Hrebiniak and William F. Joyce, *Implementing Strategy* (New York: Macmillan, 1984), pp. 204–9.

Figure 13–4
Annual incentive system with long-term perspective

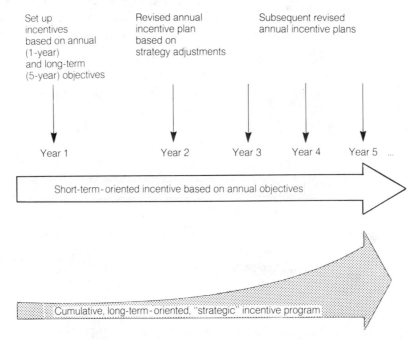

necessary for successful implementation of the strategy. This helps integrate short- and long-term considerations in strategy implementation by linking adjustments necessary in supporting revised, long-term considerations to next year's reward structure. The second component in the management reward system in Figure 13–4 is an incentive based on cumulative progress toward strategic objectives. It is shown as increasing in size or amount over time, which reinforces a long-term, strategic perspective. Incentives such as stock options, deferred bonuses, or cumulative compensation indexed to future performance indicators are ways this reward component could be structured. The key ingredient is an incentive system linked to longer-term progress toward strategic goals. This approach reinforces the interdependence of performance over the five-year period rather than the importance of any one year.

These incentive priorities (long-term versus short-term) should vary depending on the basic nature of the strategy. Figure 13–5 provides the results of a recent study illustrating this point. Comparing the importance of 11 criteria used in determining bonuses for SBU managers, the researchers found that long-term criteria were more important determinants of bonuses in SBUs with "build-oriented" strategies than in SBUs with "harvest-oriented" strategies. Short-term criteria were important in both types of SBUs, although these criteria were much more important than long-term criteria for determin-

Figure 13–5
Perceived importance of various performance dimensions in determination of SBU general manager's incentive bonus

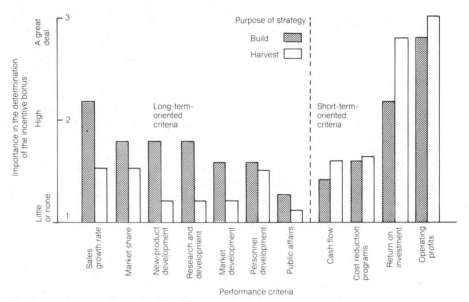

Source: Anil K. Gupta and V. Govindarajan, "Build, Hold, Harvest: Converting Strategic Intentions into Reality," *Journal of Business Strategy,* Winter 1984, p. 43.

ing incentive structures in harvest-oriented SBUs. Strategy in Action 13–3 illustrates how top executives at two multibusiness companies that participated in this research link reward structures for their SBUs to each SBU's basic strategy.

Another refinement suggested in constructing incentive systems that reward long-term (strategic) as well as short-term thinking is the use of *strategic budgets.*[11] In this approach, strategic budgets are employed simultaneously with operating budgets, but the objectives and plans associated with each budget vary a great deal. The focus of the operating budget is control and evaluation of business as usual. The strategic budget specifies resources (and targets) for key programs or activities linked to major initiatives that are integral to the long-term strategy. Concerned that executive incentive plans can and should give more explicit weight to strategic activities, proponents of a strategic budget approach suggest three basic steps:[12]

---

[11] Peter Lorange, *Implementation of Strategic Planning* (Englewood Cliffs, N.J.: Prentice-Hall, 1982); and "Strategic Control: Some Issues in Making It Operationally More Useful," in *Latest Advances in Strategic Management,* ed. R. Lamb Warren (Englewood Cliffs, N.J.: Prentice-Hall, 1986).

[12] Yavitz and Newman, *Strategy in Action,* p. 179.

Strategy in Action 13–3
Linking Incentive Compensation to Strategy in Large Multibusiness Firms

Recent research suggests large firms are moving away from uniform (usually "bottom-line") profit criteria to determine incentives in favor of multiple criteria linked in some way to business unit strategy. Below are reports from two multibusiness firms:

At a $5 billion producer of specialty chemicals and metal alloys, the strategic plan for each business is prepared before the annual budgeting process. The objective of the annual budgeting process, however, is not just to prepare an operating budget but also what executives in this firm refer to as a *strategic budget*. The latter "budget" lists specific strategic actions that the business unit manager would, in line with the long-range strategic plan, need to undertake during the coming year. Examples of items in such a strategic budget are: "increase market share from x percent to y percent," "prepare a strategic plan to reposition product P by such and such date," "find a buyer for subunit A," and so on. Managers are required to submit progress reports on a quarterly basis on accomplishments vis-à-vis this strategic budget. On a yearly basis, these accomplishments are evaluated for the purposes of determining the second half of a manager's incentive bonus. The link between the strategic mission and the incentive system then becomes a straightforward task—one part of the bonus is linked to certain items in the annual operating budget, and the other part to certain other items in the annual strategic budget.

At a $5 billion producer of electronics components and equipment, 25 percent of every SBU manager's bonus is based on corporate performance ("we want them to take a broader, corporatewide perspective") and the remaining 75 percent is split equally between the SBU's bottom-line and nonfinancial objectives. A group vice president detailed how this incentive system operates: "I have three units. I essentially get the same data on each. But in the nonfinancial objectives— more so than in the financial ones—I try to evaluate the three units against their strategic missions. For instance, for [business with a build strategy], I look for acquisitions planned, progress on capital projects, market share, and so forth. For my other two units [with maintain and harvest strategies], I focus on pricing, elimination of low-margin items, cost control, and the line. It is in these nonfinancial objectives where you can differentiate the performance criteria by strategy."

In firms that appear to have made the maximum progress toward matching the incentive system to strategy, the bonus is usually split into two parts: one

Continued on Page 429

> **Strategy in Action 13–3** (*concluded*)
>
> based on financial figures—such as earnings, return on investment, and cash flow—and the other based on the manager's accomplishments with regard to certain "strategic milestones" derived from the long-range strategic plan.

Source: Adapted from Anil K. Gupta and V. Govindarajan, "Build, Hold, Harvest: Converting Strategic Intentions into Reality," *Journal of Business Strategy*, Winter 1984, pp. 39–47.

1. Measure progress toward strategic targets separately from results of established operations.
2. Determine incentive awards separately for established operations and for progress toward strategic targets.
3. Devise a long-term, stock option equivalent to encourage revisions of strategy and entrepreneurial risk taking.

Common to each of these reward and sanction approaches is growing recognition of the need for a two-tiered incentive system linked to short-run and long-term considerations. The relative emphasis in terms of reward linkages should be determined by the focus of the strategy. For businesses with growth-oriented strategies, for example, incentive systems weighted toward long-term payoffs are more appropriate. Strategy in Action 13–4 illustrates a clear emphasis on this type of executive reward system among *INC* magazine's top 100 growth firms. Each incentive emphasizes long-term value based on either stock appreciation, length of the option, or a combination of both. While this emphasis is appropriate, short-term operating objectives deserve attention so that short-term performance is geared toward long-term objectives. For businesses pursuing more immediate strategic goals, the incentive emphasis should shift accordingly. In harvest business units of large firms, for example, greater emphasis on short-term, easily quantified performance indicators appears to be the basis for reward systems designed to evaluate strategic results.

Summary

Two fundamental perspectives—strategic and operational control—provide the basis for designing strategy control systems. Strategic controls are intended to steer the company toward its long-term strategic direction. Premise controls, implementation controls, strategic surveillance, and special alerts are four types of strategic control. Each is designed to meet top management's need to track the strategy as it is being implemented, detect underlying problems, and make necessary adjustments. These strategic controls are linked to the environmental assumptions and key operating requirements necessary for successful strategy implementation.

Strategy in Action 13–4
Linking Bonus Compensation to Strategy: What the *INC* 100 Fastest-Growing Companies Grant

Type of long-term compensation	Definition	Number of INC 100 companies	
Investment:			
Incentive stock option	Right to purchase company stock at a set price over period not to exceed 10 years; price must equal 100 percent of fair market value at grant with optionee limited to $100,000 (plus unused carryovers) per year in aggregate exercise cost, must be exercised in order of grant; capital gains at sale if acquired shares held at least one year after exercise and two years after grant.	New plan Continuing plan Total	29 54 83
Nonqualified stock options	Rights to purchase company stock at a set price over a stated period, often years; typically, price is 100 percent of market value at grant, but can be less. Gain at exercise is taxable income.	New plan Continuing plan Total	2 55 57
Stock purchases	Short-term rights to purchase company stock, typically at a discount from market value and/or with financing assistance from the company. Shares may be subject to transfer restrictions.	New plan Continuing plan Total	2 7 9
Noninvestment:			
Stock appreciation rights	Right to receive in stock and/or cash appreciation the gain in market value of specified number of shares since grant, typically granted in conjunction with stock options.	New plan Continuing plan Total	1 8 9
Stock grants (restricted stock)	Grants of stock, typically subject to transfer restrictions and risk of forfeiture until earned by continued employment with the company.	New plan Continuing plan Total	— 1 1

Source: "Beyond the Paycheck: Compensating for Growth," *INC*, September 1983, p. 110.

Operational control systems identify the performance standards associated with allocation and use of the company's financial, physical, and human resources in pursuit of the strategy. Budgets, schedules, and key success factors are the primary means of operational control.

Operational control systems require systematic evaluation of performance against predetermined standards or targets. A critical concern here is identification and evaluation of performance deviations, with careful attention paid to determining the underlying reasons and strategic implications for observed deviations before management reacts. Some companies use trigger points and contingency plans in this process.

The reward system is a key ingredient in motivating managers to emphasize execution and control in steering the business toward strategic success. Companies should emphasize incentive systems that ensure adequate attention to strategic thrusts. This usually requires a concerted effort to emphasize long-term performance indicators rather than solely emphasizing short-term measures of performance. Short- and long-term performance considerations must be integrated to ensure performance consistent with the company's strategy and to provide a basis for monitoring future short-run performance against objectives incrementally linked to long-term strategic outcomes.

Questions for Discussion

1. Distinguish strategic control from operating control. Give an example of each.
2. Select a business that has a strategy you are familiar with. Identify what you think are its key premises. Then select the key indicators you would use to monitor each premise.
3. Explain the differences between implementation controls, strategic surveillance, and special alerts. Give example of each.
4. Why are budgets, schedules, and key success factors essential to operations control and evaluation?
5. What are key considerations in monitoring deviations from performance standards?
6. How would you vary an incentive system for a growth-oriented versus a harvest-oriented business?
7. Why do strategists prefer reward systems similar to that shown in Figure 13–4? What are the advantages and disadvantages of such a system?

Bibliography

Bales, Carter. "Strategic Control: The President's Paradox." *Business Horizons,* August 1977, pp. 17–28.

Bower, Joseph. "Planning and Control." *Journal of General Management* 1, no. 3 (1974), pp. 20–31.

Camillus, J. C. "Six Approaches to Preventive Management Control." *Financial Executive,* December 1980, pp. 28–31.

Christopher, W. "Achievement Reporting—Controlling Performance against Objectives." *Long-Range Planning,* October 1977, pp. 14–24.

Diffenbach, J. "Finding the Right Strategic Combination." *Journal of Business Strategy,* Fall 1981, pp. 47–58.

Hobbs, John, and Donald Heany. "Coupling Strategy to Operating Plans." *Harvard Business Review,* May–June 1977, pp. 119–26.

Horovits, J. N. "Strategic Control: A New Task for Top Management." *Long-Range Planning,* June 1979, pp. 2–7.

Lenz, R. T. "Determinants of Organizational Performance: An Interdisciplinary Review." *Strategic Management Journal* 2 (1981), pp. 131–54.

Lorange, P., and D. Murphy. "Considerations in Implementing Strategic Control." *Journal of Business Strategy* 4 (1984), pp. 27–35.

Merchant, Kenneth A. "The Control Function of Management." *Sloan Management Review* 23, no. 4 (1982), pp. 43–55.

Newman, W. H. *Constructive Control: Design and Use of Control Systems.* Englewood Cliffs, N.J.: Prentice-Hall, 1975.

Rappaport, Alfred. "Executive Incentives versus Corporate Growth." *Harvard Business Review,* July–August 1978, pp. 81–88.

Rockart, J. F. "Chief Executives Define Their Own Data Needs." *Harvard Business Review,* March–April 1979, pp. 85–94.

Schreyögg, G., and H. Steinmann. "Strategic Control: A New Perspective." *Academy of Management Review* 12, no. 1 (1987), pp. 91–103.

Yavitz, B., and W. H. Newman. *Strategy in Action.* New York: Free Press, 1982, chap. 12.

Chapter 13 Cohesion Case Illustration

Guiding and Evaluating the Strategy at Holiday Inns, Inc.

Holiday Inns' corporate strategy sought to focus the company's growth in the two business sectors of hotels and casino gaming while seeking to divest businesses that were not directly tied to this new hospitality focus. That meant divesting Trailways, Delta, and eventually Perkins.

The business strategy of the hotel group centered on both product and market development, the intent being to expand the company's participation in all segments of the evolving lodging industry in a profitable, leadership fashion. The business strategy of the gaming group focused on market development, seeking to ensure a leadership position for the company's Harrah's operation in each of the four U.S. markets for legalized gambling as well as in any newly legalized markets.

Several controls used by Holiday Inns executives to guide and evaluate these two business-level strategies will be illustrated below.

Strategic Control

Premise Control

The company's renewed focus on hotels centered on accelerated, steady expansion of the number of franchised Holiday Inns properties in domestic and international urban markets. This decision to initially emphasize continued Holiday Inns expansion rather than immediate expansion into other types of lodging chains (budget, high-priced, etc.) was based on the company's market research-derived premise that for the next five years or more, the mid-priced segment of the lodging industry would remain the place where 75–80 cents out of every lodging dollar would be spent. At the same time, management was preparing the company for expansion (via newly named chains) into various segments of the lodging industry when the demand became more convincing. So they carefully monitored this premise on which the initial lodging strategy was predicated; if they detected a change in the size of the mid-priced segment as well as acceleration in the growth of one or more of these other segments (which they considered a strong possibility at some future date), Holiday Inns' top management would alter the initial strategy to the extent of implementing aggressive development of new chains (or brands) designed to compete in these faster-growing segments.

By 1985, this premise control had led Holiday Corporation (the corporate name was changed to reflect the company's emphasis on several lodging chains—or *brands,* as they called them) to move by acquisition or internal development into five different lodging segments. They were as follows:

Holiday Inn Hotels—the current leader in the full-service, mid-priced market segment.

Holiday Inn Crowne Plaza Hotels—hotels that offer extra amenities and personalized services in selected urban areas.

Embassy Suites Hotels—the world's largest all-suite hotel system, offering spacious suite accommodations and extra services. Established via acquisition.

Hampton Inn Hotels—a limited-service hotel chain providing streamlined facilities without restaurants in the rapidly growing budget segment. Internally developed with heavy franchising emphasis.

The Residence Inn Hotel—a recently acquired, unique system of residential-style, all-suite properties designed for guests staying five days or longer.

Implementation Control

One of the key strategic thrusts of Holiday Corporation's strategy of maintaining and expanding its leadership position in the lodging industry has been to intensify the level of franchising associated with its lodging chains. By so doing, the company felt it would be in a position to more rapidly and aggressively move into attractive or growing locations since the requirement for capital in a very capital-intensive business would be supplied by the franchisee, not the Holiday Corporation. Therefore, the company could invest its capital in the means necessary to sell and manage each lodging network rather than in the land and buildings necessary to secure each new site.

In 1985, two years into the plan, corporate management monitoring the success of this thrust concluded that while it was working, its impact on return on stockholder equity could be accelerated. The original thrust had the gradual effect, as the number of franchises relative to company-owned properties increased, of improving ROE by replacing operating income generated by ownership of properties with higher-return income from franchise fees and assessments requiring less capital investment. But managers monitoring the implementation of this key strategic thrust concluded that its impact could be accelerated by doing two things:

1. The company could begin to sell off selected lodging properties to interested investors and retain a management contract with them to operate the property as a Holiday Inn Hotel. Interested, passive investors

(such as pension funds or insurance companies) got an attractive yet secure investment with reasonably guaranteed returns—the historical track record of the facility gave clear evidence of its income-producing capability. And the Holiday Corporation was able to sell an asset for many times its book value, keep control of the location and continue to derive income via management fees, and use that additional, sizable revenue ($87 million in operating income and $328 million in cash flow in 1985 alone) to support expansion of its several lodging and gaming businesses.

2. The company could increase its leverage of the company's still-extensive asset base to increase the capital available to support corporatewide growth.

They therefore changed its conservative debt/invested capital ratio policy from a required ratio of 30–40 percent to a ratio of 45–60 percent.

Implementation control, focused on one strategic thrust having to do with increasing ROE and market presence via increased franchising, led Holiday Corporation to adjust two other thrusts—debt policy and management services—so as to fine-tune the direction of the company's chosen strategy.

Strategic Surveillance

An interesting example of Holiday Corporation's benefit from the use of strategic surveillance occurred with regard to its attempt to develop a satellite communications network, HI-NET, as a state-of-the-art offering linking its lodging facilities—particularly those catering to convention business—to provide teleconferencing, in-room entertainment, and other as yet unforeseen benefits. Top executives viewed being first with this technology (in the lodging and gaming industries) and at the forefront of this technology as essential competitive advantages for its future as a market leader. Consistent with this assumption, several executives regularly read satellite communications information, attended trade shows, and otherwise strategically surveyed events in this area.

This surveillance led two Holiday Inns executives to become aware of an emerging company, Communications Satellite Corporation, which was very much at the technological forefront of satellite and microwave communications. Subsequent investigation led to a long-term joint venture between the two firms to develop the HI-NET communications satellite network into the world's largest privately owned satellite communication system. Partly as a result of strategic surveillance by several Holiday Corporation executives, the firm was able to speed up the development of its HI-NET system and was more likely to ensure its use of the field's latest technology.

Special Alert Control

Holiday Corporation's gaming business, Harrah's, was committed to a strategy of rapid market development so as to maintain and expand its leadership position in the U.S. gaming industry. Building from its dominant position in Nevada markets, Harrah's moved quickly in an effort to become a dominant force in the newly legalized Atlantic City market. It developed its own Harrah's property and bought a 50 percent interest in another property owned by Donald Trump, the Trump Casino Hotel, so as to be able to further dominate the Atlantic City market should it continue its explosive early expansion.

At the same time, Harrah's executives carefully monitored two indicators of the future direction of the Atlantic City market—supply of gaming floor space (to include the number of tables and slot machines) and number of Atlantic City visitors—on a monthly basis. Uncertain about the stability of the Atlantic City gaming environment, these factors were monitored so as to alert Harrah's management about changing market fundamentals that would seriously erode potential profitability in the new gaming market. By 1986, the growth in market demand had not kept pace with supply additions of 12.5 percent and 12.8 percent in the two previous years, thus alerting Harrah's management to reevaluate their degree of emphasis on this market as a realistic source for continued rapid growth in profitability and market share. This in turn led to a slight change in strategy, with Holiday Corporation deciding to sell its 50 percent interest in the Trump Casino in Atlantic City, to finalize a 15,000-square-foot expansion of its Harrah's Marina in Atlantic City, and to initiate construction of a hotel/casino in Laughlin, Nevada, which is a new, rapidly growing gaming market.

Operations Control

Each of the hotel businesses and the Harrah's casino gaming business use several types of operational control to monitor and evaluate the implementation of their strategies on a year-to-year basis. We will briefly describe two operational control systems within the hotel group that serve this purpose: expenditure budgeting and quality control.

Expenditure Budgeting System

The Holiday Inn chain has adopted an expenditure budgeting system, which it calls *operations management systems (OMS)*, to control the profitability of each Holiday Inn. The purpose of this system is to monitor and control profitability at individual inn locations by providing weekly budgets for the use of hotel resources that reflect the cyclical nature of occupancy patterns throughout the year. This OMS budgeting system provides the local managers, called innkeepers, with projected staff scheduling needs, energy control (based on weather forecasts), departmental (inn, restaurant, and lounge) expenditures, and usage, inventory control, and quality assurance needs for each week throughout the year to help control profitability yet attempt to ensure the full-service level of quality portrayed in Holiday Inns' mission and promotion. The weekly budgets are updated monthly, and innkeepers report they are very helpful in making the day-to-day management decisions necessary to keep profitability in line.

Quality Control

The Holiday Inns chain puts major emphasis on its efforts to maintain and control the quality of its 1,800 plus locations. It is essential that continued, careful efforts be made to ensure that each facility offers standardized, high-quality accommodation and service. At the heart of the system used to do this is a staff of 30 full-time inspectors, who travel over 1.5 million miles each year and perform approximately 5,000 unannounced, biannual inspections of properties in the Holiday Inns system. Many properties are actually inspected three times a year through this program, where the inspector makes a 24-hour, unannounced inspection of up to 1,100 different items ranging from the quality of a mattress to the greeting from a waiter to the cleanliness of bar utensils. Hotel properties failing two inspections in a row are removed from the system. Chairman Mike Rose proudly reported in 1986 that "To reinforce our commitment to continually improving product quality, we eliminated from our Holiday Inn system 59 hotels that did not meet our standards or our customers' expectations of quality for Holiday Inn Hotels last year."

Reward Systems at Holiday Corporation

A basic, corporatewide objective at Holiday Inns is to achieve an annual return on stockholders' equity of between 18 and 20 percent over the planning period. This objective represents the basic objective pursued by each business unit's strategy. Top management at the Holiday Corporation implements several reward systems designed to encourage executive and employee performance in this direction. Selected programs are as follows:

Employee Savings Plan

The company instituted in 1985 a program whereby all employees could contribute up to 16 percent of their earnings on a pre-tax basis, which would be matched by the company and used to purchase Holiday Corporation common stock in the employee's name. The company's matching contribution would vest (become fully controlled by an employee leaving the company) in eight years.

This plan has two effects consistent with the company's hospitality businesses and their dependence on personalized attention by individual employees to project the proper full-service image. First, it links every employee's financial savings program at least partially to the successful operation—profitability and sales growth—of each lodging or gaming property. And the company's matching contribution has the effect of leveraging the employees' potential benefits if they provide good service (and the stock does well). Second, it ties employees motivated by this program to the company for at least eight years—enough time to identify and keep highly productive employees while resulting in no cost to the company if some employees, hopefully those that don't measure up, leave before eight years.

Executive Stock Programs

The company has two plans under which executives and key employees are awarded shares of stock or stock options in the company's common stock. One program awards shares of common stock subject to forfeiture restrictions ranging from two to six years, which restrictions are in turn linked to the time horizons associated with key strategic programs the recipients are responsible for implementing. A second stock option program grants key management personnel the option to purchase the company's stock at a price equal to its market value at the date of the grant. Obviously, both programs link key executives' financial rewards to improved stock performance. Furthermore, each program takes effect over time, which further links reward to long-term, strategic success.

Long-Term Performance Plans

Holiday Corporation also has a long-term performance plan under which contingent awards of cash and shares of common stock are granted to key executives. Awards are paid only if the company's financial performance *over a four-year period* meets or exceeds standards determined by the Executive Compensation Committee of Holiday Corporation's board of directors. This program focuses rewards on the long-term performance of the company and the strategies executives develop.

All of these reward systems are clearly designed to link the actions of employees and key executives with the company's long-term objectives.

Epilogue

A Summary of Key Decisions Made by Holiday Inn Executives in Positioning the Company for the 1990s

Become a Narrowly Focused, "Hospitality" Company

The first key decision made by top management at Holiday Inns, Inc., was to redefine the company from being a broadly diversified, transportation-related company to a much more narrowly focused, hospitality company. The following comments made by key Holiday Inns executives serve to explain this fundamental corporate change. Roy Winegardner, commenting to *Business Week:*

> We are in the process of reshaping Holiday Inns into a different company. Holiday Inns is actually a hospitality company—a concept that will limit its scope to lodging, entertainment, and food. . . . In the future, the company will get into as few businesses as possible, and only those that have good growth, high returns, and are synergistic with our main business—hotels.

Mike Rose, to the New York Society of Security Analysts:

> We concluded that we simply could not provide the right kind of management to the wide variety of businesses we were in at the time, so we set about divesting ourselves of those that did not fit with our hospitality strategy.

Divest Businesses in the Transportation Group, the Products Group, and the Perkins Restaurant Chain

Between 1979 and 1986, Holiday Inns, Inc.'s top management systematically sold off virtually all businesses not directly involved with either its hotel group or its gaming group. In each case, they sold going concerns and waited for the right opportunity to sell so as to minimize their losses associated with getting out of the business.

Trailways was sold in 1979; Delta Steamship was sold in 1985; and the Perkins chain was sold in 1986. Selected products group businesses were sold as opportunities arose throughout this time period. The products group became essentially the procurement device for the hotel group and also provided facilities-planning services to the entire lodging system.

Shift to a Product Development Strategy within the Hotel Group

Holiday Inns' key decision looking to the 1990s was to focus solely on lodging and gaming. The essence of the initial strategy was to encourage steady growth in the Holiday Inn Hotel chain and rapid growth of the Harrah's hotel/casino business. Early comments by Chairman Mike Rose were as follows. Speaking to New York security analysts in the early 1980s:

> The key to our long-term direction is the fact that our hotel business will be our core business for the future. . . . The mission of the hotel group is to grow Holiday Inns' leadership position in the broad, midscale segments of the lodging industry, to grow our consumer recognition as the preferred brand in the lodging industry. . . . While we think the percentage growth of demand will be highest in the high-price or image segment, in absolute terms demand for rooms in the moderate-price segment will grow three times faster than in either the high-price or low-price segments.

By the late 1980s, the strategy shifted from a major emphasis solely on Holiday Inns as the hotel focus to the development of several different lodging chains, each targeted at a specific segment of the maturing lodging industry. Each chain, including Holiday Inns, was now referred to as one of the company's hotel *brands* or *products*. Seemingly, to lessen the emphasis on, and identity solely with, Holiday Inns, the company reorganized itself as Holiday Corporation. The following remarks made by Mike Rose in 1986 reflect this significant shift in strategy:

> Under our new name, Holiday Corporation, 1986 was a year of great accomplishment for our company. Holiday Corporation is now a multiple-brand hospitality company specializing in hotels and hotel/casinos. We intend to concentrate on the hotel and hotel/casino businesses, developing profitable market segments within those businesses where we either enjoy leading positions or see our way clear to establishing a leading position. In January, we acquired a 50 percent interest in the Residence Inn system, which enjoys a leadership position in the extended-stay market. Our other new hotel brands, Embassy Suites and Hampton Inn, are experiencing exceptional growth. And our core Holiday Inn brand as well our Holiday Inn Crowne Plaza brand are enjoying exceptional growth. We have designed distinctive hotel products that meet the specific needs of well-defined customer segments. All of our brands are intended to be leaders in their segments, which allows them to use sophisticated marketing techniques to increase market share despite intense competition.

Decrease Capital Intensity and Increase Leverage

In the early 1980s, management was committed to a conservative debt policy and a continuation of its standing policy of maintaining a 4-to-1 franchise/company-owned ratio in ownership of hotel facilities. Note the following comment by Mike Rose to security analysts in 1982:

> We can see significant opportunities for unit growth in our hotel business, both domestically and abroad. Our intent is to develop through a combination of franchisee growth and parent company investment. We expect to maintain the current relationship of four franchise units for each parent unit into the 1990s. . . . We intend to remain conservative in our debt policy, keeping a debt/invested capital ratio between 30 and 40 percent, which maintains excellent extra borrowing capacity.

By the late 1980s, perhaps in an effort to more easily increase ROE while at the same time speeding up the growth of each new brand in the face of greatly intensified competition, Holiday Corporation had significantly changed its posture toward company-owned properties and leverage. This can be seen in the following remarks made by Mike Rose in 1986:

> Our plan calls for accelerated disposition of assets as we reduce the capital intensity of our businesses. Operating income generated by ownership of properties will be replaced in part by high-return management and franchise income. . . . After thorough study, we raised the company's target for its debt/invested capital ratio to 45–60 percent. This higher leverage is supported by the value of the company's assets and strong cash flow. . . . We want to own fewer properties while significantly increasing the number of franchised properties and properties where we have long-term management contracts. . . . This allows us to expand our market positions using limited amounts of the company's capital.

General Index